A GUIDE TO
TREKKING IN NEPAL

A GUIDE TO
TREKKING IN NEPAL
FIFTH EDITION

STEPHEN BEZRUCHKA
THE MOUNTAINEERS • SEATTLE

First edition 1972; second edition 1974; third edition 1976; all by Sahayogi Press, Kathmandu, Nepal

Fourth edition, published January 1981, and fifth edition, published 1985, in the United States, by The Mountaineers, 306 2nd Avenue West, Seattle, Washington 98119.

Fourth and fifth editions made possible through the courtesy of Sahayogi Press, Kathmandu, Nepal.

Published simultaneously:
    In Nepal by Sahayogi Press, Tripureshwar, Kathmandu
    In the United Kingdom and Europe by Cordee, 3a De Montfort St.,
       Leicester, England LE1 7HD
    In Canada by Douglas & McIntyre Ltd., 1615 Venables Street, Vancouver,
       British Columbia V5L 2H1

Manufactured in the United States of America

Book design by Marge Mueller

Cover photo: Trekking below Annapurna South on the lush southern side of the range. Photo by Gordon Wiltsie.

Title photo: Dhaulagiri towers above the Kali Gandaki Valley, seen en route to Annapurna Base Camp. Photo by Peter Banys.

Library of Congress Cataloging in Publication Data

Bezruchka, Stephen.
    A guide to trekking in Nepal.

    Bibliography: p.
    Includes index.
    1. Hiking—Nepal—Guide-books.   2. Nepal—
Description and travel—Guide-books.   I. Title.
II. Title: Trekking in Nepal.
GV199.44.N46B49   1985   915.49'6   84-20576
ISBN 0-89886-094-6

Nepal is there to change you, not for you to change it. Lose yourself in its essence. Make your footprints with care and awareness of the precarious balance around you. Take souvenirs in your mind and spirit, not in your pockets. Nepal is not only a place on the map, but an experience, a way of life from which we all can learn.

CONTENTS

Mount Everest—first climbed in 1953 by Sir Edmund Hillary and Tenzing Norgay. (Stephen Bezruchka)

FOREWORD

I first visited the Khumbu area of Nepal in 1951 and took part in the initial reconnaissance of the great icefall and the southern approaches to Everest.

I can clearly remember my first walk up the Everest valleys—the unbelievable summits, the dense forest around Tengboche, alive with colorful birds and nervous musk deer, the upper valleys clothed in dark green juniper and azalea. It was a unique experience and everything was so incredibly beautiful.

What a change there is today! The summits are still there of course—floating high above man's mess and destruction—but the Khumbu valley is now an ecological slum. Erosion is everywhere; tins and trash clutter up the paths and campsites. You are lucky if you see a single juniper; the forests are being destroyed, and the traditional culture is being crushed by the insidious economic machine.

As you trek through Nepal, you have to be blind if you cannot see the changes taking place. Population pressure pushes agricultural terraces higher and higher on steep hillsides; there is widespread and growing erosion; and "tourist" routes are clearly defined by cigarette packages and used toilet paper.

Nepal is still very beautiful—surely one of the world's great trekking paradises. But those of us who take advantage of these charms have great responsibility. We can play an active part in Nepal's future by making positive efforts to leave the mountains and walkways cleaner than we found them, taking care not to abuse local customs and traditions, and limiting our use of energy to a minimum so there may be something left for future generations.

Nepal must be saved—and we can help do it.

Sir Edmund Hillary

The fortress village of Jharkot. (Ane Haaland)

PREFACE

Nepal, a tiny Himalayan kingdom, is economically one of the poorest countries of the world. Yet it is the fabled Shangri-la for thousands of tourists and seekers who visit each year. They come in far greater numbers than to other countries of the Himalaya. Most are not disappointed and find great wealth in Nepal.

Travel along the routes that are popular with trekkers has changed considerably since I first came to Nepal in 1969. There are more and more facilities, signs, hotels, latrines, imported foods, and improved trails, all of which make it easier for the trekker. And there is much more opportunity for companionship with other visitors. Some feel that the popularity of trekking and the changes made in a few areas to accommodate tourists have rendered the country less attractive. The mountains will never be less spectacular, but the actions of the visitors will have great impact on the people living in those mountains. These actions may improve the experience of both visitor and Nepali, or may make it worse.

This book encourages the visitor to interact with Nepal in a manner that is sensitive to local customs and oriented towards preserving the experience of trekking in Nepal. Detailed information is provided to help you choose a trek and prepare for it. Informative trail descriptions are given for all the popular treks as well as others that may appeal to those wishing to experience Nepal without many other tourists. And most importantly, it is vital to follow the cross-cultural information in Chapter 4 so that trekking in Nepal continues to be the fabled experience it has been and still is. Language learning tips are given in Chapter 6. An audio cassette tape is available to help you learn rudiments of the language before you trek and to provide a resource during your trip. Information on ordering this is on page 143 at the end of Chapter 6. Finally, there is material on the country and the people, as well as information on further resources to help you continue learning about Nepal.

There are many different ways of trekking in Nepal. These are outlined and the advantages of each are pointed out. The aspiring trekker must determine which of these styles best suits his or her needs, time constraints, and funds. The information given here is valuable no matter whether you are going off on your own to a less traveled area, or taking an expensive, organized group trek to a popular site. Other than this book and the language tape, I have no financial interest in trekking in Nepal, so I won't try to persuade you to travel in one mode or another, but I do want you to be as well informed as possible so you can make that decision yourself.

There are other ways of learning about and interacting with Nepal. In some areas, courses on trekking are available. Friends and acquaintances who have been to Nepal are a good information resource. There are now Nepal friendship societies in various countries, and the nearest Nepalis embassy or consulate can help you locate them.

Nepal is in the public eye much more than before. Place names in Nepal are being used as product brand names. Many photographs for advertising outdoor products, obviously taken in Nepal, help sell these items. The King of Nepal has recently visited numerous countries, generating attendant publicity.

Adventurers still attempt various "firsts" in Nepal. Mountain climbers seeking first ascents began this trend. And while there are few unclimbed peaks left in Nepal, plenty of new routes remain. Being the first outsider to visit a location or perform an activity used to be important. Now most rivers have been rafted, and the base of Everest has been reached by a runner and even by a bicyclist. A river draining earth's pinnacle has been descended by canoe and by swimmers. What next? Perhaps the first to Base Camp by pogo stick or by wheelchair? It matters not; there is plenty to enjoy in Nepal, even if you are not a "first" person.

It will be evident, once you get on the trail, that the country is going through a time of change, especially along the well-traveled routes. The information in this guide is as current as I can make it. But your comments and suggestions can help improve future editions. In spite of revisions, errors remain. One woman wrote me that the stated time of twenty minutes between points A and B could not be right; she was sure it took seventy minutes. She agreed with my times elsewhere and had walked the section in question twice. I checked my notes and, of course, she was correct. Please send updated information and corrections to me care of the publisher.

I once read a book by Yvon Chouinard, the acknowledged master of ice climbing, and later took a seminar from him. What I learned most from that experience was that he meant every word and every sentence he wrote in his book. The same applies to this volume. All the information and suggestions are based on my own personal experience and that of friends who have lived and trekked in Nepal.

Many people have helped me in producing this book. I won't list those who assisted in previous editions, though I continue to be grateful for their help. Thanks to: Ross and Kathy Anthony, Tom Arens, Peter Banys, Tizzy Bennett, Binny van Bergen, Inger-Marie Bjønness, Bronwen Bledsoe, Arlene Blum, Brot Coburn, Steve Conlon, Penny Dawson, Andrea Dite, Hugh Downs, Marsha Dupar, Ned Espey, Pema Gyaltsen, Kathryn Gorrie, Mary Lynn Hanley, Lance Hart, Julie Howell, Kristen Johnson, Ambika Joshi, Anjan Joshi, David Kukla, Robert Lee, Vivian and Walter Leitner, Robert Matthews, Jonathan Miller, Kevin O'Connell, Elizabeth Page, Karen Payntor, David and Kathy Peterson, John Pilkington, Jennifer Read, Robert Rieffel, Johan Reinhard, John Rosen, Barry Rosenbaum, Kami Temba Sherpa, David Shlim, Bruce Silverstein, Peter Spear, Hugh Swift, Bala Ram Thapa, Jamie Uhrig, Steve Wagner, Alan Wald, Will Weber, Gary White, and Don Whittaker.

Mr. R.K. Sharma of Sahayogi Press in Nepal has supported the book from its conception. My good friend Donald Messerschmidt is always helpful. The staff of The Mountaineers Books continues to be a joy to work with. Sandy Marvinney helped shape the manuscript. Marge Mueller did the maps and design. Ann Cleeland, Stephen Whitney, and Donna DeShazo helped in many ways.

To all who helped, I am very grateful.

SECTION I
ABOUT TREKKING

Trail scene west of Pokhara. (Stephen Bezruchka)

Namaste, *the traditional greeting, done with hands pressed together, will welcome every traveler in Nepal. (Ane Haaland)*

WHAT TO EXPECT

A hundred divine epochs would not suffice to describe all the marvels of the Himalaya.

Sanskrit proverb

What kind of experiences will you have in Nepal? Think of waking up early one morning and directing your gaze to the north. It is quite cloudy, but for some reason, you lift up your eyes. There it is—the triangular rock and snow face of Machhapuchhre, glistening in the sun through a hole in the clouds. But it is not even 23,000 ft (7000 m) high! How could it look so big? Or you are walking along the trail when you suddenly hear, "Good morning, Sir," spoken in perfect English. You turn around, astonished, to see an ordinary-looking Nepali. Yes, the speaker is a Gurkha soldier, retired from the British Army. The two of you pass many miles talking together. Or it is the day's end and you are resting after the walk, looking at a Western book or magazine that you carry. Soon you are surrounded by children who gaze intently at the pictures. You want to tell them that the world those pictures represent is not better than theirs. Or after you have walked for eleven days, you reach the top of a hill and suddenly see Mount Everest and Ama Dablang. Everest is over 6000 ft (1800 m) higher, but you hardly notice it; Ama Dablang excites you all the time you are near it. Or it is spring and you have toiled to get far above the valley. The rhododendrons make the mountains look like a paradise. They are red in many places; yet the colors can be light, and even beautifully white. Every day there will be many times like these when you will forget the miles you have yet to go, the vertical feet yet to climb, the load on your back. And you will vow to return.

Nepal is a land of unparalleled variety. Imagine a rectangle, 500 miles by 150 miles, divided lengthwise into three strips. The northernmost strip is mountainous; it includes eight of the ten highest mountains in the world. This Himalayan region is sparsely settled by people who speak languages of the Tibeto-Burman family and practice Tibetan Buddhism. The southernmost region, which is the narrowest of the three strips, is called the Tarai. It is an extension of the Gangetic plain of northern India. This area is populated by people who speak Indo-European languages and practice Hinduism. The animals of the south belong to a different realm than the animals of the north. In between the two outer strips lies an interface region of hills and valleys. The inhabitants speak languages of both the Tibeto-Burman and Indo-European families and generally practice Hinduism with many Buddhist and shamanistic influences.

Climatically, the country has subtropical, temperate, and alpine regions, determined by elevation. It contains examples of most of the vegetation zones of the world.

The economy is basically subsistence agriculture. Nepal has most of the statistical characteristics of the world's poorest countries in terms of per capita income, literacy, and infant mortality. The World Bank ranks Nepal as the fourth poorest country in the world. The high rate of population growth—doubling time is

A well-provisioned hotel for trekkers near Pokhara. (Stephen Bezruchka)

about thirty years—threatens to outstrip food production. Another serious problem is deforestation due to the search for wood for fuel and construction. The result is erosion and loss of topsoil. Nepal's population in 1981 topped fifteen million, and its annual growth rate is approximately 2.7 percent. Although I returned from Nepal in 1970 with a doomsday outlook, I have seen many positive changes over the years, as well as some negative ones, so the situation does not seem hopeless. Historically, the Nepali people have worked through their problems satisfactorily, and I see no reaon to doubt their ability to continue to do so, as long as we visitors don't interfere.

Nepal is the world's only Hindu monarchy. The King, Birendra Bir Bikram Shah Dev, is a direct descendant of Prithvinarayan Shah who unified the country in the 1760s. For over a hundred years, until 1951, Nepal was ruled by a sequence of hereditary prime ministers, the Ranas. During this period Nepal was essentially cut off from outside influences. Because of its forbidding mountains to the north and deadly malaria endemic in the Tarai to the south, Nepal was never successfully invaded by a major power.

After the Chinese occupied Tibet in 1959, many Tibetans fled to India and Nepal where they settled in refugee camps. The northern border of Nepal was closed for some time, but restrictions now have been relaxed somewhat so that trade goes on, though it is not the extensive commerce it once was. Most Tibetans in Nepal have successfully adapted to their new environment.

After an attempt at democracy in 1959, the country was ruled by a system of participatory councils, but with real power vested in the King. In the spring of 1980 a popular referendum was held to determine if the country should allow multiple political parties. The proposal was defeated. It remains unclear how Nepal's government will change as a result of the popular pressures that are becoming more commonplace in Third World countries.

Nepal was closed to foreigners and foreign influence until 1951 and did not officially open its doors to tourists until a few years later. But by 1981, over 110,000 tourists were visiting the country each year, and massive amounts of foreign aid had started Nepal on the road to modernization and development. Major contributors of aid are India, China, the Soviet Union, and the United States. It remains to be seen whether this economic assistance will improve the lot of Nepali farmers. In the past, most aid has been given primarily for political reasons, although Nepal is a non-aligned country and has declared itself a zone of peace. So far most of Nepal remains largely untouched by the ways and ideas of the West.

It is this land of contrasts that beckons those who are willing to travel, as the Nepalis do, on foot. Indeed, walking is the only means of reaching most destinations, since Nepal still has the fewest miles of roads in proportion to area or population of any country in the world. The trails that trekkers use are the public transportation and communication routes for the local people.

Trekking, as described here, means travel by foot for many days. During this time, travelers can spend nights either in the homes of local people or in recently constructed simple hotels, or they can camp by themselves. They can eat either local food or food they have brought with them. In fact, on many journeys through populated areas to lonely heights, it is customary to try all of the above variations. Most of Nepal is not wilderness as the term is understood in the West. Trekking routes pass through rural, sparsely settled areas, the homeland of the Nepali people. Visitors need to be cognizant of local values and culture, a subject expanded upon in Chapter 4.

In recent years the number of tourists visiting Nepal has leveled off, but the number of trekkers continues to increase. In 1981, almost 30,000 trekking permits were issued. If this number discourages you from going, realize that by choosing one of the rarely visited areas (see end of Chapter 2), you can almost be assured of not meeting another trekker.

Trekking is a very healthy activity, although not without its hazards. It is strenuous and burns calories, so that many overweight people shed their excess load along the trail. Smokers may cut back on their consumption of cigarettes. And everyone feels his or her muscles strengthen and firm up. To be sure, there are hazards and lower standards of hygiene. Furthermore, modern health care is not available in the hill and mountain areas. But when sensible precautions are taken, few get sick in Nepal. To the contrary, most people find it physically and spiritually enlightening.

Camp below the Trashi Labsta. (Stephen Bezruchka)

1 TREKKING STYLES AND RELATED ACTIVITIES

There are three basic approaches to trekking, but within each there are many variations as well as some related activities that can be enjoyed during or between treks. The style you choose depends on your budget, time available, and personal preferences. In addition, the areas you wish to visit dictate certain choices. Finally, your choice depends on what you want from your trek.

Trekking Without a Guide

This mode, also know as the "live on the land" approach, is very popular among budget-conscious travelers as well as those who wish to live among the people of Nepal during their treks. This is a good way to learn Nepali, if traveling off the popular routes. You can sleep and eat with the local people or, in areas where there are no inhabitants, carry your own food and shelter. Along the popular routes, your main human contacts may be with other similar-minded trekkers. Food can often be purchased at the last inhabited place on your route, but be sure to check availability beforehand. Local porters can be hired at this stage or at the start of a trek. If you have porters, they can keep you on the right trails.

Trekking along the popular tourist trails (see summary at end of next chapter) has changed considerably since 1969, when I first came to Nepal. Enterprising Nepalis have established hotels that provide rooms for trekkers and offer international menus. Villagers are very likely to run after you or at least shout if you take the wrong turn on a trail. While this has diminished the sense of adventure, it has made it easy for people to travel without a guide, carrying their own small loads. Of course, by avoiding these popular trails, it is still possible to experience Nepal as it was before these changes.

In some areas, for example from Pokhara to Thak Khola, or in Khumbu, more luxurious accommodations and eating places cater to trekkers. These establishments provide Western style food and comforts. They are, of course, more expensive than the facilities found along the trails less popular with tourists. But they do allow trekkers to travel without a great deal of hassle.

With few people in the party, large distances can be covered quickly if necessary or desired. Such travel, especially on the standard treks described in this book, can be very rewarding and expenses can be quite low. Daily costs, not including any porters, are usually less than $3 per person.

Disadvantages of this mode of travel include spending considerable time in Kathmandu organizing affairs, getting lost occasionally—especially when traveling off the standard routes, and often being limited in the areas you can travel to.

Trekkers who choose to travel without a guide are more likely to be disappointed in some of their expectations than those who have their treks catered through a professional agency, although most people seem to manage quite well. But the advantage of trekking without a guide is that learning to deal without the cultural props you grew up with can be a very educational and enlightening exper-ience. Attempting to view the world through Nepali eyes may be the best lesson trekking in Nepal has to offer.

Trekking With a Guide

This mode of travel can mean arranging and outfitting a large trek just as a professional agency would do. Or it might mean simply hiring a guide to accom-pany a small group. A guide can keep the party on the correct trails and may sometimes cook, carry a load, or attend to other chores. Porters, that is people hired strictly for load-carrying, can be taken on along the trail when necessary, or hired in Kathmandu before starting a trek. The guide can take care of this. Parties may camp all the way; or they may eat and sleep in local homes or hotels, and camp only where necessary. Those camping all the way must carry considerable food and equipment. A guide can be hired either privately, or through a trekking agency. The agency can also make other arrangements, such as providing equip-ment and porters. Guides can often be hired at points along the trek for difficult portions and high passes, although this can't be assured in advance.

Parties wishing more of a spirit of adventure—and a savings on wages—can hire an inexperienced guide. Such a person may be an older Sherpa who has been a porter for treks and mountaineering expeditions, or a youngster eager to break into the business. Such people can be excellent and will often do much more than guide—they can cook, carry things, and help in other ways. On my first trek in Nepal in 1969, I hired a young inexperienced Sherpa. We both learned a great deal and enjoyed ourselves immensely. He has since gone on to become an excellent guide, and now with his brother runs a company that supplies dehydrated foods to trekkers.

The advantage of trekking with a guide is that it allows considerable flexibility in the choice of route, diversions, and scheduling. There is also a greater oppor-tunity for interacting with the local people encountered en route, especially if the party and the number of assistants (guides and porters) are small. However, ar-ranging all this after arriving in Nepal can be time-consuming, frustrating, and somewhat difficult, and it is sometimes helpful to seek the assistance of a local trekking agency.

Trekking in a modest style is a good means of getting money into the hands of people in the hills of Nepal, since the villagers who provide food, run the inns, and work as porters benefit directly. This may be a more effective means of economic assistance than international aid. Costs for this style are less than for professionally arranged treks, and depend on the number of assistants hired.

Trekking With a Professional Agency

While initially only Mountain Travel, founded in 1965 by the indomitable Himalayan veteran, Lieutenant Colonel James Roberts, was able to offer compre-hensive trekking arrangements for the traveler, many similar businesses operate today (see Addresses in Appendix).

Many travel agencies and organizations based in other countries organize groups for treks to various regions of Nepal. The actual arrangements for the treks are customarily handled by one of the approved trekking agencies in Nepal. No listing of non-Nepali agencies is given here, but information about them can be ob-tained from travel agents in your own country. Even though a particular trekking agency in Nepal works with an affiliated agency in your country, you can usually deal directly with the Nepali agency if you prefer. A list of these is provided in Appendix A.

This mode of travel is expensive but it offers a degree of luxury that is not available in the others. Treks are organized for both large and small groups and are usually conducted by Sherpa guides called Sirdars, who are often famous for their mountaineering exploits on Himalayan expeditions. The guides speak sufficient English to allay fears of language difficulties. A large retinue of porters ensures that nothing essential to the comfort and well-being of trekkers is left behind. The parties usually camp in tents near villages and skilled cooks prepare fine meals. Most of the necessary equipment is provided. These parties often have someone with medical expertise along, and emergencies can usually be handled more quickly than in less experienced groups. There is also no need to spend time planning for all these arrangements in Kathmandu.

Such parties usually have to stick to a pre-determined route and schedule, so there is less leeway for interesting diversions or layovers. Members of large parties must generally keep together. Trekkers in professionally organized parties are usually rather insulated from the local people encountered en route. Indeed, the participants tend to relate exclusively to one another, to the guides, and to other employees of the trek.

This kind of travel is especially suited for those who have neither the time nor the desire to make their own arrangements, but wish to enjoy the scenery of the country. The costs, exclusive of air fares and charters, run from about $20 to $100 per person per day and vary according to the length of the trek and the number of people in the party. Arrangements must usually be made before leaving your own country, either directly or through agents. In contrast to people who prefer other styles of trekking, those who embark on this type of trek are paying for comfort and security.

Some people argue that an agency trek is preferable since your food is carried from Kathmandu and does not deplete local resources. On such treks, however, all of the food for the porters is purchased along the route, and some food for trekkers may be purchased locally as well. The argument that Sirdars for trekking groups will get the best prices for local foods does not always hold up. When the primary concern is that the trek go well, costs can mount. I have seen cooks and Sirdars for trekking groups pay far more than the going price for local food items. As a consequence, the price for villagers goes up too. Traveling on your own or only with a few employed people reduces the impact on local food resources.

Finally, much of the money to support an agency trek leaves Nepal to pay for imported food and equipment. There is little sharing of profits with the locals. An estimated eighty percent of Nepal's dollar earnings from tourism is spent to import goods and services required by visitors. This figure seems high, but it does spell out the situation. I don't mean to discourage travel with agency treks, but it is best to decide what your hopes, needs, and means are and to travel accordingly.

Choosing a Trekking Style

It is basically true that "anybody" can trek in Nepal—if they try to match their experience to the difficulty of the journey they plan. Given the tremendous travel expense, time commitment, and for many, a once-in-a-lifetime opportunity, ambition can easily outstrip ability. It used to be that trekking in the Himalaya was at the high end of the spectrum of walking, backpacking, and mountaineering. Often, mountaineers experienced on ranges such as the Alps, Rockies, or Sierra became "mere" trekkers in the Himalaya, where routes carried them thousands of feet above the summits of their home ranges.

But these days, a disturbing trend is changing the nature of trekking in Nepal. Less experienced hikers are electing to undertake harder treks. More and more people are spending their first night ever in a sleeping bag on a trail in Nepal. Walking in the mountains is a skill that requires some training and experience. In the last year or so, the number of tourists who have fallen from trails (fatally and non-fatally) is up dramatically. Inexperienced hikers are becoming incapacitated by severe musculoskeletal problems that could have been prevented by adequate training.

Trekking should be regarded as an expedition: you are often days from any form of outside help, and unless you are experienced and confident of your self-sufficiency skills, first treks should be on established tourist trails that offer a minimum of difficulty and no dangerous passes. The scenery in Nepal is no less exotic because other outsiders have seen it before you. As your experience, skills and confidence grow, you can plan more challenging, isolated, and adventurous treks.

MORE TIME THAN MONEY

If you crave adventure, have plenty of time but limited money, want to adapt your schedule to circumstances, and want to interact with local people as much as possible, then organize your own trek, especially if you want to travel one of the popular routes.

MORE MONEY THAN TIME

An organized trek with one of the well-known agencies may be for you if you have a limited amount of time yet want to cover a major route and can accept limitations in flexibility. An agency trek may be an attractive option if you enjoy the idea of camping in Nepal with food prepared to familiar tastes and with all arrangements made for you. One disadvantage of such treks is the relative lack of close contact with the local people.

Of course, the dichotomy is not quite so cut and dried. Many agencies allow some flexibility in scheduling, and with increasing competition they try to adapt treks to your needs.

Trekking Alone

Those trekking alone would be wise to hire a guide or a porter, especially on trails with few foreigners. If traveling alone along the popular trails, you will find it easy to meet up with similar-minded people. Plan to touch bases with them periodically for support. It is also easy to meet and join up with other trekkers in Kathmandu.

Women should not travel alone but should try to find a female guide or porter. Nepalis find it difficult to understand why foreigners, especially women, would travel alone—indeed Nepali women wouldn't. Local people seem to consider a woman walking alone to be a witch or person of low morals. The same caution applies to men, although it is more common to see a Nepali man traveling alone.

There have been rare instances of attacks on trekkers, usually those who are alone, camping in remote areas. I can no longer state that you are perfectly safe from human harm in Nepal, but if you follow the principles outlined in Chapter 4 and are sensitive to your hosts, you should have no problem. Travel in Nepal is certainly safer than in most other countries, including your homeland!

Trekking With Small Children

Small children need not be left at home in order for the adults of a family to enjoy a trek in Nepal. Certainly a trek with children will be different from one without children, but it need not be any less enjoyable or memorable. In fact, children can be real icebreakers in an alien land; they provide a common link with which the local people can identify.

Although when I first came to Nepal in 1969 no one trekked with children except occasional expatriots working there, now you often see families along the trails. The Nepali village people are open and friendly for the most part, and the sight of a trekking family will interest them. Indeed, while you eat, they will often care for the child, holding, comforting, and playing with it. Although a small child may initially be overwhelmed by the interest of outsiders, an exciting cultural exchange can be encouraged if the child becomes accustomed to the local people. Flexibility in the itinerary is particularly important if the family hopes to achieve this communication. Many of the difficulties encountered in trekking with children in Nepal can be overcome if the family tries some overnight trips hear home. In fact, I would not recommend that a family attempt trekking in Nepal if they have not done overnight hikes together at home. In this section, problems specific to Nepal will be discussed, and in Chapter 5 there is an important section on health care for children. It should be read concurrently.

Also, it is probably best not to travel with very young children, perhaps those under five years of age, unless parents have prior trekking experience in Nepal. If a child is over five, it is advisable to have more than one child along for companionship. Families who wish to trek independently of an agency will find it easiest to take one of the popular routes where lodges catering to trekkers offer separate rooms, and the Nepali staff can help care for the children at mealtimes.

Don't assume that treks must be modest in scope. One family with children, aged four and six, trekked with another family with a child of six. They covered almost 500 miles in fifty-five days from Pokhara to Baitadi in the extreme western part of Nepal. This trek was more ambitious than most people would choose to undertake with children of that age, but for them it was a wonderful experience that none of them will forget. The two families, by carrying moderate packs themselves (30 to 50 lb, 13 to 23 kg) and living off the land insofar as possible, were able to get by with only two porters. They never carried any of the children except across streams or rickety bridges. Thus the pace was slower than that of normal adults, but they compensated for this by increased attention to peripheral activities such as photography and birdwatching. The children appeared to thrive on the physical exercise. They received lots of personalized attention from their parents and were constantly stimulated by new sights and activites. At the end of the day, they had little energy left and usually fell asleep soon after dinner.

It may not be inappropriate to consider taking older children out of school for a trek. Understanding school officials will probably agree that what the children learn on the trip far outweighs any loss in book learning. Parents can help children keep journals of their activities and adventures, which will aid them with their writing and provide a resource for later use.

Take your children trekking. They may enjoy Nepal as much as you. (Stephen Bezruchka)

Younger children need not be left at home. Infants can trek, though I would recommend that only breast-fed infants be taken. One trekking family with a two-year-old found it most convenient that the child was still breast feeding. In Nepal children nurse at their mother's breasts until they are quite old. Certainly this is the most sanitary method of feeding, and it has many other health benefits.

Families with younger children have carried them in a back- or front-style pack carrier. A back carrier with an elevator seat is probably best. Other families hire a porter, the best being a woman—a Sherpani or hill Nepali. It will be difficult to hire just one woman. Two together could porter and help take care of the child. Most such women have children themselves and enjoy singing and playing with the child. They usually prefer carrying the child in a *Doko,* a conical wicker basket, using a tumpline. A foam pad for the inside and an umbrella attached to the basket rim for shade keep the child comfortable. It is not unreasonable to carry a child up to 44 lb (22 kg) in this manner. Some children, especially active ones, may not tolerate being carried in a basket by a stranger. The method you choose depends on your personal preferences. Certainly carrying your own child can contribute to an important relationship with him or her.

Children in diapers need not be a problem. Some parents prefer disposable diapers. Never dispose of them in a hearth fire in a Nepali home. Burn them out of sight of others and bury the ashes. Infants might need six a day, while two a day should be enough for semi-toilet-trained toddlers. A few disposable diapers may come in handy in case of diarrhea, even for a toilet-trained child. Disposable diapers are not available in Nepal. Actually, I feel it is preferable to use cloth diapers, which either you or the porters wash. It is not a chore that a porter can be expected to do, but an arrangement can be worked out beforehand. Your porter will probably prefer to wash the diapers in a stream away from town and out of sight of the villagers. Try to avoid pollution of streams when washing diapers. Bring a string for a clothesline, soap and clothespins. Drying diapers would be very difficult in the monsoon. In fact, it is probably not advisable to trek with young children at that time. Nepali childen never use diapers as we know them. A "potty" or chamber pot for toilet-trained children may be helpful. Otherwise, unfamiliar surroundings may make defecation difficult for them.

Food for children can vary a great deal. The children of one trekking family soon became willing consumers of *daal bhaat,* the local rice and lentil dish. Those on treks organized by professional agencies have few problems if the cook prepares familiar foods. A greal deal depends on the parents' attitude and their children's food fussiness. It may be wise to keep some favorite snacks handy.

Parents who have hiked with their children under various conditions should have no difficulties choosing clothing for them. The new synthetic-pile garments, worn over a zippered pajama suit, may be the best choice for cold days. Such clothes are warm, light in weight, and quick drying.

Most children, like many adults, find it difficult to be continually stared at. This is the case when staying in a Nepali home that is not set up as a hotel with separate rooms for trekkers. To avoid this problem, take a tent or choose one of the popular treks with lodges or hotels along the way. A tent gives your children a familiar place to go, away from the prying eyes of the crowds that always assemble to stare at the funny little white children. Children may find it reassuring to sleep between their parents when staying in unfamiliar surroundings.

Your children may be surprised to see that Nepali children have few toys. It is wise to bring a few items to keep your children amused since they won't be as inspired by the beauty of the countryside as you. Playing with toys with the Nepali children could be fascinating for your children, but avoid setting an unfortunate precedent by indiscriminately giving out toys to local children. Nepali children are quite happy with the toys they have, and they could become quite depressed if they knew about the toys they don't and can't have.

Be aware of the physical hazards in Nepal. There are plenty of places inside homes, along the trails, and in the fields where a slip or fall could be disastrous for a child. Dogs (particularly rabid ones) represent an occupational hazard for trekkers in Nepal, and even more so for children. Exercise extreme caution around all dogs and villages as options after being bitten are few and unpleasant. Although they are not known to be carriers of rabies, water buffalo frequently have surly dispositions and delight in charging small children.

Altitude may affect children more than adults. Also it may be difficult to ascertain whether it is altitude or some other illness that is causing symptoms in infants and young children. (See "Altitude Illness" in Chapter 5.) Like most aspects of trekking in Nepal, the experience of going as a family can be rewarding and enlightening if you prepare yourself adequately.

Trekking in the Monsoon

In Nepal all paths and bridges are liable to disappear or change at no notice due to monsoons, act of Gods, etc.

Note on trekking map, 1972

Although many consider it out of the question, trekking during the rainy season has been discovered by a select few "Nepalophiles." There are several reasons to consider joining these eccentrics. Many people can come to Nepal only during the Western summer holidays, which correspond to the monsoon. Some want to trek when popular trails are not packed with foreigners. Others are interested in the plant and animal life that is most spectacular at this time. It is undeniably a most beautiful time of the year. Everything is lush and green. The clouds perform dramatically, and periodically part to reveal the splendor of spectacular vistas. Mist-shrouded mountain views during the monsoon may be unforgettable. The high country is alive with activity as people pasture their animals on the upper slopes.

During the monsoon, Nepal is much like it was years ago, except that now there are better bridges, portable radios, more supplies available, and children who may remember to beg when they see you. You can plan your route either to get behind (north of) the Himalaya (north of Pokhara), or to the far west (RaRa), or into the Himalaya (Khumbu) to experience less rainfall. See the climatological data in the next chapter.

There are problems, however. Everything tends to get soaked. Trails are often very muddy, always wet, and sometimes treacherous. It is always hot and muggy at low altitudes though more comfortable higher up. Distant views are clouded most of the time. Bridges sometimes wash out, necessitating time-consuming and difficult detours. What may have been a trickle in the dry season becomes a deep, fast torrent in the monsoon. Travel thus often involves fording rivers. At times you may have to wait a day or two for the water level to drop enough for a safe ford. To make matters worse, leeches populate the forests at higher altitudes (see Chapter 5), while mosquitoes abound at lower elevations.

Yet, just as you adjust to trekking in Nepal during the dry season, so you can adapt your lifestyle to the monsoon. Certain items of equipment are essential: a waterproof cover for your pack, sheets of plastic for the porter loads, an umbrella, and footwear with good traction, preferably new waffle-soled training flats or boots with flexible Vibram soles. Skirts for women, preferably with a hem about calf length, and shorts for men are the most practical clothing. Although women should wear skirts in towns for cultural reasons (see Chapter 4), many prefer to wear pants on monsoon-soaked trails and only change into skirts when they stop for the evening in a village. Most waterproof rain parkas and cagoules are not very useful—if you do not get wet from the outside, you will soak in sweat from the inside. The new gear made from Gore-Tex, a fabric that breathes, yet is waterproof if kept clean, may be suitable for the monsoon when at higher altitudes. Gore-Tex jackets with underarm zips allow considerable ventilation, as do pants with side zips. Pile clothing or garments of synthetic, down-like material are useful in the wet high altitudes.

In planning a monsoon trek, do not plan on covering too much distance in a short time. It is hard to equal dry season trekking times. Many of the trails will be different during the monsoon. Drier ridges are usually taken instead of the flooded valley bottoms. Take time to enjoy village life, to sample the fruits and vegetables in season, and to enjoy the prodigious plant life. And do not tell too many people how much you enjoyed it!

Mountaineering

Among the first outsiders to come to Nepal were mountaineers looking for ways onto the highest summits. Much of the early descriptions of the countryside comes from them. The history of climbing on the highest peaks is itself fascinating, and has been well chronicled by Louis Baume in *Sivalaya* (see Recommended Reading).

Besides the many expeditionary peaks, there are eighteen minor peaks, called trekking summits, which can be climbed by trekkers if they get the proper permits. The fact that they are called trekking summits in no way implies they are trivial. Some are difficult and dangerous, and a few have only recently had first ascents. These summits are not suitable for trekkers who do not have substantial experience in alpine climbing. Further information on these climbs can be obtained from mountaineering journals, trekking agencies, and the climbing community.

To attempt one of these peaks, application must be made to the Nepal Mountaineering Association (NMA), G.P.O. Box 1435 Ram Shah Path, Kathmandu. Permission is granted for one month, and may be extended. This period applies only to the time spent at or above base camp. Applications are on a first-come, first-served basis and are not transferable. A fee must be paid, and for groups exceeding ten members an extra charge is levied for each additional climber. The charge for the time extension is twenty-five percent of the original fee. Fees are payable at the time of application and are non-refundable. Climbers can apply after they arrive in Nepal.

A Sirdar, or guide, registered with the NMA must accompany each party. He must be provided with a salary, food, and tent accommodations. If he is required to go above base camp, he must be furnished with climbing equipment and clothing, and insured to Rs. 75,000. All climbing must be clean: hardware must be removed and camps left clean. Finally, a report must be submitted to the NMA upon return. Applications should include the climbing fee and the following information: the name of the peak; the period of time for which the permit is requested; the route (peaks can be climbed by any route); the name and nationality of each member of the party; the name, nationality, passport number, and home address of the leader; the appointed representative in Kathmandu (usually a trekking agency); and the name and organization or address of the guide or Sirdar.

The trekking peaks, grouped according to area and using the term *Himal* which means range, are:

Khumbu Himal

Imja Tse (Island Peak) (6189 m)
Kwangde (6187 m)
Kusum Kangru (6369 m)
Lobuje (Lobuche) East (6119 m)
Khongma Tse (Mehra Peak) (5820 m)
Mera Peak (6437 m)
Pokalde (5806 m)

Rolwaling Himal

Pharchamo (6318 m)
Ramdung (6060 m)

Langtang Himal

Ganja La Chuli (5846 m)

Ganesh Himal

Paldor Peak (5928 m)

Manang Himal

Chulu East (6059 m)
Chulu West (6583 m)
Pisang (6091 m)

Annapurna Himal

Singu Chuli (Fluted Peak) (6390 m)
Hiunchuli (6441 m)
Mardi Himal (5586 m)
Chuli (Tent Peak) (5500 m)

If you have been to Kala Pattar and other high altitude trekking destinations in Nepal and are looking for new "summits," are trekking peaks for you? If you are not a mountaineer, by and large the answer is no. While some are not technically difficult, they do involve mountaineering skills, unlike almost all the treks described in this book, which require just walking. Considerable familiarity with climbing on rock, snow and ice, camping on snow, and the understanding of objective hazards is necessary.

The general rules and regulations for expeditionary peaks are too lengthy to document here. These regulations can be obtained by writing the Ministry of Tourism, His Majesty's Government, Kathmandu. Essentially, a license must be obtained by application to the Ministry of Tourism "with the recommendation of a reputed and recognized mountaineering institution in the appropriate country, or the embassy of that country in Nepal." Usually this is the national alpine club, if one exists. A royalty of Rs. 10,000 to Rs. 15,000 must be paid, and the party must take a liaison officer chosen by the government. There are rules governing what he must be provided and paid; these rules also describe his duties and functions. There are similar rules regarding the Sirdar and high altitude porters. Penalties for disregarding the rules include banishment from Nepal for three to five years or disqualification from climbing in Nepal for five to ten years. An institution that disregards the rules can be disqualified from sponsoring climbs for three years.

The current list of all expeditionary peaks follows. There are restrictions on some of them.

Ama Dablang (6856 m)	Ganesh Himal II (7150 m)
Annapurna I (8091 m)	Ganesh Himal III (7132 m)
Annapurna II (7937 m)	Ganesh Himal IV (7102 m)
Annapurna III (7555 m)	Ganesh Himal V (6950 m)
Annapurna IV (7525 m)	Gangapurna (7454 m)
Annapurna South (7237 m)	Gauri Shankar (7150 m)
Api (7132 m)	Gurja Himal (7193 m)
Baruntse (7220 m)	Gyachung Kang (7922 m)
Baudha (6672 m)	Gyalzen Peak (6705 m)
Bhrikuti (6720 m)	Himalchuli (7893 m)
Bobaye Himal (6808 m)	Himalchuli North (7371 m)
Chamar (7177 m)	Himalchuli West (7540 m)
Chamlang (7319 m)	Himlung Himal (7126 m)
Changla (6715 m)	Hongde (6556 m)
Cheo Himal (6812 m)	Jagula (5785 m)
Chobuje (6689 m)	Jethi Behurani (6849 m)
Cholatse (6440 m)	Jongsang Peak (7473 m)
Cho Oyu (8153 m)	Kagmara I (5960 m)
Cho Polu (6734 m)	Kanchenjunga (8593 m)
Churen Himal (7375 m)	Kanchenjunga Central (8496 m)
Dhampas (6012 m)	Kanchenjunga South (8490 m)
Dhaulagiri I (8167 m)	Kande Hiunchuli (6627 m)
Dhaulagiri II (7751 m)	Kangbachen (7902 m)
Dhaulagiri III (7715 m)	Kangtega (6809 m)
Dhaulagiri IV (7661 m)	Kanguru (6981 m)
Dhaulagiri V (7618 m)	Kanjeralwa (6612 m)
Dhaulagiri VI (7269 m)	Kanjiroba (6882 m)
Dorje Lakpa (6990 m)	Keryolung (6681 m)
Everest, Sagarmatha (8848 m)	Khangsar Kang (Roc Noir) (7485 m)
Ganesh Himal I (7406 m)	Khatang (6853 m)

Kirat Chuli (Tent Peak,
  Kanchenjunga Himal) (7365 m)
Kumbhakarna (Jannu) (7710 m)
Lamjung Himal (6986 m)
Langshisa Ri (6300 m)
Langtang Lirung (7246 m)
Langtang Ri (7239 m)
Lhotse (8511 m)
Lhotse Shar (8383 m)
Lobuche West (6145 m)
Lonpo Gang (Big White Peak)
  (7083 m)
Madiya Peak (6800 m)
Makalu (8481 m)
Makalu II (Kangchungtse) (7680 m)
Manapathi Himal (6380 m)
Manaslu (8156 m)
Manaslu North (7157 m)
Nala Kankar (6935 m)
Nampa (6754 m)
Nepal Peak (7168 m)
Ngadi Chuli (Peak 29) (7541 m)
Nilgiri Central (6940 m)
Nilgiri North (7061 m)

Nilgiri South (6839 m)
Numbur (6954 m)
Nuptse (7879 m)
Omi Kang Ri (7992 m)
Patrasi (6860 m)
Phurbi Chhyachu (6658 m)
Pumori (7145 m)
Putha Hiunchuli (7246 m)
Saipal (7031 m)
Shartse Himal (7502 m)
Shey Shikhar (Junction Peak)
  (6139 m)
Sisne Himal (6945 m)
Sita Chuchura (6611 m)
Taboche (6542 m)
Tarke Kang (Glacier Dome) (7193 m)
Thamserku (6623 m)
Tilicho (7132 m)
Tripura Hiun Chuli (Hanging Glacier
  Peak) (6550 m)
Tukuche Peak (6920 m)
Varaha Shikha (Fang) (7647 m)
Yalung Kang (8420 m)

River Running

Over the last ten years, many of the great rivers of Nepal have been run by rubber rafts, canoes, kayaks, and other craft. There is nothing unique about rivers in Nepal as far as such activities are concerned. There are the usual difficulties in transporting the boats to the starting point and arranging to have them picked up at the destination. Rivers commonly rafted include the Trisuli and the Gandaki. You can arrange motor transportation to and from these rivers. Another popular choice is the Sun Kosi. You can go by vehicle to the starting point, but you must fly back from Biratnagar after the journey. Rivers like the Bheri, the Marsyangdi, and the Arun offer more challenges because of logistic problems. Others like the Karnali are extremely challenging.

While some professional river runners have done expeditionary trips independently, most people deal with agencies in Nepal that specialize in rafting (see Appendix for Addresses).

Running

Running, which has become very popular in the West, has in some measure come to Nepal. While few Nepalis run regularly along the trails, stories abound of incredibly short times taken by Nepalis, usually as mail runners for mountaineering expeditions. Jay Longacre became known in much of Nepal as "The American Runner" for his 4¼-day run from Kathmandu to Kala Pattar near the base of Mount Everest, a journey that takes more than 15 days to trek. Few people will want to challenge that record, but some may wish to combine running with trekking. The following information is based on Jay's experiences in Nepal.

Three Devils Rapids on the Trisuli Khola. (Ane Haaland)

Most of the information for trekkers applies also to runners and won't be repeated here. The problems of altitude illness are very important and the cautions in Chapter 5 must be heeded. Physical conditioning does not prevent these problems. Runners, if they are alert to the symptoms, should at least be able to descend quickly to safety. If they persist in ascending despite serious symptoms, their risk is certainly greater. However, most runners won't be able to continue running, even with mild symptoms.

One danger of steep mountain running is the possibility of falling off the trail. If a runner stumbles, he should try to fall on his hands and knees onto the dirt. If he tries to remain upright, he may lurch off the trail and down the mountainside. To prevent injury, runners must master the techniques of running downhill. To avoid falling and injuring joints, a runner must shorten his stride, strike heel first with the knee slightly bent, and lean backward as little as possible. Practice it on hills near home first.

Proper shoes and clothing are basics for a pleasant run. Ripple-soled running shoes are preferable to waffle-soled shoes. The latter tend to wear quickly and to grip the trail too well, permitting feet to slide within the shoes. This causes blisters. Running without socks may help prevent blisters and it enables the runner to walk through water and across rivers easily.

Basically there are two ways of running outside the major cities and towns in Nepal: long solo runs covering two or more days and 50 mi (80 km) or more; and daily runs of more than an hour, alone or with a group, along or close to one of the main trekking trails. On long solo runs, you should retain a Sherpa guide (not a porter) to meet you at the end of your run with extra clothes and other needed supplies. On the run itself you need to carry sunscreen, petrolatum jelly, soap, face mask, wool mittens, one suit of long wool underwear, cap with a long bill, nylon all-weather suit, Nepali money, cup, sleeping bag, water bottle, iodine, map, pen, notebook, flashlight, sunglasses, extra clothes, and this book. All of this will fit into a small pack, and needn't weigh more than a few pounds. Wear shorts, tee shirt, and running shoes.

For daily runs along a main trekking route, hire a Sherpa guide to carry your sleeping bag and supplies. He can help by explaining the trails and by leaving earlier to wait for you at difficult or confusing areas. On these daily runs, you need only carry a cup, soap, petrolatum jelly, sunscreen, camera, iodine, and water bottle.

It is important to force yourself to drink frequently to prevent dehydration, even if you don't feel thirsty. It is unlikely you could drink too much.

Runners have greater difficulty with anal irritation than do trekkers. After each bowel movement, wash to help prevent irritation. Use the water in your bottle if necessary.

Bicycling

Nepal may never be the most popular spot for cycle tourists, but the spectacular scenery, almost traffic-free roads, and curious, hospitable Nepalis make the country a cycling haven. Donald Whittaker of Vancouver, Canada, recently bicycled from Kathmandu to Kala Pattar, the first person to do so. If you think bicycling the trails of Nepal may be for you, here are some of Don's suggestions:

Touring the country on the rather limited road network is easy enough with any properly outfitted ten-speed bike. Riding the trekking routes is also quite feasible, although it is recommended that you use an all-terrain bike (ATB) with fat, knobby tires, a low gear range, an extra-strong frame, and good stopping, cantilever brakes. Most importantly, the bike you take should be in top running condition, and you should be prepared to handle any mechanical problem that might arise, for the bike shops in Kathmandu only have parts for rather low-tech Indian and Chinese one-speed bikes. Bring along a few spare tubes, a spare tire, extra spokes, brake and gear cables, puncture kit, a pump, and possibly an extra rear gear changer, as well as any tools needed to work on the bike.

The choice of a route is important. The route from Kathmandu to Everest goes against the grain of the land, and requires considerable bicycle carrying. Other routes going up the Kali Gandaki, or even the Annapurna circuit, would offer easier stretches. Some cyclists have flown to Lukla and bicycled up from there. This option involves considerably fewer ascents and descents than bicycling all the way from Kathmandu.

Riding an ATB on the trekking trails is not always easy, but it is an interesting and often thrilling alternative to walking. The bike, fitted with a rear pannier carrying your day's needs, should weigh no more than forty pounds. Such a bike, so outfitted, is quite manageable for the motivated trekker to carry and ride. On the rougher sections of the trail, the bike can be carried over your shoulder, or on your back by using a tumpline. Pushing the bike over rough sections is not always easier, but it does give your shoulder or back a rest. The condition of the trail and your level of fitness will determine how much ground you can cover per day. You can expect to go about three-quarters to three times the speed of a walking trekker.

Coordinating your ride with a porter carrying your gear is not a problem. Just plan to meet at points along the day's trek for tea, lunch, and so forth. You must realize, though, that most natives along the trail have never seen a bicycle before,

Giving rides to children along the trail. (Don Whittaker)

so you'll be a real spectacle—something that might detract from a quiet mountain experience.

A small, light security cable is a good idea to discourage unauthorized test rides when you're not around your bike. If you carry any exposed items that might attract attention, keep an eye on your bicycle, or better still, remove that gear and keep it with you when you leave the vehicle.

Three last tips: invest in a bell, it speaks a universal language. Beware of yaks on the trail; they get very nervous around a bike and may run you off the trail. It is best to stop, dismount on the uphill side of the trail, and let them walk by. The same advice goes for buffaloes and other bovines, though yaks are the most temperamental. Finally, don't forget to ride on the left-hand side of the prayer walls. Happy trails!

Himalayan Weight Loss Treks

Are you in adequate physical shape but want to lose ten to twenty pounds, never be hungry while doing so, and want to keep the weight off? Undertake a twenty-day trek along a popular trail, carry your own pack, and eat as much *daal bhaat* twice a day as you wish. It works!

2 CHOOSING A TREK

Just go on and on... Do you see the mountain ranges there, far away? One behind another. They rise up. They tower. That is my deep, unending, inexhaustible kingdom.

Henrik Ibsen, *The Master Builder*

In choosing a trek, many factors must be considered. Important among them are the time available, the strength and ability of the members of the party, and the desires of the trekkers. Certain treks offer majestic mountain scenery; others a glimpse of hill life in Nepal; still others spectacular floral displays. Routes can be linked to provide many different experiences. Some entail entering potentially dangerous mountain terrain. Finally, the time of year is very important, as certain treks are difficult, if not impossible, during heavy snowfalls. Others are very uncomfortable in the pre-monsoon heat.

Weather

The usual trekking season lasts from October to May. During the remainder of the year, the monsoon makes traveling wet and offers little in the way of mountain views. In addition, leeches abound.

During October and November the skies are clear and good views can be expected. Occasional short storms may occur and the temperature often goes below freezing at night above 10,000 ft (3050 m). This is the most popular time for trekking.

December and January are the coldest months, but there is little snowfall. Again, excellent clear views are common. Temperatures constantly plunge below freezing at night above 10,000 ft (3050 m), and below 0°F (-18°C) at altitudes above 14,000 ft (4300 m). Some inhabitants of the northern Himalayan region head south for the winter at this time. It can be a hauntingly beautiful time of the year to trek.

February and March bring warmer weather, but more frequent storms and considerable snowfall at higher altitudes. Birds and flowers, especially the rhododendrons, are seen at the lower altitudes. Toward the end of March, haze—caused by dust from the plains of India—and smoke from local fires often obscure distant views. In addition, it becomes much warmer in the regions below 3000 ft (1000 m).

April and May are less suitable for trekking because of the heat—sometimes 100°F (38°C)—at altitudes below 3000 ft (1000 m). Also the haze mars distant views of the peaks. During these months, however, you encounter many species of plant and animal life not seen at other times. As the season progresses, the magnificent rhododendrons bloom at higher and higher altitudes until the flowers reach the tree line. Occasional pre-monsoon storms clear the haze and cool the atmosphere for a few days. While temperatures below freezing can be encountered above 12,000 ft (3600 m), it becomes quite warm below 8000 ft (2500 m) and almost oppressive below 3000 ft (1000 m).

CLIMATOLOGICAL DATA FOR SELECTED TREKKING TOWNS

(First line: Precipitation [mm]. Second line: Temperature—Max/Min [°C])

Town (Altitude [meters])	Jan.	Feb.	March	April	May	June	July	Aug.	Sept.	Oct.	Nov.	Dec.
Kathmandu (1336)	18	11	33	54	83	270	383	338	160	62	7	2
	19/2	21/3	25/7	28/10	30/4	29/18	28/19	28/19	27/17	27/12	23/7	20/2
Trisuli (541)	20	23	29	57	90	319	463	474	265	107	14	
	22/7	25/8	30/13	34/17	33/19	33/21	32/20	32/20	31/18	30/15	27/12	23/8
Langtang (3307)	2/-11	3/-10	8/-6	14/-2	17/2	18/7	19/9	18/8	16/7	15/2	9/-8	8/-10
Pokhara (833)	26	25	50	87	292	569	809	705	581	224	19	1
	19/6	21/8	26/12	30/15	30/18	29/20	29/21	29/21	28/20	26/17	23/11	20/7
Lumle (1520)	28	45	52	194	318	902	1522	1339	932	294	23	2
	13/5	14/6	19/10	22/13	22/14	23/17	22/17	23/17	21/16	20/14	16/9	13/6
Marpha (2955)	14	13	27	22	26	44	63	58	45	58	7	2
	10/-1	12/0	15/3	18/5	19/7	21/11	21/12	21/12	20/11	17/7	14/2	12/0
Jomosom (2800)	20	18	23	15	11	17	41	54	35	37	2	2
	12/-3	13/-1	16/2	20/4	23/7	25/12	25/14	25/14	23/11	19/5	15/1	13/-2
Jumla (2424)	32	40	43	27	40	70	162	173	92	39	1	4
	11/-2	13/-3	17/0	22/3	24/6	24/13	23/15	24/15	23/12	24/6	19/-4	15/-5
Jiri (2003)	18	20	47	71	139	381	599	605	337	93	15	3
	13/0	15/1	19/4	22/8	22/12	23/16	23/17	23/17	22/15	20/10	17/4	14/1
Namche Bazaar (3450)	26	23	34	26	41	140	243	243	165	78	9	39
	7/-8	6/-6	9/-3	12/1	14/4	15/6	16/8	16/8	15/6	12/2	9/3	7/-6
Tengboche (3867)	13	24	23	25	29	95	280	265	140	72	9	2
	4/-9	5/-9	9/-6	12/-4	14/-1	14/3	14/5	14/4	13/2	12/-2	8/-7	6/-7
Ilam (1300)	10	8	18	62	139	321	463	280	215	81	8	2
	16/9	18/10	23/14	25/16	25/17	25/18	25/18	25/19	25/17	25/16	21/12	18/8

Depending on the year, travel in the high country can be difficult because of heavy snowfalls, especially during January, February, and March. Passes, such as the Trashi Labtsa, the one near Gosainkund, and the Ganja La heading north into Langtang, are best attempted in autumn through December, or in later spring.

Trekking in the monsoon (June to the end of September) can be undertaken by the keen or experienced. Rain, mist, and fog can be expected almost daily, but occasionally clouds part to give spectacular views of the mountains. The flora are usually at their most colorful.

It is important to keep in mind that mountain weather is highly unpredictable. Classical signs of a storm approaching, such as a cirrus-clouded sky or a fall in barometric pressure, can be misleading.

The table on page 34 gives precipitation and maximum and minimum temperatures for various trekking locations. You can estimate temperatures for other nearby locations by a simple formula. For a rise of 100 m the temperature falls 0.65 °C; or for a rise of 1000 ft it falls 3.5 °F. Metric units are used with conversion scales below.

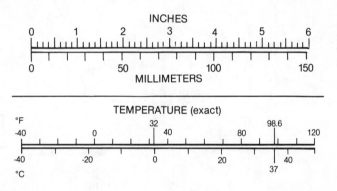

Helambu, Gosainkund, and Langtang

The trekking most accessible to Kathmandu is in Helambu, Gosainkund, and Langtang, all north of the capital city. There are trails linking the three regions, and as many can be visited as time and conditions permit. The minimum time for a brief visit is a week. Two weeks would allow you to combine two of the regions, and in three weeks you could enjoy the entire area.

Helambu is the region closest to Kathmandu. It is best approached from the northeast rim of the Kathmandu Valley. The name refers to a region at the north end of the Malemchi Khola (river). It is inhabited by people calling themselves Sherpas, though they are not closely related to the famed Sherpas of the Everest area. This region south of the main Himalayan chain provides an example of typical hill life in Nepal. A circuit can be made through the area with minimal backtracking if snow does not prevent travel on one high-level stretch. The trails are fairly good and only a few sections are difficult to follow. Cooked food and lodging are easily available, except on the high-level stretch. The route begins in areas of Hindu influence and goes through Buddhist villages. Side trips are possible and linkups can be made with Gosainkund and Langtang, weather conditions permitting. There are distant views of the Himalaya on the high-level stretch in good

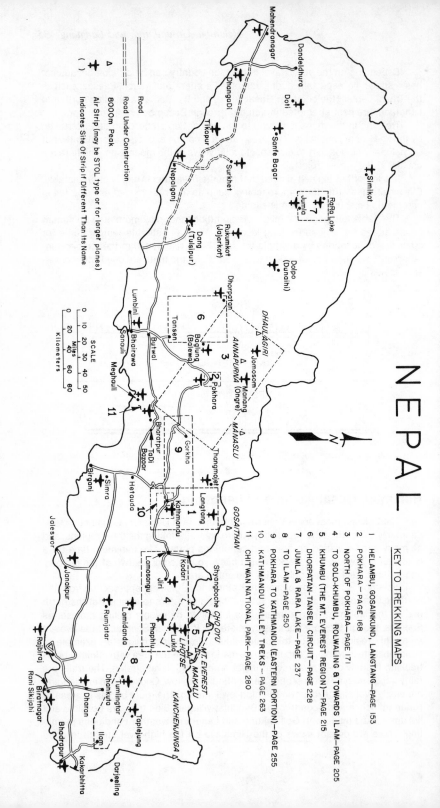

NEPAL

KEY TO TREKKING MAPS

1 HELAMBU, GOSAINKUND, LANGTANG—PAGE 153
2 POKHARA—PAGE 168
3 NORTH OF POKHARA—PAGE 171
4 TO SOLO-KHUMBU, ROLWALING & TOWARDS ILAM—PAGE 205
5 KHUMBU (THE MT. EVEREST REGION)—PAGE 215
6 DHORPATAN-TANSEN CIRCUIT—PAGE 228
7 JUMLA & RARA LAKE—PAGE 237
8 TO ILAM—PAGE 250
9 POKHARA TO KATHMANDU (EASTERN PORTION)—PAGE 255
10 KATHMANDU VALLEY TREKS — PAGE 263
11 CHITWAN NATIONAL PARK—PAGE 280

Road
Road Under Construction
8000m Peak
Air Strip (may be STOL type or for larger planes)
Indicates Site Of Strip If Different Than Its Name

SCALE

Kilometers
0 10 20 30 40 50
0 20 40 60 80
Miles

weather, except during late spring when they may be obscured by the haze. Rather than backtrack to Kathmandu, you could vary your exit to reach the Kathmandu-Kodari Road, either at Panchkhal if you head south from Tarang Marang, or at Baliphi if you take the Panch Pokhari side trip.

Gosainkund is the site of seven lakes that lie south of a major ridge between Helambu and the Trisuli river to the west. The area is uninhabited for the most part, but every August as many as 50,000 pilgrims crowd into the area for a festival near a lake that figures prominently in Hindu mythology. Trekkers may wish to visit this area from Trisuli Bazaar and, if conditions permit, cross a moderate pass to link up with Helambu. In the spring when rhododendrons are in bloom, it is a spectacular area. Below the lakes to the west, but above the Trisuli, is a cheese factory and a little-used Buddhist temple. Trekkers heading into this area must be self-sufficient.

Langtang is a Himalayan valley that lies north of both Helambu and Gosainkund. It is inhabited by Tibetan people and provides a glimpse of mountain life. Trails are straightforward, yet you can head east in the Langtang Valley beyond the last habitation to spectacular remote mountain areas, taking various side trips. Food and lodging are available for the most part. Linkups with Gosainkund are reasonably simple; but those with Helambu require crossing a substantial pass. Either way, you must be self-sufficient. There is an airstrip in the Langtang Valley at Kyangjin where planes can be chartered. They can be used to leave the area, but should not be taken in because the altitude gain is too abrupt. Most of Langtang and Gosainkund has been included in Langtang National Park in an attempt to preserve their beauty.

North of Pokhara

The area north of Pokhara is popular both with trekkers new to Nepal and with veterans. Expect to meet people from many different countries. The mountain scenery is as spectacular as any in Nepal, especially on the high routes. The many different ethnic groups are as interesting, if not as famous, as the Sherpas of Khumbu. Some of the areas provide perhaps the finest native cuisine in rural Nepal. One ethnic group, the *Thakali*, run numerous inns and hotels in the area. They have adapted their menu in many cases to the palates of foreign trekkers and can provide food and accommodations for those who wish to avoid local diets and the lodgings used by hill Nepalis. Finally, and perhaps most significantly, most of the treks in this region traverse through many different ecological zones. They begin with the customary terraces of the hills, encounter rain, deciduous, and pine forests, pass through arid, desert-like country similar to the Tibetan Plateau, and even reach alpine areas. Remarkable transitions through different areas, each with its customary animal life, can be made in a week or less.

Perhaps the most famous trek is from Pokhara to the Kali Gandaki river and up it to the Thak Khola region and to Jomosom, the administrative center of Mustang District. This route does not go higher than 10,000 ft (3048 m) and is not too strenuous. Along the way there are plenty of inns and hotels that cater to single trekkers or small parties. The trek is quite suitable for those traveling without guides or porters. The trail goes through an incredible variety of vegetation and follows one of the deepest gorges in the world—that between Annapurna and Dhaulagiri. On this route you are likely to encounter colorful mule caravans made musical by the tinkling of neck bells. Several side trips out of the Kali Gandaki Valley are possible. They are strenuous, but they reward tired hikers with spectacular views. This is a justifiably popular trek, and the only way to avoid

Getting a haircut in Tatopani. (Ane Haaland)

meeting other trekkers all along the trail is to take the side trips. Ten days is the minimum time for a round trip to Jomosom. Most parties prefer to take two weeks and travel up to Muktinath (12,475 ft, 3802 m), an ancient pilgrimage site a day beyond Jomosom.

The Annapurna Sanctuary, the basin southwest of Annapurna that is the source of the Modi Khola, is a fine objective for those who wish to trek only a short time, yet include a trip into alpine country. There is not quite the same variety in vegetation as on the trek up the Thak Khola since you never get north of the main Himalayan chain. The *Gurung* villages en route are particularly colorful. Ten days is the minimum time. Snowfall and avalanche hazards may make it difficult, if not impossible, to reach the sanctuary in winter. During the peak season, cooked food and shelter may be available for the entire journey, though it may not be adequate for the demand.

Manang, the region north and east of the Annapurna massif, is a third worthwhile objective north of Pokhara. This area was finally opened to foreign travel in 1977. The people of the villages of Manang are traders and many of them, world travelers. The scenery north of the main Himalayan chain is spectacular. It takes over a week to reach the town of Manang. There are no *Thakali* here running the kind of hotels and lodges for tourists that you find on the trail to Jomosom. If you don't travel with an organized group, you are more apt to eat in people's homes or in simple *bhaTTi* (inns). Some people have told me that they preferred Manang to Thak Khola for this reason. Beyond, a high pass, the Thorong La, leads over to Muktinath. This pass can be difficult or impossible in the winter and early spring because of snow. But for those able to cope with the high altitudes, the pass allows a complete circuit of the Annapurna massif without backtracking. While you can usually travel to Manang carrying only minimal food and shelter, it is necessary to be self-sufficient to cross the Thorung La. While some facilities may be available on both sides of the pass, they may not meet the demand during the popular season.

The classic trek in this region, combining Manang and Thak Khola in a circuit, covers more than 150 mi (240 km) and requires at least three weeks. The Thorong La pass is best crossed from Manang to Thak Khola in order to take advantage of better campsites and allow enough time for acclimatization. It is feasible to include the Annapurna Sanctuary on the circuit. There is an airstrip at Jomosom, and scheduled or charter flights from Kathmandu can shorten treks. You should not fly to Jomosom and then attempt the crossing to Manang unless you spend enough time acclimatizing. The altitude gain is too abrupt for safety. Similarly, there is now an airstrip in Manang at Ongre with scheduled flights. For the same reason entering this area by plane is not recommended.

Many trekkers with little time make a circuit from Pokhara to GhoDapani, down to the Kali Gandaki, to Baglung, and then to Pokhara. Other such circuits include: to Ghandrung via Chandrakot and return via Dhampus; to GhoDapani and return via Ghandrung. A pleasant short trip would be to walk to NagDAADa via Sarankot or Phedi, then to KAADe, to Dhampus and return. There are many other fine possibilities.

This area provides great ethnic and geographic diversity together with spectacular mountain scenery. A trek here can be as easy or as difficult as you wish.

Pokhara can be reached from Kathmandu by foot, road, or air, or from India by road or air. Flight delays to or from Pokhara are common during the peak tourist season, so it is best to make reservations as far in advance as possible. A week or more may be necessary.

Solu-Khumbu

Solu-Khumbu is the district south and west of Mount Everest. It is populated by Sherpas, an ethnic group that has achieved fame because of the exploits of its men on mountaineering expeditions. Khumbu is the name of the northern half of this region, which includes the highest mountain in the world and many of the 8000 m (26,247 ft) summits. Most of Khumbu is part of Sagarmatha National Park. Solu, the southern portion, is less rugged, but it has many interesting monasteries and villages.

The attractions are the majestic mountains, the villages in the high mountain valleys, the associated monasteries, and the interesting inhabitants. The area is popular, and outside of the monsoon, many trekkers are encountered. Some potential visitors might be put off by this, but where else can you find so many of the world's highest mountains together with communities of people living among them? By contrast, the inhabited areas of the Karakorum in Pakistan are few and the villages are far from the great mountains there. Actually, fewer than 6000 people a year visit Khumbu, while many more crowd into small areas of well-known European and North American mountain parks in a weekend! While you can count on meeting many trekkers on the standard route to the base of Mount Everest (except in the monsoon, when there will be no one else there), it is quite possible to spend time in Khumbu and its environs without meeting other trekkers. For almost two weeks one autumn I did not see a single trekker on part of my wanderings in Khumbu and on the trek out. And I didn't concoct a devious route to avoid people.

To avoid getting altitude sickness in Khumbu, make sure you stay a night or two in Pheriche. (Dave Hardenbergh)

This should not be taken as a plea to get more trekkers into Khumbu, merely a statement that while it is popular, you needn't always feel crowded.

A survey of trekkers conducted in October 1978 rated the popularity of the following trails according to number of trekkers (in order from highest to lowest): Namche Bazaar to Pheriche; Pheriche to Lobuche; Namche Bazaar to Khumjung-Kunde; Namche Bazaar to Thami; Lobuche to Kala Pattar; Namche Bazaar to Gokyo, to Phortse, to Chhukhung, to Gokyo's Kala Pattar, to Everest Base Camp, to Island Peak, to Trashi Labtsa, to Pass 5420 m.

Travel to and from Khumbu can pose logistic problems. Royal-Nepal Airlines (RNAC) has scheduled flights from Kathmandu to Lukla, an airstrip located one to two days south of Namche Bazaar, the entrance to Khumbu. While getting flights to Lukla can be a problem, finding a seat back to Kathmandu can be even more trying since weather sometimes delays landings for weeks! Several hundred trekkers can be stranded there, with their patience wearing thin as they find themselves belatedly close to the pressures of modern civilization. There are other airstrips in the region, but the one at Shyangboche, close to Namche Bazaar, is even higher and best avoided for flights in. For most trekkers, it is not useful for flights out, as the planes landing there do so only to service the Everest View Hotel. Trekkers who land at high altitudes such as at Lukla and venture into the rarefied altitudes are at greater risk of altitude illness. Thus it is preferable to walk to Khumbu, and to fly out if you can tolerate delays. Part of the pleasure of walking to Khumbu is in enjoying the beautiful countryside of hill Nepal and in anticipating your arrival in Khumbu as you follow the footsteps of many mountaineering expeditions.

Two week is the minimum time I would recommend spending in Khumbu if your goal is the foot of Everest. If you walk from Lamosangu on the Kathmandu-Kodari Road and fly back, the entire trip takes three to four weeks. Walking to and from Khumbu makes the trip at least a month and probably more. By walking in, the trekker samples midland Nepal as well as the Sherpa country. Many trekkers find the walk to Khumbu better than the destination itself. Other approaches to Khumbu on foot include walking to Rolwaling from Barabise on the Kathmandu-Kodari Road or crossing the Trashi Labtsa Pass. Another attractive exit is to walk southeast to Ilam. Also you can enter and leave from the Tarai. Finally, airstrips at Phaphlu in Solu, at Rumjatar and Lamidanda in the south, and at Jiri in the west can shorten approaches or exits.

For those planning to trek on their own, there should be few problems obtaining cooked food and shelter on the standard route to Khumbu, and, except for the last day, on the trek to the base of Mount Everest. However, shortages do occur at times, and it is best to carry some food in reserve. While a Sherpa guide or porter may not be absolutely necessary, there is a great advantage in having one whose home is in Khumbu. He can often give you a hospitable base of operations, and hospitality in the area.

The Khumbu trekking area offers a visit to the homeland of the Sherpas, a chance to get close to the highest mountain in the world, as well as the feeling that you are surrounded by peaks.

Western Nepal

Generally, the part of Nepal west of the Kali Gandaki river is not often visited by trekkers. The facilities for trekkers are few and distances are great. There are very few roads suitable for launching treks and, unless you charter a plane, air transportation is difficult. Food is sometimes impossible to obtain. Except for the treks near the Dhaulagiri Range, there are few trails that provide views of spectacular mountains. In fact, Dhaulagiri is the only 8000 m peak in Nepal west of the Kali Gandaki. The feeling of being right in the mountains that is common in, say, Khumbu, is rare here.

In spite of the difficulties, the rewards are many. The hills of western Nepal are characterized by majestic forests and interesting vegetation. Population pressures have yet to contribute to extensive deforestation. The country is very rugged, and in the northern reaches, has a feeling of openness. The people are very interesting. The farther west you go, the less contact they have had with Westerners. This can create difficulties in getting their cooperation.

One trek is a circuit from Pokhara to Dhorpatan, returning via Tansen, the capital of an old kingdom. It can be walked in less than two weeks. From Tansen you can either return to Kathmandu by road via Pokhara, or motor to Bhairawa in the Tarai and fly from there. The trek can be shortened using regular RNAC flights to Balewa near Baglung, and charters to Dhorpatan. Food and lodging are available along most of the route. There are excellent views of the Dhau'agiri Range and you can take side trips into more mountainous country.

Another trek is a circuit from Jumla to RaRa Lake, the site of a national park. Jumla is reached by scheduled planes, but getting a seat on a return flight can be difficult due to weather problems. Food and shelter must be carried on the week-long circuit. Finding the way can be a challenge, so those on their first trek in Nepal should hire a guide if they are not on a professionally organized trek.

In general, if this is your first visit to Nepal, choose one of the other treks unless you have some specific reason for wanting to trek in western Nepal. On the other hand, if you are a veteran trekker, and are looking for new, exciting, interesting experiences, go west and enjoy them.

Other Treks

The treks described in Chapter 11 include an exit from Khumbu across the Trashi Labsta, a high pass to the west (18,885 ft, 5755 m), and through Rolwaling to the Kathmandu-Kodari Road. The pass is strenuous and hazardous, and unsuitable for neophyte trekkers. Sir Edmund Hillary once said it was one of the hardest passes he had ever crossed. Some mountaineering experience is required, and food and shelter must be carried. The trek takes a minimum of ten days. It is best attempted in the early autumn or late spring. The route can be followed in reverse to visit the Rolwaling Valley, an incredibly steep-walled valley inhabited by Sherpas. It is a fine objective in its own right, although it is not advisable to cross from Rolwaling to Khumbu because of the abrupt altitude gain. Careful parties can do it successfully if they take time to acclimatize.

Another exit from Solu-Khumbu, this one suitable for all trekkers, is the walk from Namche Bazaar to Ilam. It takes about ten days and is best done during the winter when there is little haze from the plains of India to obscure the view. Also, the weather in the lowlands is coolest at this time.

The trek between Pokhara and Kathmandu, like that to Khumbu, goes against the grain of the land, but the difference in elevation between the ridges and the valleys is much less. It is an easy and convenient trip for those who wish to eat local food and sleep in Nepali homes. The scenery is typical of the hills of Nepal, and there are spectacular views of distant high mountains. The trek is also interesting from a historical point of view, especially the town of Gorkha from where the founder of modern Nepal, King Prithvinarayan Shah, made conquests in the eighteenth century. Indeed many of the places along this route figure strongly in the story of the unification of the country. It is quite a short journey, a matter of five or six days if you take a jeep or bus between Trisuli and Kathmandu. There is now a spur road from AAbu Khaireni on the Kathmandu-Pokhara Highway to Gorkha, so it can be even shorter. People who do not want to take the road or wait for a plane to or from Pokhara can follow this route. It is a good introduction to trekking in Nepal. The Pokhara-Kathmandu road runs about a day's walk south of the trail and is much less scenic.

There are many possibilities for short treks in and around the Kathmandu Valley. Several of these are outlined in Chapter 11.

In contrast to treks to hill and mountain regions, a trip to Chitwan National Park provides an example of the country, people, animals, and vegetation of the Tarai. Like other treks described in this book, it can be done economically. About five days is an appropriate time to spend on the round trip from Kathmandu.

There are, of course, many fine trekking areas that are currently restricted. Nevertheless, many unrestricted areas not described in this book provide excellent trekking. Areas you might consider include the Arun Valley in the east, even going up to the Makalu Base Camp on the upper Barun Khola Valley, and to the Hongu Basin. Areas in central Nepal include the Bara Pokhari Lekh north of Chiti,

The South Face of Lhotse to the left, and Imja Tse (Island Peak) to the right, from Dingboche. (Dave Hardenbergh)

the upper Chepe and Darondi Kholas, and the area south of Ganesh Himal as well as crossing the Rupina La. There are many possibilities in the west, among them heading up the Mayagdi Khola to French Col, and Dhampus Pass to Thak Khola. But before trying one of these, get some experience on the more popular treks.

In the future, areas of Nepal previously closed to trekkers may be opened up. Many of the restrictions were imposed due to the disdain for the prevailing rules and limits shown by earlier travelers. If all trekkers abide by the regulations, there may be fewer restrictions imposed on travel due to the transgressions of a few.

After gaining some basic experience in Nepal on some of the treks described in this book, the person yearning for adventure can easily strike out to visit places where few outsiders have been. The opportunities are endless.

Summary of Treks

Easiest
    Chitwan National Park
    Pokhara to Kathmandu
Moderate
    Dhorpatan circuit
    Gosainkund
    Helambu
    Jumla to RaRa Lake circuit
    Langtang
    North of Pokhara to Jomosom
    Rolwaling Valley

More difficult
> High altitude wanderings north of Pokhara, in Khumbu and beyond Rolwaling
> High passes such as the Ganja La, Trashi Labsta (most difficult and hazardous) and Thorong La

Shortest (a few days)
> Initial part of most any trek, e.g. Pokhara to NagDAADa and return via Sarangkot
> Flying to Shyangboche, Langtang, Lukla, Dhorpatan, or Jomosom; walking a day or two without altitude gain; and flying back

Around a week
> Gosainkund
> Helambu
> Khumbu—flying in and out, but not going to Everest Base Camp or Kala Pattar
> Langtang
> Pokhara to Ghandrung circuit
> Pokhara to GhoDapani circuit
> Pokhara-Kathmandu
> RaRa Lake circuit

Two weeks or more
> Dhorpatan circuit
> Combining two areas north of Kathmandu
> Khumbu—flying in and out, and visiting the Everest Base Camp and Kala Pattar
> To Manang and back from Pokhara
> Rolwaling
> To Thak Khola heading north from Pokhara, returning the same way

Three weeks or more
> Dhorpatan circuit with side trips
> Helambu, Gosainkund, and Langtang
> Khumbu with plenty of side trips or walking from Kathmandu and back
> North of Pokhara with lots of side trips or the Annapurna circuit

Most spectacular mountain scenery
> Annapurna circuit
> Khumbu
> Upper Langtang Valley
> Manang
> Side trips north of Pokhara such as Annapurna Sanctuary, Annapurna Base Camp, Dhaulagiri Icefall, Tilicho Tal, or Dhampus Pass
> Upper Rolwaling Valley

Good springtime introduction to flora, especially rhododendrons
> Dhorpatan circuit
> Gosainkund, Helambu, and Langtang
> RaRa Lake circuit
> Rolwaling
> Solu-Khumbu

Greatest cultural and geographic diversity
> Pokhara to Muktinath or Jomosom
> Annapurna circuit

For those seeking new adventures
    Monsoon treks—even in areas you have visited before
    Far west treks
    Take your family (spouse, parents, children).
    Don't go with an agency if you have done so previously.
    Don't hire any guides or porters who speak English.
    Focus on a specific interest (hang gliding, birding, photography,
        architecture, etc.)
    Go on a pilgrimage at the time Nepalis visit pilgrimage sites.
    Climb a trekking peak if you have the requisite mountaineering experience.
    Check Appendix D, After Trekking, What Next?

Most popular treks in decreasing order (based on number of trekking permits issued in 1981)
    Thak Khola to Jomosom (14,435) (this may include crossing to Manang)
    Khumbu (5804)
    Helambu (3051)
    Annapurna Sanctuary (2180)
    Langtang (1437)
    Manang (438)
    RaRa (10)

Most popular time to trek (in decreasing order based on number of permits issued)
    October
    November
    March
    April
    December
    February
    January
    September
    May
    August
    June
    July

Treks with few other trekkers
    Dhorpatan circuit
    Khumbu to Ilam
    Pokhara-Kathmandu
    RaRa Lake
    To Rolwaling

Playing the shehnai. *(Stephen Bezruchka)*

3 PREPARATIONS

All obstacles are blessings of the guru.

A *BhoTiya* saying

Remember this saying when in Nepal, for despite all your careful preparations, some "serendipitous accident"—a phrase coined by Hugh R. Downs—may occur. The message in this chapter is "be prepared," but most of all, be prepared to be flexible and to make the best of all circumstances. Trekking in Nepal, like any other activity, is usually more successful if the participants are prepared, and if they have some idea of what to expect. Those who know before they leave home that they want to trek in Nepal should attempt to equip themselves adequately before they leave. The many people who decide to trek only after they arrive in Nepal must acquire equipment there. Since this is not always easy, it is better not to come totally unprepared.

Visas and Permits

Most travelers to Nepal need a visa. This can be obtained from one of the Nepali Embassies and Consular Services in eighteen countries throughout the world. The visas are valid for up to one month. Two passport-size photographs are necessary for the application, and travelers should bring a dozen or so for use in formalities.

Visas valid for one week only are issued at entry points to Nepal. The main entry points are: (1) Kathmandu, for those arriving by air; (2) Kodari along the Nepal-Tibet border (currently not used by tourists, but may be opened if travel to the Tibetan Region of China becomes established); (3) Birgunj across from Raxaul, India, on the main road from India to Kathmandu; and (4) Sunauli across from Nautanwa, India, near the town of Bhairawa on the road from India to Pokhara. Other border points with India, less used by tourists, are: DhangaDi, Jaleswor, Kakarbhitta, Koilabas, Mahendranagar, Nepalganj, and Rani Sikijahi. Travelers coming by road need a *carnet de passage* for their vehicles. There is also bus service on the main roads.

Nepali Embassies and Consular Services are located in Edgecliffe, Australia; Vienna, Austria; Dacca, Bangladesh; Brussels and Antwerp, Belgium; Rangoon, Burma; Peking and Lhasa, Peoples Republic of China; Cairo, Egypt; London, England; Bonn, Dusseldorf, Frankfurt, and Munich, West Germany; Paris, France; Hong Kong; New Delhi and Calcutta, India; Tokyo, Japan; Beirut, Lebanon; Islamabad, Pakistan; Bangkok, Thailand; Washington, New York, and San Francisco, United States; and Moscow, Soviet Union.

Trekking regulations change from time to time, so it is wise to check by writing to one of the trekking agencies. At present, permits are required for all areas except the Kathmandu and Pokhara valleys and Chitwan National Park. Several areas of Nepal, mostly those on the northern border, are restricted, and permission to trek there is not granted. It is important to respect these restrictions, as many have been imposed after indiscretions by trekkers.

Under current regulations, trekking permits are issued at the Central Immigration Office of the Home and Panchayat Ministry, His Majesty's Government (HMG), at Maiti Devi (Dilli Bazaar) in Kathmandu, and in Pokhara at the airport. A visa extension is issued first, then a trekking permit for one trek at a time. The places that you are permitted to go are stated on the permit and are standardized for the popular treks. A general prescribed route must be taken. In applying, state the northernmost town in each major valley as well as names of towns with police check posts. Two passport-size photographs are required and a fee is levied. Bring a supply of passport photographs with you to Nepal and a black-and-white negative to print more if necessary. The trekking permit must be presented at all police check posts along the route and annotated by the post nearest to the destination. It is a good idea to have the permit annotated at all check posts to verify that you have in fact traveled with the permit. This procedure may be helpful in getting visa extensions. With the increasing number of "incidents" occurring to trekkers, it is especially important to check in at police posts in case you end up missing or being sought in an emergency. The police provide a service to trekkers. The permit must be surrendered on return to Kathmandu. A trekking agency can handle many of the formalities.

The limit for tourist visas is three months. Extensions for one month at a time can be obtained through the Central Immigration Office in Kathmandu. An initial visa for one month can be obtained from Nepali Embassies abroad, or a one-week visa can be obtained at an entry point to Nepal. Extensions can usually be granted only in Kathmandu or Pokhara, though occasionally it may be possible to obtain one-week extensions at a police post.

Visa and trekking permit formalities tended to take some time in the past. Now they can usually be obtained the same day if you apply early. All government offices are closed on Saturday, the weekly holiday. Other holidays are frequent.

It cannot be too heavily stressed that you should attempt to put forward a pleasant image in dealing with the immigration officials. They do not understand the ways, habits, dress, or customs of many Westerners. They are wary of people who attempt to get visa extensions indefinitely under the pretext of trekking, but who, in fact, wish to become residents of Kathmandu Valley. Be considerate, dress neatly, and try to minimize the element of distrust that Nepali officials may have of foreigners. You will have fewer problems if you do so.

Four areas of Nepal have been designated national parks. They are the Langtang, RaRa, Royal Chitwan, and Sagarmatha (Everest) national parks. Foreigners must pay a fee and obtain a park permit at the entrance. Buying wood from locals or taking it from the forests is illegal in the parks. All travelers are required to carry non-wood stoves and fuel. Violators can be arrested and fined. The flora and fauna are protected.

Maps

Modern topographical maps suitable for trekking are difficult to find for areas of Nepal. The country was surveyed between 1924 and 1927 by clandestine workers for the Survey of India. They ventured through the country with concealed survey instruments and did a creditable job. While the altitudes on their maps are usually not correct, the relative features of the topography south of the Himalaya are portrayed well. But the trails are not always marked accurately. The 1:250,000 series (one inch = 3.9 miles) of this survey is not generally available. Like most

Indian cartographic materials, its distribution used to be restricted to official agencies. In the United States, the U.S. Army Map Service, Corps of Engineers, has printed these maps under the title Series U502. Copies of these maps are sometimes available from the sources listed at the end of this section. They can also be ordered from the Library of Congress, Photoduplication Service, Washington, D.C. 20540; or the Cartographic and Architectural Branch, National Archives and Records Service, 8th and Pennsylvania Avenue NW, Washington, D.C. 20408. The sheets most useful to trekkers are:

NG 45— 3 *Kanchenjunga* (toward Darjeeling)
NG 45— 2 *Mount Everest* (Kathmandu to Khumbu and Rolwaling)
NG 45—14 *Tingri Dzong* (north of above sheet)
NG 45— 1 *Kathmandu* (Gorkha to Kathmandu and north)
NG 45—13 *Jongkha Dzong* (north of Kathmandu)
NG 44—16 *Pokhara* (north and west of Pokhara)
NG 44— 4 *Tansing* (south of above sheet)
NG 44—11 *Jumla* (Jumla to RaRa Lake)

These maps can be seen at major map libraries. Some government offices in Kathmandu have maps from this series on display.

A scaled-down version of the Survey of India maps on the scale of 1:506,880 (one inch = 8.0 miles) is available to the public. These maps, Series U462, are published by the British Ministry of Defense. They can be seen at His Majesty's Government (HMG) Tourist Office in Kathmandu. A blue non-topographical version with recently built roads and airstrips is also sometimes available. A further scaled-down updated version on the scale of 1:780,000 (one inch = 12.3 miles) is available from American-Nepal Maps, c/o M. S. Holloway, 5831 Hampton Court, San Diego, Calif. 92120. Either of these versions gives general impressions of the topography, but few towns are marked and the delineation of the trails is not quite accurate. Nevertheless, they are the best general maps of Nepal available.

Recently a map has been produced from land satellite imagery covering Nepal on the 1:500,000 scale. It is available from International Mapping Unlimited, 4343 39th Street NW, Washington, D.C. 20016. Although not too helpful for trekking, it depicts the country very well.

Maps produced for aircraft navigation are available from: Distribution Division (C-44), Office of Aeronautical Charts and Cartography, National Oceanic Survey, Riverdale, Maryland 20840. They portray the topography well, but do not show most villages or trails. In the 1:500,000 (one inch = 7.9 miles) series, four sheets cover Nepal—PC-H-9A, 9B, 9C, and 9D. In the 1:1,000,000 (one inch = 15.8 miles) series, ONC-H-9 covers all of Nepal.

The Survey of India completed an aerial survey of Nepal in the early 1960s to produce maps on a scale of 1:63,360 (one inch = 1.0 mile). They are excellent, but almost impossible to find because of restrictions on distribution.

Several series of maps produced in Nepal have appeared recently. The first, entitled Annapurna and Dhaulagiri Himal, was done accurately by Dr. Harka Gurung on the scale of 1:253,440 (one inch = 4 miles) and indicates ridges, trails, and drainage features in an easy to use fashion. It is out of print, but occasionally available. This series was followed by several others: first the Mandala Maps, and then other series from several sources, including the recent Survey of India maps. Contours, trails, and towns are shown on most of them, but the altitudes, trails, and towns are not always accurate as they were drawn by people who haven't trekked. They are dyeline copies of artwork, and the copies are poor. Nevertheless, they are sufficient for most trekking purposes. Maps to cover most of the commonly trekked areas are available sporadically. Titles include: *Kathmandu, Helambu, Langtang, Gosainkund; Pokhara to Jomosom, Manang; Lamosangu to Mount Everest; Kathmandu to Pokhara; Jomosom to Jumla and Surkhet; Jugal Himal; Khumbu Himal; Kanchenjunga, Makalu, Mount Everest;* and *Jumla to RaRa.* The series is currently called "Latest Trekking Maps."

Other productions are expected. A recent series, published by M.L. Maharjan, has a map covering the Annapurna region. Another covers the Everest trek and beyond to the Arun, while one of Nepal has maps covering the popular treks as well. Another useful map is *Royal Chitwan National Park Map,* published by Tiger Tops.

Because of extensive mountaineering interest in the Khumbu region, there are excellent maps of it and of some nearby areas. Currently the best available are six published by Kartographische Anstalt Freytag-Berndt und Artaria, Vienna, Austria. The *Tamba Kosi-Likhu Khola Nepal* sheet covers about five days of the hill portion of the trek to Khumbu. The *Shorong/Hinku* sheet covers the next portion to just below Namche Bazaar. The *Khumbu Himal Nepal* sheet covers the region from Namche Bazaar north. The *Lapchi Kang Nepal* and *Rolwaling Himal (Gaurisankar) Nepal* sheets cover the trek from the Kathmandu-Kodari Road to Rolwaling and beyond. The *Dudh Kosi* sheet covers the southern part of Solu. These modern topographic maps on the scale of 1:50,000 (one inch = 0.8 mile) are produced by the Research Scheme Nepal Himalaya and are accurate in almost all respects. An earlier version of the *Khumbu Himal* sheet was published in 1957 as *Mahalangur Himal.* It covers only an area close to Mount Everest and has a scale of 1:25,000 (one inch = 0.4 mile).

Currently in production in the same series are sheets covering Langtang/ Jugal Himal and Khumbakarna Himal. The latter will cover the area east of the *Khumbu Himal* sheet. Another sheet in the series covers the Kathmandu Valley. These maps are occasionally available in Kathmandu. They can also be purchased from the mail order sources listed below. They are expensive, but map lovers will find them hard to resist. In this text, they are often referred to as the Schneider maps, after the mapmaker.

There is a series of ecological maps published by the Centre National de la Recherche Scientifique (CNRS), and can be ordered from Librairie de vente du CNRS, 295 rue Saint-Jacques, 75005 Paris, France, or SMPF, 16 East 34th Street, 7th floor, New York, N.Y. 10016. They are useful because they show vegetation zones and contain some ethnographical information. Presently available are:

Carte Ecologique du Nepal Region Annapurna-Dhaulagiri 1:250,000 (one inch = 3.9 miles)
Carte Ecologique du Nepal Region Jiri-Thodung 1:50,000 (one inch = 0.8 mile)
Carte Ecologique du Nepal Region Kathmandu-Everest 1:250,000
Carte Ecologique du Nepal Region Tarai Central 1:250,000
Carte Ecologique du Nepal Region Ankhu-Khola-Trisuli 1:100,000 (one inch = 1.6 miles)
Carte Ecologique du Nepal Region Biratnagar Kanchenjunga 1:250,000
Carte Ecologique du Nepal Region Jumla Saipal 1:250,000
Carte Ecologique du Nepal Region Butwal-Mustang 1:250,000
Carte Ecologique du Nepal Region Dhangarhi-Api 1:250,000
Carte Ecologique du Nepal Region Nepalganj-Dailekh 1:250,000

Many accounts of mountaineering expeditions include maps that are useful to trekkers. Map sellers handling many of the maps not published in Nepal include: Edward Sanford Limited, 12-14 Long Acre, London WC2E 9LP, England; Geo Center GmbH, Honigwiesenstrasse 25, Postfach 80 08 30, D-7000 Stuttgart 80, West Germany; Geo Buch, Rosental 6, D-8000 München 2, West Germany; Reise und Verkehrsverlag, Gutenbergstrasse 21, Stuttgart, West Germany; Zumsteins Landkartenhaus, Liebkerrstrasse 5, 8 München 22, West Germany; Libreria Alpina, Via C. Coronedi-Berti 4, 40137 Bologna, Zona 3705 Italy; Bradt Enterprises Inc., 95 Harvey Street, Cambridge, Mass. 02140, USA.

The maps in this book are intended to help the reader visualize the route descriptions. They are drawn to scale and have the towns and trails described in the text. Except for major ridge features and drainage systems, little else is depicted. Town placements are often somewhat arbitrary, since some towns have houses spread out rather than clustered together. Trekkers not especially interested in maps should find them adequate, but those who appreciate good maps should try to obtain the Schneider maps and may also enjoy the book, *Maps of Nepal* by Harka Gurung, listed in Appendix C.

Finally, don't expect most Nepali people to be able to read maps, even the roughly fifteen percent who are literate. They do have a superb spatial sense of the land, a quality few of us possess. Tapping this resource, should it be necessary, is one of the joyful challenges of traveling independently.

Equipment

Although much of the equipment is the same, trekking in Nepal is different from backpacking as the term has come to be known in North America and Western countries. My equipment preferences are based on considerable and varied experience in Nepal. Much of the equipment described is current "state-of-the-art" gear. This is not really necessary for trekking, but it is important to have equipment adequate for the conditions. I have used many different types of gear while trekking in Nepal, sometimes going quite simply, though never as simply as the local Nepalis.

To minimize customs hassles and delays, trekkers should carry equipment with them into Nepal if possible, rather than shipping it separately. If you must ship equipment and supplies into Nepal, arrange for at least the last part of the journey to be by airfreight. Delays are fewer that way and customs duties are generally less. Shipping by sea is fraught with risk. Be prepared for delays no matter how you ship. The only sure way to have the gear you want when you want it is to bring it all with you. I have waited over a month to receive an airfreight shipment! In such circumstances, check daily at the airport or employ someone to check for you. But even then expect delays.

After your trek you can ship your goods out of Nepal in various ways. Airfreight is reliable, but expensive, except for large shipments. Surface parcel post is slightly less reliable. The best shipping agencies in Kathmandu do a good job of packing and mailing goods, and the bureaucratic hassles and time involved in doing it yourself can be eliminated.

Camping and mountaineering equipment used by Sherpas and climbers on mountaineering expeditions is often available for sale or rent in Kathmandu, Pokhara, and Namche Bazaar. The number of shops selling and renting a variety of equipment has proliferated greatly in recent years. Much of it is new gear unused on expeditions. Prices vary from cheap to outrageous, and the quality is not uniform. Many trekkers sell their equipment after their treks by means of notices in restaurants and hotels. The variety of equipment available, like everything else in Kathmandu, is never constant. Some people are able to pick up everything they need in the city, but it is safer to come at least minimally prepared.

If you don't own items such as good down sleeping bags, jackets, foam pads, and packs, or if you have other travel plans that make it difficult to bring your own equipment, plan to rent. I would not advise renting footwear, so do bring your own broken-in shoes and boots. When renting equipment, don't leave your passport as collateral, you may need it.

FOOTWEAR

Comfortable footwear is a must, but opinions vary widely on what types are best. I prefer a Vibram-soled mountaineering boot for the high country where snow, ice, or rock is anticipated. But at most other times I wear a pair of rubber-soled leather scampers, or light, flexible Vibram-soled boots with uppers above the ankles, or waffle-soled running shoes during the monsoon. I wear wool socks over a light, thin pair of synthetic socks. It is difficult to find footwear to fit large feet (size 11 American or 44 European) in Nepal. Make sure that your boots or shoes are well broken in before the trip. On long treks, there may be considerable wear, especially to the uppers. Bring stitching material and Barge cement or epoxy glue for the soles. In snow or wet weather, appropriate waterproofing material is needed.

Some trekkers wear high-top hunting boots all the time. I find them unnecessarily restrictive and uncomfortable as well as hot and sweaty. Others swear by sneakers, running shoes, or tennis shoes. Rubber-soled shoes with fabric uppers are very cheap and easily obtainable in Nepal. The Chinese-made variety is quite durable. These shoes are rarely found in the bazaars outside the Kathmandu Valley, and even then, only in small sizes. They work quite well, but I would be cautious wearing them in hot weather because the feet may sweat a great deal and develop blisters quickly. I also find that they provide little support under the sole of the foot. Running shoes are popular and quite suitable below the snowline. Such shoes, with good shock-absorbing heels, are excellent for downhill travel. Those with waffle soles, if new, provide excellent traction during the monsoon. However, this type of footwear is not suitable for snow. If you plan to cross high passes, take along substantial boots for snow and cold. Trekkers with inadequate footwear have suffered serious frostbite. Some companies making running shoes are producing a more substantial leather and fabric hiking boot with shock-absorbing heels. Such boots may be very good for the hills—if they are strong enough to last. Some trekkers have reported accelerated wear with these boots, especially glued soles coming apart.

A type of footwear known variously as a thong or a chapal, consisting of a sole with a strap passing between the toes and over the front of the foot, is widely available in Nepal. It is unsuitable for constant walking, but can be comfortable off the trail. It is good to have some sort of light footwear to change into at the end of the day.

The amount of wear and tear on your footwear over a month's trek in Nepal can't be overestimated. Sturdy equipment that will last the duration is necessary, and you must be prepared to make repairs.

If boots or shoes are irritating your feet, experiment with various ways of lacing. Try lacing tightly to the instep, then tying a knot and lacing loosely the rest of the way. On some boots, avoiding some of the first lacing holes and lacing diagonally may prevent painful infolding of the leather. Always tighten the laces for a steep descent.

Individuals prone to ankle sprains should always wear boots that go over the ankle and provide support. Those troubled with knee problems, especially when going downhill, should wear boots or shoes with shock-absorbing heels. Sorbothane heelpads sold for running shoes may be helpful.

The secret of foot care is in the socks. The outer pair, which should be soft and woolen to absorb moisture, should be changed frequently. Thick outer socks made of synthetic material (acrylic or nylon) should be avoided since they do not absorb sweat well and often lead to blisters. But synthetic socks as thin inners are excellent. The nylon anklets worn by women might serve well. Thin slippery socks worn within heavier ones allow the feet and the inner socks to slip around inside the outer socks. This decreases stress and helps prevent blisters. A plastic bag over the inner sock may prevent the inside of the boot from getting wet from sweat and help keep feet warm in cold, snowy conditions. Some people advocate changing socks twice a day or more, keeping a pair drying outside the pack. Try this if you are having trouble with your feet. Be sure to take enough pairs, say four to six, for the journey. Also take some wool for darning. Again, large size socks are unavailable in Nepal. For prevention and care of blisters, see Chapter 5. In the high, snowy regions, gaiters or spats of various types can be useful in keeping snow out of boot tops.

CLOTHING

Loose trousers for men, long skirts for women, and shirts with pockets are good basic garments. Wool clothing is traditionally chosen because it feels warm when wet. Knickers, also called plus-fours, are versatile for men since they can be ventilated easily. Long thermal underwear is good at high altitudes, especially during the winter months. Wool has traditionally been considered best for these garments, but new synthetic fabrics such as polypropylene keep moisture away from the skin and are more comfortable when the wearer sweats. Sweaters, worn with an outer nylon shell, provide wind protection and variable degrees of warmth depending on the number of layers. A down jacket is a light, efficient alternative to a sweater, but down is useless when wet. Synthetic, fiber-insulated clothing is good for wet weather. Recent improvements in clothing are the warm, efficient, synthetic pile garments. Like wool, they are warm when wet, but also dry out quickly. Some advocate down pants for sitting around in the cool high campsites; synthetic pile pants are also good. Garments that can be easily put on over existing clothing are the most versatile. A hat is important on cold days since considerable heat can be lost from the scalp because of its particularly good blood supply. A hat with a wide brim is best at high altitudes in order to shade the eyes from the sun. Dark glasses or goggles are also essential at high altitudes, especially on snow where the sunlight is exceptionally intense. Such eye protection should have eye shields to prevent light from coming in from the sides. They should absorb all ultra-violet light and at least ninety percent of visible light. If you wear eyeglasses or contact lenses, bring a spare pair and a copy of the refraction prescription. Mittens are better than gloves for cold weather. Fingerless gloves or ones made of thin silk or synthetic material are good for operating cameras or attending to other intricate details in the snow. Thermolactyl mitts (not gloves) I find excellent, enabling me to use my fingers for various tasks yet keep them sheathed and warm.

The Doko *is a means of carrying almost anything or anybody. (Ane Haaland)*

It is difficult to stay dry while walking in rainy weather. Those wearing water-proof garments tend to sweat inside them. The new Gore-Tex fabrics are a definite improvement over the old coated nylon gear because they are waterproof if kept clean, yet breathe better than other waterproof fabrics. Jackets and pants with zip-pered areas under the arms and down the legs are preferable, since they have bet-ter ventilation. In the hundred-percent humidity of an intense rainfall, no clothing can breathe, so you will probably get wet from the inside no matter what. In those circumstances, light clothes and an umbrella or loose fitting poncho may be the best compromise. Serviceable bamboo-shafted umbrellas are available in Kathmandu. Trekkers often use them for shade in the hot sun, and they are essen-tial for the monsoon.

Men should bring shorts for the hot, low altitudes. Skirts for women should be light synthetic or cotton fabrics for the lowlands, but wool for the high country (For the rationale behind skirts for women, see the next chapter.) A bathing suit can be useful, but modesty should prevail.

Since individuals vary, it is difficult to give specific details regarding how many garments of a particular type will give the required warmth at a particular temperature range. Many of the temperature ranges encountered are familiar. Most people can expect to be reasonably comfortable at high altitudes, with thick wool pants, two sweaters, a wind jacket, mittens, a hat, wool socks and heavy boots. You may feel chilly in the morning, when it could be well below freezing, yet sweat later in the day, as you exercise in the sun. The climatological data in Chapter 2 should help you plan what to bring.

SLEEPING GEAR

A good sleeping bag is essential for those who contemplate going to the cold, high elevations. A down or synthetic-fiber mummy bag is usually necessary for comfort at temperatures below freezing. Recently, bags have been produced with a silvery reflective lining material that improves efficiency. A bag with a full zipper is more versatile because it is comfortable at cool, high altitudes and in warm, low country. A washable sleeping bag liner solves some hygiene problems, and the liner alone may be all you'll need most of the monsoon season at low altitudes. An air mattress or foam air bed provides a comfortable night's sleep, and to me, at least, is worth the extra effort needed to carry it. The short, rubberized nylon models, extending from the knees to the shoulders, weigh little and are sufficient. Bring a repair kit for it. Some prefer a foam pad or nothing at all. A sheet of plastic under the sleeping bag helps keep equipment clean and dry. This is a good item even in hotels and on the floors of village houses.

Those who plan to sleep outside or in a tent at low temperatures (below freezing, or on snow or ice) should be aware that a sufficient thickness of insulation is necessary under you as well as over. Most sleeping bags do not provide enough since the filler compresses under the weight of the body. Anything that can trap air and provide a quarter to a half inch of insulation is sufficient. An ideal item is a closed cell foam pad. Of course, jackets, clothing, rope, rugs, packs, or other items can serve as well.

For those going only to low altitudes, or planning a trek in the monsoon below 7000 ft (2150 m), a lightweight blanket may be sufficient.

SHELTER

Your route and preferred style dictate whether you need a tent. If you prefer to camp, or desire privacy even occasionally, a tent is necessary, except along certain routes where hotels with private rooms are common. A tent is a must at high altitudes if there is no shelter. A lightweight nylon tent good enough to withstand high winds and snow is necessary for the high passes, but a lean-to made from a sheet of plastic and some cord can weather some of the heaviest of storms if properly pitched. Bivouac sacs used by mountaineers are light, efficient shelters good for occasional use. In some areas you can stay in herding huts called *goTh*. Shelter can sometimes be found in caves or beneath overhanging rocks. Be sure you have enough adequate shelter for all the members of your party if you are going to high altitudes. It is not unheard of for porters to die of exposure and hypothermia in the parties of thoughtless trekkers. My relationship with porters has always been better when I showed them the tent they will use in the high passes before we left our point of departure.

Campsites are quite variable. Near villages, terraces that are harvested or in fallow make ideal campsites. Clearings in the forest can be very pleasant.

Monastery courtyards and *dharamsala* (resting houses for native travelers), as well as alpine meadows, are all possible sites. Be sure to obtain permission to use people's land. Finding a place to camp is usually not a problem for a small group, but finding water may be difficult. Ridges and hillsides may lack water, especially before the monsoon. Trek descriptions in later chapters indicate where water is a problem.

PACKS

Traditionally, the most suitable and comfortable carrying device for trekking is the contoured pack frame made of aluminum or a light alloy. The load is placed in a bag that attaches to the frame. Frames with padded waistbands allow you to transfer the weight from your shoulders to your hips. Waterproof nylon bags with outside pockets are best since they allow easy access to selected items during the day. The sleeping bag is usually stuffed in another bag and attached to the frame below the pack bag. Recent models of internal frame packs and soft packs are equally suitable. As with much other outdoor gear, recent models are ergonomic, that is, designed to be very efficient. With soft packs, the load must be arranged carefully in order to be comfortable. Equipment and supplies that the porters carry can be packed in sturdy duffel bags, preferably ones that can be locked.

While I understand the "carry it all yourself" philosophy, it makes little sense to burden yourself down like a pack animal and then wear yourself out carrying the load. There may be little for you to enjoy except the feeling that you did it. Porters are quite inexpensive, and by hiring them, you contribute directly to those who need it. I, for one, feel I must always carry something. I usually limit myself to forty or fifty pounds (I weigh 190 lb), but I reduced this when going above 12,000 ft (3657 m). I did make the mistake of starting off on my first trek with fifty or sixty pounds on my back and, after some days, I developed back strain that didn't disappear for quite a while. So start off light and gradually get used to carrying a load. Members of mountaineering expeditions do this.

COOKING GEAR

Light nesting pots are available in Kathmandu. Two or three should suffice for a small group cooking together. Spoons are the ideal general purpose utensil, and pocket knives are a good accessory. Quality Swiss pocket knives are hard to come by in Kathmandu. A combination salt and pepper shaker is useful if you season your food. Plastic scouring pads are handy for cleaning pots, but steel pads are easier to find in Kathmandu.

Because travelers have placed great pressures on the scant forests remaining in the high altitude areas, regulations require that all trekkers and their porters, cooks, and guides be self-sufficient in the national parks. And I strongly recommend that trekkers use kerosene stoves at all times when they cook for themselves, especially in the high altitude areas. Kerosene is the only fuel available in the hills. Even then its availability is sporadic outside of popular places like Namche Bazaar. Furthermore, its quality is low and at times unsuitable for burning in some stoves. So fuel must sometimes be carried from Kathmandu. The quantity needed depends on whether snow must be melted for water, the efficiency of the stove, and the number in the party. About three liters will last a party of three for a week if snow must be melted. Plastic jerry cans for fuel are available in Kathmandu. Kerosene stoves of Indian manufacture are readily available in Kathmandu; though adequate, they are generally bulky and heavy. The light Swedish stoves are some-times found in stores selling trekking and climbing gear. In my experience, the Swedish stoves seem to operate well at high altitudes on the impure kerosene found in the hills. The MSR stove, the most efficient kerosene design, used to be finicky on impure kerosene. Be sure to carry appropriate spare parts and a funnel containing a wool filter. Try the stove out before you leave.

MISCELLANEOUS

A medical kit is essential (see Chapter 5).

Food is best packed in plastic bags and then put into labeled cloth bags tied with string. Plastic bags can be purchased in Kathmandu. Be sure to take extras. (Sheet plastic is also available. It is a good item for protecting porters and loads in the rain.) Cotton bags can be sewn by a local tailor, but nylon stuff sacks are, perhaps, a better choice.

Take along enough stuff sacks to store all your gear so it is easier to keep track of your goods. They can be packed in a duffel bag or a porter's *doko* (basket). A sturdy, zippered duffel bag that locks is ideal for a porter to carry. For security reasons it is not advisable to leave loose items in the basket. Some people find large plastic garbage bags (brought from home) useful. On long treks during the monsoon, I use them to protect the contents of those duffel bags that don't need to be unpacked too often.

It is important to consider what might break down and carry appropriate spare parts. A sewing kit is indispensable and a sewing awl for heavier items may be very useful. Epoxy glue can repair most things if used discriminately. In Kathmandu, ask for the brand, Aryldite, in stores carrying Indian products. A pair of pliers can be useful; the combination wrench, pliers, and screwdriver originally made for ski troops, is ideal. A pocket knife with a few gadgets on it will also come in handy.

Bring several handkerchiefs for colds and upper respiratory infections, or learn to blow your nose Nepali style. Petrolatum jelly is good for cold-weather chapping.

A water bottle of at least one quart (liter) capacity should be carried for each person in the party. Water is often scarce and must be treated before use. Buy plastic jerry cans and bottles with good stoppers and screw tops in the Kathmandu bazaar. Take biodegradable soap in a container. A washcloth or towel and a tooth-brush are good to have. A small flashlight or torch is very useful—the plastic kind is warmer to handle in cold weather. A headlamp is a pleasant luxury. Indian D-cell batteries are about the only kind usually obtainable outside of Kathmandu. Take candles to read by at night, matches in a waterproof container (or a lighter), and toilet paper. Consider earplugs for noisy hotels.

It is wise to have at least one compass in the party. Magnetic declination in Nepal is less than two or three degrees west in most places and can be overlooked for most map work. A pair of binoculars, an altimeter, and a thermometer can be helpful. A star chart can help you identify constellations in the clear night air. A watch with a chronograph can help you compare your walking times with those in this book.

Insects are not usually a problem in the high country, but those traveling extensively in the lowlands during the warmer months or during the monsoon should use mosquito netting while sleeping and insect repellents (the ones with N,

N-diethyl-meta-toluamide are the best) while traveling.

Consider taking a portable tape recorder to capture the local music and other sounds of Nepal. Cassette tapes of various manufacture and D, C, and AA batteries are available in Kathmandu. On occasion, I carry a quality recorder and a professional stereo microphone to capture the memorable sounds of Nepal. If your recorder has a built-in microphone, get a separate one, preferably with a low-pass (voice) filter and a windscreen.

If you are a proficient musician who plays a portable instrument, consider bringing it along. A harmonica, recorder, or flute can help break the ice in a village and elicit "good vibrations." Porters may balk at carrying a piano, but Jonathan Miller, cello recitalist and Boston Symphony musician, took a compact, battery-operated cello that enriched everyone he played for.

Most trekkers carry reading matter and writing materials. Rereading years later a journal kept on a trek can be a most rewarding experience. Bring a picture book about your country to share with Nepali people you encounter. Photographs of your family are great fun to share. Order the language tape mentioned in Chapter 6. And bring this book, an essential item. If its weight seems excessive, tear out the pages of the route descriptions that don't apply.

The equipment game can be, and often is, carried to extremes. Naturalist Ed Cronin describes how, relying on the Boy Scout spirit of preparedness, he emerged from the plane at a remote airstrip on his first trip to Nepal. He was dressed in his custom-designed field jacket, complete with dashing epaulets and eleven pockets offering precise space for various necessities from compass to moleskin to a waterproof container of matches. Around his neck he carried two camera bodies and a host of lenses and light meters as well as a pair of binoculars and a tripod. Descending laboriously from the plane, he noticed that all eyes were on him. "I thought at the time this was because I was new and lacked a sunburn, but later realized it was because I carried more wealth on my person than the average porter. . .could accumulate in a lifetime," he said. He later described all the difficulties he had walking with this paraphernalia.

For many reasons, including some important ones to be discussed later, be reasonable in what you bring, and keep most of it packed until needed.

Photography in Nepal

"Photography is a magical process that has given Sahibs all over the world the chance to rest under the guise of business," states Cronin. This is most certainly true, but I also find it valuable as an art form expressing my impressions of Nepal and as a means of sharing my experience with others. And years later, it helps me remember.

Inexperienced photographers should bring a small, simple 35mm automatic camera and flash, or comparable equipment in 110 or disc format. An instant picture or self-developing camera may make you popular with some people, but I would be cautious in its use. Often, after I snap the shutter on my 35mm camera, people along the popular trails wait thirty seconds and approach me for the photograph. If you use an instant camera, everybody will pester you for their photograph. Most people will do best bringing 35mm single-lens-reflex equipment. It is especially suited to candid photography, and with a suitable array of lenses, a flash and tripod, you can handle most situations. Large-format cameras can provide incredibly sharp images that come close to doing justice to Nepal's scenery.

Chamber music artist Jonathan Miller, who plays in the Boston Symphony Orchestra, shares his music by playing a traveling violoncello. (Jonathan Miller)

A trekker once remarked that if you are walking along a trail in Nepal with a camera, lose your step, and fall, and in the process accidentally trip the camera shutter, you will get a good photograph. It does take a little more work, a lot more if you want top images, but this comment underlines the notion that Nepal is very photogenic. Problems in getting good results stem from the immense scale of the terrain, contrasty light and poorly lit home interiors.

Wide-angle lenses help capture the grandeur of the mountain landscape, but their use demands attention to the foreground for good results. Details of mountains, especially if shrouded in cloud, can be dramatic if taken with a telephoto lens. The range of light intensities in bright sun makes good results almost impossible except in the early morning or late in the day. So either restrict your photography to the oblique filtered light close to sunrise and sunset, or consider using polarizing and split-density filters and, in either case, bracketing the exposures.

This last process means making exposures above and below what your light meter reading shows and choosing the best result later.

It is most important to know which exposure conditions will throw the built-in light meter in your camera off and to adjust accordingly. This problem commonly occurs when taking portraits in the midday sun. When the face is positioned so the overhead sun casts strong shadows across the eyes, there is little except fill-in flash that will help. If possible orient the subject to avoid these shadows. When the background is very bright, as with the sky or snow, the camera meter reading will be too low and the subject will be dark and underexposed. When the background is too dark, in a forest for example, the opposite may occur. In these circumstances take a meter reading at very close range, directly off the subject's face, or, if on bright snow, use the flat of your hand for a reading. With automatic-only cameras, exposure compensation, if available, will help surmount this problem. Lacking that option, adjust the film speed. Practice before your trip so you won't lose good pictures or waste film.

Battery-dependent cameras will cease to function if the battery fails. Carry plenty of spares. If your camera operates mechanically without the battery and you have no spare, the following principle for determining exposure will help. When shooting in the midday sun, unobscured by clouds, a setting of f:16 and a shutter speed close to the ASA film speed will produce good results. For example, with ASA 64 film, set the camera to f:16 and $\frac{1}{60}$th second. If on snow, set it to one stop less, e.g. f:16 and $\frac{1}{125}$th. In hazy conditions, open up one stop to f:11 and $\frac{1}{60}$th. On cloudy days, open up two stops to f:8 and $\frac{1}{60}$th. On overcast days or in open shade, open up three stops over the basic reading for bright sun to f:5.6 and $\frac{1}{60}$th. Any combination of lens opening and shutter speed that produces the needed exposure will work.

The fascinating activities in the dark interiors of Nepali homes are difficult to photograph. Long exposures using a tripod and fast film can work, while a carefully used flash can handle other situations. The harsh light of direct on-camera flash rarely produces pleasing effects. Creative use of bounce light is better. Even a piece of white paper held obliquely to the flash head and positioned to reflect light on the subject can work. Flash equipment should be chosen with bounce versatility in mind. Fast film and bare-bulb flash produces the softest light and best results. Old fashioned flashbulbs used this way are ideal. To capture the striking art on dark monastery walls, two flashes from either side at a 45° angle to the camera are necessary to avoid light reflections. A flash meter, off-the-film flash metering, and experience are necessary to get good results with this technique.

Accept the challenge of varied photographic conditions in Nepal. Subjects in mist or fog often produce striking images. Overexposing slightly may help under such conditions. The monsoon season is ideal for capturing moody landscapes, and even photographing in the rain can produce rewarding results. An umbrella can keep you and the camera dry. A macro lens allows striking closeups of the prodigious monsoon flora and insects. Long exposures at night in the unelectrified villages of Nepal can provide striking images.

The camera I use is a Pentax LX, chosen because it is rugged, well sealed for the monsoon, provides off-the-film metering in the automatic mode, yet functions mechanically when the battery fails. Off-the-film flash metering is also useful, not only in difficult interior situations but also for macrophotography. A spot meter helps deal with exposure problems. The lenses I find useful in Nepal are 20mm, 28mm, 50mm, f:1.2 for low light situations, 100mm macro, 70-210mm zoom, and 400mm. Of course I often go light with one body and two lenses (a 28mm and

100mm) but the above is my burden when I so choose.

A chest pack to hold the camera and several lenses keeps the equipment close at hand. I often carry a substantial tripod with a reversing center piece, but a camera clamp attached to a pack, ice axe, or stick can double as a tripod. I use polarizing filters and carry a split filter, hoping one day to get the ideal rhododendron in bloom sharply framed against a mountain scene. A winder is useful in capturing the smile that follows the shutter release in posed pictures of Nepalis. Lens-cleaning equipment and spare batteries are a must. I find Kodachrome film excellent for outdoor photography but use Ektachrome 400 indoors.

Food

Some people are surprised to discover that Nepal has no large scale organized food distribution network with supermarkets and the like. The type of food available in the hills varies depending on the place and the season. It is also somewhat dependent on who has gone before you. Many locally grown items are available during the autumn harvest time, but in late spring vegetables and other commodities may be scarce. Fruits, a real treat, are available in season. On the more popular routes, such as in Khumbu, Helambu, Langtang, Thak Khola, and some parts of Manang, many items normally only available in large cities can be purchased. Cooked meals available at inns are described in the next chapter.

Below, the starred (*) items are sold in most hill bazaars, and can sometimes be purchased in people's homes. The remainder, except as noted above, can only be bought in Kathmandu, Pokhara, or cities in the Tarai. Although the metric system is being introduced, the traditional system of measure is used here where appropriate. Volume is measured in *maanaa*. One *maanaa* equals twenty ounces or 2½ cups (0.7 l). Eight *maanaa* equal a *paathi*. The basic unit of weight is the *paau*, about half a pound (0.2 kg). Four *paau* equal a *ser*, and three *ser* equal a *dhaarni* or six pounds (2.7 kg).

Rice* is the staple food of richer Nepalis, but it is not easily obtainable in the northern regions. It is measured by volume. Most Nepalis eat large quantities of rice daily. Try to buy the kind with unbroken grains. Other grains are occasionally available. Popcorn can now be purchased in Kathmandu.

Lentils,* or chick peas, are made into a soup called *daal*. It is poured over rice to make the staple meal. A *maanaa* of lentils should last two or three people for about three meals.

Assorted vegetables* are obtainable locally. A list of them is given in Chapter 6. They are eaten in comparatively small amounts by the Nepalis, except in Solu-Khumbu and Langtang where entire meals usually consist of potatoes.

Noodles are rarely found outside of Kathmandu, Namche Bazaar, Langtang, and other areas of Tibetan influence.

Tea* is the staple drink, usually taken sweet with milk. Five hundred grams should last two or three people most of a month. In Khumbu and other areas of Tibetan influence. Tibetan tea is served with butter and salt. It is delicious, but it is an acquired taste.

Coffee is sold only in the instant variety from India.

Sugar* is sold either by weight or volume. It is a comparative luxury and is sometimes hard to find in the hills. About twenty *paau* should last a small party for almost a month.

Milk is best carried in powdered form. If mixed dry with sugar before adding hot tea or coffee, it should dissolve well. Several kilograms should last a month.

Threshing rice. (Donald Messerschmidt)

Cans of condensed sweetened milk are sometimes sold in the hills. Milk powder is often sold along the popular trekking trails. Fresh milk should be heated to the boiling point before being consumed.

Salt* of the finely granulated iodized variety is available in Kathmandu. Only coarse rock salt is available in the hills. Both are measured by volume.

Pepper* and other spices should be bought in Kathmandu. Many unfamiliar, exotic spices are used in the hills.

Oats are another item that lend variety to a diet. They are available in Kathmandu.

Cheese is usually available at the dairy on New Road or Lainchaur in Kathmandu. It is made from yak's milk in Langtang. Canned cheese made in India is also available. Cheese can be purchased at certain times at plants in Langtang, at Thodung, at Tragsindho, and at Sing Gomba near Gosainkund.

Butter can also be purchased at the dairies in Kathmandu. It does not keep long if unrefrigerated. Indian butter is available in cans. In the hills clarified butter called *ghiu** is available.

Peanut butter and various **jams** are a treat, but the ones that come in glass jars must be repackaged as it is not practical to carry glass.

Biscuits* made by the Nebico Biscuit Company in Kathmandu are excellent, as are the more expensive Indian cookies manufactured under license from British affiliates, but the latter are more likely to be stale.

Candy* is a good source of quick energy during the day. Try the milk bonbons made by Nebico. Buy them in the kilogram package. Chocolate bars of Indian manufacture are available.

Roasted flour* is a common food in the hills. It may be of wheat, barley (*tsampa*), corn, or millet. Mixed with water and spices, it is sometimes the only food you can get.

Soup mixes, cooked and poured over rice, make a good substitute when *daal* is not available. The Indian brands are not as good as those made in the West. However, most American groceries can be obtained only from the U.S. Commissary by embassy and Aid for International Development employees. Got any friends?

Eggs* are available wherever there are laying chickens. This includes most places except the high mountain areas (above 10,000 ft, 3050 m).

Dehydrated foods suitable for trekking and mountaineering expeditions are produced in Kathmandu by Trekkers Foods, G.P.O. Box 2389 Kathmandu. (At the time this book went to press, this company was the only producer of dehydrated foods in Kathmandu.) These foods are of good quality, are quite reasonably priced, and require less fuel to cook than many other foods. They are available in many supply stores in Kathmandu and some in Pokhara. Products currently available follow, but those marked with the symbol (**) are not available in the autumn or winter: powdered soup (tomato, onion, and cream of tomato, spinach, and potato); dried vegetables (carrots, onions, spinach, cauliflower,** cabbage**); dried fruits (pineapple, apple, naspati—like pear, persimmon,** mango,** papaya**); granola; muesli (a breakfast cereal); wheatmeal porridge and tomato drink powder. New products may be available in the future.

Many luxury items such as Indian-canned fruits, vegetables, and meat are sold in Kathmandu, but they are quite heavy. Shops in areas of the city frequented by tourists sometimes carry imported foods. Foods taken on mountaineering expeditions find their way into shops in the appropriate areas—for instance, around Namche Bazaar, north of Pokhara, and near Langtang. The variety and quality vary greatly.

You may want to bring other items from home that aren't usually available in Nepal—drink mixes, soup mixes, freeze-dried meats, vegetables, mustard powder, popcorn, and desserts. Of course, none of them are necessary, but it may be enjoyable to celebrate at certain times during the trek. I personally like to take powdered grapefruit drink.

Any non-burnable containers (metal, glass, plastic) that you carry into the hills will have to be compacted and carried out.

Note that few meat items are mentioned. Most Westerners are used to meals centered around meat, but this is not so in Nepal. Occasional bits of meat may turn up among the vegetables and you can ask to have a small dish served to you with your *daal bhaat.* You can buy a chicken in the hills and have it cooked. Where meat is available, it must be requested separately—at a small extra cost. If you are in good health, you can survive and remain quite healthy without any meat. For more on nutrition, see Chapter 5.

Guides and Porters

Sherpas are an ethnic group who have become famous for their exploits on mountaineering expeditions. The term Sherpa, as commonly used by Nepalis, does not stand for a specific job description, but for a group of people who originally migrated from eastern Tibet and settled in the Solu-Khumbu region of Nepal. They have often been employed by trekkers as guides (Sirdars), cooks, and porters. But the term sherpa, especially when used for foreigners, at times refers to anyone of any ethnic group who does those tasks. People of ethnic groups other than Sherpas—*Tamang* and Tibetans, for instance—are increasingly being used as guides. Many of them are quite capable.

People trekking in Nepal for the first time will generally have fewer problems if they have a guide or Sirdar. It may be difficult to hire one during the busy autumn season. The current rate for guides is at least Rs. 35 per day with food provided by the trekker. Guides often demand considerable equipment and since this custom is becoming established, you may find it difficult to avoid. These experienced people do not carry loads, and usually do not cook either; they confine their activities to guiding, hiring porters, and attending to various logistical matters. Most guides speak some English, and some speak varying degrees of French, German, Japanese, and other languages due to their close contacts with foreigners on treks and mountaineering expeditions.

Sometimes younger people with little experience or knowledge of English, who are nevertheless enthusiastic and quite capable, can be hired for less. Such people are, in a way, more desirable, especially for the trekker who wants as few assistants as possible and wants to learn some Nepali. Sometimes these workers may carry a porter's load and do some cooking in addition to guiding.

For a large party not eating locally, a cook, and perhaps a helper, are needed. The guide can usually suggest a Sherpa cook. Porters are also hired by the guide, or by you if you do not have a guide. The wages are higher in the western part of Nepal and for work in high-altitude areas. But it is often possible to make a contract with a porter to carry the load a certain distance, an arrangement that may work out to be cheaper than a daily wage. Porters usually carry their own food. They can be hired through the trekking agencies in Kathmandu, or in other areas at airstrips, restaurants, and hotels frequented by foreigners. They can also be hired at staging areas for treks. Some trekkers prefer to bring reliable people with them from Kathmandu to the beginning of a trek. Porters hired locally may be Sherpas or Tibetans in Khumbu, Tibetans in Pokhara, *Gurung* north of Pokhara, *Tamang* in Kathmandu, or people of other ethnic groups, depending on the area. I find the Hindu caste porters less satisfactory than the hill ethnic groups. Others have found this true for guides as well. Women as well as men can be good porters; a few women have become guides. Some porters on the large treks prefer the companionship of their friends to that of the trekkers. Look for porters who might enjoy closer contact with trekkers.

Porters carry their loads—usually around 65 lb (30 kg)—by means of a tumpline or *naamlo,* a band going around the load and around the forehead. You need only put the load in a sack or duffel bag. Or porters use a *Doko,* a conical basket available for a few rupees throughout much of Nepal. Anything can be carried in it, and an outer wrapping of plastic can keep the load dry when it rains. Even if you give your porters a modern pack frame to carry, many of them will disregard the straps and waist belt in favor of a tumpline, which supports the weight from

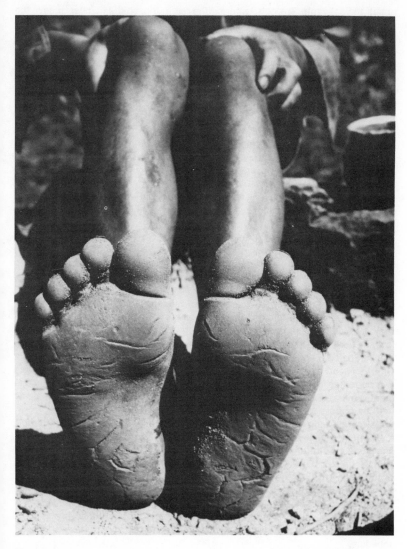

The hardy soles on a porter's feet never wear out. (Stephen Bezruchka)

their foreheads. Indeed, for those accustomed to it, this may be the most efficient and comfortable way to carry a heavy load. Try a tumpline with your pack and gradually increase the weight it supports. Items carried by porters receive rough treatment, and it is best to carry fragile items yourself.

All transportation costs such as bus or plane fares to the actual beginning of the trek are the responsibility of the trekker. In addition, if the trek does not leave an employee at his home or point of hiring, you are obligated to pay for his return, at half the daily rate. Travel is faster on the return trip, so the number of days the journey will take should be agreed upon in advance.

With numerous mountaineering expeditions and large groups requiring many porters along the major trails, especially to Everest, it may be difficult to find porters at the start of a trek or several days into it. And you may have to pay quite an inflated rate. While you can sometimes hire people in remote places such as at the last settlement below a pass, their rates may also be quite expensive. You have few options at this point, and the porters looking for work likely have many. Economics works in Nepal!

Large groups organized by trekking agencies commonly follow day-to-day itineraries or "stages," stopping at agreed-upon points. Porters hired for such routes may insist that you pay them the daily rate for the usual stages—a fixed sum for the distance to be covered—instead of the days you actually walk. In such circumstances I would advise trying to find other porters who are more flexible. Sometimes you may not be able to get around paying the stage rate, but since this amount often does not include pay for the return journey, the stage rate may work out to be similar to a daily rate.

Do not give an unknown guide a large advance, perhaps two or three days wages at the most. Even if your guide is looking after the porters, you should, at the start of a trip, make the wages clear with them yourself to avoid possible misunderstandings later. Have the guide keep an account book. Also do not loan your guide or porters money in contrived circumstances if you expect to get it back. If you feel insecure about your potential guide, ask for references and try to verify them.

When you hire porters and Sherpas, you are taking responsibility for them. If they get sick or injured, see to it that they get suitable medical attention. Many lowland porters have never been on snow or in below-freezing temperatures. They may not be aware of conditions in the places you want to take them. Provide them with footwear, clothes, bedding and shelter if necessary. Equipment for porters can be rented in Kathmandu. Make sure the porters understand that the equipment is a loan, not a gift. An advance of two or three days wages may be paid so that the porters can purchase needed items.

The following scene is all too common. The sahib is in his tent, comfortable and warm in his down sleeping bag sitting on a thick foam pad. His down jacket and pants are stuffed in the corner. Outside, huddled together by some rocks used as a windbreak, his wet, shivering porters do not sleep a wink all night. The sahib wonders why they are so slow the next day.

If you have a guide, it is his responsibility to see to the needs of the porters, but this does not relieve you of responsibility. Recently several porters died needlessly on high passes in storms after they were abandoned by guides. In a storm, it may be prudent to sit low and wait it out rather than try to cross a pass to keep on schedule.

Some people advise trekkers to give guides and porters cigarettes occasionally, or even regularly. Smoking is well established in Nepal, but I feel that it is unethical to further this unhealthy habit, especially for those who don't smoke. If you do smoke, it may be unreasonable not to share your cigarettes. But don't make a habit of buying cigarettes for the employees. There are many other ways to share your satisfaction with them on the trip and to show your appreciation for their efforts at its end. Give them a smile, a look through your camera, binoculars or this book or a gift. Good gifts include used clothing, pocket knives, pencils, paper, discarded containers, sewing needles, and strong thread.

Do not overlook the possibility of using animals to carry loads. This is especially feasible in Khumbu and other northern regions. On one occasion we used a yak and on another, a *zopkio*—the sterile male offspring of a cow mated with a yak. The animals are remarkably sure-footed, but the *zopkio* has a much better disposition than the yak, which requires pulling and pushing at times. However, the yak can withstand more cold than the *zopkio*. Either can carry a hundred pounds or more. In some areas horses can be used. Sometimes a person whom you may want to hire as a porter will carry nothing, but use a pack animal. In this case, the person is paid as a porter, or two, depending on the load carried by the animal. Be sure that the arrangement is clear beforehand.

SLEEPING COOLIE

On his back a fifty-pound load,
spine bent double,
six miles straight up in the January snow,
naked bones,
two rupees worth of life in his body
to challenge the mountain.

Cloth cap black with sweat
and worn to shreds,
body swarming with lice and fleas,
mind dulled.
It's like sulphur, but how tough
this human frame.

The bird of his heart panting,
sweat and breath.
On the cliff his hut, kids trembling:
hungry griefs!
No greens to eat; his wife combs the woods
for weeds and nettles.

Beneath the snow peak
of this more than human hero's mountain,
conquering nature, with a hoard of pearls—
the sweat on his forehead—
and above only the lid of night
bright with stars:
in this night he is rich with sleep.

Laxmiprasad Devkota, 1958
(1909–1959) Nepal's foremost poet

Aircraft

Small Short Takeoff and Landing (STOL) aircraft can be chartered to small airstrips in many parts of Nepal. Helicopters can also be chartered for travel to trekking sites, although this is rare for most tourists. Helicopters are used more commonly for sightseeing and rescue. The planes are single engine Pilatus Porters carrying 900 to 1100 lb (400 to 500 kg) or Twin Otter planes carrying more than twice that load. Charters are arranged in Kathmandu through the offices of Royal Nepal Airlines (RNAC), which also has regularly scheduled flights to many small airstrips. These are usually cheaper than charters, but you can only be sure of the reservations from Kathmandu to the place in question. Reservations for the return trip can be made in Kathmandu, but this is usually not very helpful, and everything has to be rearranged at the remote airstrip. For example, it is notoriously difficult to get a reservation back to Kathmandu from the STOL strip in Jumla.

By making arrangements to fly, it is possible to complete treks in a shorter time and occasionally to prevent backtracking. In addition, the views are often incredible, and the thrill of a spectacular landing is not quickly forgotten. However, this mode of travel is expensive.

Charters are usually arranged to bring a party into a high altitude area. The quick gain in elevation can be very fatiguing and the time lost recuperating from the sudden rise can sometimes equal the time necessary to trek to the area. Even more important for quite a few trekkers, such rapid elevation gain has resulted in death from altitude illness, especially high altitude pulmonary edema. Hence, given the choice, it is better to arrange a charter to return from the area and to acclimatize by walking in.

Cars, Buses, and Trucks

> *A fast approach by plane robs the journey of anticipation; a slow approach by road always begins with the hope of a pleasant trip, and continues with the hope of simply reaching the destination.*
>
> George Schaller, *Stones of Silence*

Private bus companies provide service over Nepal's main roads. The routes most often used by trekkers are Kathmandu to Barabise and Lamosangu for treks east; Kathmandu to Trisuli for treks north; Kathmandu to Pokhara for treks north of Pokhara; and Bhairawa to Pokhara for western treks. Further information is given in the route descriptions. Riding on these buses is usually an unforgettable experience. They often tax the trekker as much as two weeks' walk with a pack. Most trekkers are willing to put up with the slow, pitching buses in order to save time. Trekkers may sometimes be able to purchase rides on trucks transporting goods; this may even be preferable to the crowded buses. It may make sense for a large party wishing to transport all its gear, porters, and trekkers to the start of a trek to hire taxis or other private vehicles. Trekking agencies, of course, usually make these arrangements and provide pickup services.

You can shorten treks by taking the jeeps and buses that travel on the now numerous spur roads off the main routes. In certain places you may find this preferable to taking the trail, in others not. I sometimes describe alternate routes that avoid the roads. It is up to you to decide whether to see Nepal from a bone-jerking vehicle or by sauntering along a trail.

Money

Nepali currency is the medium of exchange in Nepal. In the not too distant past, bartering was the common means of trade and commerce in the hills, although Indian coins were occasionally accepted. Ten years ago trekkers were advised to take mostly coins of low denomination. Now I recommend taking one-, five-, ten-, and fifty-rupee (*rupiyAA*) notes as well as five or ten rupees in five-, twenty-five-, and fifty-*paisaa* coins. There are 100 *paisaa* in a rupee. A rupee is

An enterprising Tibetan selling artifacts alongside a popular trail. (Stephen Bezruchka)

equal to about seven cents (U.S.) at the 1984 exchange rate. In Solu-Khumbu, Thak Khola, and other areas of wealth, 100-rupee notes can often be changed. I have even been asked by locals to change 1000-rupee notes. I would advise against using large bills (Rs. 100 or more). If you must, don't flash them, but handle them discreetly and only use them if little change is to be made. In wealthy areas some trekkers manage to do business with foreign currency such as U.S. dollars. But this is illegal except at certain locations. It is easiest to exchange currency at banks in Kathmandu and Pokhara. While banks do have branches in most of the district centers, exchanging foreign currency at them can be time consuming and difficult, if not impossible. But like most encounters with Nepali bureaucracy, it is fascinating.

Many trekkers barter clothes and equipment for Nepali crafts, meals, and lodging. Western goods can also be exchanged for cash at times. The local people like to obtain useful foreign goods in this way. I usually travel with minimal gear that is difficult to replace in Nepal and do most of my commerce with cash. Some who are in Nepal for short periods of time exchange, sell, or give away much of their clothing and equipment toward the end of their trek.

It is best to take new currency on your trek. Exchange worn tattered notes for crisp new ones in Kathmandu. People in the hills will often refuse a ragged, torn note. Similarly coins that are worn thin may be refused. As for the amount of money to take, it depends on your style of trekking. If everything has been arranged by a prepaid trekking company, little money is needed. If you are traveling without porters or guides and eating food locally, $2 to $3 (U.S.) per person per day takes care of the necessities. Carry enough funds for contingencies. Generally you get a great deal of value for the money spent in Nepal. Don't lose that perspective.

The prices throughout this book are based on 1984 rates. Although you may well find the prices higher when you reach Nepal, you'll at least have some idea of what to expect.

Addresses for Receiving Mail in Nepal

The best, in order of preference, are (1) your trekking agency, if you have one, (2) your embassy, (3) American Express, if you use their traveler's checks, and (4) Post Restante.

Equipment List

R   *items you may be able to rent in Nepal*
P   *items you can hope to purchase in Nepal, though you may not be able to
         count on the quality*

Essential for all trekkers

         walking shoes, well broken-in
  P   socks; several pairs of heavy wool outer socks and a few pairs of light nylon
             inner socks
  P   skirts; mid-calf to above the ankle
  P   pants; baggy ones are best (for women, only between settlements)
  P   shirts, blouses, T shirts
  P   hat with wide brim
R,P   sleeping bag adequate for temperatures encountered (may be provided by
             some trekking agencies)
         repair kit to deal with all your gear
  P   water-purification materials (see Chapter 5)
  P   water bottle; at least 1-litre capacity
R,P   backpack with outside pockets to handle smaller items
  P   stuff sacks (nylon is best) for organizing equipment
  P   medical kit (see Chapter 5)
  P   flashlight (torch) with spare batteries and bulbs
  P   handkerchief
  P   toiletries (soap, washcloth, toothbrush and paste, dental floss, comb,
             shampoos)
         passport
         trekking permit
         this book

P   rupees in small bills and coins
P   pen or pencil, ink, paper and envelopes (to write an emergency message should the need arise)
      pocket knife, perhaps with can opener and scissors
P   plastic bags; several sizes, with rubber bands
P   nylon line (parachute cord)
      blister-prevention materials (moleskin)
      feminine hygiene materials
P   matches or cigarette lighter
      spare eyeglasses or contact lenses if you wear them
P   umbrella if traveling in warm sunny lowlands

For treks to cold, snowy, and high places

P   wool or pile hat; balaclava
R,P wool sweaters, or pile or down jacket
P   wool or pile pants
      long underwear of polypropylene and wool
      mitts (possibly gloves) with water-resistant shell and warm, light inner lining for dexterity
P   windproof outer garments, pants, and jacket
      boots, well broken-in and waterproofed
P   gaiters to keep snow out of boots
P   ice-axe, rope, and crampons for glacier travel
P   glacier goggles, with spares, including enough for Nepali employees
P   sunscreen; zinc oxide for lips

If trekking with an agency (check with the manager regarding items in the other categories)

P   duffel bag; sturdy, zippered, lockable with all your gear stowed inside; to give to your porter

If trekking independently, where hotels catering to trekkers exist all the way

P   toilet paper
P   makeshift shelter (plastic sheeting)
P   some food for contingencies

If trekking independently and relying on *bhaTTi*

R,P air mattress or foam pad
P   toilet paper
P   plastic ground sheet
P   some food for contingencies

If trekking independently where you may camp and rely on your own food at times

R,P tent
P   toilet paper
P   sturdy duffel bags, zippered and lockable, for gear
P   kerosene stove
P   kerosene
P   fuel containers, fuel filter
P   nesting pots
P   cups, plates, spoons
P   scouring pad

P   alcohol in a plastic container (for priming stove)
R,P   shelter, warm clothing, and cooking facilities for your employees if you will
     be in remote areas
P   food, packed appropriately

Monsoon treks

       training flats with new waffle soles
P   umbrella
       waterproof (Gore-Tex) jacket with underarm zips
       waterproof rain chaps or pants (optional)
       large, heavy-duty plastic bags and several smaller ones
P   plastic sheeting for covering porters' loads, and other uses
       insect repellent
       patience
       adaptability

Optional gear

       specialty food items
       bathing suit
       shorts for men
       shaving paraphernalia for men (battery operated or safety razor)
       altimeter
       compass
       thermometer
       watch with a chronograph and alarm
       binoculars
       spotting telescope and tripod
P   maps
       star chart
       headlamp
P   candles
P   reading material
P   journal or diary
P   stationary, air letters, post cards
       a picture book about your country or favorite activities
       photographs of your family, friends, and activities
       photographic equipment, film, appropriate spare batteries
       tape recorder, batteries, blank tapes
       headphones
       prerecorded tapes
       microphone
       language tape (see Chapter 6)
       musical instrument
       games
       belt bag or fanny pack for easy access to selected items while walking

4 INTERACTING WITH NEPAL

Madam, this is Nepal. In America you can be a bird in a gilded cage. Here the bird is free. And for that there is a price.

A Nepali to an inconvenienced and angry trekker

For many years, few indulged in trekking in Nepal, and their impact on the country was rather small. But the large numbers of people who have begun trekking in recent years are causing many changes, good and bad, in the landscape and the people of Nepal. Generally, trekkers are unaware of these changes until, reflecting later, they wonder what is happening.

This chapter, then, attempts to provide not only basic information on day-to-day trekking, but also food for thought on how to help preserve the character of trekking in Nepal.

Trekking Life

Variables such as the type of trek, the size of the party, and the area visited all affect the way you organize your daily trekking activities. Trekkers employing Nepali assistants are advised to adhere to a schedule compatible with them. Trekkers traveling in areas where there are few foreigners and who wish to eat local food, must also adhere to the local schedules.

Though local schedules vary depending on the area and the village, the following general outline gives you some idea of what to expect. In the hills, Nepali people get up around sunrise, sometimes have a brief snack, then work until the mid-morning meal about 10 A.M. Work then continues until the late afternoon, and is followed by the second meal of the day. A snack immediately preceding this meal is not uncommon. Since activities coincide with the period of daylight, people tend to go to sleep soon after sunset. In the mountains a more Western schedule is common. People wait until it warms up a little before engaging in much activity. They generally eat three meals a day.

Thus, a reasonable schedule for trekkers not too insulated from the Nepali lifestyle is to begin around sunrise, or just before. After a snack or hot drink, begin walking in the cool morning until 9 or 10 A.M. Then stop at a *bhaTTi* (local inn) for food, or cook your own along the trail. If traveling away from the trails frequented by foreigners and eating in the local inns, the food is *daal bhaat*, a large quantity of rice, with a lentil soup poured over it. There are usually some cooked vegetables available, and occasionally you may be able to get an egg or some meat. Unlimited quantities of *bhaat* (rice) are included in the meal, but the *daal* (lentils) and vegetables are rationed. The food requested in a *bhaTTi* is usually not cooked until after you order, so the entire food stop takes approximately two hours. In some inns catering to trekkers, ready-cooked food is available.

If you eat in traditional inns or *bhaTTi*, or even in hotels that cater to Western-

Washing glasses at a tea stall. (Steve Conlon)

ers, please realize that the standards of hygiene do not compare to those in restaurants at home. They don't even come close. That is the price you pay to reap the benefits of being in Nepal. The sanitation on treks run by professional guides also varies considerably, but you may be able to exercise some influence there.

Sometimes, away from the popular trekking areas, rice is not available, and you may have to eat *saatu, dherdo,* or *piTho,* terms for roasted flour (corn, millet or wheat) made into a thick paste by adding boiling water. Eat it with a spicy sauce and vegetables if available.

Spoons are seldom available in a *bhaTTi* frequented by Nepalis. You must either provide your own or eat with your right hand as Nepalis do. It is not considered impolite to make slurping noises while eating, and a burp is often taken as an appreciation of the meal. Sometimes, while waiting for a meal to be cooked, you can obtain a snack (*khaajaa*) such as roasted corn (it does not pop like the Western variety). Often tea is available too, but the farther north you go along trails frequented mostly by Nepalis, the more scarce it becomes. In many areas of Buddhist influence in the northern regions, only Tibetan tea served with butter and salt is available. Large quantities of this broth are consumed by the *BhoTiya* of this region, and you may acquire a taste for it, too. Along certain northern routes frequented by trekkers, tea with milk and sugar is often available.

In Khumbu as in most mountain areas, the diet can be mostly potatoes. They are made into a stew (*shakpa*), or pancakes (*riki kur*), or mashed and served with a spicy sauce (*riltok sen*), but most often they are boiled and eaten after peeling the skin off. Other features of the Sherpa diet, also common to other *BhoTiya,* are *thukpa,* a noodle soup, and *tsampa* (roasted barley flour). *Tsampa* is eaten either as a watery porridge (*chamdur*), made by pouring tea over it, or as a drier form (*pak*) poured into the tea.

Just as tea shops can be found only in certain areas, local inns are often limited to regions settled by *Thakali,* the traditional innkeepers, though people of other ethnic groups also run them. *BhaTTi* are especially scarce in the west. When you cannot find one, villagers are often willing to provide food and shelter in their own houses. This generally is not possible, however, in Brahman and *Chhetri* dwellings. To ask, you must first attract the attention of someone inside the house (never go in without being invited). Call out a suitable term of address (see "Nepali for Trekkers") and wait for someone to appear. Then make your request.

It may be difficult to find people prepared to cater to trekkers on the less frequented trails, but on the popular trails it is much easier. En route to Khumbu and in Khumbu, Langtang, Helambu, Gosainkund, and north of Pokhara, many establishments cater specifically to trekkers. They often sell foods carried in from big towns and bazaars, and hoteliers will generally cook meals for you at other than the usual Nepali times. Most of these places have signs; others can be found by asking around. A variety of non-Nepali meals are available, depending on local supplies. This is not gourmet cooking, and the local people do not eat it. If you find you do not like *daal bhaat,* you can avoid it by staying on the popular trails and eating in such hotels. Those who sample local foods may be surprised by the tasty variety and become converts to this simple cuisine.

It is important to realize that innkeepers, in spite of their lengthy menus, usually only have one stove to cook on. If they are cooking rice or another dish, they cannot immediately produce two pancakes with jam for another trekker. However, rather than explain this, they will take the order and cook it in turn. The impatient trekker gets angry and unnecessary ill feelings are generated. Try to size up the situation and adjust your order to what is already being cooked or, even better, learn some tips from the Nepalis on patience.

With the first meal of the day in your stomach, the rest of the day's trail awaits your feet. Along the way you may pass tea shops and stop for refreshment. Trekkers may pass pastures and shepherds in the high country, and may be able to obtain some fresh milk, yogurt (*dhai*) or whey (*mAl*).

During the day's walk, you may pass through several villages and farming areas, cross major rivers, climb to the crest of one or more ridges, and descend down into the valleys again. When trekking without a guide, it is necessary to constantly ask the name of the current village and the way to the next village. There are few trail signs in Nepal, and finding the route is a matter of asking the way as the Nepalis do. Indeed, Nepali people traveling in unknown areas are constantly asking the way and exchanging news. Often you may be confused by the answers Nepalis give to your questions. If so, repeat the question or phrase it differently until you are satisfied with the response. The problem may be your pronunciation. Ask the next person on the trail, too. It's all part of the fun of trekking and finding your way in Nepal. Along the more popular routes local people make a commotion when they think you are on the wrong trail. This can create problems when you deliberately wish to take a side trip. When asking the way, keep in mind both the next town's name as well as a larger, well-known town farther along. Often the names of small settlements may not be known, but everyone knows the names of big centers, even though they may be a few days' walk away. Because of a lack of standardized spelling, names on many maps may lead to improper pronunciation.

Nepalis are eager to please Westerners and in their enthusiasm to do so, often give incorrect answers to questions. For example, a Nepali might say that a particular destination you ask about is close when it is actually a long way off. Or he might say that the trail you are on goes to the place you are asking for, rather than upset you by telling you the truth. And people who don't understand your questions sometimes answer nevertheless. Learning to get around these problems is all part of the experience. It isn't insurmountable or fraught with hazard.

Trails in the high country where there are no settlements are a different matter. Travel along these is seasonal. Most Nepalis go there only during the monsoon when few trekkers are afoot. Animal trails may be confused with human trails.

Moving office furniture creates a traffic jam on the trail. (Stephen Bezruchka)

Forest, fog, or whiteout may make finding the route difficult or impossible. Trekkers have often become lost in such circumstances, and it is easy to remain lost for several days, especially if trying to bushwhack to a trail you don't know. If lost, backtrack to a point you know, rather than trying to push onward. It is prudent to travel with a guide in such country. Often one can be hired locally for a few days.

Trails vary considerably with the seasons. During and soon after the monsoon when the rivers are still swollen, travelers take ridge trails rather than those following the valley floors. But in the dry season, November through May, many trails on ridges are abandoned in favor of more direct river routes. Sometimes during the well-traveled dry season, tea shops spring up along the river routes. In addition, shortcuts across dry paddy fields are favored over the well-worn trails. These shortcuts can be numerous and at times misleading, but they are still preferable in most cases. By contrast, in warmer weather and during the monsoon, tea shops and *bhaTTi* reappear in the high country, where there are few trekkers. Economics has dictated the converse too: tea shops appear where trekkers tend to go in large numbers.

During the day you may pass many Nepalis who ask where you are coming from and where you are going. The accepted form of greeting or taking leave of a person is to place the palms of your hands together in front of your face as if to pray and say *namaste* or *namaskaar*. The latter is more respectful and formal. Both have the connotation of "I salute the god within you." Children will often badger you with endless greetings. Always use the less formal greeting with children.

In the late afternoon or sooner, look for a place to stay. Asking for a meal in the evening is equivalent to asking for a place to sleep. Along the popular routes, there is usually a hotel fee for sleeping in places that cater to foreigners. But in *bhaTTi* in the rest of the country, a place for the night is included in the charge for a meal. Hotels for foreigners often have extra sleeping space, and often separate rooms with beds can be obtained. Some places have wood stoves or fireplaces for warmth and hot showers! Charges are reasonable in view of the wood used. In the more typical *bhaTTi,* you sleep on the floor, often with many other travelers. Sometimes when the *bhaTTi* is particularly crowded, you may be shown a hayloft or other more simple accommodation. I sometimes prefer to sleep on porches outside the houses, as chimneyless and windowless interiors are often quite smoky. This is obviously impractical in most high, cool areas. Establish the prices for items when you order so you will not be surprised at the bill. Find out the going prices from other trekkers and try to not pay more.

If stopping to cook your own food along the trail during the day, expect to take two hours. Setting up camp in the evening takes half an hour, and breaking it the next morning takes almost an hour. Trekkers on trips organized through an agency will tend to have customary meals at the usual times. Lunch is usually prepared by the cooking staff who then go on ahead. The staff sets up and breaks camp and makes sure that the trekker keeps to the correct trail. The Sirdar and other staff may be able to enrich the experience by explaining things seen, and also things not seen.

Trekkers traveling in the high country often stay at *goTh*, temporary shelters used by shepherds. Some are quite substantial structures, while others are only four walls or just the frames for the walls. When the shepherds bring their animals up to graze during the hot monsoon months, they bring mats to cover the frames. *Yersa* in Khumbu are groups of *goTh* used by those who pasture yak and sheep. If there is any doubt about whether these shelters will be available or if privacy is desired, it is safest to carry a tent.

It is especially important to check in at police posts along the way, should you need to be traced in an emergency. To get a small group processed at a police check post takes half an hour. Do not produce your passport unless absolutely necessary or there may be further delays. Be patient and courteous in dealing with officials.

Don't always be in a hurry, eager to cover as much ground as possible. Sometimes, stop at noon and watch village life or explore the surroundings. Consider spending an entire day in someplace that is *not* the highest, the most spectacular, the most beautiful, and just let things happen.

Cross-Cultural Clues for the Survival of Trekking in Nepal

> *To expect Nepalis to conform to and accept outsiders' ways is the most extreme form of cultural arrogance.*
>
> Donald Messerschmidt

The fullest enjoyment of Nepal in all its myriad aspects comes to those who attempt to transcend the cultural and linguistic differences between themselves and their Nepali hosts. Such people are more easily accepted into the social framework of Nepal, and there are many rewards.

In the past, many trekkers have offended their Nepali hosts. They have also misunderstood the actions and feelings of Nepalis, and the foreigner's reactions have made a bad situation worse. Others have taken great advantage of traditional hospitality without considering the consequences. Still others, realizing how much further their money will go in this country, have made a big display of their wealth. They have handed out large (for Nepal) sums of money, and given away many of their possessions. Trekkers have disgraced religious customs and shown great disrespect for their host's beliefs. The local people have adapted somewhat to this breach of courtesy and ethics by these foreign travelers. Indeed, Nepalis along the popular routes expect foreigners to behave in this manner. Partly for this reason, traditional Nepali hospitality is less obvious along these trails. Some trekkers complain that Nepal isn't all it was billed to be and search for new unspoiled places to desecrate. The Nepali people will not let you know of their displeasure — it isn't their way. But amongst themselves they will have less respect for you and less desire to treat you as an honored guest. But should you make the effort to stand apart from the other trekkers, to respect the Nepali people and their customs, they will relate to you in positive ways you couldn't have imagined. You will find yourself more respected in turn.

This section, perhaps the most important part of this book, is an attempt to provide you, the guest in Nepal, with the understanding to act in ways that constitute reasonably acceptable behavior to your hosts. Most of the information has been subtly gleaned from Nepalis, or from the experiences of sensitive visitors to Nepal. If your attitudes are right, and your practices are acceptable, then a few *faux pas* will be overlooked. All of us in Nepal have, at times, acted incorrectly. How do you think I've obtained most of the information presented here? But once you have learned acceptable norms of behavior, the benefits should make the effort worthwhile. Encourage others who have your confidence to do likewise. This is essential if trekking in Nepal is to continue to be one of the supreme experiences in social-cultural peregrination.

Nepal is a complex social mosaic, with Hindu and Buddhist traditions over-

Appropriate dress for trekking. (Stephen Bezruchka)

laying animistic and shamanistic beliefs. Many of the customs stem from Hindu concepts of purity and ritual pollution. As hill Nepal becomes increasingly Sanskritized, these concepts become more important. While the *BhoTiya*—Buddhist highlanders of Nepal—have their own customs that must be respected, they too are becoming increasingly affected by Hindu religion. There are basic rules governing acceptable behavior in Nepal that have knit the social fabric together over centuries. These rules are not difficult. Basically, you need only observe what Nepalis around you are doing and act accordingly. What follows classifies and expounds on this.

DRESS

The dress code for men is as important as that for women but is often neglected. For example, men wearing shorts have low status in Nepal. Men should never bare their chests, except when bathing discreetly. Wear a shirt at all times.

Women should attempt to wear long skirts, mid-calf at least, as often as possible. It is important that women do not expose their legs. Wearing long underwear is helpful if your skirt is shorter than mid-calf. Baggy pants, although not ideal, are much better attire for women than are clothes that expose their legs. Shorts are not acceptable for women.

For women, a *lungi* or tube of material can be purchased in any cloth shop in Nepal and custom-sewn in ten minutes into a suitable garment. Perhaps easier to wear is the *AAgi,* or *chubaa,* a long, sleeveless *BhoTiya* dress that ties in back. You can sometimes purchase a ready-made cotton one. Or it can be made from wool or polyester. Long skirts brought from home are also excellent. Some women have made them of denim, or with beautiful patterns. An elastic waistband or draw-string is helpful for washing discreetly. If you wear baggy pants for the arduous part of the day's walk, change into your skirt in the evening when in a village or when dealing with Nepali people.

Several women on one trek reported a phenomenal difference in acceptance by Nepalis depending on whether they wore skirts, pants, or shorts. One woman who started trekking in a skirt decided it wasn't necessary and changed into shorts. In an hour she was accosted by a Nepali man. Another changed from wear-ing shorts into a skirt and found that, rather than being stared at as a curiosity, she felt more accepted by Nepalis. In questioning neophyte women trekkers who wore long skirts, I found that *everyone* felt much more accepted by the people, which tremendously enriched their experiences. There is also a significant difference between wearing a skirt and wearing pants, as these women have learned.

Trekkers who have questioned Sherpas or other Nepalis about appropriate attire have countered my arguments by quoting their answers. The Nepalis always answer to please, even though their feelings are offended. Donald Messerschmidt, the author of Chapter 13, was talking with a shopkeeper in Tirkhedhunga when a French couple walked by, dressed as if on the Riviera, the man in a tiny brief, the woman in a skimpy bikini. The shopkeeper asked Don what country they came from. Don, having heard them speak, replied France. The shopkeeper then asked, "What's the matter, don't they have cloth in their country?" Consider how you might feel if a Papua New Guinea highlander male, wearing only a penis shield, walked near your home and spoke to you. Would you treat him in a friendly manner and invite him inside? Nepalis feel equally put off by the dress of many foreigners.

BATHING

Trekkers often like to relax in hot springs or swim in rivers or lakes. Nepalis are usually very shocked if this is done with genitals exposed. Women should not bare their breasts, especially those who have not borne children. Men may go bare-chested while swimming or bathing, but not at other times. If you wish to swim in the nude, do so out of sight of Nepalis. Also be modest while washing yourself within view of others. Women wearing skirts can bathe discreetly when not alone by using the skirt as a tent. Clothes can be changed under it too, and an elastic waistband or drawstring makes it easy if your skirt is not too bulky.

BARGAINING

To understand the custom of bargaining, which is almost universal in Asia, one must realize that it is a game, not an impediment to friendship. Westerners, by contrast, often harbor bad feelings after the bargaining process. Yet once a price is agreed upon, it is "fixed." Language trouble can also create misunderstandings. I can well remember bargaining with a taxi driver to take me to the start of a trek out of the Kathmandu Valley. He named a price, and I began to bargain with him, but named a higher price, as my command of numbers in Nepali was poor. He quickly agreed, and it was only as the ride began that I realized my mistake. Never-theless, I paid the price I had agreed upon.

Try to find out the going price for an item before you begin bargaining. Failure to do so hurts everyone. As an example, if a Nepali will sell an egg to his neighbor for Rs. 2, but finds he can get Rs. 3 from a trekker, he will be less likely to sell that egg to his neighbor. Thus the price of eggs goes up. The Nepali is hurt, but not the trekker, to whom the difference in price is negligible. Such inflation has become quite common, and it behooves the trekker to always pay the lowest going price in any transaction.

Bargaining effectively takes time, so be leisurely and relaxed. Don't show too much interest in the item and certainly don't begin by offering the top price you are willing to pay. If you are hung up over the last stages of the bargaining process, remember the monetary exchange value of the amount in dispute. Sometimes it may just be a few cents and not worth the haggle for something a local wouldn't buy. Also remember that prices are fixed for certain items, usually food and commodities, especially along well traveled routes, and bargaining is not appropriate.

EATING

Hindus are concerned about ritual pollution of food when it is touched by anyone outside their caste or religion. As a foreigner, you are outside the caste system. Often you are considered an outcaste or untouchable. Thus, do not touch any cooked foods on display, though it is usually all right to handle uncooked foods such as fruit and raw vegetables. When drinking from a container used by others, avoid touching your lips to it; pour the liquid into your mouth. Similarly, when drinking from a water bottle, do not touch your lips to it—at least not in sight of your hosts. Wait for food to be served to you rather than helping yourself. Do not give leftovers to your hosts, even though they may be rare delicacies brought from home. Do not offer a person anything from which you have taken a bite or sip. This is the *juTho* concept of food—if any food is touched by someone's mouth, the entire plate is contaminated and the utensils must be washed before anyone else uses them. By the same token, all leftover food or drink must either be thrown away or fed to animals. The only exception is that a wife may eat from her husband's plate. Hence, do not accept more food than you can eat, and in a tea shop, make sure you put your empty glass where the Nepalis put theirs. Furthermore, since Westerners are considered outside the Hindu caste system, trekkers who visit Brahman houses or villages can expect to be served food apart from others, usually outside their host's house. They will not be allowed to sleep in a Brahman house. In general, don't offer to share food in a group of Nepalis unless you have enough for everyone.

Don't touch food with your left hand. Nepalis use the left hand for cleaning after defecating, and it is offensive for them to see food in it. Eat with your right hand and use your left for picking up a glass or holding something nonedible. Before and after meals, you will be offered water and a place to wash your hands and rinse your mouth. Wash your hands separately, or your left one not at all. Your right hand may be used to wipe your mouth, never your left. Give and receive items with your right hand. In eating *daal bhaat* and vegetables, the meal is served in separate containers, so keep them that way, except for small portions that you mix on your plate prior to eating. It is, of course, possible to eat with a spoon or chopsticks, which may be available along the more popular trekking trails. But try eating with your right hand. It's fun! It's also the most popular way of consuming food in the world.

GIFT-GIVING AND GENEROSITY

In dealings with people, pay the going rate. Never walk off without paying. In tipping people for their services, be reasonable. Some people tip much more than the salary they are paying. This only reinforces the belief that the sahib does not know the value of his money, and thus should be relieved of as much of it as possible. Bringing small gifts for people who have helped you along the way is a good idea. Such people may also appreciate a look through your camera or binoculars or at the pictures in this book. Allowing people to look through picture books from home (those with farm scenes go over best), post cards, or to see photographs of your family, will be a generous gesture. But displays of generosity should be limited to appreciation for something *extraordinary* that has been done for you. And gifts should emphasize the transcendent values of friendship, knowledge, and health over material wealth. Read the next section to understand why. But beware of the long-term repercussions of anything you do. When a friend of mine who was working in family planning in Kathmandu in 1969 suggested that I distribute condoms during my treks, it seemed a great idea. Reluctant to demonstrate their proper use to adults, I blew them up as balloons for children. This was a highly successful public relations gesture, but I learned later that people following my path were besieged with requests for condoms and balloons. Currently such litter abounds. Bring small useful items like strong sewing thread, needles, cloth, and rope.

BEGGING, AND DEALING WITH CHILDREN

Give me one pen, miThai, *bonbon. Give me one rupee.*

The sounds of Nepali children the trekker hears today

Trekkers may sometimes encounter beggars to whom it is appropriate to give. There are few traditional beggars in the hills, but occasionally *saddhu,* or holy men, travel through begging as part of their lifestyles. Monks and nuns occasionally beg. Food such as rice is an appropriate gift for them. Sometimes destitute people are encountered and gifts of clothing, food, and occasionally money are appropriate. Note the actions of Nepalis around you when deciding whether to give.

It is instructive to watch patterns of begging develop along the trekking trails over the years. When I first came to Nepal in 1969 there was little begging in the hills, and the two who did were children who wanted candy. Yet children and others along the trekking trails are now constantly begging for candy, money, pens, and cigarettes. A few hours walk off these trails, people do not beg at all. In areas such as Thak Khola where many types of trekkers are seen, people who beg tend to approach those who appear to be well-to-do. When I visited Manang after only a few rather lavishly organized treks had been through that area I was constantly besieged. Indeed, it was expected that I should give freely to everyone, presumably because earlier parties had done so. Intransigent trekkers like me have had children throw stones at them for not giving in to begging. Yet over the pass in Thak Khola the pressure to give was much less, presumably because the children and others realize their requests will be better rewarded by trekkers in large groups.

Why do trekkers give money, pens, cigarettes, candy and other items to children? Clearly they like the happy smiles they receive. And in Nepal, foreigners can feel generous without having to give very much. Others feel guilty about the great gulf in material wealth between themselves and Nepali people. If you are one of these, realize that you are making beggars out of children who once were spontaneously happy. To encourage and support begging is an important example of the cultural arrogance that characterizes many tourists. Do you want everyone in Nepal to lose their self-respect, a quality that you probably admire so much? If

Nepali children in school. (Ane Haaland)

everyone stopped reinforcing inappropriate begging, it would cease in a generation, or less. To sample the experience without begging, take a trek away from popular areas. You'll be convinced.

Nepalis have had good dental hygiene in the past, due mostly to their low consumption of sugar. Don't work against this by giving candy. Indeed, the amount of tooth decay in the Khumbu area from recent consumption of sugar in the form of candies has increased dramatically. There are plans for remedial dental work there. Heavy cigarette smoking is a major factor contributing to the high rate of lung disease in Nepal. Don't encourage smoking by handing out cigarettes, especially to children. A few enlightened Nepalis will not allow smoking inside their inns! Handing out money to everyone who asks for it further propagates the image of the fat, rich tourist who does not have anything better to do with it. Giving money for posing for pictures is similarly not a good idea. Parents of Nepali children are usually quite ashamed to learn that their children have been begging, and they try to stop it, except in areas where begging has been so reinforced that parents have become a type of pimp.

You will find many other trekkers giving to begging children. Suggest tactfully to them that they not do so and explain the reasons. This will be a significant step in trying to help the Nepalis maintain their self-respect. It will help return Nepal to the trekking paradise it once was.

When approached by a beggar, either walk away disinterested or, for begging children, use one of the phrases in the chapter on Nepali for trekkers. Don't taunt or ridicule the beggar. Sarcasm is not understood in Nepal.

Sometimes trekkers are approached to donate large sums of money for village construction projects. I have not had this experience, even when I was traveling through an area where other trekkers had mentioned this soliciting, so I can't vouch for the honesty of these ventures. In some places Nepalis will approach you to plant a *tika* (red mark) on your forehead or garland you with flowers, for which they expect you to pay. Avoid such people if you don't want the product.

"Oh money come to me"

This may become the mantra of the future in Nepal if we who are fortunate to travel here don't exercise care and sensitivity.

THEFT AND OTHER INCIDENTS

> *Tourism is thus not only the goose that lays golden eggs, but it also fouls its own nest.*
>
> Dr. Kamal Kumar Shrestha, Nepali chemist

When the first trekkers came to Nepal, the reaction among the hill people was uniform. The visitors were given hospitality and respect, and their actions were watched carefully. With the passage of time and many travelers, patterns of interaction developed. As the kinds of people who came to trek changed, so did the Nepalis' reactions.

The first travelers were interested in mountaineering or research. Some people, generally well-to-do, came just to see the country. All traveled similarly, with large numbers of porters, much equipment, and imported food. They tended to be quite generous, both with their money and their equipment. Lavish tips and presents were offered. More often than not, local feelings were not respected, and customs were violated. Travlers began to be viewed as a source of income and goods. Since they were usually able to pay outrageous prices for Nepali goods and services, this came to be expected. Traditional hospitality remained and has to this day, but it is much less spontaneous and more dependent on money, especially along the more frequented routes.

At the other extreme, in the late 1960s and early 1970s, very budget-conscious travelers and "hippies" came onto the scene. Their actions and customs were different from those of the earlier travelers. Often they lived and kept themselves in a dirtier state than many of the Nepalis. Their drug habits were also viewed with suspicion. While Nepalis have used marijuana and hashish for years, it is used in moderation and only among some older people in society. The new travelers would sometimes run off without paying for food or services. Occasionally, they would even steal precious items. Indeed, once Nepalis realized that art objects had value other than religious, they too began to steal them to sell on the black market.

The result of all this is that trekking in many areas has become essentially a commercial venture in which attempts are made to relieve travelers of their goods and money. Nepal used to be famous as a place where travelers had absolutely no worries about theft and violence. Now some trekkers complain of theft. Petty vandalism and thievery of packs and luggage left on tops of buses is no longer rare. Tents left unattended have been robbed, and some have even been slit open and robbed while occupied. Misunderstandings have resulted in attacks, robberies, and a few deaths. Among the incidents have been attacks on trekkers camping alone in areas with few people, attacks by porters, and instances where trekkers enjoying a view from an exposed area have been pushed off a precipice. Perhaps there is no increase in the incidence of such episodes, but with ten times the number of trekkers they are no longer unheard of.

However, clearly some trekkers have been insensitive to local customs, have mistreated their porters, and have behaved in a manner outside the norms of Nepali experience. The increasing numbers of trekkers have made such behavior more visible. In the past Nepalis would not steal because others would see them with the item and everyone would know, especially if it was an imported good. But now, in popular trekking areas, theft is more common because there is greater display of wealth, everyone is more mobile, and it is easier to get rid of stolen property. There has been a considerable change in cultural values among some people living in the areas most heavily influenced by trekking, in part because our display of wealth is often greater than a Nepali could ever accumulate in a lifetime. The Nepalis believe that trekkers don't value their money because they don't try to get the best prices. Since they are so willing to pay too much, others try to relieve them of their seemingly unvalued money and possessions. It would not be unreasonable to expect criminals to move to the most profitable areas. "Why do you rob banks, Willy?"—"That's where the money is." Remember, however, that the risk of attack and robbery in Nepal is much less than in your home country. But I can no longer state that it will not happen.

Try to prevent petty thievery by keeping a watchful eye on your possessions. Don't display large sums of money. Carry around exposed to view only the equipment that you expect to use a great deal. Try to have all your gear stowed inside your pack and duffel bag, and keep the pockets done up. Lock items whenever possible. Discreetly inventory your gear in the morning and afternoon; it will be less likely to disappear through porter mishap. When traveling by bus with your belongings in the luggage rack on top, either have someone in the party ride with them, or be watchful of people climbing on top when the bus stops. It helps to keep all easily removed items buried deep inside the luggage. In populated areas don't leave your tents unattended.

Another aspect of travel in Nepal that contributed to its popularity was the availability of cheap labor. Porters could be hired for very low rates. Trekkers who could not afford it at home could have servants to do many of the distasteful and laborious chores of camping and backpacking. Porters and assistants were sometimes thought of as less than human. This was evident in the lack of responsibility that many took toward their employees. Porters often carried their loads through the cold and snow with no shoes, clothing, or bedding. A considerable number died in the service of trekkers, usually in high areas during bad weather. At times porters who were sick or injured were abandoned by the sahibs.

Treat your porters with respect. Make sure they have equipment and food sufficient for the undertaking.

MEDICAL TREATMENT OF LOCAL PEOPLE

In the past, medical facilities were very scarce in Nepal, and foreigners were almost the only source of Western medicines. It became traditional to consider each passing traveler a doctor, and indeed, many people, both medical and nonmedical, used to devote a considerable part of their energies to treating the ills of the local people. I feel that this effort is probably not warranted, and may even do more harm than good. To begin with, it helps destroy confidence in health care services developing in rural areas. Besides the facilities staffed by doctors along the trails, there are many health posts manned by auxiliary health workers. It is very doubtful that ephemeral medical care such as a trekker could dispense would result in a cure or significant benefit to the sufferer. Furthermore, the idea that a little medicine might help a sick person and enable him or her to get to proper medical aid just does not hold up. Based on my personal experience as a doctor working in a remote area of Nepal and on discussions with other medical personnel, giving medicine to someone whom you wish to refer to another facility is almost certain to deter that person from acting on the referral. Finally, the idea that a little aspirin won't hurt anyone is untenable because, since it will not effect a cure, it may help destroy confidence in Western medicine. In a country with many different medical practices, it is best to introduce those aspects of Western medicine that definitely work. This may seem like a very inhumane and hard-nosed attitude, especially for a physician, but it is in Nepal's best interests.

However, this advice does not apply to your porters and other employees. If a problem presents itself that you can confidently manage, you should treat them to the best of your abilities. Otherwise, if the condition is serious you are responsible for obtaining proper medical care for that person.

MISCELLANEOUS CUSTOMS

The fire and hearth are considered sacred in Sherpa homes, and in those of most other *BhoTiya.* Thus do not throw any refuse, including cigarettes into a hearth. This is also the case in high-caste Hindu homes. Sherpas and other *BhoTiya* believe that burning or charring meat offends the gods. Even if you have the opportunity, do not roast meat on an open fire.

Shoes are considered the most degrading part of your apparel, so keep them on the floor or ground. Remove them before putting your feet up on anything. Shoes, especially leather ones, should always be removed before entering any kind of temple, *gomba,* or monastery. Do not touch anyone with your shoes. The greatest insult you can give a Nepali is to kick him or her with your shoe. Follow the example of your host in deciding whether to remove shoes before entering a Nepali home. If in doubt, remove them. When sleeping in a temple or *gomba*, don't point your feet at the images.

Don't wash your feet in water that will flow into a water-driven prayer wheel. If you must wash your feet in such a stream, do it after the water has passed through the entire series of prayer wheels. The head of an adult Nepali is the most sacred or ritually clean part of the body. You should never touch it. Similarly, don't touch anyone with your left hand.

Before sitting down on the ground, you will almost always be offered a mat to sit on. When sitting, do not point the soles of your feet at anyone. Nepalis will not step over your legs and feet. Be sure to draw them up to make a path for anyone coming or going. As you go farther north, these concepts of purity and pollution become more relaxed. Watch your hosts and adjust your habits accordingly.

While traveling, you may pass Buddhist *mani* walls containing tablets with prayers carved on them in handsome Tibetan script. Walk by them, keeping them on your right, as Buddhists would do as a sign of respect. Similar treatment is given to the *chorten* and stupas, commemorative mounds sometimes modeled after those at Swayambhu or Baudha. If in doubt as to whether a structure is one of these, keep it on the right as you walk by. When visiting a monastery or *gomba*, a donation of money for the upkeep is expected as a gift. In paying respects to the

A completed mani *stone is carried to its destination. (Dave Hardenbergh)*

abbot of a monastery, offer him a ceremonial scarf, or *kata*, obtained from another monk. Note that many Hindu temples will be out-of-bounds for non-Hindus.

Many Western habits are offensive to Nepalis. Some, such as shaking hands, using dry toilet paper, carrying around a used handkerchief, and eating without washing seem unsanitary to them.

OTHER CONCERNS FOR THE TREKKER

Respect people's desires not to be photographed. Many, especially elderly villagers, believe that being photographed can shorten their lifespans. Sometimes if you talk with them a while, they will consent. After you show them pictures of your family, they may be more willing to be photographed. Or let a recalcitrant subject take a photograph with your camera. After he snaps the shutter, he may change his mind and let you photograph. Otherwise there are many who enjoy being photographed, and their smiles will grace your pictures for years. Don't promise to send copies of photographs to people unless there is a reasonable chance that you can do so. Sending photographs through the mail in Nepal is completely unreliable unless the letters are registered, and even then I wouldn't advise it. Better to send them with another traveler, or through your trekking agency in Kathmandu.

Some people who come to Nepal are attracted by the freely available marijuana and hashish. The plant grows as a weed in much of the country. Traditionally, older shopkeepers consumed it now and then at the end of the day. Young Nepali people never used it when I first came to Nepal in 1969. Now in their desire to copy foreign habits, they indulge. Some trekkers smoking marijuana on the trails will offer it to wide-eyed young children. Consumption of this drug is a personal adult decision. I feel it is wrong to try to entice youngsters to use it. So please be discreet in your use of marijuana.

Many trekkers purchase art and craft objects in the hills. Sometimes they buy valuable old art objects, usually at modest prices. This is expressly illegal; it is prohibited to remove any valuable old items from their origins. Even transporting idols and artifacts can result in imprisonment, and this has happened to several trekkers. Steadfastly deny any interest in old art, for if you don't, you encourage Nepalis to steal objects from sanctuaries, monasteries, or temples in order to sell them to foreigners. Theft of such items by trekkers themselves is totally reprehensible.

Some Nepalis have taken to fraudulently "antiquing" art. The old-appearing *thangka* (scroll painting), brought out of a chest in Helambu and sold as an antique, is common. So-called old jewelry peddled by *BhoTiya* is another example. It may even be difficult to obtain government permission to export fraudulently antiqued works of art or objects of religious value. Permission must be obtained from the Archaeological Department in Thapathali in Kathmandu.

Beware of other amazing items for sale. Once in Manang I was shown what appeared to be a huge (ten-carat or more) diamond that its owner said he found lying on the ground near a mountain glacier. He went to great lengths to "prove" to me that it was not glass and said he wanted only Rs. 300 for it. I was entertained, but not convinced. There are many good locally made craft items in certain areas. Purchasing these at the going prices is certainly beneficial to the local economy.

Conservation

Take nothing but pictures, leave nothing but footprints.

Sierra Club motto

In addition to the effect trekkers have on the people of Nepal, they may leave a profound impact on the countryside. Nepal's limited supply of firewood is being rapidly consumed and there are few reforestation projects. As a result, Nepal's biggest export is probably the extremely valuable topsoil being eroded away into rivers to be washed into India. Trekkers increase the demand for wood, especially in alpine areas where forests are being cut down near tree line to provide it. In addition, *goTh*, temporary herding huts, are sometimes dismantled by trekkers or their porters who need firewood for warmth and cooking. Use of wood for trekking, especially in the high altitude areas, must stop if trekking is to be a resource-conserving activity. Some may argue that wood is a renewable resource, while kerosene is a non-renewable fossil fuel. True, but in Nepal the deforestation problem is far too severe to be further worsened by trekkers. The local people need the wood for themselves, and even for them, it won't last forever.

When camping, especially in the frail alpine meadows, be careful not to add to erosion problems. It takes many decades to produce the vegetation that can be carelessly torn away by a boot or killed by a tent. Similarly, when following trails, stay on the path and do not cut switchbacks. If the vegetation surrounding the trails erodes, it is much more likely that the trail will wash out during the torrential monsoon.

For some popular trails, the route description might as well read, "Follow the line of sahib's garbage—film boxes, food wrappers, foreign cigarette boxes, tin cans—for a week to reach the superb alpine pastures and majestic viewpoints." Many parties have littered areas of Nepal so that they are reminiscent of the over-used campsites, trails, and countryside of North America. It is really not necessary to provide labels from many foreign lands for the bored trekker to read. Carry your wrappers and other items throughout the day, and burn them in the evening. A number of trekkers have begun collecting garbage around inns or as they walk along, burning it when they stop. This practice is to be encouraged. It will not only help reduce the litter but perhaps also provide a good example for the Nepalis. Remember, however, not to throw any items into your host's hearth fire. Metal and glass containers can often be given as gifts to villagers. But along the popular trails this gesture is no longer as appreciated as it once was because of the abundance of containers. Consolidate and carry out non-combustible items (metal, glass and plastic). Burial is no longer an option. Twenty years ago in North America, the wilderness ethic was to bury garbage or place it under stones. In popular areas every stone came to have some litter under it and every shovel pitch unearthed garbage. In alpine areas the soil is too shallow to allow burial.

Nepalis discarded little in the past that did not quickly decompose. Even to-day Nepali people eat off a sal leaf plate when in the forest away from home. When they discard it after a meal, it causes no environmental problems. But as we bring glass, metal, and plastic containers, and wrappings, the local people will similarly toss them away without a second thought if they aren't useful. Don't give them the opportunity to do this. Remember that your actions will be a model for Nepalis and that you owe it to trekkers following you to provide them an experience uncluttered by your litter. Carry your non-burnables back to Kathmandu.

Disposing of body wastes is another problem facing trekkers. Those on large organized treks often erect enclosed latrines at campsites. The feces and other material are then buried. This commendable practice avoids the unsightliness and potential for disease of piles of feces, each with a topping of toilet paper. Travelers who are not on organized treks that provide portable toilets should ask if there are communal latrines (*chaarpi*) in the villages, or if a family has one. One of the many positive changes over the past decade has been the establishment of latrines in certain heavily trekked areas. There are latrines in many of the villages in Thak Khola and other areas. Although not always maintained, they are often excellent facilities. Most homes in Khumbu have a convenient latrine arrangement on top of the hay pile situated in an alcove off the second floor, or more recently, a separate latrine near the house. However, in most of Nepal, you will have to do as the Nepalis do. Usually, they perform their eliminations before dawn or after sunset in various places near the village. They carry a *loTaa*, or container of water, to wash themselves. I recommend that you find a corner of a field or other sheltered spot away from running water and bury your feces, or at least cover them with stones. Burn the toilet paper. Keep a cigarette lighter or matches in a bag with your toilet paper. Sadly, so much of the countryside next to the popular trails is festooned by Western prayer flats—soggy, brightly colored toilet paper, or tampons and other feminine hygiene materials. Always burn and bury them.

Often you will find pariah dogs that eat feces—indeed these are often sum-moned by villagers to clean up after young children. Disgusting as it may seem to non-Nepalis, it is certainly preferable to some alternatives. Whatever you do, be sure to exercise appropriate modesty and get out of sight of others. You never see a Nepali in an act of defecation. I wish I could say the same for trekkers. Nepali women and men often urinate discreetly by hunkering in their skirts. Some women trekkers find this quite appropriate if wearing long skirts with no underpants. But urination generally poses few problems. Women should be careful to dispose of tampons and applicators properly since they have been turning up as children's toys! Note that feminine hygiene products are not available in the hills.

Finally, in whatever you do, realize that you are not alone. If you carry off one *mani* stone from a prayer wall, saying that one less will make no difference, realize what would happen if everyone did so. If we who travel in this exotic country respect its culture and customs, perhaps its spectacular countryside and the experience which we have found so worthwhile can be preserved for the benefit of Nepalis and the enjoyment of future trekkers.

Essential Do's and Don'ts

DO

—wear a shirt if you are a man
—wear a long skirt or baggy pants if you are a woman
—take responsibility for your employees
—keep your valuables secure, locked up if possible
—keep prayer walls and chortens on the right when passing them
—pay the going price for food and other goods
—give away useful containers to villagers
—burn combustible garbage
—carry out unburnable garbage
—draw your legs up while sitting on the floor so Nepalis can pass by you
—leave donations when visiting monasteries
—use kerosene stoves wherever you can
—smile—Nepalis tend to smile to relieve possible embarrassment; a return
    smile quickly eases tensions

DON'T

—give to beggars unless Nepalis also do so, and give the amounts they do
—give money or items to people who have not done special favors for you
—give medicines to the local people
—point the soles of your feet at anyone
—touch anyone with your shoes
—touch any Nepali's head
—give or receive food with your left hand
—eat off another's plate
—give food to Nepalis if you have touched it
—touch your lips to a drinking container that is to be used by others
—accept more food on your plate than you can eat
—walk out of a hotel or *bhaTTi* without paying your bill
—throw garbage in your host's fire
—defecate or urinate indiscreetly
—offer recreational drugs to Nepali children or adults
—travel alone
—be sarcastic to Nepalis

5 HEALTH CARE

I suffered increasingly from mountaineer's foot—reluctance to put one in front of the other.

H. W. Tilman, *Nepal Himalaya*

Trekking in Nepal need not be a great risk to your health in spite of what many Westerners may think. If the preventive measures described here are strictly followed before and during your stay in Nepal, you should enjoy reasonably good health. Field treatments and procedures are given for the medical problems you may encounter in the hills. These are based on my own experiences as a physician who has worked and trekked in the hills of Nepal, and on discussions with other experienced trekkers.

What follows may seem frightening to would-be trekkers who are used to the professional medical care available in modern society. In Nepal you may be a week's walk or more from a doctor. Tens of thousands of trekkers have followed precautions similar to those outlined here and have had a most enjoyable and healthy journey. Awareness and prevention are the keys. A lot of information is provided, some of which may cause anxiety. But it is better to have advice available should it be needed, rather than to disclaim any potential for illness. For most people, trekking is not dangerous; it is the beginning of a new vitality.

Preparations and Post-Trek Precautions

Many people come to Nepal with no hiking experience and, though in poor condition, take on their first trek, walk a hundred miles or more, and thoroughly enjoy themselves. Some treks are more conducive to doing this successfully than are others. Still, I strongly recommend that those planning to trek undertake a conditioning program. Running several miles a day is about the best single conditioner. Taking hikes uphill with a heavy pack is a good activity to put variety into the regimen. Bicycling, cross-country skiing, swimming, and other aerobic activities are also excellent. But all of them must be started months ahead of time and carried on regularly with increases in the amount of exercise each week. Toughen your feet and break in your footwear through progressively longer hikes. Applying tincture of benzoin to your feet over pressure points may toughen the skin.

Before you leave for Nepal, visit your physician and get necessary inoculations. The following immunizations are recommended: Sabin trivalent polio, typhoid, and tetanus-diphtheria. These vaccinations should be recorded on a World Health Organization-approved International Certificate of Vaccination that can be obtained from the health department in your country's national government offices. The live oral typhoid vaccine available in parts of Europe and South America may be preferable to the dead vaccine given by injection elsewhere. Immunization against measles, mumps, and rubella is recommended for those not previously infected or vaccinated. Rabies exists in Nepal and you may wish to get the new but expensive diploid cell vaccine. I have not heard of a trekker contract-

This traditional medical practitioner in western Nepal will chant and beat his drum for many hours to drive out the evil spirit causing disease in a sick child. These shamans coexist with the modern medical practices slowly being introduced. (Stephen Bezruchka)

ing rabies, but animal bites do occur and the risk is there. The cholera inoculation is not particularly effective but you may want this protection. Typhus is present in Nepal and you may wish to be immunized against it. This vaccine is no longer available in the U.S.

Obtain a tuberculin test, and consider the BCG immunization against tuberculosis. A knowledgeable physician can time these inoculations properly. They should begin several months before departure. Have a thorough physical examination and let your physician know the nature of the activities you will be engaged in and the altitudes you hope to reach. Visit a dentist to have potentially disabling dental problems cared for. There has been no easily accessible good dental service in Nepal.

Those with active chest and heart diseases that limit physical activity should avoid going to high altitudes. Individuals with the following conditions definitely should not go to high altitudes: primary pulmonary hypertension, cyanotic congenital heart disease, absence of the right pulmonary artery, chronic pulmonary disease with arterial unsaturation, coronary artery disease with severe angina or cardiac failure, congestive failure with arterial unsaturation, and disablingly symptomatic cardiac arrhythmias. These conditions are described in specific medical terms so the risks can be accurately assessed by your physician. Show this list to your physician if you believe you have one of these conditions.

Recently some people who had serious pre-existing diseases have died while trekking. Those with sickle cell disease or sickle cell trait greatly increase their risk at high altitudes. People with recurrent deep vein thromboses and pulmonary emboli should also avoid high altitudes, but those with essential hypertension tolerate high altitudes well. Our knowledge of the effect of high altitudes on people with mild or moderate chronic disease, as well as on the elderly, is woefully inadequate. Information on drug effects at high altitudes is similarly lacking. Certainly many people in their 60s and 70s have trekked at high altitudes in Nepal with no problems. If you are in that age range or older and enjoy good health and physical conditioning, by all means consider trekking in Nepal, at least at moderate altitudes. You could later consider trying the high passes. Anyone with chronic diseases not discussed here should seek the advice of a knowledgeable physician and, if given the go-ahead, should first make supervised visits to high altitudes in his or her home country. Similarly, those who wonder if they have the physical stamina for trekking should first take backpack trips in hilly areas before planning a trek in Nepal.

Those with stable chronic diseases who can undertake strenuous exercise can certainly trek. Some such people may wish the security provided by an organized trek with a doctor along. Others may have enough self-confidence to trek in small groups without physicians. To my knowledge, people with diabetes, recurrent cancer, amputations, arthritis, and other conditions have enjoyed trekking.

Many physicians are not too familiar with emporiatric (travelers' health) problems. If yours isn't, state and local public health departments usually have knowledgeable people whom you can consult.

Ask your physician about taking malaria suppressants. Malaria used to be endemic in the Tarai, but today it has been somewhat controlled in most areas. Nevertheless, incidents of malaria continue to occur. The usual form of protection is to take the suppressant chloroquin, 500 mg weekly. Except during the monsoon, the chances of contracting malaria while trekking in the hills and mountains are slight, especially above 4000 ft (1200 m). But you may wish to take the drug as an additional protection. If so, start taking the pills two weeks before you reach the first area where there is a chance of getting malaria. Do not discontinue them until two months after you have left all infected areas and until you are in an area where good medical care is available in case an attack occurs after you stop the drug. There may now be some chloroquin-resistant *falciparum* malaria in Nepal.

Discuss the medical supplies mentioned here with your physician. Drugs and most supplies can be bought cheaply in Kathmandu. Moleskin, iodine water purification tablets, and modern sunscreens may only be available in the United States and Europe. Moreover, a few items available in Kathmandu, such as elastic or adhesive bandages, are inferior to those made in the West.

Finally, arrange to get an immune serum globulin (gamma globulin) injection just before you leave home. This provides partial protection against infectious hepatitis, long feared by travelers to Asia. Currently, the U.S. Public Health Association advises 5 ml every four months for adults regardless of body weight or 2 ml for two months' protection. If traveling for more than four months, you can get a gamma globulin injection at 1 P.M. any Wednesday at the Kalimati Clinic in Kathmandu. Gamma globulin does not offer complete protection, but lessens the risk remarkably, so that if you follow other safeguards while in Nepal, you will probably not end up in a hospital hepatitis ward.

Some people are expressing concern about AIDS (acquired immune deficiency syndrome) and the possibility of contracting it from a gamma globulin injection. Immune serum globulin (gamma globulin), a blood product, has not been known to transmit any disease. Although the epidemiology of AIDS is not understood, the risk of acquiring it from a blood transfusion is less than one in 1,000,000. There is clearly a greater risk in *not* getting the injection and thereby contracting hepatitis.

In summary, every trekker should have current immunization status for polio, typhoid fever, tetanus, diphtheria, measles, mumps, and rubella, and should obtain immune serum globulin. I recommend rabies vaccine but suggest that malaria prophylaxis not be taken, except possibly, for lowland treks during the monsoon.

After you return home from trekking, you should have your stool examined for ova and parasites. It is a good idea for all travelers returning from Asia to have their stool examined even if they never had diarrhea there. Several people have written to me, pleased that they followed this recommendation, as tests showed parasitic infestations that were easily treated. You should also repeat your tuberculin skin test if it was previously negative.

Health Care of Children

For those trekking with children, it is essential that a knowledgeable physician or other health professional be consulted before you leave home in order to get specific information appropriate to your children and their needs. See this person well in advance—several months may be necessary—to ensure that the required immunizations can be obtained in time. If it is decided that your children should take chloroquin as a malaria prophylactic, pills of appropriate size can be obtained at stops en route, in Hong Kong for example, or sometimes in Nepal. Small-dose tablets are not easily available in the United States or Canada.

The greatest health risk for children trekking in Nepal is the hazard of fecal-oral contamination. Children at oral stages tend to put everything in their mouths. Human and animal feces are everywhere, and tend to get into the hands and mouths of children. The problem is compounded because children with diarrhea and vomiting can get dehydrated quickly. Since there are essentially no medical care facilities in the hills, each family is on its own. Take solace in knowing that most trekking families have no problems.

Prevention is the key. Watch what your child puts in his mouth. Iodize or boil all water for drinking and feed your child only cooked food. Keep materials for making oral rehydration solution on hand in case diarrhea or vomiting develops. If the liquid losses in stool or vomitus are replaced gradually, no serious problems should result. Oral rehydration powder has been formulated by the World Health Organization and provides the substances lost. In Kathmandu this oral rehydration powder, called Jeevan Jal (meaning life-liquid) can be purchased in drug shops. Mix one packet with four cups (one liter) of boiled or iodized water, and feed it to the child a little at a time by spoon or cup. Try to get the child to drink at least as much liquid as he has lost. Check for signs of adequate hydration such as normal frequency and amount of urination, moisture on the lips and mouth, and fairly normal behavior. If in doubt, get the child to take more fluids. Do not use opiates or other similar drugs to "plug up" diarrhea in children. Do not use tetracycline drugs in children under age eight. If you lack a commercial oral rehydration powder such as Jeevan Jal, a substitute can be made up almost anywhere. Add one three-finger

A Tarai shaman prepares to suck an object that is believed to cause illness out of his patient's body. (Johan Reinhard)

pinch of salt and a three-finger scoop of sugar to one *maanaa* (2½ cups or 570 ml) of boiled or iodized water. Add some orange or lime juice if available.

In 1983–84, there was a meningitis epidemic in Nepal that appears to be concentrated in the Kathmandu Valley. If this epidemic persists, it may be wise for children coming to Nepal to be immunized with the meningococcal bivalent vaccine, effective against the prevalent organism in Nepal. Ask your physician about this. Adults are usually resistant to the disease.

Colds and other upper respiratory infections are very common in Nepal, and your children may get their share. One family found a bulb syringe handy for clearing their two-year-old's snotty nose.

Children's doses for drugs are not given here. They vary, of course, with the age and weight of the child. Be sure to discuss which drugs to take, and their doses with your health consultant. Liquid doses are best for young children.

The hazards of high altitudes are no less for children than for adults, except that it may be more difficult to determine whether a particular child's health problem is due to altitude or to some other cause. One family recently took their twenty-one-month-old child to 16,500 ft (5000 m) without difficulty, after appropriate acclimatization. I have seen Sherpa mothers carry their one- or two-month-old babies over 19,000-ft (5800-m) passes. And a woman who was six months pregnant ascended to 24,000 ft (7300 m). Such extremes are not recommended. Families should limit their treks to 13,000 ft (4000 m). With infants, 10,000 ft (3050 m) might be a safe limit. Little is known about altitude illness in infants and young children. But the general consensus is that unless born at high altitude, children probably tolerate ascent to heights less well than do adults. All people with children who venture to high altitudes should descend immediately if there is any difficulty in acclimatizing. The safety margin in waiting out the minor symptoms of altitude illness is significantly less in children than in adults.

The Medical Kit

A very basic medical kit is proposed here so that trekkers will be reasonably prepared for problems. Most of the items can be purchased quite cheaply in Kathmandu. Since the greater part of its contents will remain unused, it can be considered a kind of insurance. In most developed countries, prescriptions are required for some of the drugs. An understanding physician should give you these if you carefully explain why you need them. Do not use these medications when medical assistance is available nearby. In most cases the procedures outlined here are only field approximations, and proper diagnosis is very important.

Names of drugs are always a dilemma. While the official or generic names are generally the same throughout the world, the advertising or brand names vary greatly from place to place. The generic names are used here whenever possible.

My recommended medical kit—enough for a party of two—includes:

Moleskin—Felt padding about one millimeter thick with adhesive backing, used for the prevention of blisters. About half a square foot per person should be enough. It is not available in Kathmandu, but adhesive tape or zinc oxide strapping can be used as a substitute.

Bandages—One roll of two-inch cotton gauze, one roll of two-inch adhesive tape, and five to ten adhesive bandages per person for small wounds.

Elastic Bandage—One three-inch roll for relief of strains and sprains.

Thermometer—One that reads below normal temperatures (for diagnosis of hypothermia) as well as above (for fever).

Miscellaneous—Scissors, needle or safety pin, and forceps or tweezers.

Plastic Dropper Bottles—One-ounce size for iodine and tincture of opium. These are best brought from home as the ones available in Nepal tend to leak. If your pharmacy no longer carries empty plastic dropper bottles for dispensing compounded ear, eye, or nose drops, buy a plastic dropper bottle of nose drops and dump the contents.

Water Purification Chemicals—Tetraglycine hydroperiodide or iodine in various forms (see next section).

Iron Pills (Optional)—Ferrous Sulfate tablets (200 mg) for women only. Take one per day, and discontinue after your trek.

Nose Spray or Drops—Phenylephrine HCL (one-half percent) for stuffed noses and sinuses. In Kathmandu a product called Fenox (one-fourth percent active substance) is available in convenient 15 ml dropper bottles. Put two drops of the more concentrated solution in each nostril two or three times a day when symptomatic and when changing altitude.

Nasal Decongestant (Optional)—For those used to taking these tablets for colds.

Antihistamine—For treating symptoms of colds and hay fever. If you do not have a favorite, try chlorpheniramine maleate tablets (4 mg).

Aspirin or Similar Drug—Twenty-five tablets (five-grain, 325 mg) of aspirin for relief of minor pain, for lowering temperatures, and for symptomatic relief of colds and respiratory infections. Acetaminophen (paracetamol) is an appropriate substitute for those who can't tolerate aspirin and may be preferable at altitude.

Codeine—Fifteen tablets (30 mg) for relief of pain, cough and diarrhea. A good multi-purpose drug.

Anti-motility Agent—Tincture of opium (the most concentrated), 1 oz (30 ml), or camphorated tincture of opium (less concentrated, but the only form available in Kathmandu), 8 oz (250 ml). More expensive alternatives (see next section) include Lomotil and loperamide tablets. Codeine also works well.

Antibiotic—Two different ones should be carried, a cephalosporin (Cephalexin or Cephradine are cheapest), and co-trimoxazole. Carry forty capsules of a 250-mg cephalosporin. If allergic to penicillin, you might also be allergic to a cephalosporin, as there is a ten percent rate of cross-sensitivity. Erythromycin in a 250-mg capsule would be the best choice for allergic individuals, but it may cause stomach upset in some. Dosage for either drug is one or two every six hours. Bring co-trimoxazole (trimethoprim 160 mg and sulfamethoxazole 800 mg) in so-called double-strength tablets, abbreviated TMP/SMX later in this chapter. Bactrim and Septra are common advertising names for this drug. Bring twenty of these tablets. The dose is one every twelve hours. Tetracycline (forty 250-mg capsules) would be a less satisfactory alternative to TMP/SMX.

Antiprotazoan—Twenty tinidazole 500-mg tablets are the best drug to self-treat presumed giardia infections while trekking. It is not currently available in the U.S. but can be purchased in Nepal.

Antihelminth (worm medicine)—Six 100-mg tablets of mobendazole. One tablet morning and evening for three days will take care of most worm infestations in a porter. You won't be there long enough to require treatment in Nepal.

Anti-inflammatory Agent—To be considered if you are prone to arthritic complaints or tendonitis. Aspirin is the best choice for those not previously afflicted. For the others, ask your doctor about phenylbutazone or indomethacin.

Sunscreening Preparation—One with a Sun Protection Factor (SPF) of ten to fifteen in order to get adequate protection from the sun on snow slopes at high altitudes. Zinc oxide, an opaque ointment, is the only effective sunscreen available in Nepal. Sunscreens are best applied one or two hours before exposure, and reapplied after heavy sweating. Be sure to apply them over all areas that can receive direct or reflected sunlight, especially under the nose, chin, and eyebrows. Lip balms containing effective sunscreens should also be used.

Topical Ophthalmic Antibiotics—For instance, Ten Percent Sodium Sulfacetamide (15 ml) made by Royal Drug in Kathmandu. Many antibiotic products are made for treatment of conjunctivitis or eye irritations, but in choosing one, avoid all penicillin products since the chance of becoming sensitized to them is great if they are used on the skin. The same goes for any antibiotic if you may want to take the active ingredient internally. Good choices of ophthalmic antibiotics are those that contain bacitracin, chloramphenicol, neomycin, or polymixin. Avoid any that contain steroids such as betamethasone, cortisone, dexamethasone, hydrocortisone, prednisone, or others.

Malaria Suppressant (Optional)—Chloroquin, for instance, if you and your doctor think it is necessary.

These items are considered a bare minimum by some, too much by others; they are clearly adequate for most situations. Other items are mentioned in the next section, and can be added if desired. I would never go into the hills without tincture of opium, aspirin, iodine, a sunscreen, and an antibiotic. Physicians accompanying a group to high altitudes might find a stethoscope and an ophthalmoscope useful.

Pregnant women should consult a physician regarding medical problems they might encounter and use of these or other drugs.

Health and Medical Problems

The vast majority of diseases that plague the trekker in Nepal are transmitted by food or water contaminated by infected human or animal feces. You should assume that all water and uncooked foods in Nepal are contaminated. Prepare food and water properly to render them harmless.

WATER

The safest procedure is to boil drinking water vigorously for ten minutes. This kills all bacteria, viruses, and parasites. The next best is to treat the water with iodine, which kills most organisms including giardia cysts. There are several methods of adding the required amount of iodine to water. One is to add two drops of two percent Tincture of Iodine to 8 oz (one cup, 250 ml) of water, stir, and wait ten to thirty minutes before using. If the water is cloudy, add twice the amount of iodine. The iodine can be carried in a small plastic dropper bottle. The other method involves using tetraglycine hydroperiodide tablets, also called water purification tablets iodine (Globaline, Potable Aqua). Add one tablet to a quart (liter) of water. After it has dissolved, stir the water and leave it for twenty minutes before using. The Tincture of Iodine method is best suited for small quantities, while the tablets are useful for water in canteens. I use iodine tincture exclusively because it is cheap and convenient.

Another technique for iodination of water is to place 4 to 8 g of crystal iodine (USP grade resublimed iodine) in a 1-oz (30-ml) clear glass bottle with a plastic top. Fill the bottle with water and shake it vigorously. Allow the crystals to settle to the bottom. Add half the bottle of solution to each quart (liter) of water, and wait for fifteen minutes before consuming the water. Refill the bottle, and reuse it. This technique can be used about 1000 times before the iodine is depleted. If the water is unusually contaminated, allow it to stand for forty minutes before using. The iodine crystals themselves could be fatal if swallowed inadvertently. Be very careful using this method. People with no access to a chemical supply store may find iodine crystals difficult to obtain, but sometimes a drugstore can supply them. A final option is a ten-percent solution of povidone-iodine, a disinfectant used in hospitals and available in many drugstores. Use two to three drops per glass of water (250 ml) or eight to ten drops per liter. Lugol's Iodine is a solution sometimes used in Nepal, rather than the tincture. The quantity used is half that of tincture. Try any method using iodine at home first to make sure you are not allergic to it. Such allergies are rare but not unknown. Ingestion of large quantities of iodine during pregnancy could harm the fetus.

The effectiveness of iodination depends on the temperature of the water. At 20° C (68° F) all methods work, while at 3° C (37° F) the tablets are the only method that works effectively to kill giardia cysts. Conceivably, letting the iodine drops or crystals work longer (up to an hour) in such cold water may make its use effective.

Several new products that treat water by passing it through a device are available. I have no personal experience with any of these devices and can see no advantage to the trekker in using them unless he is allergic to iodine and purchases one that filters water effectively. The standard water filters used in homes and restaurants in Asia are not effective by themselves in filtering out bacteria, viruses, and parasites.

On organized treks, trekkers are sometimes told the water they are given has been boiled, when in fact it hasn't. I always assume that "boiled water" has not been boiled, unless I have supervised it.

You must be cautious with all water ingested, even that used for brushing teeth. Water used for cleaning open wounds is best boiled first and left to cool. Get used to the idea that if it does not taste like iodine, it is not water (unless it has been boiled). Bottled soft drinks and beer of reputable brands are considered safe.

Chlorine (Halazone) is widely used as a water purification agent, but it is not as effective as iodine because the spectrum of organisms it kills is smaller. Chlorine is useless against amebic cysts, while iodine has been shown to kill these hardy creatures. Most trekkers will probably decide to add iodine to their water rather than boil it.

FOOD

Thoroughly cooked foods can be considered safe, but only if they are eaten soon after cooking. Fruits and vegetables that are eaten uncooked must first be washed and peeled under sanitary conditions. Leafy vegetables must be cooked, since it is not clear how effective it is to wash them in an iodine solution. Thus peel it, cook it, or forget it.

Food prepared by Nepalis can be assumed to be safe if it has just been cooked and not allowed to be contaminated by flies. Contamination is possible from the plates the food is served on, but this is very difficult to control.

Milk should always be heated just to the boiling point and allowed to cool before drinking, unless it is known to be already pasteurized. Curds are made from boiled milk and can be assumed to be safe unless recontaminated. This can easily occur, especially if flies have been allowed to sit on the surface. Scraping off the top layer should then be sufficient. If milk has been diluted with water, it is

Milking a yak. (Dave Hardenbergh)

necessary to boil the mixture for ten minutes. Buttermilk and cottage cheese, especially when prepared by herdsmen in their alpine huts, can be considered fairly safe. The dairy in Kathmandu pasteurizes its milk. Most of the ice cream in Kathmandu is risky.

It is difficult to follow rigorous advice concerning alcoholic drinks. To be safe, avoid them all. *Rakshi,* distilled from a fermented mash, is perhaps the safest since it has been boiled. The *Thakali* frequently serve *daru,* a *rakshi* that is very much like sake. The common fermented drink is called *chang* by Sherpas and Tibetans, and *jAAR* by other Nepalis. Unless the water from which it is made is known to be pure, it is possible to get sick from it (a hangover notwithstanding). However, many trekkers will find it very difficult to abstain.

Honey is often obtained in the hills from beehives located on cliffs. The bees are smoked out by Nepalis dangling on primitive ladders made of reeds. If this honey is from rhododendron flowers, it may contain a potent neurotoxin (poison). Locals are often aware of this. Cooking the honey is reputed to destroy the toxin. On one of my treks in a remote region we obtained some cliff honey and later consumed part of it. An hour later, my companion began to feel ill and then became comatose. He required rescue, but recovered fully. We subsequently cooked the honey, but days later his Nepali companion ate some and developed similar though less severe, symptoms. Be careful of unknown local honey.

NUTRITION

The University of Hawaii *Nepal Health Survey* concluded that the dietary intake of Nepalis is adequate, except that it is deficient in vitamins A and C and riboflavin. However, clinical signs of deficiency are occasionally observed only with regard to vitamin A. Iodine deficiency is also found in the hills, and people with goiters are sometimes seen.

A survey of trekkers' diets in Nepal showed that many are inadequate in protein and caloric intakes. Rice and lentils (*daal bhaat*) in large quantities are a reasonable source of calories and protein. Trekkers should make sure that they periodically eat green vegetables and pigmented fruits and vegetables to get sufficient vitamins A and C. Those worried about their protein intake because of the relatively meatless diet should ask at Nepali homes for some roasted soybeans (*bhaTmaas*). These are pleasant to munch on along the trail and they contain more protein per unit weight than any other food, including meat. Eggs are also available at the lower altitudes.

Learn a lesson from your porters who consume vast quantities of rice. This is necessary to provide the calories needed for walking, and the protein for repair. Sometimes ascents are measured in the amount of rice needed to carry a certain load up a specific hill. So eat plenty and then some!

For insurance, some trekkers might want to take a vitamin pill daily. Women might also want to take an iron pill daily, as the local diets do not contain much iron. Women do lose a significant amount of iron monthly through menstruation. However, neither of these supplements should be necessary for healthy trekkers who spend a few months walking around in the hills.

DIARRHEA AND DYSENTERY

Diarrhea and dysentery are the most common problems among trekkers. The term diarrhea as used here means frequent passage of loose stool. Dysentery means forms of diarrhea in which the stool often contains blood and mucus. Sufferers may also have stomach cramps and fever. Diarrhea is much more common among trekkers than dysentery and can be caused by toxin-producing intestinal bacteria or parasites such as *Giardia lamblia* or other bugs.

General principles in either situation are to note the number and nature of the stools and to begin taking clear fluids such as water, weak tea with sugar, juice, clear soup, or soda pop that has been left to stand until the carbonation is gone. Avoid dairy products. Drinking lots of fluids is necessary to avoid dehydration. Perhaps the best liquid to take is an oral rehydration solution. Jeevan Jal, a powder manufactured in Nepal by Royal Drug Company, contains the needed salts. Mix one small bag with a quart (liter) of water and drink it in small sips. If the diarrhea is particularly bothersome, take ten drops of tincture of opium in a small amount of water after each loose stool, up to five times a day. A teaspoon of the deodorized tincture (paregoric), two or three Lomotil tablets, or loperamide tablets can be substituted. Codeine in 60- to 120-mg dosage works effectively too. Treatment with opiates and synthetic anti-motility agents may actually prolong illness in those afflicted with certain forms of dysentery, so don't take them indiscriminately.

If these medications relieve the symptoms, return to solid food gradually. If you continue to have two or three loose stools a day with no blood or mucus but feel well enough to continue, omit taking the tincture of opium and go on. Usually the diarrhea will subside of its own accord. On the other hand, if you have dysentery, especially with nausea, vomiting, and fever, rest and begin the antibiotic. Cotrimoxazole (TMP/SMX) is the best choice if available. Take one tablet every twelve hours for five days. People with such symptoms will rarely be able to continue at the time, but with rest and constant intake of fluids, the symptoms should disappear in a few days. It is important to continue fluids, even if only small portions can be taken at any one time.

Another effective remedy for non-giardia diarrhea is a bismuth subsalicylate suspension such as Pepto-Bismol. It has also been shown to work as a prophylactic agent. No side effects have been reported. The dosage of 60 ml (4 tbsp) taken four times a day is effective for either purpose, but this necessitates carrying enough for a cup a day. But a half pound (225 g) a day (not counting the weight of the container) works out to some 15 lb (7 kg) for a month's trek. Tablets of this material are available and may also be effective, but this hasn't been studied.

If your diarrhea is accompanied by burps of rotten-egg-like gas, then the protozoan parasite *Giardia lamblia* may well be the cause. This parasite seems to be more prevalent on treks around and north of Pokhara though it is common elsewhere in Nepal too. Stools will often contain mucus and smell like rotten eggs or sulfur, as will expelled gas. I used to advise not treating with the medicine specific for giardia until an accurate microscope diagnosis was made. However, a new therapy seems safe and quite effective, and trekkers may wish to treat suspected cases of giardiasis after symptoms have persisted for a week. Take two grams of tinidazole (which is not yet available in North America but can be purchased in Kathmandu) as a single dose. The dosage may have to be repeated in twenty-four hours. Some trekkers have developed giardia neuroses, thinking that each loose stool has been caused by this comical looking flagellate. There are other causes of foul-smelling burps. For these people, taking tinidazole every few days could be risky.

Another way of treating the common, non-giardia diarrhea that trekkers get is to take a tablet of co-trimoxazole (TMP/SMX) with the first episode of diarrhea. Those allergic to sulfa drugs should not use co-trimoxazole. If the diarrhea persists, a tablet every twelve hours for a day or two may be necessary. This is not a recognized treatment protocol, and as a physician I admit that such a low dose could mask other illness. I began this mode of treatment in Nepal years ago by taking one tetracycline capsule at the onset of diarrhea. I recommended it to others who confirmed its seeming effectiveness. However, tetracycline can cause an increased sensitivity to sunlight, resulting in a pronounced rash and sunburn. Tetracycline should also be avoided by children and pregnant women. Co-trimoxazole is a better drug for this and other reasons, so I am changing my recommendation in this edition.

A five-day course of antibiotics for diarrhea has been shown to work in one study, which used either co-trimoxazole (trimethoprim 160 mg and sulfamethoxazole 800 mg, TMP/SMX) or trimethoprim 200 mg twice a day. Other antibiotics and shorter courses (such as mentioned above) may be sufficient but are currently unproven.

There are many other treatment regimens for diarrhea and dysentery. In fact, almost every traveler knows of several. One drug, a combination of diphenoxylate and atropine, has been marketed and heavily promoted under the trademarked name Lomotil. It is used much the same as tincture of opium, but it has not been shown to be superior, in spite of its much higher cost. A newer similar drug, perhaps slightly better, is loperamide. An old favorite is the widely touted iodochlorhydroxyquin marketed under the name Entero-Vioform. People take it either prophylactically or for diarrhea. However, a study of people using this drug for prophylaxis in Mexico showed it was no better than a placebo (sugar pill). And a recent study has implicated this drug in causing eye and nerve damage. I would not recommend it. I similarly would not recommend the use of the drug Mexaform.

Other drugs have been used for prophylaxis of traveler's diarrhea. Sulfa drugs and neomycin as well as bismuth subsalicylate have been shown to be of some benefit in controlled studies. Other recent studies have confirmed the prophylactic benefit of the tetracycline drugs. Doxycycline, available under various brand names, was the particular drug studied. A dose of 100 mg (one capsule) taken once a day with meals to avoid side effects, is effective according to two studies. Another study has shown similar benefits to TMP/SMX (co-trimoxazole) taken as a single (double-strength, i.e. trimethoprim 160 mg plus sulfamethoxazole 800 mg) tablet *once* a day. Use of a drug for longer than three weeks is not recommended. Doxycycline should not be used by pregnant women, children under eight, or people allergic to tetracyclines. These drugs are quite expensive, often costing a dollar a day. Individuals taking such drugs may theoretically risk other infections with resistant strains of bacteria such as salmonella and shigella. Another theoretical risk is the development of resistant strains of enteropathogenic *E. coli* bacteria (the causative agent of most forms of traveler's diarrhea). Cases of photosensitivity have occurred among people using doxycycline for prevention of diarrhea in Nepal. They become sensitive to the sun, and are sunburned much more easily than others on the trek. If you suspect this is happening to you, discontinue the drug immediately. These reactions are more common with this drug than with tetracycline. As with any drug, the potential hazards should be weighed against the potential advantages. I do not recommend these drugs as prophylactics except to those who have previously had incapacitating traveler's diarrhea, or who are very worried about getting it. Prophylaxis may be appropriate for those people without gastric acid (achlorhydria), since they are at greater risk. Since the usual forms of diarrhea affecting trekkers are self-limiting, most people can get by quite well by treating episodes as they occur.

ALTITUDE ILLNESS*

> *If you are not feeling well at altitude, it's altitude illness until proven otherwise.*
>
> David Shlim

Problems with altitude can strike anyone, even at relatively low altitudes such as 8000 ft (2450 m). Indeed some have died from altitude illness at this level. But in general, trekkers going to higher altitudes quickly are more severely affected. People who fly to a high altitude and then proceed to an even higher area or cross a pass should be especially wary. Examples include flying to Lukla and Shyangboche and going on to Everest Base Camp; flying to Jomosom and crossing the Thorong La; or flying to Langtang and crossing to Ganja La. Statistically, some symptoms will be felt by two-thirds to three-fourths of those going to high altitudes, especially to 14,000 ft (4200 m) or above. Those hiking up will have fewer problems than those flying up. Serious illness occurs in perhaps less than two percent of people who go to high altitudes.

Altitude illness can be prevented by acclimatization, that is by a gradual rate of ascent, allowing sufficient rest at various intermediate altitudes. It is a totally

---

*Much of the information here on altitude illness is taken from *Mountain Sickness* by Dr. Peter Hackett (see Recommended Reading). He has perhaps more experience in dealing with altitude illness in Nepal than any other physician.

preventable problem. The proper amount of rest and rate of ascent vary greatly from individual to individual, and even over time in the same individual. For example, one person who previously had climbed Mount Everest later had difficulties at lower altitudes from ascending too rapidly. Dr. Charles Houston, who has done extensive research at high altitudes, says a cautious rate of ascent that would ensure comfort and safety for almost anyone is to take five days to reach 11,000 ft (3350 m) and six more days to reach 15,000 ft (4500 m). Above 15,000 ft (4500 m), climb 500 ft (150 m) a day. However, most parties could safely go at a slightly faster rate, allowing one day of acclimatization for every 3000 ft (900 m) gained between sleeping sites above 10,000 ft (3000 m). This is feasible only if everyone is on the lookout for the signs and symptoms of maladaption to high altitudes. If the party acts appropriately should anyone develop altitude illness, serious problems can usually be avoided.

For example, in ascending to Everest Base Camp, Kala Pattar, or anywhere above 15,000 ft (4500 m) allow at least two rest and acclimatization days. One stop could be at 11,000 ft (3350 m), and the other at 14,000 ft (4250 m). On these days, people who feel good could take an excursion to a higher point, but return to sleep at the same altitude as the night before. In Khumbu a rest day at Namche Bazaar or Tengboche, followed by another at Pheriche, would be the minimum requirement. Then spend a night at Lobuje, and ascend to Kala Pattar the next day, returning to Lobuje for the night. Climb high and sleep low.

There are other factors besides a slow rate of ascent that help in acclimatization. A large fluid intake to ensure good hydration is a key. Four quarts (liters) or more a day of liquid are usually necessary. Urine volume should always exceed one pint (one-half liter) daily, preferably one quart (one liter). The urine color should be almost clear. A strong yellow color indicates that more fluids should be drunk. Some trekkers and Himalayan climbers find that measuring urine output daily with a small plastic bottle helps ensure adequate hydration. A simpler way to measure urine output is to wait until you are absolutely bursting before urinating. The volume is then close to half a liter. Empty a full bladder at least twice a day. One sign of adaptation to altitude is a good natural diuresis (passage of lots of urine). If this is not found, be cautious. An easy way to judge the presence of dehydration is to compare heart rates standing and lying down, with a thirty-second interval between. If the rate is twenty percent greater in the standing position, the individual is significantly dehydrated and should consume more fluids. This can be water, tea, soup, or broth. Alcoholic drinks should be avoided by dehydrated individuals, and at high altitudes by everyone. Besides being detrimental to acclimatization, the effects of alcohol at high altitude may be impossible to distinguish from symptoms of altitude illness.

Proper nutrition is another factor in acclimatization. Caloric intake should be maintained and the diet should be high in carbohydrates. The tasty potatoes found at high altitudes in Nepal are an excellent source of carbohydrates. A good appetite is a sign of acclimatization. Avoid an excessive salt intake at high altitudes; indeed cut back somewhat if you habitually consume a great deal of salt. Don't take salt tablets.

Rest is also important. Over-exertion does not help acclimatization. Give up part of your load to Sherpas and other high altitude dwellers who are already well acclimatized and can carry loads with ease. Avoid going so fast that you are always stopping short of breath with your heart pounding. A rest step and techniques for pacing yourself by checking your heart rate are described in the introduction to Section II. Plan modest objectives for each day so that you will enjoy your stay in the heights.

Many people who frequent the mountains and often make rapid changes in altitude find that forced deep breathing helps reduce the mild symptoms of altitude illness. However, if done to excess, it can produce the hyperventilation syndrome in which shortness of breath, dizziness, and numbness are present. Breathing in and out of a large paper or plastic bag for a few minutes will relieve these symptoms.

Finally there is a drug that may help in coping with high altitude in certain situations. Acetazolamide (Diamox) has been shown to be beneficial in those who fly to high altitudes. The dose is 250 mg by mouth twice a day begun two days before the flight and continued for three days after ascent. It can also help when begun upon arrival at high altitude by plane, and may have some benefit to those who walk to high altitudes. Side effects often noted are an increased urine output, and some numbness and tingling. Trekkers flying into a high altitude area such as Lukla, Shyangboche, Langtang, Dhorpatan, Jomosom, or Manang might consider taking it. But even they should not use it routinely because of the side effects and, perhaps more importantly, because of the false sense of security it may provide. Users may not heed the early warnings of grave problems and continue ascending to their deaths. The drug only prevents certain symptoms and not the serious life-threatening ones. An interesting recent study has shown that dexamethasone prevented the symptoms of acute mountain sickness in subjects exposed to altitude in a hypobaric chamber. There is no experience with this drug in a trekking environment. Furthermore, this drug could potentially cause serious side effects that could have grave consequences in a remote area. Its use is not recommended; it is mentioned here only for the sake of completeness and because some people may have heard of this drug.

Other drugs used for prevention are at best controversial and studies on their effectiveness are conflicting. Furosemide, also called frusemide (Lasix), has been studied by the Indian Army and found to be helpful, but all the other studies attempting to confirm it have in fact found it to be harmful as a prophylactic. Antacids to alkalinize the urine have been proposed as part of a comprehensive program to acclimatize but at present there is no controlled evidence to support their use.

Most people trekking to high altitudes experience one or more **mild symptoms of altitude illness.** The symptoms include:

—Nausea
—Loss of appetite
—Mild shortness of breath with exertion
—Sleep disturbance
—Breathing irregularity, usually during sleep
—Dizziness or light-headedness
—Mild weakness
—Slight swelling of hands and face

As long as the symptoms remain mild, and are only a nuisance, ascent at a modest rate can continue. Symptomatic treatment with medicines may be helpful. If several of the mild symptoms are present and the climber is quite uncomfortable, ascent should be halted and the victim observed closely. If there is no improvement after a few hours, or after a night's rest, descent on foot should continue until the symptoms are relieved. Then ascent at a more gradual rate can be considered.

Serious symptoms of altitude illness are a grave matter. They include:
—Marked shortness of breath with only slight exertion
—Rapid breathing after resting—twenty-five or more breaths per minute
—Wet, bubbly breathing
—Severe coughing spasms that limit activity
—Coughing up pinkish or rust-colored sputum
—Rapid heart rate after resting—110 or more beats per minute
—Blueness of face and lips
—Low urine output—less than a pint (500 ml) daily
—Persistent vomiting
—Severe, persistent headache
—Gross fatigue or extreme lassitude
—Delirium, confusion, and coma
—Loss of coordination, staggering

If anyone in your party develops any of these symptoms, he or she should descend IMMEDIATELY, on the back of a porter or animal to avoid undue exertion. Dr. Peter Hackett states, "There are three rules for treatment: descent, descent, descent!" The victim should be kept warm and given oxygen if it is available. After a descent of several thousand feet, relief may be dramatic. At the point where relief occurs, or lower, rest a few days. Then consider ascending cautiously again.

The clearest symptoms of significant altitude illness to watch for in *yourself* are:
—breathlessness at rest
—resting pulse over 110 per minute
—loss of appetite
—unusual fatigue while walking
The clearest ones to watch for in others are:
—skipping meals
—anti-social behavior
—the last person to arrive at the destination (i.e. people having difficulties with the walking)

It cannot be stressed too strongly that you *must* descend at the onset of serious symptoms. If in Khumbu, go to the hospital at Kunde, or to the Trekker's Aid Post in Pheriche, if that is on your descent route. A pressure chamber to simulate the effects of descent is being tested in Pheriche at times, so this could hold some hope for the future. Don't stop descending in Pheriche unless the victim is considerably better. Trekkers have died in Pheriche from not heeding this guideline. Don't wait for a helicopter to rescue you. Many trekkers, including Olympic athletes, doctors, and experienced climbers, have died in Nepal from altitude illness because they failed to heed symptoms when they occurred. A disproportionate number of physicians, who should know better, have died from altitude illness in Nepal. Don't be another statistic in this totally preventable problem.

———————

The essential material on altitude illness has already been covered, and what follows is for trekkers who are particularly interested, or who are suffering from altitude illness.

Altitude illnesses observed in Nepal include: acute mountain sickness (AMS), high altitude pulmonary edema (HAPE), peripheral edema (PE), cerebral edema (CE), high altitude retinal hemorrhage (HARH), and high altitude flatus expulsion (HAFE).

AMS commonly comes on after being at high altitudes for one to two days. A variety of symptoms are experienced, most often a persistent headache, usually present on awakening. The mild symptoms listed here also occur. Irregular or periodic breathing during sleep, called Cheyne-Stokes respiration, is common. The rate and depth of respiration increase to a peak, then diminish, stopping altogether for fractions of a minute, then increasing again. If none of the serious symptoms are present, there is no cause for concern. Young people seem to be more susceptible to AMS. Physical fitness *per se* is of no benefit. This is true for most altitude illness. The treatment is to deal with each symptom with whatever means you have, and to ascend slowly or rest, depending on the severity of the problem. Acetazolamide, if available, is worth trying in treating the symptoms of AMS, although its effectiveness has not yet been documented. Try a 250-mg tablet before bed and upon arising to see if it helps the headache and malaise. It may also help ensure a good night's sleep. (Do not take sleeping pills at high altitude; they may worsen symptoms and be dangerous.) It is important to make sure that mild weakness does not progress to the serious symptom of gross fatigue or extensive lassitude in which the person becomes unable to care for himself. Don't leave such a person alone, for the mild condition may progress and the victim can become helpless.

Tests for coordination should be taken. An easy one is called tandem walking. See if, after resting, the person can walk a straight line by putting the heel of the advancing foot directly in front of the toe of the back foot. Slight difficulty is tolerable if 12 ft (4 m) can be covered in a straight line. If in doubt, compare the individual with someone who is having no difficulty. In exhaustion, hypothermia, or intoxication, mild degrees of loss of coordination (ataxia) can be seen, but there should be no staggering or falling. Another test is to have the person stand, feet together, arms at the side (or in front), and eyes closed. If the person sways considerably, significant loss of coordination (ataxia) is present. Again, use a non-affected member of the party as a measure. Ataxia is a sign of serious illness, possibly cerebral edema (CE), and the person should descend while he is still able to do so under his own power, but always with someone else. Even if this condition is diagnosed at night, descent should begin immediately.

HAPE, the presence of fluid in the lungs, is a grave illness and is probably present if the respiratory problems on the above serious symptoms list are noted. The heart and breathing rates are useful clues. Do not delay in descending with individuals with these symptoms as death can be only a few hours away. Usually there are also some signs of AMS. Trained people using stethoscopes may hear sounds called rales in the lungs of trekkers with no symptoms. This is common and no cause for alarm. It may be difficult to differentiate HAPE from lung infection. In fact, both may be present. If there is any doubt, especially if the person is getting worse, descend. Individuals with chest disease are more susceptible to HAPE as are people who have previously suffered from it. People under age twenty-five are also more susceptible. Those with upper respiratory infections or common colds are probably not at any increased risk. Oxygen and morphine may be beneficial, but it appears doubtful that other drugs used to treat pulmonary edema at sea level are effective. If descent is impossible, oxygen and morphine could be tried as a last resort. One altitude illness expert, Dr. Herbert Hultgren, has recently published a study suggesting that mild to moderate HAPE at a relatively low altitude (12,300 ft, 3750 m) can be treated by bed rest alone. This was done by trained clinicians in a modern hospital in Peru, however, and cannot be recommended as the therapy of choice in Nepal. Descend!

PE—swelling around the eyes, face, hands, feet, or ankles—is present in some degree in many visitors to high altitudes. Women seem to be affected more than men, but this doesn't appear to be related to the menstrual cycle or to taking birth control pills. The hands are the part of the body most often affected. Rings on the fingers and constricting clothing or pack straps should be removed or loosened. Swelling of the feet and ankles should be treated by rest and elevation of the legs. Facial swelling, especially if severe enough to shut the eyes, requires descent. In general, check for other symptoms, and if any of the serious ones are present, descend. Otherwise, if the swelling is not especially uncomfortable or disabling, cautious ascent can continue. But such swelling can be an early indication of failure of the body to adapt to high altitudes. A diuretic to increase urination can be administered if swelling is a problem, but again, watch for other serious symptoms.

CE or swelling of the brain is a serious disorder that has killed quite a few. It usually occurs after a week or more at high altitudes and begins with mild symptoms that progress to the serious ones. Usually the heart and lung symptoms are not prominent. Characteristic features are severe lassitude, lack of coordination, and total apathy, leading to coma and death. Do not leave such a person alone assuming that he is tired. Check for ataxia (loss of coordination) and descend. Oxygen and steroids may be useful adjuncts in treatment. For those trained in the use of an ophthalmoscope, swelling of the optic nerve in the eye can be an indication of problems. Difficulty with the tandem walking test is probably better as an early sign.

HARH or bleeding in the retinas of the eye is more common at extreme altitudes than at those the trekker is likely to reach. But it does happen to trekkers occasionally and usually is symptomless unless the vision clouds somewhat, or the bleeding is near the macula or center of visual acuity in the eye. Double vision or noticeable blind spots are sufficient cause for descent. Vision clears and bleeding resolves at lower altitudes.

HAFE, the production of increased amounts of intestinal gas, seems endemic up high. This recently described ailment does not seem to be serious but does cause problems to those around the sufferer. There is no effective treatment or known prevention.

All this may seem frightening to the trekker bound for the heights, but the information has to be put in perspective. If you have previous high altitude experience, you have some idea of what to expect (though altitude illness continues to strike groups led by Himalayan "experts"). If you have not been to high altitudes, don't be scared away from enjoying the mountains of Nepal. Be prudent. Ascend at a rate appropriate for the entire party—that is at the rate appropriate for the individual having the greatest difficulty. Know the symptoms of altitude illness and what to do about them. If descent becomes necessary for some members of the party, make sure they are not sent down alone, but are cared for by responsible, informed people. Don't always assume that your hired employees understand altitude illness. There have been incidents in the past when people with obvious serious altitude illness were put into tents to rest unobserved and were discovered dead in the morning. With people better informed today, this shouldn't happen. Above all, use common sense. You are not in Nepal to race up to base camp even if it kills you, but to enjoy the country and its people in all their varied beauty. Finally, give yourself permission to not be the high altitude wanderer, summiter, and pass crosser, should you be one of the many who cannot tolerate high altitudes well. This group includes many renowned climbers and athletes and does not reflect a lack of character or endurance.

FOOT CARE

It is easier to prevent foot problems than to treat them. Well-fitting boots or shoes and proper socks are a must (see Chapter 3). Blisters tend to form on the same spots time and again, so prophylactic application of moleskin or adhesive tape is beneficial. Tincture of benzoin can be applied to the skin to toughen it. The tape or moleskin tends to spread the friction over a larger area and reduce local shear stress between layers of the skin. When you feel a tender or hot spot on the skin while walking, stop and investigate. Put a generous piece of moleskin or adhesive tape over the area. Don't remove it for several days; otherwise you may pull some skin off with it. Rather than wait for hot spots to develop, begin your trek with moleskin applied to potential trouble areas.

It is important to keep the feet dry. Change socks frequently in hot weather, and do not wash or soak your feet too often. By keeping feet dry, you develop callouses over pressure points, and this protects your feet against blisters. Sometimes callouses can get too thick and cause painful problems. Soaking them in warm water will soften them, and they can sometimes be peeled back with a knife.

Once a blister has formed, there are two schools of thought on what to do. Some advocate leaving the blister alone, in fact protecting it by cutting a hole of the same diameter as the blister in a piece of moleskin and applying that around the blister. Several thicknesses of moleskin may be necessary in order to have the moleskin level with the top of the blister. Eventually the blister will go away of its own accord. The alternative is to drain the blister with a needle. Sterilize the needle in a flame until it turns red hot and allow it to cool. The needle should be inserted at the edge of the blister right next to the good skin. Then apply a sterile dressing or some moleskin. I prefer the latter routine. Some trekkers have found the product Spenco Second Skin useful in preventing and treating blisters.

Do not go barefoot in Nepal. The risk of picking up infections is great. Hookworm is spread this way.

STRAINS, SPRAINS AND SAHIB'S KNEE

As muscles flex, they shorten and move joints by means of tendons that attach to bones. Ligaments are fibrous tissue straps that cross joints and hold them together. Sprains are tears or stretching of ligaments while strains are tears in muscles. The tendons may get stretched, torn or inflamed too. For most trekkers, the prolonged, continual walking necessary to reach a distant point causes more wear on their musculoskeletal systems than they are used to. If you gradually increase the amount of activity, your body will toughen up and adjust. Even so, the amount of toil can cause problems, especially in those not well conditioned. People who push themselves to walk long distances every day, especially with heavy packs, will find their poorly prepared body protesting. Strains, especially in the thigh and calf muscles, make climbing and descending painful. Knees will rebel, especially on the downhill portions, if the cartilage (the shock-absorbing pads in the joint) gets too much pounding. "Sahib's knee" is the result. Those with weak cartilage lining the kneecap (chondromalacia patellae), women being more commonly afflicted, will especially have pain climbing and descending. When tired, or not paying attention to the trail, anyone can twist and sprain a joint, most commonly the ankle.

Treatment for strains and sprains is similar. When they occur, control internal bleeding by icing or cooling the affected part, elevate and compress the injured area. Compression can be achieved by means of adhesive tape or an elastic bandage, if available. Severe injuries will require rest for a few days. For strains in the bulky muscles of the thigh, there may be little you can do except to lighten the load and ease up on the amount of ground to be covered. This advice applies to sprains as well. Aspirin for pain will help, as will the application of moist heat several days after the injury has occurred.

Individuals with pre-existing knee or ankle problems should strengthen the muscles that pull across the joint by doing isometric exercises before they trek. Those with a tendency to ankle sprains will want to wear sturdy, over-the-ankle boots and do exercises to strengthen their peroneal muscles. Others prone to knee injuries will be wise to work on their quadriceps muscles, and wear footwear with shock absorbency in the heel.

Everyone should pay attention to reducing the impact on the descent. Absorb the shock by bending the knee when the lower foot contacts the ground. Take short choppy strides. Once the quadriceps muscles get into shape, this method is much less tiring than keeping the knee straight. Turn your feet sideways on steep descents. Watch how Nepali porters descend. Be sure to keep your shoes or boots laced tightly during descents to avoid toe blisters. If you take long strides with your legs fully extended, the cartilage pads in the knee joint and the supporting ligaments will absorb the shock, pre-disposing you to "sahib's knee." If this occurs, apply the treatment principles outlined above.

HYPOTHERMIA

This condition, often termed exposure, occurs when loss of body heat exceeds gain, and body core temperature drops. The body gains heat by digesting food, from an external source, and through muscular activity, including shivering. Loss occurs through respiration, evaporation, conduction, radiation, and convection. The combination of physical exhaustion and wet or insufficient clothing, compounded by failure to eat, dehydration, and high altitude, can result in death in a very short time, even at temperatures above freezing. People venturing into cold, high regions must take adequate steps to prevent hypothermia, and should be able to recognize its signs and symptoms. Be especially alert to its development in lowland porters who may be inadequately clothed for cold.

Obese people are better able to insulate their bodies against the cold than are slim individuals—a rare advantage to being overweight. Small adults and children are especially prone to hypothermia.

Initial symptoms of hypothermia are marked shivering and pale skin, followed by poor coordination, apathy, confusion, and fatigue. As temperature drops further, speech becomes slurred, and the victim has difficulty walking. Even at this stage, an external source of heat is needed to warm the victim. Further lowering of core temperature results in cessation of shivering, irrationality, memory lapses, and hallucinations. This is followed by increased muscular rigidity, stupor, and decreased pulse and respiration. Unconsciousness and death soon follow. Symptoms can appear in a few hours after the onset of bad weather, and the situation can quickly progress to the point where the victim cannot perform the functions necessary for survival. Hypothermia is easily diagnosed with a low-reading thermometer. Mild degrees of hypothermia are present when body temperature is below 94 °F (34.4 °C).

Treatment consists of applying heat rapidly to the person's body core. Remove wet clothing and put the person in a sleeping bag together with a source of heat—a warm naked person. If possible feed the victim warm drinks and sweets. Set up a tent, dig a snow cave, or seek shelter. On one of my treks, a companion developed hypothermia on a high rainy pass. Taking turns, we carried him down to a pasturing shelter where I put him in my sleeping bag with me to warm him up. He recovered the next day.

FROSTBITE

Frostbite is a condition of frozen body tissues. Fingers, toes, ears, noses, and chins are most commonly affected. Fortunately it is rare in trekkers because the temperature extremes necessary are not usually encountered for long periods of time. But it has happened, especially on high passes and trekking summits. Inadequate boots and experience are the most common causes. So-called easy passes can become frostbite traps after unseasonal snowfall. Beware of someone's developing frostbite or hypothermia if your party is moving slowly over easy ground, due to fatigue, or is being delayed by route-finding difficulties or by having to help another member. Prevention is a matter of having adequate clothing and equipment, eating adequate food, and avoiding dehydration and exhaustion. Extreme altitudes increase the potential for the problem, as does a previous history of frostbite. Frostbite can occur at relatively warm temperatures if there is significant wind and if the victims are inadequately equipped and suffer from dehydration and exhaustion. Affected tissues initially become cold, painful, and pale. As the condition progresses, they become numb. The trekker may then forget about the problem, with serious consequences.

An earlier reversible stage is frostnip. At this stage the affected area becomes numb and white. Treatment consists of rapid rewarming by placing the part against a warm area of the body—an armpit, a hand, the stomach of the victim or another trekker. Once normal color, feeling, and consistency are restored, the part can be used, providing it is not allowed to freeze again. A part of the body that has suffered frostnip before is more likely to get frostbite again.

Once an extremity has become frozen and seriously frostbitten, it is best to keep it that way until help and safety can be reached. A frozen foot can be walked on to leave the cold area. Do not rub snow on the frozen area. Once feasible, the treatment is rapid rewarming in a water bath between 100° F (37.7° C) and 108° F (42.2° C). Thereafter the victim requires expert care in a hospital and is not able to walk until treatment is completed. Like most medical problems associated with trekking, prevention is far better than treatment.

HEAT INJURY

Not only does travel in Nepal pose problems in coping with extreme cold, but also in dealing with extreme heat. Both can happen during the same trek if it is from the hot lowlands to the cold, windy, snowy heights. Heat produced by the body is eliminated mostly by the skin through evaporation of perspiration. Acclimatization to heat takes about a week. When the body becomes able to sweat more without losing more salt, the ability to exercise in a hot environment improves. Maladaptation to heat can be prevented by an adequate intake of fluids and salt. Thirst mechanisms and salt hunger may not work adequately, so extra salt and water should be consumed. In humid regions where evaporation is limited, it is a good idea to rest in the shade during the hottest part of the day. Cover the head and wear light colored clothing to reflect sunlight.

Signs and symptoms of heat exhaustion are a rapid heart rate, faintness and perhaps nausea, vomiting, and headaches. Blood supply to the brain and other organs is inadequate because of shunting of blood to the skin. The patient's temperature is normal. If the victim is treated with shaded rest, fluids, and salt, recovery is usually rapid.

Heat stroke is a failure of the sweating and heat regulation process, usually because of fatigue of the sweat glands themselves. The victim rapidly becomes aware of extreme heat, then becomes confused, uncoordinated (ataxic), delirious, or unconscious. Characteristically, the body temperature is very high, 105° F (40.6° C), or higher. The skin feels hot and dry and does not sweat. Treat immediately by undressing the victim and cooling him by any means available. Immersion in cool water, soaking with wet cloths, and fanning are all appropriate. Massage the limbs vigorously to promote circulation. Continue cooling the body until the temperature is below 102° F (38.9° C). Start cooling again if the temperature rises. The victim should be watched closely for the next few days. Strenuous exercise should be avoided.

ANIMAL BITES

Loud, threatening dogs are sometimes met along the trail. They rarely attack, but just to be sure, carry a long stick and pass them assertively. I particularly remember the angry dogs in Jubing. Often you meet large Tibetan mastiffs, but they are usually chained, except possibly at night and near herders' camps.

In case of an animal bite, treat by washing the site immediately with soap and water as well as salt and water. Wash and irrigate the wound for half an hour or more. In animal experiments, washing alone has been shown to be effective in preventing rabies after inoculation of a wound with rabies virus. Irrigation with a quaternary ammonium solution (cetrimide or benzalkonium chloride, also found in the antiseptic Savlon) within twelve hours has also been found effective in animal tests. Those who have had rabies vaccine before coming to Nepal face less risk than others but should get post-exposure inoculation as well, although they do not need rabies immune globulin.

If rabies is suspected, speed of evacuation is essential so that the vaccine can be administered as soon as possible. Once symptoms occur in the person bitten, it is too late to begin treatment. The decision to seek help may be difficult if the animal bite is unprovoked and the animal appears healthy. If other animals in the area have been acting strangely recently, there may be an epidemic. In order to contract rabies, it is necessary that the animal's saliva penetrate the skin, either through the bite itself or through a previous wound.

Try to capture the beast and keep it alive for seven to ten days. If the animal is healthy after that, you do not have to worry about rabies. A dead animal's brain can be examined for rabies by medical personnel, but this is not as reliable as direct observation of a live animal.

Often a dog's bite can be explained considering the circumstances surrounding it. In such cases, it is wise to inquire seven to ten days after the incident to see if the animal has undergone any unusual changes. But in case of an unprovoked, unexplained attack, get yourself and the animal, if possible, to Kathmandu as soon as possible. Two incidents of dog bite occurred during our treks in 1969 and 1970. Once a person entered a courtyard quickly, and without looking, thrust a leg

Even the body heat in your finger will attract a leech. (Stephen Bezruchka)

near a bitch that was nursing her pups. Circumstances explained the bite and observation of the animal several days later alleviated any worries. Another time, I heard squeaking noises coming from a covered basket and went over to investigate. As I crouched down to look, the mother of the litter in the basket sank her teeth into my posterior! Again explainable.

Leeches, abundant in the forests above 4000 ft (1200 m) during the monsoon, are attracted to byproducts of respiration and drop off as you pass under them, or attach as you brush by leaves or rocks, or crawl up from the ground. The best way to deal with leeches is to pick them off as soon as they latch on. When you feel a very localized cool sensation anywhere on your skin, stop immediately and investigate. It may be around your ears or neck, or just above your ankle. In leech-prone forests, stop periodically and search. You may find it amusing to tease the critters with your finger as they scan their suckers while attached to a leaf or rock.

Once attached to your skin, they may often be pulled off. Holding a lighted match or cigarette to them also works well, as does some salt or iodine generously applied. The resulting wound may bleed considerably. Control this with pressure and watch for signs of infection later. I no longer recommend any leech repellents, but feel that dealing with individual offenders makes most sense.

SMALL WOUNDS AND INFECTIONS

It is important to clean with soap and water any wound that breaks the skin. Avoid using the common antiseptics, as they may damage healthy tissue. A large wound should be covered with a sterile dressing that should be changed periodically until a good clot has formed and healing is well underway. It is then best left uncovered. Small wounds, especially if not gaping or occurring over joints, are best left uncovered. There is less risk of infection.

A wound infection is often the result of contamination and is evidenced by signs of inflammation (redness, swelling, tenderness, warmth) and pain a day or more after it occurs. In this case, soak the wound in hot water for at least fifteen minutes. Afterwards, cover it with a sterile dressing. With severe spreading infections, antibiotics should be taken. For abscesses such as boils or carbuncles, the treatment is similar to that for wound infections, except that antibiotics probably do little to help unless the boils are a recurring problem. Drain the abscesses by soaking them in hot water for fifteen minutes five or six times a day. They will usually spontaneously open but you may have to assist the process with a sharp knife.

CONSTIPATION

This is not nearly the problem diarrhea can be. A bulky diet usually prevents difficulties with bowel movements. If constipation does occur, drink plenty of fluids. Try a cup or two of hot water, tea, or coffee upon waking in the morning. In rare cases, mild laxatives may be needed. Better to just wait until the bowels do the job on their own.

BURNS, SUNBURNS, AND SNOWBLINDNESS

Burns are common among Nepali infants who walk or crawl too close to a fire and fall in. The severity of a burn depends on its area, its depth, and its location on the body. First degree burns are superficial—they do not kill any of the tissue, but produce only redness of the skin. Second degree burns kill the upper portion of the skin and cause blisters. In third degree burns damage extends through the skin into the underlying tissues. First degree burns require no treatment, but for the others, wash the area gently with iced or cold water, if possible, and cover with a sterile dressing. Ointments are of no use and may increase the danger of infection. Burns that cover more than twenty percent of the body surface are usually accompanied by shock, which is a serious threat to life. Attempt to get the injured person to drink plenty of fluids mixed with salt. Aspirin or codeine, two tablets every six hours, may help relieve pain. There is little you can do for extensive burns except evacuate the person to medical help.

Sunburn is common among trekkers visiting high altitudes where there is less atmosphere to filter solar radiation, and where snow and ice can reflect additional radiation. Effective sunscreening agents are listed as contents of the medical kit. Be sure to protect the lips and under the chin and nose when on snow. When sunburn occurs, it should be treated in the same way as any other burn.

Eye protection in the form of dark glasses is needed on snow, and generally at high altitudes. In an emergency, lenses made of cardboard with a thin slit to see through can be used. Hair combed over the face, a method favored by Sherpas and Tibetans, is effective. Otherwise, snowblindness, a painful temporary condition, can result. The condition gets better in a few days. Darkness and cold compresses over the eyes may help relieve pain. A poultice of tea leaves can provide some relief too. Patch the eyes tightly so the lids don't move. For severe pain, take aspirin or codeine, two tablets every six hours.

COMMON COLD

Upper respiratory infections including the common cold are very prevalent in Nepal. Medical science does not seem to offer any widely agreed upon remedies. Linus Pauling, a Nobel Prize-winning chemist, has popularized taking large doses of vitamin C to prevent a cold, and to cure it in its early stages. But there is certainly less than universal confidence in this method. There are plenty of other ways to deal with a common cold. Rest if possible, drink plenty of fluids, and take two aspirin tablets every four to six hours. Do not smoke. Gargle with warm water and salt for a sore throat. Decongestants have been used for years by many people. Recently some evidence from experiments has suggested that the antihistamine chlorpheniramine maleate may be helpful in reducing the annoying symptoms of nasal stuffiness associated with a cold. You may want to try taking a tablet (4 mg) four times a day. I would avoid decongestants containing many different drugs. People with high temperatures should not continue trekking. Normal temperature is 98.6°F (37°C), but there is no reason to be concerned if temperatures measured orally remain below 100°F (38.9°C).

COUGHING

Coughing normally brings up sputum and is beneficial in ridding the body of it. Sometimes, however, an annoying cough occurs that even after a few days, does not produce sputum. If this happens, take one or two tablets of codeine (30 mg), every six hours for a day. Do not attempt to suppress those coughs that produce some sputum. Read the section on altitude illness to make sure you are not dealing with a form of it. General measures in treating an annoying cough include drinking plenty of fluids and breathing moist air. The latter is difficult in dry mountain areas. Hard candy or throat lozenges may provide some relief at night.

In addition to altitude illness, serious coughing could be due to a pneumonia. An affected individual would have high fevers, sputum thick with pus and streaked with blood (but not frothy) and often localized chest pain that is most severe at the end of a deep breath. The sick person is usually too ill to travel. Treatment consists of antibiotics, aspirin for high fever and pain, and plenty of fluids.

CONJUNCTIVITIS

This is an inflammation of the delicate membrane that covers the surface of the eye and the undersurface of the eyelid. The eye appears red and the blood vessels on its surface are engorged. The flow of tears is increased and exudate may be crusted in the margins of the eyelids and eyelashes. Irritation from the ubiquitous smoke in Nepali homes is a common cause, especially among the Nepalis. Apply ophthalmic antibiotic ointment or solution beneath the lower eyelid next to the eye every four hours until the symptoms disappear.

GYNECOLOGIC PROBLEMS

Women plagued with vaginal yeast infections when taking antibiotics might bring along appropriate vaginal suppositories. Those prone to urinary infections could consider carrying extra medicine for this problem. Women who decide to take prophylactic antibiotics for diarrhea should not have urinary infections unless harboring resistant organisms.

Trekking is very strenuous and women who have been on the trail for many months may find that their menstrual periods stop. This is not serious; they will resume again with lessened activity. Vaginal bleeding may be profuse after one or two missed periods and will necessitate resting until the bleeding stops. Note that tampons or sanitary napkins are not available in the hills.

WORMS

You probably won't be bothered by a worm infection while in Nepal. But your porters may tell you they have passed worms. It is likely that there are more inside.

A broad-spectrum worm medicine such as mebendazole (mentioned in the medical kit list) may be of some benefit. The porters will, however, get reinfected. Mebendazole is also a good drug to try if your porter complains of abdominal pain. Do not pass it out to villagers, for reasons explained in the previous chapter. And be sure to get your own stool examined when you return home. Trekkers do pick up worm infections. Although the common roundworm will die of old age and you will be rid of him if you avoid reinfection, this is not necessarily true of other intestinal parasites.

APPENDICITIS

Sometimes trekkers, out in the remote hills, worry about appendicitis. The chances of it occurring are very slight, so this information is offered only for your peace of mind. The pain usually starts in the mid-abdomen, soon shifts to the right lower quadrant, and becomes accompanied by nausea. Persistent diarrhea is rare with appendicitis. In a case where appendicitis is suspected, give fluids, an antibiotic, and evacuate the patient. Cases of acute appendicitis may respond to antibiotics and even improve without treatment.

DENTAL PROBLEMS

Dental problems are unlikely among trekkers if they see a dentist before going to Nepal. For simple toothache, a small wad of cotton soaked in oil of cloves and inserted in the appropriate cavity often relieves pain. Codeine and aspirin, two tablets every four to six hours, help relieve severe pain. Abscesses characterized by swelling of the gums and jaw near the site of the toothache, and often accompanied by fever and chills, call for extraction. In the interim, take an antibiotic.

SINUSITIS

Sinusitis is an inflammation of the sinuses, often following a cold. It is characterized by headaches of a dull nature, pain in the sinuses, fever, chills, weakness, and swelling of the facial area. Some or all of these symptoms may be present. For severe symptoms, record the fever and chill temperatures, rest, drink plenty of fluids, and take two aspirin every four hours for the fever and phenylephrine nose drops three times a day. Start an antibiotic if the temperature is less than 97 °F (36.0 °C) during a chill or more than 101 °F (38.3 °C) when feverish. This course should be continued for seven days no matter when the symptoms subside.

PSYCHOLOGICAL AND EMOTIONAL PROBLEMS

But at times I wondered if I had not come a long way only to find that what I really sought was something I left behind.

Tom Hornbein, *Everest, The West Ridge*

Trekkers and travelers to exotic countries can, and sometimes do, have emotional problems adjusting. Reasons are many: being separated from friends and familiar places; adjusting to a very different environment; being seemingly surrounded by poverty, filth, and disease; realizing that you are essentially alone a week or two from "civilization" and 15,000 mi (24,000 km) from "home" by plane; being sick and not eating well; being dirty and unkempt; consuming "recreational" drugs; and realizing that trekking is not all it was cracked up to be. (I can well remember squatting in the bush with diarrhea on the first few days of my first trek in Nepal on my first journey away from North America, and pondering whether this was my reaction to being separated from my familiar environment.)

As with most health matters, prevention is the key to not getting "burned out." Steps for prevention depend on the individual. For some, it may be ensuring that you are with friends with whom you can share the experience. For those who are fastidious in their personal habits, it may mean a daily bath, shaving every day or every other day, keeping hair combed, and putting on a clean change of clothes every few days. For some it may mean acceptance of the reality that the schedule they have set for themselves is too ambitious, or that difficulties in adjusting to altitude will prevent them from getting to that famous viewpoint or crossing that pass. For all, it should include being aware of what is in store during the trek and being prepared for it psychologically as well as physically.

What if you are getting quite depressed or close to a "nervous breakdown"? First, do some familiar, relaxing, comforting routines, such as bathing, shaving, washing your clothes, or putting on clean ones. If alone, find other trekkers to join. If carrying a heavy load, hire a porter. If sick and weak, rest and eat better foods frequently during the day. If consuming marijuana and other mood altering drugs, stop them. If appalled by the conditions in Nepal and among the Nepalis, take comfort in the fact that you can leave if you choose. If your mood does not improve, head back to Kathmandu or Pokhara by plane if possible. But be careful not to end up waiting a week for a plane when you could have walked in three days. If you have trouble adjusting to conditions in Nepal, don't go to India.

Few people end up having to curtail their trek in Nepal for these reasons. Rather, many will undergo a "culture shock" upon returning home as, based on their experience in Nepal, they question the values of the environment they have grown up in. But trekking in Nepal is not for everyone. If it isn't for you, don't despair. There are many other superb activities elsewhere waiting for you.

> *Oh mommy, take me home.*
>
> The mantra of the burned-out trekker

Emergency Care and Rescue Facilities

Nepal's health plan involves setting up hospitals staffed by physicians in each of the seventy-five districts. They are intended to provide secondary health care. Primary health care is provided by health posts scattered throughout each district. These are staffed by paramedical personnel and provide basic facilities. Tertiary care is provided by a few major hospitals throughout the country, with the best in Kathmandu. However, to date, district hospitals are set up in only about forty-five places. None of these can provide health care to a standard that even approximates that available at home.

If faced with an emergency in the hills, you must choose between trying to reach one of the hospitals or clinics listed here and trying to get word to Kathmandu to effect an air rescue. If an air rescue is necessary, head for a STOL landing strip if one is near, or send to Kathmandu for a helicopter. Most STOL airstrips do not have frequent or even regular service, so a fixed-wing aircraft should be sent for. Air rescue by fixed-wing aircraft is usually impossible during the monsoon.

HOSPITALS, AID POSTS, AIRSTRIPS, AND RADIO STATIONS

Helambu, Gosainkund, Langtang

The only facilities available are at the government hospital in Trisuli where there is also a radio and telephone to Kathmandu. A STOL strip is located near Kyangjin in the Langtang Valley. The nearest radio station is on the Bhote Kosi at Rasuwa Garhi on the Tibetan border or in Dhunche. In winter, the STOL strip in Thangmojet across the Bhote Kosi may be the only recourse. There is also a little-used strip at Likhu near Trisuli.

North of Pokhara

There is a regional government hospital, radio service to Kathmandu, and an airport in Pokhara. Radio stations are located in Chame, Kusma, Baglung, Beni, and Jomosom. STOL strips are found in Jomosom, Ongre, and in Balewa south of Baglung across the river from Kusma. There are district hospitals in Baglung, Besisaha, and Jomosom. A Trekkers' Aid Post operated by the Himalayan Rescue Association at Ongre is staffed by a doctor during much of the popular trekking season.

Solu-Khumbu and Rolwaling

There are radio stations at Jiri, Namche Bazaar, Tengboche, Pheriche, Lobuje, Salleri, Charikot (south of Rolwaling), and Lamobagar (north of the Rolwaling River). STOL strips are found at Jiri, Phaphlu, Lukla, and Shyangboche. There are government health facilities in Jiri, Namche Bazaar, Phaphlu and Charikot. A hospital built by Sir Edmund Hillary and staffed by New Zealand physicians is found in Kunde. There is a Trekkers' Aid Post operated by the Himalayan Rescue Association at Pheriche. It is staffed by a doctor during most of the trekking season.

From Namche Bazaar toward Darjeeling

There are radio stations at Chainpur, Khanbari, Taplejung, Phidim, Bhojpur, Terhathum, Dhankuta, Dharan, Ilam, and Chandragari, and STOL strips at Tumlingtar, Lamidanda, Bhojpur, Chandragari, and Taplejung. There are government hospitals in Chainpur, Taplejung, Bhojpur, and Dhankuta. The British Military Hospital is at Dharan.

Pokhara to Kathmandu

In addition to the facilities in Pokhara and Trisuli already mentioned, there are radio stations in Gorkha and Kuncha; a STOL strip at Palungtar near Tadi Pokhari; and a government hospital at Gorkha. The United Mission runs a hospital at Ampipal.

Western Nepal

In addition to the facilities in Baglung and Beni already mentioned, there are radio stations in Jumla and Tansen. STOL strips are found at Dhorpatan, Jumla, and RaRa Lake. There is a government hospital in Jumla.

The radio stations listed here are civilian operated, part of the telecommunication system. The messages are delivered through the Telecommunication Central Office in Kathmandu. In addition, there are other wireless systems in operation, but their use is normally restricted. In an emergency, it may be possible to use them. Ask at police check posts or army installations.

EMERGENCY MESSAGES AND RESCUES

In writing a message and organizing a rescue, it is important to provide the proper information and make sure it reaches the proper place. It is wise to send several messages to different organizations to ensure that at least one is delivered. Addresses should be as specific as possible to speed delivery. Rescue messages should be sent to one or more of these:

—The trekking agency that organized the trek, if applicable.

—Royal Nepal Airlines Corporation, Charter Division, RNAC Building, New Road, Kathmandu (Phone: 214511, extension 147 or 137).

—The embassy or consulate of the victim.

—Himalayan Rescue Association, G.P.O. Box 435, Ghantaghar, Kathmandu (Phone: 216514).

The message should contain the following information:

—Degree of urgency. **Most Immediate** means death is likely within twenty-four hours. **As Soon As Possible** is used for all other cases in which helicopter rescue is justified.

—The location, including whether the victim will remain in one place or be moved down along a particular route. If the pickup place is above 10,000 ft (3000 m), give the altitude. Generally, 17,000 ft (5000 m) is the limit for helicopter pickups.

—Medical information, including the type of sickness or injury, and whether oxygen or a stretcher (as for back injuries) is needed.

—The name, nationality, age, and sex of all people to be evacuated.

—The sender's name and organization, along with information on the method and source of payment for the rescue. Generally, RNAC will not fly rescues without written assurance of payment. This can sometimes be provided by the embassy of the victim.

A rescue can take several days, especially if a runner has to be sent with the message, or if there is airplane trouble. It is wise to move the person along the route, waiting each day until 10 A.M. to start. In each sleeping place, a large smoky fire should be built each morning, and a landing site cleared and marked with a large X, preferably using international orange garments.

The cost of a helicopter rescue is high—an hour of helicopter time costs over $500. This has to be borne by the party involved, unless rescue insurance has been taken out previously. Some trekkers might wish to obtain a comprehensive travel, accident, and rescue insurance policy before they leave home. Some of the general insurance companies in Kathmandu may be able to provide this, but I have had no personal experience with them. If you have not dealt with a trekking agency, it may be prudent to make yourself known at your country's embassy in Kathmandu, in case they receive a rescue telegram. Westerners working in remote areas in Nepal have posted bonds in Kathmandu to pay for a rescue should it be needed. It all depends on your inclination and life-style.

In the tragic event that a porter or trekker dies, be aware that RNAC will not transport corpses on their planes. You might be able to charter a helicopter or porter the body out, though you may find it very difficult to hire porters to do this. It is best to cremate the body. If possible this should be witnessed, preferably by a local policeman, village headman, or person not associated with your trek. Record the person's name and address and keep the ashes for relatives.

6 NEPALI FOR TREKKERS

> *Refusal to accept anybody else's language as worth knowing*
> *reflects the same narrow-gauge kind of head, the same stubborn*
> *ignorance as that of the fundamentalist I heard about who de-*
> *nounced people speaking in other tongues, saying "If English*
> *was good enough for Jesus Christ, it's good enough for them."*
> *The story is apocryphal in both senses.*
>
> Flora Lewis

Nepali is an Indo-European language that is really not very difficult to learn. Here an attempt is made to introduce the trekker to enough Nepali words and phrases to get by in the hills. It is especially advisable for those trekking without an English-speaking guide to make some effort to learn minimal Nepali. Nevertheless, people have trekked without guides and without any knowledge of the language.

Indeed, along the popular routes, many of the people the trekker encounters will speak a few words of English. Nevertheless, your experience with Nepal will be much more intimate if you attempt to speak the language. Trekkers who have used this chapter in previous editions have found it very helpful in increasing their understanding and enjoyment of the country. Now that more Nepalis are speaking English, it is even more important to try to speak some Nepali so as to be given a warmer welcome by the people you meet.

Some trekkers find it useful to tear these pages out and keep them close at hand. I have also produced a language tape incorporating all this material as well as place names. Trekkers who want to further increase their knowledge of Nepali will find the tape very useful. I have been very impressed with the language spoken by those using the tape recommended in the previous edition. The trekkers also felt it made a considerable difference in how they were received by their Nepali hosts. While preparing for your trek, use the tape to get a feeling for the sounds of the language and to learn some basic words and phrases. If you take a small tape recorder with you, bring the tape and use it as a reference when needed. Information on ordering the tape is available at the end of this chapter.

The problem of learning the language is complicated by the lack of suitable books for the trekker. The best aids available at present are the Summer Institute of Linguistics' *Conversational Nepali* course, the book *Basic Course in Spoken Nepali*, and the *Basic Gurkhali Dictionary* (see Recommended Reading). Without some principles of grammar, the dictionary is of little use. Brief phrase books, which occasionally become available in bookstores in Kathmandu, are of some value.

Pronunciation

Nepali is written in Devanagari script, but a system of transliteration to the Roman script is used here. Many of the letters denote their usual sounds. Only the special sounds are described.

STRESS

The stress usually falls on the first syllable (**chaá mal**) unless the first syllable has a short vowel and is followed in the second syllable by a long one. Then the stress falls on the second syllable (**pa kaaú nos**). The single most common pronunciation error made by the casual student is *not* putting the emphasis on the first syllable.

VOWELS

a   like the *a* in *balloon*. Never like the *a* in *hat*.

aa   long like the *a* in *father* or *car*.

i   like *ee* in *beer*, the short and long forms are pronounced similarly.

u   like *oo* in *mood* or *root*, again with long and short forms similar. Never like the *u* in *mute*.

e   like *a* in *skate* or like the French *e* as in *café*.

ai   a diphthong with first element like the *a* in *arise* and the second like the *y* in *city*. Together, somewhat like the *ay* in *laying*, but not like the sound of the word *eye*.

au   a diphthong in which the first element is like the *a* in *arise* and the second like the *u* in *put*.

o   like *o* in *bowl* or *go*.

aau, aai, and eu   not diphthongs, but vowels pronounced separately one after the other.

CAPITALIZED VOWELS

Capitalized vowels (**A,E,I,O,U**) indicate nasalization of that sound.

DENTAL AND RETROFLEX CONSONANTS

t   pronounced unaspirated with the tip of the tongue on the teeth as in the French *petite*.

T   like the *t* in *little*, with the tongue slightly recurved when it meets the roof of the mouth.

d   dental like the French *d* in which the blade of the tongue is pressed behind the upper teeth.

D   pronounced with retroflexion of the tongue. Turn the tongue back in the mouth, press the underside of it against the palate and pronounce the *d* in *dog*.

R   also pronounced with retroflexion of the tongue.

ASPIRATED CONSONANTS

Nepalis differentiate between aspirated and unaspirated consonants. This is quite difficult for native English speakers. Aspiration is indicated by an *h* following the consonant. Consciously avoid breathing hard or aspirating on the consonants that are not followed by an *h*.

The exception to the above rule in the transliteration scheme employed in this book applies to *ch* and *chh*. Only the latter is aspirated.

chh   press the blade of the tongue behind the upper teeth and try to say *ts*. At the same time exert strong breath pressure so that when the tongue is released from the teeth, there is a loud emission of breath. Listen to a native Nepali speaker. It is like the *tch-h* in pi*tch h*ere.

ch   the unaspirated form as in *chalk, Chinese*.

MISCELLANEOUS

k	like *c* in *cat*.
y	like *y* in *yeast*.
s	like *s* in *song*.
j	press the blade of the tongue against the upper teeth with the tip of the tongue pointed down and say *j* as in *January*. It is somewhat like *dz* and is especially found in words coming from Tibetan dialects.
ph	like *f* in *full*.
p	less aspiration than ph.

Other consonants should present little difficulty. When two consonants come together, be sure to pronounce them individually.

Grammar Notes

Listening to and practicing the sounds of Nepali are basic to communication in the country. Next, you need some vocabulary and the ability to speak in phrases. To help you, lists of useful words and phrases are given later in the chapter. In this regard, too, the language tape offers invaluable assistance. In addition, you can adapt the sample phrases to your particular needs by following the indicated sentence structure and plugging in other words from the vocabulary lists. At some point, however, you may want information on grammar to increase your fluency. You will find such information in this section. You don't have to get bogged down in this material until the need arises because you can do quite well by just learning the sounds and phrases.

SENTENCE STRUCTURE

Subject-object-verb is the usual order in Nepali. This holds true for questions as well, but a rising vocal pitch at the end of the sentence indicates the interrogative mode.

Plurals and gender can be neglected by the trekker, as they often are by Nepalis. Verbs are declined and, for the trekker, a few tenses and forms will suffice. Nouns and pronouns used as subjects of transitive verbs in the past tense have the suffix **-le**.

PRONOUNS

I	**ma**
we	**haami**
he, she, it (familiar)	**u**
he, she (polite)	**wahAA**
they (familiar)	**uniharu**
they (polite)	**wahAAharu**
you (familiar)	**timi**
you (polite)	**tapAAI**

Trekkers should always use the polite forms of address, except with children and animals. I'll never forget the time I addressed a dog using the polite honorific. The laughter traveled throughout the entire village.

VERBS

Verbs are listed in the infinitive form, ending in **-nu**. A neutral form used with any pronoun, or noun subject, whose tense is near the present, is formed by changing the **u** to **e**, e.g.

jaanu to **jaane** meaning, go
ma kaaThmaanDu-maa jaane   meaning, I am going to Kathmandu;
I   Kathmandu   to   go

or,
tapAAI kahAA jaane?   meaning, where are you going?
you   where go

This last example is formally incorrect but tolerable from a foreigner.

Polite imperatives are formed by deleting the **-e** from the infinitive and adding **-os**, e.g.

dinu, to give in; **chiyaa dinos**   meaning, please give tea.
                tea   please give

Negatives can be formed by prefixing **na-** to the verb, in this imperative form, e.g.

naaaumos   meaning, don't come.

The present tense is made by deleting the **-nu** from the infinitive and adding one of the following suffixes (the example used is the verb **garnu**, meaning, to do):

		AFFIRMATIVE	NEGATIVE
I	**ma**	**garchhu**	**gardinA**
we	**haami**	**garchhAU**	**gardainAU**
he, she (familiar)	**u**	**garchha**	**gardaina**
he, she (polite)	**uhAA**	**garnu hunchha**	**garnu hunna**
they (familiar)	**uniharu**	**garchhan**	**gardainan**
they (polite)	**wahAAharu**	**garnu hunchha**	**garnu hunna**
you (familiar)	**timi**	**garchhau**	**gardainau**
you (polite)	**tapAAI**	**garnu hunchha**	**garnu hunna**

There are actually slight differences depending on categorizations of the verb stem, but we shall neglect this detail.

The first perfect participle (e.g. having gone), formed by deleting **-nu** from the infinitive and adding **-eko,** can be a general purpose past and present progressive tense. The formation is slightly different for verbs whose infinitives end in **-aaunu**, **-anu**, or **unu**. The respective forms usually replace with **-aaeko**, **-eko**, and **-eko**. The form of the verb to go, **jaanu**, is **gaeko**, and that of the verb to be, **hunu**, is **bhaeko**. The negatives are formed by prefixing **na-**, except for **bhaeko**, which is **bhaena**. For polite expressions, use the infinitive and **bhaeko**, or **bhaena**, e.g.

tapAAI kahAAbaaTa aaunu   bhaeko meaning, where have you come from?
you   where from   to come   have

The verb to be, is special and has two forms. One form has no infinitive; its third person singular is **chha**, meaning there is or it is, or in the past tense, **thiyo**. It indicates possession, or location. Negatives are **chaaina** and **thiena**, respectively, e.g.

kitaab   tyahAA   chha   meaning, there is the book.
book   there   is

The other verb to be, **hunu**, has the present form **ho**, and the past, **bhayo**, with negatives **hoina** and **bhaena**, respectively. It defines, e.g.

mero	**desh**	**kaanada**	**ho**	meaning, I come from Canada.
my	country	Canada	is	

Confusion may arise as to which to use, and the full declension is not given. Most Nepalis will understand what you are trying to say.

Future tenses vary depending on the likelihood of the action happening. For the spoken language, the form usually used adds suffixes; using the verb **garnu**, meaning to do, as an example:

I	**ma**	**garUlaa**	meaning, I (probably) will do.
we	**haami**	**garAUlaa**	
he, she (familiar)	**u**	**garlaa**	
they (familiar)	**uniharu**	**garlaan**	
you (familiar)	**timi**	**garaulaa**	

The easiest way to form the negative is to prefix **na-** to the appropriate form of the verb. For the polite forms, use the imperatives mentioned earlier. The form mentioned earlier ending in **-ne** is suitable for the future tense as well, e.g.

kahile	**jane**
when	will you go?

MISCELLANEOUS VERBS

The verb **hunchha**, used following an infinitive at the end of an interrogative sentence (indicated by rising voice inflexion) can mean Is it okay to _____?

ghar	**bhitra**	**aaunu**	**hunchha?**	meaning, can I (implied) go inside the house?
house	inside	to go	is it okay?	

To express can or may, in a sense of physical possibility, you use the infinitive end in **-na**, rather than **-nu**, and follow it by a form of the verb **saknu** (to be able to do), e.g.

baaTo	**maa**	**chhirna**	**sakchha?**	meaning, Is it possible to get
trail	on	to get through	it is possible?	through on the trail?

Similarly, to express "must," use the infinitive ending in **-nu**, and the verb **parchha**, e.g.

bholi	**aaram**	**garnu**	**parchha**	meaning, I (implied) must rest tomorrow.
tomorrow	rest	to do	must	

The phrases **man parchha** and **man laagchha** both mean like. All of the verbs in this section are used with subjects that have the suffix **-laai**, e.g.

malaai	**Nepal**	**man parchha**	meaning, I like Nepal.
me (to)	Nepal	like	

PREPOSITIONS

In Nepali, prepositions are post positions; that is, they are suffixed to the noun.

in, on, to, at (locating)	**-maa**	
to, for	**-laai**	(this is also added to the subject of impersonal verbs)

e.g. **ma-laai paani caahinchha** meaning, I need water.
    for me   water   needs

for the sake of	**-laagi**	from	**-baaTa**
inside, in	**-bhitra**	around (approximately)	**-tira**
outside	**-bahira**	before	**-agaaDi**
with	**-sita, -sAga**	under, below	**-tala**
of (indicating possession)	**-ko**	after	**-pachhi**

With some pronouns, the word is changed somewhat.

mine	**mero**	whose	**kasko**
yours	**timro**	for me	**malaai**
for this	**yasko**	yours (polite)	**tapAAIko**
his, hers (familiar)	**usko**	theirs (polite)	**wahAAko**

With this skeleton of grammar, you should be better able to understand the phrases in this chapter and modify them to suit your needs.

Practice Before You Go

> *To acquire a language is to learn the spoken utterance. The natural receptive medium is, therefore, the ear, not the eye. It is an art very much akin to music.*
>
> G. G. Rogers, *Colloquial Nepali*

The following may seem formidable if you are just going on a short trek. Do not be daunted. It is here in case you need it. You will find, however, that a minimal knowledge of the language is indispensable on the trail where most people normally cannot speak or understand much English.

If you have a few days in Kathmandu before you set off, you can practice a little in a familiar and exceedingly helpful environment.

First ask your hotel receptionist or some friendly waiter in a restaurant you frequent to read the word list to you. Repeat it after him until you get a feel for the pronunciation. This should take about 15 minutes and will probably make you instant friends with your Nepali helper. Then try it out. For example, practice your Nepali in a restaurant.

Say:
　　chiyaa　dinos
　　tea　　　please give me

or:
　　bill　dinos
　　bill　　please give me

or:
　　menu　dinos
　　menu　　please give me

Later when it is time to pay, say:
　　khaanaa　-ko　kati?
　　food　　　for　how much

raising your voice pitch at the end of the sentence to indicate a question. Have the person answer in Nepali rather than English. People are usually more than happy to repeat the Nepali number for you and translate it into English. If you feel clumsy or shy about any of this, always smile. It works like magic to ease every situation. Smiling is the Nepali way of getting over tense or slightly embarrassing situations.

When you go to a bazaar and wish to buy an item, point to it and say:

yasko   kati?
for this   how much?

The person may answer in Nepali or English, but try to come away from the transaction able to understand the Nepali number.

If you do this each time, you should soon be able to understand spoken Nepali numbers, or at least the main ones. This is a tremendous asset on the trail where people often do not know the English numbers.

If you do not understand, or want something repeated, say:

hajur
excuse me

By the time you reach this stage, you will already be experiencing the hospitality that even the tiniest knowledge of Nepali inspires.

Now try asking for directions:

paaTan   jaane   baaTo   ho?
Patan   going to   road   is it?

meaning: Is this the road to Patan? On the trail where there are no road signs, this direction-finding question is essential.

Now add some vocabulary to the skeleton. If you do not want much food, say:

ali ali   dinos
very little   please give

Ask for **dhai** instead of yogurt, **paani** instead of water. Ask for the time, bargain, use the terms of address.

By asking questions in Kathmandu, you can get used to hearing some of the many types of responses. Basic communication in Nepali will lose some of its terrors, and you will be far more competent in dealing with situations in the non-English-speaking world on the trail.

It's easy. Now go straight to your hotel receptionist and begin reading the word list with him.

There are opportunities for language instruction in Kathmandu. Among organizations that may help you locate instructors or language classes are:

Nepal Studies Center in Naxal, Phone 212551
Nepal Language Services in Gyaneshwar, Phone 213166
Experiment in International Living in Gyaneshwar, Phone 21568
Namaste Association in Gyaneshwar, Phone 212876
LCRE in Adwait Marga, Phone 215459
United Mission in Nepal in Thapathali, Phone 212668
University of Wisconsin Program, Phone 213109
Community Services Program in Phora Durbar

While trekking in the hills, trade Nepali lessons for English lessons among people you meet when you stop to eat or sleep.

Word Lists

FOOD

apple	**syaau**	millet	**kodo**
banana	**keraa**	noodles	**chaauchaau**
beans	**simi**	oil	**tel**
beer	**biyar**	okra	**raam toriyaa**
	jAAR (Nepali)	onions	**pyaaj**
	chang (Tibetan)	oranges	
biscuits	**biskooT**	(tangerines)	**suntalaa**
bread (loaf of		peanuts	**badaam**
leavened		popcorn	**murali makai**
variety)	**pau roti**	potatoes	**aalu**
(unleavened)	**roti, chapaati**	pumpkin	**pharsi**
cabbage	**bandaa kopi**	radish	**mulaa**
carrots	**gaajar**	relish (chutney)	**achaar**
cauliflower	**kaauli**	rice (paddy)	**dhaan**
chicken	**kukhura**	uncooked but	
chilies	**khursaani**	harvested	**chaamal**
coffee	**kaphi**	cooked	**bhaat**
corn	**makai**	rice and	
cucumber	**kAAkro**	lentils	**daal bhaat**
eggs	**phul**	roasted flour	**saatu** (Nepali)
boiled eggs	**umaaleko phul**		**tsampa**
fish	**maachhaa**		(Tibetan)
flour	**piTho, aaTa**	salt	**nun**
white flour	**maidaa**	snacks	**khaajaa**
whole wheat		soybeans	**bhaTmaas**
flour	**gahUko piTho**	spices	**masalaa**
food (usually		spirits (distilled)	**rakshi**
referring		sugar	**chini**
to rice)	**khaanaa**	sweets	**miThaai**
fruit	**phalphul**	tea	**chiyaa**
garlic	**lasun**	tomatoes	**golbhEDa**
ginger	**aduwaa**	vegetables	**tarkaari, sabji**
greens (spinach)	**saag**	water	**paani**
guava	**ambaa**	drinking	
lemons	**nibuwaa**	water	**khaane paani**
lentils	**daal**	boiled water	**umaaleko paani**
limes	**kaagati**	hot water	**taato paani**
mangoes	**AAp**	washing	
meat	**maasu**	water	**dhune paani**
buffalo	**rAAngoko**	whey	**mAI**
	maasu	yogurt	**dhai**
chicken	**kukhurako**		
	maasu	**OTHER USEFUL NOUNS**	
goat	**khasiko maasu**	airport	**giraund**
dried goat	**shikaar**	baby	**naani, bachcho**
pig	**sUgurko maasu**	basket (for porter)	**Doko**
milk	**dudh**	book	**kitaab**

bottle	sisi	load	bhaari
boy	keTo	louse (plural, lice)	jumro
bridge (good		luggage (stuff)	saamaan
structure)	pul	man	maanchhe
(makeshift)	sAAghu	matches	salaai
buffalo male	rAAgo	medicine	aushadi
female	bhAIsi	mosquito	laamkhuTTe
candle	main-batti	name	naam
cat	biraalo	pass	bhanjyang
cave	wodaar	place	ThAAU
children	keTaa-keTi	plate	thaal
clothes	lugaa	porter	kulli, baariya
cow	gaai	pot	dekchi
cup	gilas, kap	religion	dharma
curved (referring		rhinoceros	gAIDa
to trail)	ghumaaune	river	khola, kosi,
daughter	chhori		nadi
day	din	road	baaTo
distance unit		room	koThaa
(2 miles)	kosh	shelter	
dog	kukur	(temporary)	goTh
downhill	oraalo	shop, store	pasal
elephant	haatti	shopkeeper	saahuji
elephant driver	phanit	sick	biraami
fire	aago	snow	hiU
firewood	daauraa	snow peak	himal
floor	bhUI	soap	saabun
flower	phul	son	chhoro
foot	khuTTo	spoon	chamchaa
foreigner	bedeshi	stone rest spot	chautaara
fork (table)	kAATaa	straight (of trail)	sidhaa
fork (of road)	dobaaTo	sun	ghaam
forest	ban	things	chij-bij
friend	saathi	toilet	chharpi
my friend	mero saathi	town	gAAU
girl	keTi	trail	baaTo
government	shri pAAch	tree	rukh
(of Nepal)	ko sarkaar	tumpline	naamlo
help	madat	uphill	ukaalo
hill	lekh, pahaaD,	village	gAAU
	DADDa	volume unit	
horse	ghoDaa	(2½ cups,	
house	ghar	600 ml)	maanaa
husband	pati	wife	patni
inn, lodging	bhaTTi	woman	aaimaai
kerosene	maTTitel		
knife (small)	chakku	**VERBS**	
(large)	khukuri		
lake	pokhri, taal	to ask for	mAAgnu
leech	juga	to ask (a question)	sodhnu
light (lamp)	batti	to boil	umaalnu
		to buy	kinnu

to carry	**boknu**	delicious	**miTho**
to cook	**pakaaunu**	different	**arko**
to defecate	**haaknu**	difficult	**mushkil**
to do	**garnu**	dirty	**phohor**
to eat, drink	**khaanu**	easy	**sajilo**
to forget	**birsanu**	far	**TaaDhaa**
to fry	**bhuTnu**	good	**raamro**
to get	**paaunu**	not good	**raamro chhaina,**
to give	**dinu**		**naraamro**
to go	**jaanu**	happy	**khushi**
to learn	**siknu**	heavy	**gahrungo**
to look for	**khojnu**	here	**yahAA**
to meet	**bheTnu**	hot (temperature)	**taato**
to need	**chaahinu**	(weather)	**gharmi**
I need	**chaahinchha,**	(spicy)	**piro**
	chaaiyo	(climate)	**nyaano**
to open	**kholnu**	inside	**bhitra**
to remember	**samjhanu**	little	**ali ali**
to repeat		long (dimension)	**laamo**
(do again)	**pheri garnu**	lot (quantity)	**dherai, thupro**
to rest (a burden)	**bisaaunu**	many, much	**dherai**
(your body)	**aaraam garnu**	near	**najik**
to sell	**bechnu**	new	**naya**
to sing a song	**git gaaunu**	only	**maatrai**
to sit, stay, stop	**basnu**	outside	**baahira**
to succeed	**saknu**	quickly	**chhito**
it is possible		slowly	**bistaarai**
(can be done)	**sakchha**	sour	**amilo**
impossible		sweet	**guliyo**
(cannot be		tasty	**miTho**
done)	**sakdaaina**	that	**tyo**
to teach	**sikaaunu**	there	**tyahAA**
to understand	**bujhnu**	this	**yo**
to wash (face,		for this	**yasko**
clothes)	**dhunu**	where	**kahAA**
to wash (body)	**nuhaaunu**	which	**kun**
to work	**kaam garnu**		

ADJECTIVES AND ADVERBS

CONJUNCTIONS

		also	**pani**
after	**pacchi**	and	**ani, ra**
again	**pheri**	or	**ki**
all	**sab**	because	**kina bhane**
always	**sadhAI**		
beautiful	**sundar, raamro**	## TIME	
clean	**saphaa**		
cold (damp, or of		now	**ahile**
liquids &		today	**aaja**
foods)	**chiso**	tomorrow	**bholi**
(weather)	**jaaDo**	day after	
(extreme		tomorrow	**parshi**
temperature)	**ThADaa**	yesterday	**hijo**
		minute	**minuT**

hour	ghanTaa	9	nau
day	din	10	das
week	haptaa	11	eghaara
morning	bihaana	12	baahra
early morning	saberai	13	tehra
afternoon		14	chaudha
(12 A.M. to 4 P.M.)	diuso	15	pandhra
evening		16	sohra
(4 P.M. to 8 P.M.)	beluki	17	satra
night	raati	18	aThaara
What time is it?	kati bajyo	19	unnaais
		20	bis
		21	ekkaais

MONEY

		22	baais
small change	paisaa	23	teis
how much	kati	24	chaubis
		25	paachis

paisaa is the smallest unit
sukaa = 25 paisaa
mohar = 50 paisaa
rupiyAA = 100 paisaa

	26	chhabis
	27	sattaais
	28	aTThaais
	29	unantis

DAYS OF THE WEEK

		30	tis
Sunday	aitabaar	40	chaalis
Monday	sombaar	50	pachaas
Tuesday	mAgalbaar	60	saaThi
Wednesday	budhabaar	70	sattari
Thursday	bihibaar	75	pachhattar
Friday	sukrabaar	80	ashi
Saturday	sanibaar	90	nabbe
		100	say or ek say

NUMBERS

		101	ek say ek
1	ek	200	dui say
2	dui	1000	ek hajaar
3	tin	100,000	ek laakh
4	chaar	10,000,000	ek kaRor
5	pAAch	½	aadha
6	chha	1½	DeDh
7	saat	2½	aDhaai
8	aaTh		

ANSWERS

Nepalis either repeat the verb you have used in your sentence to indicate agreement with you (more frequent), or they use one of the following terms:

it is (definition)	ho	okay (very polite)	haas
there is (location)	chha	okay	hajur
please sit down, stay	basnos	yes	ju
okay (polite)	hunchha	yes	A

To express a negative they might repeat the verb in its negative form:

cannot get	**paaindaaina**
cannot stay	**basnu sakdaaina**
not permitted	**hundaaina**

or they might use the negative form of the verb "to be":

it is not (definition)	**hoina**
there is not (location)	**chaaina**
no	**ahA**

Shaking of the head in a fluid motion can mean yes. You may initially think it means no.

THANK YOU

Westerners are always eager to thank people as part of common courtesy. While Nepali does have a word connoting gratitude (**dhanyabaad**), native speakers do not use it in the sense that we would. You may hear this word used by some trekkers along the popular trails, and the locals are becoming accustomed to hearing it, but it is still outside of their custom. It is best for trekkers to get used to the Nepali social custom of not thanking, except by using the English words where they are understood. Buddhist highlanders in Nepal (*BhoTiya*) do have a word (**thuDichhe** or **thuchhe**) that is used more like our "thank you."

Phrases

TALKING TO PORTERS

Here are some useful words and sentences to aid in making arrangements with porters and in giving them instructions on the trail. To avoid misunderstanding later, arrange these details before setting off: the destination; approximately how many days the porters will be needed; the rate per day and whether it includes food; pay for porters returning without a load; and whether the porters have the necessary equipment, especially if you will be traveling through snow or during the monsoon.

I am going to Namche Bazaar.
> **namche bazaar jaane.**
> Namche Bazaar go

I will need porters for one week.
> **ek haptaa-ko kulli chaahinchha.**
> one week for porters need

I will need five porters for two days.
> **dui din samma pAAch kulli**
> two days up to five porters
> **chaahinchaa.**
> need.

How much per day?
> **din-ko kati?**
> day for how much?

with food?
> **khaanaa khaaiera?**
> food eating

without food?
> **khaanaa nakhaaiera?**
> food not eating

Fifteen rupees without food is enough.	**pandhra rupiyAA khaanaa** fifteen rupees food **nakhaaiera pugchha.** not eating is enough
For returning, ten rupees per day is enough.	**pharkaaunda din -ko das** returning day for ten **rupiyAA pugchha.** rupees enough
Without load.	**bhaari chhaaina.** load there is not
With load.	**bhaari chha.** load there is
After one week.	**ek haptaa pachhi.** one week after
Do you have warm clothes?	**nyaano lugaa chha?** warm clothes do you have
Do you have a carrying basket?	**Doko chha?** carrying basket do you have
Please show me your warm clothes tomorrow.	**nyaano lugaa bholi** warm clothes tomorrow **dekhaaunos.** please show
Go quickly.	**chhito jaane.** quickly go
Go slowly.	**bistaarai jaane.** slowly go
Walk near me.	**ma-sAga jaane.** me with go
We will stop (stay or rest) now.	**ahile basne.** now stay
We will stay here.	**yahAA basne.** here stay
We will stop after one hour.	**ek ghanTaa pachhi basne.** one hour after stop
Please ask where to stay.	**kahAA basne sodhnos.** where stay please ask
Please ask about food.	**khaanaa-ko laagi sodhnos.** food about please ask
We need firewood.	**daauraa chaahinchha.** firewood need
Please cook food.	**khaanaa pakaaunos.** food please cook
tea.	**chiyaa.**
bread.	**roti.**

Are you hungry?	**bhok laagchha?** hunger strikes
Do you want to rest?	**bisaaune ki?** rest or
This equipment is a loan.	**yo saamaan mero rin ho** this kit my loan is
Please give it back after using it.	**kaam sake -pachhi phirtaa** work finished after return **dinos.** please give
Can you take me to Namche?	**malaai namche -maa laanu** me Namche to take **hunchha?** can you
We'll meet you at NagDAADa in two hours.	**haami nagDAADa -maa dui** we NagDAADa at two **ghanTaa -maa bheTchhAU.** hours in meet
Don't be late, please.	**Dhilo nagarnos.** late not please make
We may have to travel in snow.	**hIU -maa jaanuparchha holaa.** snow in to go must probably
There are three people in our party.	**haamro parti -maa tin maanis** our party in three men **chhan.** are
I am travelling alone.	**ma eklai jaanchu.** I alone go
We should stop around four o'clock.	**haami chaar baje tira baas** we four bells around stay **baschhAU.** sit
It will take two hours.	**dui ghanTaa laagchha.** two hours it strikes

ASK AND YOU WILL NOT GET LOST

Is this the road to Namche Bazaar?	**yo namche bazaar jaane baaTo** this Namche Bazaar going road **ho?** is this
How many hours to Namche?	**namche -samma kati ghanTaa** Namche up to how many hours **laagchha?** does it take?

It will take one hour.

ek   ghanTaa   laagchha.
one   hour   it will take

Is there an inn in Namche?

namche -maa   bhaTTi   chha?
Namche in   inn   is there

Can we get food in Namche?

namche -maa   khaanaa   paaincha?
Namche in   food   get

Is the trail good enough to take
or not?

baaTo -maa   chhirnu   sakchha
road on   get through   possible
ki   sakdaaina?
or   impossible

Impossible. Cannot be done.

sakdaaina.
It cannot be done

Where are you going?

kahAA   jaane?
where   go

Can I come with you?

sangaai   jaane?
with   you go

What is the name of this town?

yo   gAAU -ko   naam   ke   ho?
this town   of   name   what   is

What is the name of the next town
on the trail?

yo   baaTo -maa   kun   gAAU
this road   on   which   town
parchha?
must it be

Where is there a weekly market?

haaT bajaar   kahAA   chha?
market   where   is there

What is your caste? (ethnic group)

tapAAIko   jaat   ke   ho?
your   caste   what   is

(Strictly speaking, it is not polite to ask this, but may be tolerable from a foreigner
who has established friendly relations with a person. The answer "Nepali" usually
indicates a low Hindu caste.)

The trail going left or the trail
going right?

baaTo   baayAA   jaanchha   ki
road   left   goes   or
daayAA?
right

When is the next vehicle to Phedi?

phedi -maa   arko gaaDi   kahile
Phedi to   next cart   when
jaanchha?
go

I am going to Jomosom.

jomosom -maa   jaane.
Jomosom to   go

Is the trail very uphill?

baaTo   dherai   ukhaalo   chha?
trail   very   uphill   is
   very downhill?
   level?
      oraalo?
      tirso or **samtal?**

Where are you coming from?	**kahAAbaaTa aaeko?**
	where from have been coming
I must rest here all day tomorrow.	**bholi ma din bhari yahAA**
	tomorrow I day whole here
	aaram gar nu parchha.
	rest to make must
Let's rest.	**aaram garAU.**
	rest let's make
I have to urinate.	**pishaab garnu parchha.**
	urine make must
defecate.	**disaa.**
	stool

FINDING A PLACE TO EAT OR TO STAY

Porters can be very helpful in finding a lodging for you in town, especially if they have been over the trail before. If you are on your own, try these sentences:

Where can I get food?	**khaanaa kahAA paainchha?**
	food where get
There.	**utaa or tyahAA.**
	there
Here.	**yahAA.**
	here
Please sit down.	**basnos.**
	please sit down
Can I get food in Namche?	**namche -maa khaanaa paainchha?**
	Namche in food get
potatoes?	**aalu**
Where can I stay?	**kahAA basne?**
	where stay
Is there a place to stay in Namche?	**namche -maa baas paainchha?**
	Namche in stay get
You cannot stay.	**baas paaindaaina.**
	stay cannot
Please rest.	**aaram garnos**
	rest please make.
May we camp here?	**yahAA haami kamp garnu**
	here we camp to make
	hunchha?
	all right
Where is the toilet?	**chharpi kahAA chha?**
	latrine where is
store?	**pasal**
	shop

May we (I) stay in your house?	**tapAAIko ghar maa baas** your house in stay **paainchha?** can get
Can I (we) stay here?	**yahAA baas paainchha?** here stay can get

FOOD
ASKING AT THE HOUSE

Can I get food here?	**khaanaa yahAA paainchha?** food here get
biscuits?	**biscooT**
tea?	**chiyaa**
Please cook rice and lentils for me.	**daal bhaat pakaaunos.** lentils rice please cook
Please do not make it too spicy.	**piro nabanaaunos.** hot please do not make
Please don't put peppers in the food when you cook it.	**khaanaa -maa khursaani** food in peppers **naraakhnos.** not please put
I will eat later.	**pachhi khaane.** after eat
I will eat in two hours.	**dui ghanTaa pachhi khaane.** two hours after eat
Please make the tea without milk.	**chiyaa -maa dudh na haalnos.** tea in milk not please add
sugar.	**chini**
Please cook potatoes for me.	**malaai aalu pakaaunos.** me for potatoes please cook

DURING THE MEAL

There is a fairly strict Hindu etiquette to be observed while eating. Breach of these rules is grossly insulting. It is wise, therefore, to read about Nepali customs in Chapter 4 before you venture to eat in a Nepali home.

Please give me more rice.	**bhaat dinos.** rice please give
vegetables.	**tarkaari**
Please give me another cup of tea.	**arko ek kap chiyaa dinos.** another one cup tea please give
Give me only a little.	**ali ali dinos.** a little please give
It is tasty.	**miTho chha.** tasty it is

That is enough.	**pugyo.**
	enough

BUYING FOOD TO CARRY WITH YOU

Can I buy flour?	**piTho kinnu paainchha?**
	flour buy can I

bread?	**roti**

uncooked rice?	**chaamal**

Please give me five maanaas of flour.	**pAAch maanaa piTho dinos.**
	five maanaa flour please give

Please give me a fire so I can cook my food.	**malaai khaanaa pakaauna aago**
	me for food to cook fire
	dinos.
	please give

PAYING

How much for this?	**yasko kati?**
	for this how much

How much for food?	**khaanaa -ko kati?**
	food for how much

tea?	**chiyaa -ko**
	tea for

one day?	**ek din -ko**
	one day for

one maanaa?	**ek maanaa-ko**
	one maanaa for

I will pay only three rupees.	**tin rupiyAA maatrai dinchhu.**
	three rupees only I give

Please give me my change.	**paisaa dinos.**
	change please give

All together, how much?	**jammaai, kati lagchha?**
	altogether how much does it strike?

All right.	**hunchha**

This is too expensive.	**yo jyaadaai mahAgo chha.**
	this very expensive is

Very well, give it to me.	**la, dinos ta.**
	there please give

GETTING SOMEONE'S ATTENTION

In Nepal, people address each other using kinship terms whether they are related or not. Rather than grunting or shouting "hey you," here are some more pleasant ways of attracting people's attention. Listen and you will hear Nepalis using these terms all the time.

In addressing a person by name, it is polite to add the suffix **-ji** to the name.

When in doubt as to whether the person you address is younger or older than you, use the term for the older. Nepalis use kinship terms in addressing another often.

To get the attention of . . .

a man	**hajur.** (this also means *yes, sir* and *I did not hear you*)

a man a little older than you

o   daai or **daaju.**
hey   older brother

a woman who is a little older than you

o   didi.
hey   older sister

a man old enough to be your father

o   baabu.
hey   father

a woman old enough to be your
mother

o   aamaai.
hey   mother

a woman or a girl younger than you

o   bahini.
hey   younger sister

a man or a boy younger than you

o   bhaai.
hey   younger brother

Once you have their attention:

namaste, or more politely, **namaskaar.**
Translated literally, this greeting means:
"I salute the God in you."

TIME

People like to ask you for the time on the trail, and if you know the first twelve numbers, you can easily answer.

What time is it?

kati   bajyo?
how many   bells

It is two o'clock.

dui   bajyo.
two   bells

I will go today.

aaja   jaane.
today   go

  tomorrow.

bholi

  now.

ahile

I will stay for one day.

ek   din   basne.
one   day   stay

  one week.

ek   haptaa
one   week

Can we get bread early in the
morning?

roti   saberai   paanichha?
bread   early morning   get

What day is it today?

aaja   kun   baar   ho?
today   which   day   is it

Today is Monday.

aaja   sombaar   ho.
today   Monday   is

Tomorrow or the next day

bholi   parshi
tomorrow, the day after tomorrow

When are you going?

kahile jaane?
when   go

TO BEGGING CHILDREN

Don't beg, it's not good.

maagnu hundaaina kharaab kaam
to beg   should not   bad   work
ho.
is

Begging is bad.

maagne kharaab chha.
begging bad   is

I won't give it to you.

dindaaina.

No, you shouldn't.

hundaaina.

MISCELLANEOUS

What is the name of this?

yesko naam ke   ho?
this of name what   is

What is the name of this thing?

yo   chij   ko naam ke   ho?
this thing of name what   is

   bird?

      charo

   animal?

      janaawar

   tree?

      rukh

   plant?

      biruwaa

I only speak a little Nepali.

ma ali ali nepaali maatrai bolchhu.
I   a little Nepali   only   speak

I don't speak Nepali.

ma nepaali boldinA.
I   Nepali   don't speak

I understood.

bujhE or **bujheko.**

I don't understand.

bujhdinA.

Did you understand?

bujhnu bhayo.

Please say it again.

pheri bhannos.
again please say

Have a good trip.

raamro sAAga jaanos.
good   with   please go

Rest well.

raamro sAAga basnos.
good   with   please sit

We are leaving early tomorrow morning.

haami bholi   bihaana saberai
we   tomorrow morning   early
jaanchhAU.
go

How old are you?

tapAAIko   umer   kati bhayo?
your   age   how much has been

What is your name?

tapAAIko   naam   ke ho?
your   name   what is

My country is America.

mero   desh   ahmerika   ho.
my   country   America   is

How many children do you have?

tapAAIko   chhorachhori   kati chan?
your   children   how many are

This is my friend.

yo   mero   saathi   ho.
this   my   friend   is

   husband.

    pati

   wife.

    patni

You are very beautiful (handsome).

tapAAI   dherai   raamro   chha.
you   very   beautiful are

Your son is very beautiful.

tapAAIko   chhoro   dherai   raamro
your   son   very   beautiful
chha.
is

   daughter

    chhori

What is this?

yo   ke   ho?
this   what   is

I have three children, two sons and a daughter.

mero   tin   chhorachhori chhan,
mine   three   children   are
dui   chhoro   ra   euTaa   chhori.
two   sons   and   one   daughter

Have you seen my traveling companions?

tapAAIle   mero   saathi   dekhnu
you   my   friend   to see
bhayo?
have

   porters?

    kulli

   children?

    chhorachhori

Did it rain yesterday?

hijo   paani   paryo?
yesterday   water   fallen

   snow

    hiU

Will it rain today?

aaja   paani   parchha   holaa?
today   water   fall   maybe

   snow

    hiU

Can I help you?

madat   diU?
help   may I give

Will you help me?

malaai   madat   dinu   hunchha?
to me   help   to give   can you

| I like Nepal. | **nepaal man paarcha.** |
| | Nepal mind causes to become |

| This is a fine village. | **yo gaaU raamro chha.** |
| | this village good is |

Is this your mother?	**uhAA tapAAIko aamaa ho?**
	he/she (polite) your mother is
father?	**baabu**

| I am cold. | **malaai jaaDo laagchha.** |
| | to me cold strikes |

| Are you cold? | **tapAAIlaai jaaDo laagchha?** |
| | to you cold strikes |

| Let's go. | **la, jaaU.** |
| | (**la** is a meaningless particle that is colloquial.) |

| What to do? | **ke garne?** |
| | (a common expression) |

| Are you married? | **tapAAIko bihaa bhayo?** |
| | your wedding has it been |

I came to Nepal to sightsee.	**ma nepaal maa herna aaeko.**
	I Nepal to to see came
see the Himalaya.	**himaal herna**
	snow peak to see
wander.	**ghumna**

How are you?	**kasto chha?**
	of what sort are
	(about as meaningful as the English phrase!)

| Fine. | **sanchaai.** |
| | healthy |

| And you? | **tapAAI ni?** |
| | you (**ni** is another meaningless colloquial particle.) |

I like rice and lentils very much.	**malaai daal bhaat man**
	to me lentils rice mind
	paarchha.
	causes to become

I don't like meat.	**malaai maasu man**
	to me meat mind
	paardaina.
	doesn't cause to become

Do you want to go to Jomosom today?

tapAAIlaai aaja Jomosom-maa jaanu
for you today   Jomosom to   to go
man   laagchha?
mind   strikes
(Either **man paarchha** or **man laagchha** are heard, and mean the same.)

I follow the Christian religion.

ma   kristiyan   dharma   maanchhu.
I   Christian   religion   obey

What religion are you?

tapAAIko   dharma   ke   ho?
your   religion   what   is

May I please take a picture of you?

tapAAIko   phoTo (taswir)   khichu?
your   photograph   may I take

Can you sing a song for me?

mero   laagi   git   gaaunu   hunchha?
my   sake   song   to sing   can you

Is there someone who can dance for me?

mero   laagi   kasaile   naachnu
my   sake   anybody   to dance
sakinchha?
can

EMERGENCIES

I am sick.

biraami   chhu.
sick   I am

My friend is sick.

mero   saathi   biraami   chha.
my   friend   sick   is

Where is a hospital?

aaspital   kahAA   chha?
hospital   where   is

   police post?

    Thaanaa
    police post

   army post?

    aarmi   berik
    army   barrack

   district headquarters?

    sadar   mukaam
    headquarters   halting place

   radio?

    aabaa
    from the sky

   airstrip?

    hawai   jahaaj   giraund
    air   vehicle   ground

I have a message to be radioed to Kathmandu.

kaaThmaanDu -maa   pathaaune
Kathmandu   to   to send
samaachaar   chha.
message   there is

Please take it to Namche.

namche   -maa   puraaidinos.
Namche   to   please take

I need a person to carry me.	**ma**	**-laai**	**bokne**	**manche**	**chaahiyo.**
	me	for	carrying	man	need

Please carry me to Shyangboche.	**shyangboche**	**-maa**	**malaai**
	Shyangboche	to	me
	boknos.		
	please carry		

To speak a foreign language well. . . we must imitate and mimic the whole time. We must never imagine that our efforts will be laughed at. There are so many dialects. . . that speaking incorrectly does not sound so odd as it might in another country.

G.G. Rogers, *Colloquial Nepali*

Language Tape

A 90-minute cassette language tape is available that covers the material in this chapter, as well as the other Nepali terms used in the book, including all the place names. The words and phrases are spoken by a native Nepali, and pauses allow the listener time to repeat them.

This tape can be invaluable both when preparing to travel in Nepal and when in the country. It can be ordered by sending $10 US, payable to Stephen Bezruchka, to Nepali Language Tape, P.O. Box 122, Seattle, Washington 98111. For airmail delivery outside of Canada and the U.S., please add $2 for postage. Allow six weeks for delivery.

SECTION II
THE ROUTES

The fortress town of Jharkot in Mustang. (Ane Haaland)

There is great variety in the bridges of Nepal. (Steve Conlon)

FOLLOWING THE ROUTE DESCRIPTIONS

No one goes so far or so fast as the man who does not know where he is going.

H. W. Tilman, *Nepal Himalaya*

In the trail descriptions that follow, treks are not set out on a day-to-day basis. Instead of adhering to a schedule, each party can adjust for long rests or interesting diversions. Those committed to straight traveling can count on covering about five to seven hours of the given route times in a day, allowing a two-hour food stop during mid-morning. In the winter there is less daylight than at other times, and shorter distances can be covered.

In the route descriptions that follow, the times listed between points are actual walking times, generally those I took myself. They *do not* include any rests. This has been strictly adhered to, initially by subtracting all rest times, and more recently by using a chronograph. Over most of the trails I carried a moderately heavy pack. I almost never walked the segments in these times. Like everyone else, I rested, photographed, talked with the people, and so forth.

The times are fairly uniform in that, if a person takes ninety minutes to cover a stretch listed as taking an hour, then it will take him one and a half times as long as the time listed to cover any other stretch—providing the same pace is maintained. Some people have commented that they find the times too long, while most find them too short. The latter is usually because they do not subtract rest times from the total. The times are in boldface to make them easier to total. They help trekkers know what to expect, and thus find the way more easily, and they make it easier to plan where to eat and spend nights.

At the end of each description of a major route, I have listed cumulative walking times (excluding rests and stops) from the start of the trek to significant points along the way. Cumulative times are not listed for trail variations, side trips, or high passes.

Experienced trekkers find that often the first day on the trail seems fast. The next two or three days can be slow and painful. As the body strengthens and adjusts to the pace, the miles and hills seem to go by more effortlessly.

Everyone should learn the rest step for ascents. As you advance your uphill foot, plant it and then, before transferring your weight to it, consciously rest briefly with your weight on your downhill foot. Do this continuously and the hills come easier. On descents, tighten your shoe or boot laces so that your toes are not crammed into the front of the boot with each step. Take short steps, bending your knees to absorb the energy of the descent. Be limber. Watch the porters to see how they walk. People can easily get knee problems by not descending with bent knees. Knee injuries take a long time to heal and can be quite disabling if they occur many days away from the road.

An effective way to gauge your pace is to monitor your pulse by placing your fingertips on a wrist or neck artery. Maximal heart rate can be determined by a sustained strenuous activity for a short time (for instance running at full speed for 1½ mi or 3 km, bicycling up a steep hill, or running on a treadmill). About sixty or seventy percent of the heart rate after such exercise is an appropriate target pulse for sustained activity. Try maintaining your pace to produce this heart rate, or less, and see if you fatigue easily. Most people following this method find a speed that produces an optimal heart rate (related to oxygen consumption) which they can maintain without getting short of breath or fatigued. This may help you maintain a pace without tiring, especially climbing uphill. Some people, myself included, find this too technical and just walk at a comfortable pace.

During a walk of many weeks in such spectacular country, it is easy to let your mind wander from the task at hand, to daydream or gaze at people, mountains, or scenes. You must always pay attention to the trail in front of you and where you put your feet. This may sound obvious, but too many careless trekkers have had serious accidents or falls. As veteran trekker Hugh Swift puts it so well, "look when you look, walk when you walk." When passing animals on the trail, keep to the uphill side, where the fall is much shorter should you be nudged by a yak or buffalo. Trekkers have been seriously injured by not following this advice.

The altitudes listed in the descriptions are taken from two sources: recent maps whose accuracy can be trusted, and my altimeter, a Thommen instrument, which is affected by temperature fluctuations. The readings have not been corrected for temperature changes, but they are adequate to indicate the order of climbing or descending. Ascent rates of 2000 ft (600 m) per hour are difficult to maintain for any length of time. Most hikers find 1000 ft (300 m) per hour a reasonable rate if the trail is good and they climb steadily. Similarly, a descent rate of 1500 ft (450 m) per hour is reasonable. Altitudes are usually converted from feet into meters and are not rounded off, although they are only approximations at best and can be in error by a few hundred feet. Altitudes of most towns in the hills are difficult to interpret accurately since several hundred feet of elevation may separate the highest and the lowest parts of a town.

Routes are described in one direction only. They can easily be followed in the opposite direction. The time for a trip in the reverse direction can be figured approximately if altitude is to be gained or lost and the rate of ascent or descent is taken into consideration.

Directions in the trail descriptions are given with reference to the compass. In addition, right- and left-hand sides of rivers are indicated to avoid confusion. **Right (R) and left (L) refer to the right and left banks when** *facing downstream*. Compass directions, for the most part, are general and may be a little off in some places. However, they are adequate for finding your way.

Local village governments are improving trails because of the increasing popularity of trekking. Improved trails may take different routes from those described here, and routes can shift in popularity for a variety of reasons. I have walked most of the trails described in this book at least twice over a period of several years. Notable changes range from improvements in some trails to erosion and damage on others, and finding more villages and settlements catering to trekkers along the popular routes. Trekking times change also, usually decreasing as the trails improve through use. Detours or other changes occurring since I last walked a trail usually will not cause any problems. Please note down any changes or new information and send it to me in care of the publisher.

A *chautaara*, referred to in the trail descriptions, is a rectangular rock platform with a ledge for resting your load. Sometimes a *pipal* tree and a banyan tree are planted side by side in the center. You can look forward to these welcome structures found on many of the well-traveled routes. A *chorten* is a Buddhist religious structure, often cubical with carved tablets. The term, entrance *chorten*, refers to a covered gateway or arch decorated with Buddhist motifs. A *stupa* is a very large *chorten*. *Mani* walls are rectangular and made of stone tablets carved with mantras and prayers.

Names of towns and villages are taken from two sources: maps and other documents, and my own attempts at transliterating the names I heard. Errors crop up in both sources. One reason is the lack of a completely standardized spelling. Many names from the early Survey of India maps are quite inaccurate, especially in the northern regions. In some places when I asked four or five people the name, I heard four or five variations. Place names in Nepal are not unique. There are many Bhote Kosi's (rivers from Tibet), Beni's (junctions of two rivers), Phedi's (foot of hill), and Deorali's (passes). In addition, some villages may be called by two different names, but this should not cause much confusion in actual practice.

The pronunciation and transliteration guide in Chapter 6 indicates the correct way to pronounce the place names. It is important to place the stress on the first syllable of most words, for instance, Kathmandu, Pokhara, and Tengboche. The transliteration system is the same for words of both Nepali and Tibetan origin. The meaning of capital letters occurring within words is explained in Chapter 6. Place names and other proper nouns are capitalized in spite of the transliteration system. The only place names that would be capitalized if the transliteration scheme were followed strictly are *RaRa*, *Dumre*, *AAbu khaireni*, and *RiRi*. The correct spelling of Kathmandu in this transliteration system is kaaThmaanDu, but for the sake of convenience, the common spelling is used.

In the route descriptions, the names of some towns are in boldface. They are usually large, well-known places whose names the trekker should use when asking the way.

Many trekkers have found their greatest enjoyment from finding new trails little used by foreigners. After you get the hang of it, don't be afraid to venture forth on undescribed terrain, especially if you are trekking independently. Encouraging you to explore on your own, without route descriptions at hand, may be the best advice I can provide.

The clouds part near Langtang. (D.L. Golobitsh)

7 HELAMBU, GOSAINKUND AND LANGTANG

(Map No. 1, Page 153)

> *If you walk the trails of Nepal, you will know what Buddhist dharma is all about.*
>
> Tengboche Rinpoche

These regions are the ones most convenient to Kathmandu. Beginning from Kathmandu, the basic trek through the Helambu region makes a circuit from Pati Bhanjyang. There is an alternative exit from Talamarang to the Kathmandu-Kodari Road as well as an alternative journey out of Helambu to Panch Pokhari, and then down to the Kathmandu-Kodari Road. Visits can be made to Gosainkund and Langtang beginning at Trisuli to the northwest of Kathmandu and via routes linking them with Helambu. An alternative route goes to Langtang with the return via Gosainkund and Helambu. Langtang, Gosainkund, and the northern part of Helambu have been designated a national park with headquarters at Langtang village.

Helambu

Helambu or Helmu is the name of a region at the northern end of the Malemchi Khola Valley. The Helambu trek starts from **Sundarijal**, a small dam and hydroelectric station in the northeast corner of the Kathmandu Valley. More precisely, it begins west of Sundarijal at the end of the auto road where the large water pipe comes out of the hill.

There is no bus service to this point. A taxi could be hired. The cheapest way to go there is by bus to Baudha, boarded in Kathmandu. Stay on the bus until it reaches the turnaround point several hundred yards east of the stupa. At this point the road forks—the right branch going to Sankhu, and the left to Sundarijal. Begin on this left fork and walk **two to three hours** along the level road until it forks again near the edge of the valley. The left fork goes a short distance to a gate and the water treatment plant. Follow the right fork until it ends near a large water pipe. Cross under the pipe and proceed along its west side. Much of the way is up stairs. The trail reaches a clearing with an open building in **half an hour**. Continue until you come to a school on your left. Then just beyond, turn left to cross over the dam of a water reservoir (5200 ft, 1585 m).

Climb through wet, subtropical forest to an oak forest, and on to **Mulkharka** (5800 ft, 1768 m), a scattered *Tamang* village. The trail continues up, first in open country, then in oak forest, and reaches the few houses of **Chaubas** (7525 ft, 2233 m) in 1½ **hours**. The trail then ascends for another **half hour** to a pass, **Burlang Bhanjyang** (8000 ft, 2438 m), with a few houses below it on the north side. This pass marks Kathmandu Valley's rim, here known as the Shivapuri ridge. The trail descends through a pleasant oak forest, past one house on the left, **Chisapani** (7200 ft, 2194 m), to a flat portion where another trail joins from the right. In clear weather there are good views of the Himalaya to the north. In the spring rhododendrons bloom here. The trail continues to descend through open farmland to reach **Pati Bhanjyang** (5800 ft, 1768 m), sitting in a saddle 1¾ **hours** from the pass. There is a police check post here.

From here, there is a choice of two routes. One continues along the general ridge system heading north, and eventually descends east to the Sherpa village of Malemchigaon. The other heads east, descends to the Malemchi Khola, and proceeds up its east (L) bank toward Tarke Ghyang, situated opposite Malemchigaon on the east side of the river. The ridge route goes much higher (almost to 12,000 ft, 3658 m) than the other route, and there may be snow on its upper portions in the late winter or early spring. There are no permanent villages between Kutumsang and Malemchigaon on this route, but if you leave Kutumsang in the morning, you should reach Malemchigaon that evening. This part of the route offers excellent views of the mountains. If it clouds over, as often happens late in the day, consider spending a night up high in a *goTh* or shelter used for pasturing animals. Then hope for good views the next morning.

The circuit to the north along the ridge and the return via the east side of the Malemchi Khola Valley is described. But if the weather is bad, it is wise to head up the east (L) side of the Malemchi Khola and then, if conditions have improved, to return via the high route. In this case, follow the directions in reverse.

To head north from Pati Bhanjyang, climb up the north side of the hill forming the saddle to the left of a long house. Shortly (100 ft, 30 m), the trail forks. The right fork heads to Thakani, a *Tamang* village, and beyond to the Talamarang Khola and Malemchi Khola. This is where it meets the return path.

Take the left fork instead, climb a little, and contour for **half an hour** to reach another saddle (5800 ft, 1768 m). Continue climbing north for 1¼ **hours** to the town of **Chipling** (7100 ft, 2165 m), scattered along the hillside. Climb on, taking the uppermost fork at major junctions, up to 8050 ft (2453 m), then begin descending through the oak forest to **Gul Bhanjyang** (7025 ft, 2142 m), a *Tamang* village 1¾ **hours** from Chipling. The trail is not very direct over this portion. **A few minutes** north of the town, reach a clearing and a trail junction where the left fork contours while the right climbs near the ridge. Take the right fork. Almost an **hour** beyond Gul Bhanjyang at 7975 ft (2430 m), there is another fork. Take the left fork up to 8350 ft (2545 m) just west of the summit of the hill and descend to the few houses of **Kutumsang** (8100 ft, 2468 m) situated in a pass. Reach it in 1¾ **hours**. At the pass, you can take the right fork and contour for **ten minutes** to **Bolumje**, more houses, and perhaps a better place to stay. There are no permanent villages between this town and Malemchigaon, a day away.

In bad weather you could continue along the right fork to the Malemchi Khola Valley and proceed high up on its west (R) bank to Malemchigaon. En route, you would pass the village of Nalemgorkha and Kwagaon. This route takes about ten hours. After the last tributary, climb up a small ridge for 1500 ft (458 m) to Malemchigaon (8400 ft, 2560 m), situated in a clearing. But this route has little to recommend itself. It is steep and narrow in places, and slippery when wet.

From Kutumsang or Bolumje the trail ascends the hill to the north. From Bolumje, pass two *chorten* then reach a *mani* wall (8250 ft, 2515 m) in **ten minutes**. Climb through a prickly-leaved oak forest that becomes a rhododendron and fir forest in its upper reaches. Reach a notch containing three *chorten* (10,600 ft, 3230 m) after climbing for 2½ **hours**, mostly on the east side of the main ridge. If starting from Kutumsang, the trail initially keeps close to the ridge crest. Just beyond the notch is a clearing. Continue, keeping more level, on the west side of the ridge.

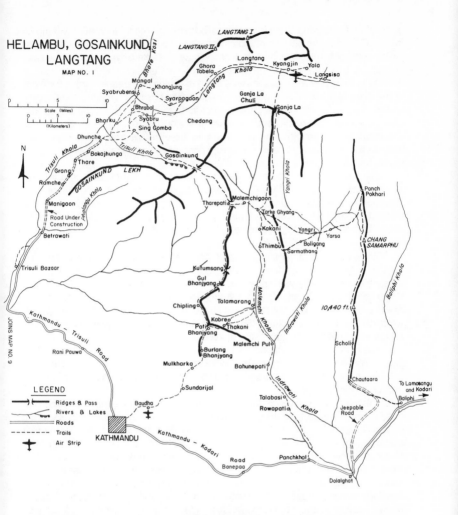

HELAMBU, GOSAINKUND, LANGTANG
MAP NO. 1

Another clearing containing some *goTh* (10,450 ft, 3185 m) is reached in **half an hour**. At the north end of the clearing, a little to the west, there is a fresh water spring. Water can be difficult to find along this ridge during dry weather. From here on, there are two route choices. One keeps close to the ridge crest, the Turin Danda, while the other contours over portions on the west side.

From the clearing, contour on the west side to reach **MangegoTh** (10,775 ft, 3285 m) in **half an hour**. This is the largest group of *goTh* before Tharepati. Continue north on the east side through pleasant rhododendron forests. Cross over to the west side in **fifteen minutes**, then contour to reach some *goTh* (11,125 ft, 3390 m) in **less than half an hour**. Continue on the west side to the ridge crest in another **forty-five minutes**. A **few minutes** beyond in a notch on the ridge (11,800 ft, 3597 m), you can look across the valley to the east and see a tight cluster of houses some 3000 ft (913 m) below you. If this town of Tarke Ghyang is east-southeast of you (slightly south of east or about 117°), you are in the correct notch. The notch is north of a *chorten* and there is now a *goTh* there, as well as a *chorten* with some faint trail markers in blue paint indicating that heading left leads to Gosainkund Lakes and right to Malemchigaon. If the village of Tarke Ghyang cannot be seen because of bad weather or haze or because you are unsure, continue north along the trail to the left of a minor summit. Then if in fifteen minutes you cross the crest of the ridge to the west side and see two clusters of *goTh*, Tharepati, 100 ft (30 m) below you, you had the correct notch. Backtrack to it. This part of the trail is confusing to most trekkers. There are many trails on this portion from Bolumje to Tharepati, so the specific one you take may be different from those described. Keep to the ridge crest for the most part. There may still be some signs in English to help locate the trails.

You can reach the notch in some **five hours** from Kutumsang, and in clear weather you should have fine views of the mountains. As mentioned before, consider spending a night in one of the *goTh* en route to enjoy views in the morning. If, instead of descending from the notch, you continue to the two clusters of *goTh* called Tharepati (11,800 ft, 3597 m) and then beyond to the north, the trail leads to the Gosainkund Lakes in a day.

To continue to Malemchigaon and the villages of upper Helambu, descend east from the notch mentioned above along a newly cut, but at times indistinct, steep trail. Eventually you enter a rocky streambed (9600 ft, 2926 m). Follow it down about 200 ft (61 m). About 1½ **hours** from the notch, at 9400 ft (2865 m), you reach a clearing with a few *goTh* and, beyond, a fork in which the right branch descends to cross a tributary (8265 ft, 2520 m) after **forty minutes**. A short climb brings you to **Malemchigaon** (8400 ft, 2560 m).

The people here call themselves Sherpas, but their relationship with the Sherpas of Solu-Khumbu is distant. The dialects spoken are also different. Here you will find a *gomba* on the east end of the town, and an interesting rock home of a hermit on the west end.

There are no more towns farther up this valley, so to go to Tarke Ghyang, proceed down to the south of the *gomba* through an entrance *chorten* and descend a small ridge. About 1000 ft (304 m) below, there are some large rocks, and farther below, a large bridge over the river. Reach it (6200 ft, 1890 m) in **one hour** from Malemchigaon. Cross to the east (L) bank and head up southward to a *chorten*. Here, turn east and climb a little until a trail branches to the right across some terraces. Continue, mostly contouring, but climb a little and cross two tributaries. After the second crossing, the trail rises more directly, and an **hour** from the bridge, reaches a small treeless *chautaara* (7200 ft, 2194 m). Another 1000 ft (304 m) of vertical climbing brings you to a *chorten* and shortly beyond, to a tight cluster of houses called **Tarke Ghyang**, another Sherpa village (8400 ft, 2560 m), 1¼ **hours** from the *chautaara*. The town's name means "temple of the 100 horses" and was taken from the name of a temple established in 1727 by a Lama who was called by the king of Kantipur to stop an epidemic in Kathmandu. As his reward, the Lama asked for 100 horses, which he brought here. The local temple, rebuilt in 1969, follows the Bhutanese style.

From Tarke Ghyang you can head east up past the schoolhouse and then north for three days to reach the Ganja La, a high pass (16,805 ft, 5123 m) leading to the Langtang Valley. Food, shelter, and fuel have to be carried, and the party should be equipped for snow climbing. This route is described in the reverse direction later in this chapter. Or, from Tarke Ghyang, you can head up to the ridge crest to the southeast and east to Panch Pokhari, a series of small lakes (about 13,000 ft, 3968 m) that are pilgrimage sites. There is a fine view from the ridge nearby. You

A Tamang *woman working the soil with a* kodaalo. *(Ane Haaland)*

can then head to the Kathmandu-Kodari Road. This is not a well-traveled route and there are few houses along the way. However, it is an alternate exit from the Helambu area. This route description follows that for the stretch from Talamarang to the Kathmandu-Kodari Road. The third route from Tarke Ghyang follows the river southward.

To take this third route, head south at the low end of the village past the large new *gomba* and rows of *mani* walls to cross a stream. Take the lower fork just beyond, and after an **hour**, cross a tributary (7000 ft, 2134 m) to **Kakani**, a small scattered Sherpa village (6750 ft, 2058 m) **half an hour** after the tributary. Upon rounding the next ridge crest, you reach a clearing in the oak forest with *chorten*, *mani* walls, and an entrance *chorten*. Descend from here into the valley of the next tributary. Rather than head east to cross the tributary upstream from the main river, the trail descends near the ridge past a large *chorten*. In 1½ **hours** from Kakani, you reach **Thimbu**, another scattered Sherpa and *Tamang* village (5000 ft, 1524 m). Below it, the trail descends for **fifteen minutes** to cross the next tributary (4550 ft, 1486 m).

The trail now follows the east (L) bank of the Malemchi Khola, close to the water for the most part, but rising occasionally to clear difficult stretches. The forest is again subtropical. In **less than an hour**, descend to a suspension bridge across the river (4050 ft, 1234 m). Do not cross it, but continue on the east (L) bank, crossing several tributaries along the way. About 1½ **hours** beyond the first suspension bridge, you come to the third bridge (3500 ft, 1067 m). Cross this to the west (R) bank and continue south on a wide trail that was once a road but is now in disrepair. There is an interesting looking Brahman village (Sarha) on the right, and 1¼ **hours** beyond the suspension bridge, you pass high above another. Then **shortly**, you descend to **Talamarang** (3150 ft, 960 m), a town with shops and teahouses.

There are two route choices from here. One ascends the tributary lying south of the village to rejoin the outward bound route at Pati Bhanjyang. The other continues south along the west (R) bank of the Malemchi Khola, crosses to the Chak Khola after five hours, and reaches the Kathmandu-Kodari Road at Panchkhal where you can board a bus for the remainder of the journey. This route takes only seven hours to the road, remains quite level, and follows a wide path almost suitable for a jeep; but it covers over twenty miles. The other route follows an ill-defined trail up a riverbed for several hours and involves a vertical ascent of 4700 ft (1433 m), followed by a descent of 2700 ft (823 m) to the Kathmandu Valley. This route takes eight to nine hours to Sundarijal and should be taken if bad weather prevents you from having good views of the peaks on the way to Pati Bhanjyang, or if you are traveling in the spring when the lower route is much hotter.

RETURN VIA PATI BHANJYANG

To return from Talamarang via Pati Bhanjyang, cross the suspension bridge over the tributary, the Talamarang Khola, and head west up its south (R) bank. There is a direct trail, which is difficult to find, up the ridge to Thakani. Instead, stay close to the river most of the time. Try to follow a small trail which meanders about the river and crisscrosses it irregularly. The forest is chir pine and chilaune again. Almost **three hours** later (4700 ft, 1433 m), cross a large landslide through which a prominent tributary from the south trickles. **Half an hour** beyond on the south (R) bank of the Talamarang Khola near the hill to the south, you come to a small water-operated mill (4750 ft, 1448 m). A trail rises near the mill and essentially climbs the ridge north of the tributary valley mentioned before. Follow the trail to the *Tamang* village of **Kabre** (5500 ft, 1676 m) which is **forty-five minutes** from the riverbed.

Continue along the ridge through oak forest past another *Tamang* village. Take the right fork beyond to head west and rise to a *chautaara* (6050 ft, 1844 m) **thirty minutes** from Kabre. The trail continues to ascend and reaches a ridge crest (6200 ft, 1890 m) in **twenty minutes** near the *Tamang* village of **Thakani**. There are good distant views from here in clear weather. The trail now crosses to the south side of the ridge and contours, heading west, for **1¼ hours** to the trail you took on the way out, just north of Pati Bhanjyang. Descend to **Pati Bhanjyang** in a **few minutes** and retrace the route described earlier to Sundarijal.

Cumulative trekking times (walking time only, does not include rests or stops) from Sundarijal to:

Burlang Bhanjyang Pass	2½ hours
Pati Bhanjyang	4¼ "
Gul Bhanjyang	7¾ "
Kutumsang	10½ "
Malemchigaon	17½ "
Tarke Ghyang	20¾ "
Talamarang	27¾ "
Return to Sundarijal via Pati Bhanjyang	34¼ "

RETURN VIA PANCHKHAL

To proceed to the Kathmandu-Kodari Road from Talamarang, cross the bridge over the tributary and continue south on a wide trail. Vehicles have succeeded in motoring most of the way on the road, but presently it is not in good repair. There are large boulders and washouts obstructing the way. You are in sal forest and non-cultivated areas for the most part.

Follow the west (R) bank of the Malemchi Khola for **1½ hours** until you see a large suspension bridge over the river and a cluster of houses on the west (R) bank. This is **Malemchi Pul Bazaar** (2775 ft, 846 m). Another **1¼ hours** brings you to **Bahunepati** (2660 ft, 811 m), the largest bazaar en route. A further **1¼ hours** along the much wider valley brings you near another suspension bridge spanning almost the entire valley floor. There is a town, Talabasi (2575 ft, 785 m), at the west end of the bridge. The road passes west of the town, heads over to the hillside on the west, and ascends it to a saddle to the west. The town of **Rowapati** (3075 ft, 937 m) is on the saddle **an hour** beyond the bridge. The trail now enters the next valley west of the Malemchi Khola containing the Chak Khola. Continue south above its east (L) bank for **1¼ hours** until you cross to the west (R) bank (2600 ft, 793 m). The trail then ascends and winds for **twenty minutes** to reach asphalt (2920 ft, 890 m). Turn right and pass mileage marker No. 47 to reach a cluster of houses by the road in **fifteen minutes**. This is a part of the town of **Panchkhal** (3100 ft, 945 m). Buses going to Kathmandu stop here every few hours.

PANCH POKHARI

For people who approach Helambu from the west or south, this route is an alternative means of return to the highway through an area south and east of Helambu. While slightly longer, it does offer some fine scenery and a ridge route that is cooler during the hot months. From Panch Pokhari (five lakes) itself, there is no view of the snow-covered mountains because the cirque the lakes are set in faces southeast. But a half-hour climb to the crest of the cirque yields a spectacular vantage point. Five or six days should be allowed for the trip.

From Tarke Ghyang, follow the main trail along the ridge crest to Sarmathang. It is a pleasant **three- to five-hour** walk via a level trail contouring around two subsidiary ridges. Panch Pokhari is on the next ridge to the east, so it is necessary to cross the Indrawati Khola in between. Descend, while going diagonally north, to **Boligang** in 1½ **hours**, passing **Samil** about halfway. The trail is rather obscure and the town, inhabited by Sherpas and *Tamang*, is notably poorer than the Sherpa villages of Helambu. Continue heading north along a better trail that reaches the town of **Yangri** near the intersection of the Ripar Khola and the Indrawati Khola in **one hour**. This town may be reached more directly from Tarke Ghyang by climbing up (2000 ft, 609 m), crossing the ridge directly, and descending via the Ripar Khola to Yangri.

Cross the river at each of the branches over somewhat treacherous bridges and take a short steep climb along a cliff between them. Instead of taking the path diverging right toward Bhotung, climb straight up through millet fields to **Yarsa** in **one hour**. From Yarsa, take the main path on the left, going gently up, but avoiding steeper alternative paths, past *chorten* and clusters of houses until you come to a rushing stream in **one hour**. Cross the stream on a bridge and then go steeply up on your left along a well-built trail. Half way up, take the steeper path (the other trail flattens) and reach the crest in **one hour**.

The trail continues gently up for **fifteen minutes** to **Dukang**, a settlement with two permanent houses and many *goTh*. This is the last human habitation for the next several days. Panch Pokhari can be reached from here in one rather long day.

Go rather steeply up to reach another ridge crest in 1¼ **hours**, then contour left for **one hour** to a stream. Here the trail is easy to lose due to floods, but proceed up the stony bed for a few hundred feet, cross a temporary bridge, and go diagonally left very steeply up the hillside. Soon the grade eases and in **forty-five minutes**, you enter pleasant terrain. Cross two streams (the last water before Panch Pokhari) and go left up across the hill. This section may be seen from the level section of the trail before the stream. In another **forty-five minutes**, gain the crest near some abandoned *goTh* and continue gently up to the left on fine rock slabs to reach the saddle (12,000 ft, 3658 m) in the Panch Pokhari ridge in 1½ **hours**. There are numerous *chorten* and a trail shelter here, but water may be difficult to find.

The trail to Panch Pokhari runs along the left side of the ridge and is generally well-built, but it has numerous ups and downs that are tiresome at that altitude. Reach one slightly dilapidated, but usable, shelter to the north of the ponds in **three hours** from the point of gaining the ridge. There is room for only three or four people to sleep on the boards, but many more could be accommodated on the dirt, and there are plenty of fine camping places. Since the area is just above the tree line, firewood is scarce. But there may be a large pile of stocks about **fifteen minutes** down the trail. A Hindu shrine and numerous Buddhist prayer flags are nearby, making it a very peaceful place. From the cirque crest (about 13,000 ft, 3962 m), there is a splendid view of the Himalaya all the way east from Langtang to beyond Everest.

The return to the Kathmandu-Kodari Road is almost entirely along a ridge route with only a couple of short climbs to break the 11,000 ft (3354 m) descent. Follow the ascent route back for **two hours** to the shelter (12,966 ft, 3958 m) in the saddle north of Chang Samarphu. The old trail went up almost to the summit, but the new route skirts the west side of the peak on a nearly level trail consisting of easy slabs. Rejoin the former trail in 1½ **hours** at the col on the south side where there are remains of some *goTh*. The next hill is also skirted on its west side in **half an hour**. Midway on this section are a couple of caves suitable for housing four or five people, but the nearby watercourses are sometimes dry outside of the monsoon. About **ten minutes** short of the next col there are some meadows that provide excellent camping and some shelter in abandoned *goTh*. Water is available at a good stream at the col, but there is no camping site any closer.

From the col, take the main trail that branches east (left). At first it is fairly level, then goes upward, crosses several streams, and reaches the crest in 1¼ **hours**. From the open, flower-filled meadows, there are fine views of the mountains. Now descend rather steeply for 500 ft (152 m), then go down more gradually over a series of bumps to reach the lowest col (10,440 ft, 3182 m) before the peak in 1½ **hours**. The remains of many fires indicate where water is found some 200 ft (61 m) east in small semi-clear pools. Camping sites as well as some small grass and leaf lean-tos are available. This is the last water for about five hours.

Proceed diagonally, going gently up, around, and down the west side of the peak (10,440 ft, 3187 m) until in 1½ **hours**, four chimney-like cairns are reached just beyond a shallow, sandy depression in the ridge. There is a good view from here of the ridge below as it goes south before doglegging southwest. The fine trail continues **one hour** down to the dogleg, then stays fairly level for another 1½ **hours**. An obvious level trail cuts off to the left (southeast) here and goes out to the end of a subsidiary ridge. Then it heads down steeply to a series of plateaus where the first houses are found and where water is probably available, though not along the trail. As you descend, the town of Scholi can be seen. Farther away, Chautaara, which has a particularly large, white building, is nestled in a saddle in the ridge.

Continuing, skirt gently down across the southwest face of a large hill where two small streams join. Cross the saddle to the east of the next hill and drop steeply down to **Scholi**. It has a small bazaar with a rest house about **forty-five minutes** from the stream crossing and perhaps 2½ **hours** from the beginning of the steep descent. From Scholi, proceed for 1½ **hours** along a very wide, flat trail which meanders along the ridge top and around hillocks, then goes more steeply down to **Chautaara**. This fairly large bazaar is the district headquarters. There is a jeep road that is sometimes open to the Kathmandu-Kodari Road. The foot trail follows the motor road east for 1½ **hours** until you come to two tea shops. From here, descend steeply to **Baliphi** on the main road where a bus to Kathmandu is available.

Gosainkund

Here is the description of a trek from Trisuli, up the Trisuli Valley to the sacred lakes of Gosainkund and beyond to Helambu. Such a circuit may be about the best possible short trek from Kathmandu. It takes a minimum of a week, and food for two or three days must be carried.

Trisuli can be reached from Kathmandu on foot in 1½ days, or by bus in four to five hours from Pakanajol in the northwest corner of Kathmandu. Consider a side trip to the old fort of Nuwakot as described in Chapter 11. From Trisuli you can proceed north up the east (L) or west (R) bank of the river.

The route up the east (L) bank has more rises and dips, but it can be motored by rugged vehicles. The route on the west paralleling the water reservoir and canal is quite flat. To take the west bank trail, climb up behind the bazaar (1775 ft, 541 m)

The tailor team in a bazaar town of eastern Nepal. (Ane Haaland)

to reach the canal flowing to the penstocks of a hydroelectric power project. Follow the road to the east of the canal. Beyond the reservoir, the water pipe crosses the river. You cross on a catwalk beside the pipe (1900 ft, 579 m) **one hour** from Trisuli. On the east (L) bank the trail joins the road and continues north through sal forest. The pipe crosses to the west (R) bank again, but you stay on the east (L) side until the road ends **half an hour** beyond the crossing near a partial dam across the Trisuli Khola. There are a few houses here, but the main town of **Betrawati** (2100 ft, 641 m) is **twenty minutes** beyond at the junction of the Phalangu Khola and the Trisuli. A road is being constructed to Dhunche and beyond. Sections of the trail will change due to local conditions and the road building. Walking times may vary as well. Currently, following the road is not advised, because of the construction. Inquire locally. Cross the suspension bridge over the tributary and climb a bit to the town of **Bogata** (2350 ft, 761 m). Now climb through an oak forest to a chir pine forest, then through open country on a wide trail to **Manigaon** (3925 ft, 1196 m) **2½ hours** from Betrawati. The trail continues north, in and out of tributary valleys, to reach **Ramche** (5875 ft, 1791 m) in **2½ hours**. Here national park entry permits must be purchased. Another **hour** brings you to the next *Tamang* village, **Grang** (6200 ft, 1890 m).

Continue contouring another **1½ hours** to **Thare** (6525 ft, 1899 m). There are good views of Langtang I and II along the way. To the north up the main valley, Tibetan peaks are visible. Another **hour** brings you to **Bokajhunga** (6200 ft, 1890 m). The trail through oak forest here is exceptionally pleasant. Another **1½ hours** brings you to **Dhunche** (6450 ft, 1966 m), a main village at the junction of the Trisuli Khola and the Bhote Kosi. There are shops and a police check post here.

From Dhunche, there are two routes to Gosainkund. The newer trail is initially the same as that heading to Langtang. Head east, taking neither of the first two left forks **twelve and eighteen minutes** from town. Contour for **half an hour**, then take a left fork (6000 ft, 1829 m) beyond His Majesty's Government (HMG) Agricultural Project below you. Descend to a cantilever bridge (5775 ft, 1700 m) some **ten minutes** beyond. Cross the Trisuli Khola, which drains the Gosainkund Lekh, to the north (R) bank, and climb up a steep, but pleasant, oak-forested gully to reach a crest with a trail junction (6450 ft, 1966 m) after **fifteen minutes**. The trail that climbs to the east heads to Gosainkund, while the one going northwest heads toward Langtang. Take the trail climbing to the east and follow it for approximately **five hours** to **Sing Gomba** (10,675 ft, 3254 m). Pass through oak forests to reach an impressive fir and rhododendron forest.

The old trail to Gosainkund heads east and contours from the water spout at the lower end of Dhunche. Do not take the right fork that ascends **forty-five minutes** beyond this. Continue past the turnoff for the new trail. In **half an hour** you reach the Trisuli Khola near some mills. The bridge here has collapsed, so you must ford the river (6375 ft, 1943 m). The trail heads east on the north (R) side. It is a climb of 8700 ft (2652 m) to the pass. The first 4300 ft (1311 m) are rather steep and there is little water. You reach **Sing Gomba** (10,675 ft, 3254 m) in **4½ hours**. At junctions, take the upper fork. The pleasant easy-to-follow trail passes through hillsides ablaze with rhododendrons in season. There are no permanent settlements until you reach the Helambu region, about a three-day trek (in good weather) beyond Dhunche. Sing Gomba is inhabited during the less severe part of the year, when people there can provide food and shelter for trekkers. An HMG cheese factory, Chauchan Bari, is located there.

From the *gomba*, head east along the south side of the ridge, following a wide trail. At first, where there was once a big burn, the slope is covered with *Piptanthus nepalensis* shrubs with yellow flowers. Then the trail enters a rhododendron and fir forest, and crosses to the north side of the ridge. In **1¼ hours**, reach a *goTh* (11,550 ft, 3520 m) where the trail is joined by the one coming up from Syabru. (If coming from Syabru, take the trail up the ridge from the village, past a water-driven prayer wheel, and follow a faint trail to gain the ridge here.) Continue for **forty-five minutes** on the north side to the few *goTh* called Laurebina (12,800 ft, 3901 m). Water is scarce here. In good weather there are views of Himalchuli, Peak 29, Manaslu, and Ganesh Himal to the west, Tibet to the north, and Langtang Himal to the northeast. Climb on, reaching a *chautaara* with poles sticking out of it (13,000 ft, 3962 m), then in a **little over half an hour**, cross the ridge to the south side (13,600 ft, 4145 m). Beyond, you begin to see the lakes. The first is Bhutkunda, followed by Nagkunda, and then **Gosainkunda**. This third lake (14,100 ft, 4298 m) is reached in **forty-five minutes**. There are two stone huts on the north shore.

Every year during the full moon between mid-July and mid-August, thousands of pilgrims and devotees come to bathe in this lake and to pay homage to Shiva. There are several legends, all similar, concerning the formation of this lake and its significance. One story is that the gods were churning the ocean, hoping to obtain from it the water of immortality. Some poison arose from the seas, and Shiva, realizing that the poison might harm the gods, drank it. The poison caused him a great deal of pain and thirst, as well as a blue discoloration of his neck. To relieve the fever and suffering, Shiva traveled to the snows of Gosainkund. He thrust his trident, or *trisul*, into the mountainside and three streams of water sprang forth which collected in the hollow beneath, producing the Gosainkund Lake. Shiva stretched along the lake's edge and drank its waters, quenching his thirst. There is said to be an oval-shaped rock beneath the surface near the center of the lake. Worshippers say they can see Shiva reclining on a bed of serpents there.

In good weather, consider climbing the hill to the north for a view. To continue to Helambu, contour the lake and ascend past four more lakes (Bhairunkunda, Saraswatikunda, Dudkunda, and Surjekunda—often they may be covered with ice) to the pass (15,100 ft, 4602 m) in an **hour**.

From the pass, descend to the southeast, keeping generally to the northeast (L) side of the valley, and head for the prominent notch in the distance. In an **hour** reach some stone *goTh* frames (13,000 ft, 3962 m). Shortly beyond, descend a ridge with a waterfall on your left. There is a campsite (11,900 ft, 3627 m) **forty-five minutes** farther. Soon the trail crosses a stream and passes by another picturesque waterfall. About **forty-five minutes** from the first campsite, there is another under the overhanging rocks of Gopte (11,700 ft, 3566 m). The notch (11,675 ft, 3559 m) you saw earlier is reached in **forty-five minutes**. Some **forty-five minutes** later, there are more overhanging rocks. The trail continues through beautiful rhododendron forests and in **half an hour**, crosses a tributary from the north (10,550 ft, 3216 m) to ascend through juniper woods. It reaches a series of *goTh* called Tharepati (11,500 ft, 3505 m) just below the ridge west of the Malemchi Khola in another 1¼ **hours**. There are good views to the north from the crest of the ridge. A trail proceeds north near the crest, and leads over a high pass to the Langtang Valley.

From the ridge (11,875 ft, 3620 m) above the *goTh*, the trail follows the crest to the southeast and drops into a notch (11,800 ft, 3597 m) from which Tarke Ghyang is visible to the east-southeast as a tight cluster of houses on the east side of the Malemchi Khola Valley some 3000 ft (913 m) below you. To the south is a hill with a *chorten*. There are two choices now: descend from the notch to Malemchigaon, or head south along the main ridge to Kutumsang. Both of these trails have been described earlier.

Cumulative trekking times (walking time only, does not include rests or stops) from Trisuli to:

Grang	8	hours
Dhunche	12	"
Gosainkunda	21½	"

Langtang

Langtang is a valley nestled in the Himalaya. It is best to carry some food in order to be able to explore the upper part of the valley. First the trip from Trisuli to Langtang, then several side trips up the valley are described. There is a high pass, the Ganja La, which links Langtang with Helambu. A brief description of this route is given. Return routes to avoid backtracking from Langtang, and linkups with Gosainkund, complete the description. An interesting and informative recent account of this area is given in Andrew R. Hall's "Preliminary Report on the Langtang Region" (see Recommended Reading).

To go to Langtang, follow the route already described to Dhunche in the Gosainkund section. The road construction up to Dhunche is continuing at least to Bharku and will go to Syabru. Eventually, the road will head northwest. Local conditions may dictate trail changes and thus may influence walking times. From Dhunche (6450 ft, 1966 m) begin working east, not taking either of the two left forks **twelve and eighteen minutes** from town. Keep level and after a **half hour** from town, at 6000 ft (1829 m), take a left fork, beyond the HMG Agricultural Project and descend steeply to a cantilever bridge (5675 ft, 1930 m) some **10 minutes** beyond. Cross the Trisuli Khola, which drains the Gosainkund Lekh, to the north (R) bank and climb up a pleasant oak-forested gully to reach a crest with a trail junction (6450 ft, 1966 m) after **forty-five minutes**. The right fork goes east to Gosainkund, while the left fork heading northwest is to Langtang. Take the left fork which forks again some **twenty minutes** later (6450 ft, 1966 m). The lower fork leads into the Bhote Kosi Valley, through a pleasant chir pine forest. After another **twenty minutes**, in sight of the next village, Bharku, there is another fork (6125 ft, 1867 m). The upper fork leads to the village and beyond to the new route into the Langtang Valley, while the left fork passes below the village to Syabrubensi and the older route to Langtang. This older route is described later as a variant for leaving the Langtang Valley. Continue to **Bharku** (6050 ft, 1844 m) **ten minutes** beyond.

To proceed on the new route, continue contouring and rising beyond Bharku through pleasant chir pine and rhododendron forests. Round a bend to a rest spot (7550 ft, 2301 m) with the first views up the Langtang Valley after 2¼ **hours**. Contour and descend another **forty-five minutes** to Syabru (6950 ft, 2118 m), a village strung out along a ridge. From Syabru there are trails ascending to Sing Gomba (three to four hours) and to Gosainkund (about seven hours). There are no settlements for at least a day's walk beyond Syabru. Shelter can be found under rocks, but food must be carried. To continue to Langtang, drop and contour across wheat fields to the east. Then descend and cross to the east (R) bank of a tributary (6375 ft, 1943 m) from the Gosainkund Lekh after **forty-five minutes**. Climb up a bit, then descend through a forest to reach the Langtang Khola (5450 ft, 1661 m) in **forty-five minutes**. A trail and several bridges cross the Langtang Khola and lead downstream to Syabrubensi. This difficult trail is passable only in the dry season, but can provide another route of return from the valley.

Continue upstream along the south (L) bank through a quite impressive gorge. In an **hour**, reach a rock shelter and cross a nearby tributary (6325 ft, 1928 m). Another **forty-five minutes** brings you to a new bridge (6700 ft, 2042 m) that is crossed to the north (R) bank. More rock shelters suitable for camping are found here. The trail continues climbing through rhododendron and prickly-leaved oak forests, to meet the old trail (7825 ft, 2385 m) from Syabrubensi in another **hour**. This older trail keeps high on the north side of the valley before descending to Syabrubensi. It is described later.

Notice how much drier it is on this side of the valley, which—because it faces south—receives more sunlight. Continue on up the valley, which widens out. **Half an hour** farther there are some *bhaTTi*, and space for camping. Forty minutes beyond is another lodge. Another **three-hour** climb brings you to the valley floor and the Nepal army post of **Ghora Tabela** (9450 ft, 2880 m). This was once a Tibetan resettlement project and may not have any permanent residents. A trekkers' lodge has been constructed here and may be in operation. Beyond, on the south side of the valley, are larch forests which turn golden yellow in the autumn.

Continue up the valley, passing several temporary settlements, then cross a tributary below a monastery after 1½ **hours**. This active monastery is interesting and worth a visit. Note the glacier-worn *U* shape of the valley here, in contrast to the water-worn *V* shape of the valley below Ghora Tabela. Another **half an hour** brings you to beautiful **Langtang** village (10,850 ft, 3307 m), site of the Langtang National Park headquarters. Tourist facilities have been constructed here. Continue on up a moraine to cross a tributary (11,800 ft, 3597 m) after another 1¼ **hours**. The views become better with further progress, and looking back, you can see the impressive Langtang Himal. Another **twenty minutes** brings you to a trail fork (12,075 ft, 3680 m). The left fork goes to Kyangjin Gomba. Shortly beyond, on the right fork, is the HMG cheese factory and the summer pasturing settlements of **Kyangjin** (12,300 ft, 3749 m). Food and lodging can usually be arranged here.

Cumulative trekking times (walking time only, does not include rests or stops) from Dhunche to:

Bharku	2½ hours
Langtang Khola	7 "
Ghora Tabela	12¼ "
Langtang National Park Headquarters	14¼ "
Kyangjin	16¼ "

UPPER LANGTANG VALLEY

From Kyangjin there are several worthwhile excursions. You can head north to reach the glacier and icefall in less than three hours. Climb the lateral moraine to the left of the glacier. Or an hour's climb to the north up a small hill provides a good view. You can also proceed farther up the main valley. The STOL airstrip (12,100 ft, 3688 m) is half an hour beyond Kyangjin in the valley floor. There are many possibilities for short climbs, mostly to the north. There is another cheese factory at Yala, a 3½-hour climb from Kyangjin. A small summit with outstanding views can be reached from the factory.

To go to Yala, head east from Kyangjin, and after about **ten minutes**, contour the hillside to the north, reaching a few *goTh* in an hour. Another **hour's** contouring and climbing brings you to another series of *goTh* (13,650 ft, 4160 m). Round the ridge crest and contour another slope for **half an hour** to another ridge (14,400 ft, 4389 m). Climb north beside a small stream to reach the buildings at Yala (15,200 ft, 4633 m) in less than an **hour**. To reach Tsergo Ri (some call this Yala Peak), an excellent viewpoint, head west from Yala, or continue circling the hill, reaching the prayer flag-festooned summit (16,353 ft, 4984 m) in **two hours**. To the south, you can see the Ganja La, a pass leading into Helambu. The surrounding peaks are quite spectacular. Many short climbs may suggest themselves to the experienced.

From Kyangjin, you can also head up the valley to Langsisa, the next to the last of the summer pasturing settlements. Cross an alluvial fan (12,250 ft, 3734 m) **twenty minutes** beyond and reach the airstrip, crossing its western end. In less than **half an hour**, reach the north (R) bank of the Langtang Khola and continue upstream. Another **forty-five minutes** brings you to a summer settlement (12,500 ft, 3810 m), and another **hour** brings you to a second. A big lateral and terminal moraine of the West Langtang Glacier looms ahead. Contour around its south terminus and reach the lone hut of Langsisa (13,400 ft, 4084 m) in another **hour**. Ahead lies the main Langtang Glacier, and the Tibetan border, a hard day's climb away (some trekking maps are grossly in error regarding the border). To the south lies beautiful Buddha Peak and the terminus of the East Langtang Glacier. Up this valley lies a difficult pass leading to the region east of Helambu. It was probably first crossed by H. W. Tilman in 1949. There are many places to explore.

There is a big reddish rock at Langsisa which, according to legend, is that color because a holy man living outside the valley lost his yak and trailed it to this place. The yak died here, however, and the Lama, wanting its hide, skinned it and spread the skin on a rock to dry. But the skin stuck and remains there on the rock to this day! This is the legend of the discovery of the Langtang Valley. "Lang" means yak, and "tang" means to follow. Hence the name. Also, a few miles up the valley to the southeast, two big rock gendarmes stand a hundred feet above the glacier. They are said to represent two Buddhist saints, Shakya Muni and Guru Rimpoche.

There are several possible linkup routes to avoid backtracking. From below Ghora Tabela, you can cross the Langtang Khola and ascend to the Chedang yak pastures and Laurebina on the main trail to Gosainkunda. This takes **two days** and requires a guide who is quite familiar with the route. You can also reach Malemchigaon from Chedang. From Syabru you can ask the way to Gosainkunda and to Sing Gomba. For experienced parties, the Ganja La leads to Helambu. This pass is normally possible from May to November, or sometimes longer in dry years. Food, fuel, and shelter must be carried for four to five days. It is necessary to have someone along who is familiar with the route, as it is quite easy to get lost in poor weather.

THE GANJA LA

To cross the Ganja La from Langtang Valley, go downstream from Kyangjin to a wooden bridge over the river. Downstream on the south (R) bank are a few huts. The trail enters the rhododendron forest and climbs to more huts, Ngegang (14,450 ft, 4404 m) in **two hours**. Another **four or more hours** brings you to the pass, which may be difficult to find. Keep to the west side of the valley coming down from the pass. The last 100 ft (30 m) to the pass (16,805 ft, 5122 m) is a scramble. Descend to the south into a basin, pick a route through the center among the moraines, and climb out of the basin. Then find the trail markers that head toward a stream. Follow the stream down to where it joins another stream to form the Yangri Khola, and follow it to some scattered summer pasturing huts (14,400 ft, 4389 m). This takes **three or four hours**. Climb out of the basin, and aim for a spur to the west of the main north-south ridge. Climb down to a series of huts in a meadow. This area is sometimes called Kelaung or Kelchung, and can be reached in **two hours** from the earlier huts. Continue south, crossing several shoulders and for the most part tending to the east side of the main ridge. Do not descend from the main high ridge. Reach another series of huts at Dukpu (13,200 ft, 4023 m) in 2½ **to three hours**. Ascend to a notch to the northeast of a prominent hill, and traverse fine rhododendron forests, crossing and recrossing the ridge crest. Pass through a clearing with a hut (10,900 ft, 3322 m) and head southwest, descending past Gekye Gomba to reach Tarke Ghyang in **three to four hours**. Routes linking Tarke Ghyang with Kathmandu have been described in the Helambu section of this chapter.

LANGTANG TO SYABRUBENSI

If you came to Langtang without visiting Syabrubensi, consider varying your exit to Trisuli slightly by following the Langtang Valley downstream, high on the north side to Syabrubensi. Descend on the usual trail from Ghora Tabela, and after **one hour**, pass a bridge over the Langtang Khola (8625 ft, 2629 m). The bridge can be used to reach Gosainkunda via Chedang yak pastures as mentioned earlier. However, continue down to reach the trail junction (7850 ft, 2393 m) in another **forty-five minutes** . The left fork descends to the new bridge and Syabru. The right fork ascends through open, steep country where you might spot some interesting animals, such as a goral or serow. The trail passes a lodge and descends to the few houses of Syarpa or **Syarpagaon** (8225 ft, 2507 m) in another **hour**. Continue contouring and climbing on the steep valley wall for **two hours** until you round a ridge to an oak and blue pine forest and the valley of the main Bhote Kosi. A **thirty- to forty-five minute** descent brings you to **Khangjung** (7250 ft, 2210 m), a scattered village with cultivated fields. At the lower end, the trail forks near a water source and *mani*. The right fork heads north to Rasuwa Garhi, while the left descends through terraces into chir pine forest to Mangal (4900 ft, 1494 m) near the bottom of the Bhote Kosi Valley in a **little over an hour**. Head downstream (south) from here, following the main trail on the east (L) bank of the Bhote Kosi for **half an hour** to **Syabrubensi** (4650 ft, 1417 m). This large town contains a settlement of Tibetan refugees as well as *BhoTiya* who call themselves *Tamang*.

There are some hot springs near here that can be used for bathing. To reach them, cross the main suspension bridge over the Bhote Kosi and head downstream on the west (R) bank for about **ten minutes** to a small hot spring. There are other bigger ones below.

SYABRUBENSI TO SING GOMBA

From Syabrubensi, cross the suspension bridge over the Langtang Khola to its south (L) bank. Heading upstream from here, you can take a trail to Syabru and on to Sing Gomba or Gosainkunda. Or you can walk for less than **ten minutes** downstream on the Bhote Kosi, take a left fork before some *mani* walls, and climb for about **six hours** to Sing Gomba and Chauchan Bari, the new HMG cheese factory (10,625 ft, 3239 m). This could provide a pleasant side trip for those basically retracing their steps to Trisuli, or it would be appropriate for trekkers who wish to visit the Gosainkund Lakes and cross over to Helambu. If taking this fork, climb steeply through chir pine forest to a *chorten* (6950 ft, 2118 m) in **two hours**. Another **fifteen minutes** brings you to a clearing with another *chorten* and good views north and west. Continue through wheat fields to **Bhrabal** (7450 ft, 2271 m) in a **few minutes**. About 125 ft (40 m) above this pleasant village, the trail intersects the trail from Bharku to Syabru at a *chautaara* and *mani* wall. However, continue climbing steeply up to the ridge, leaving terraces (8950 ft, 2728 m) after another **1½ hours** and climbing through oak forest. In an **hour** reach a clearing (10,250 ft, 3124 m) where the trail from Syabru joins. There are good views up the Langtang Valley and to the west. Climb for a **minute**, then take the right fork, which contours through blue pine forest to reach a clearing (10,450 ft, 3185 m) in **half an hour**. Here the trail to Gosainkunda, beginning from across the Trisuli Khola at Dhunche, enters. Do not climb, but continue contouring through an impressive fir and rhododendron forest to reach **Sing Gomba** and the cheese factory, Chauchan Bari (10,625 ft, 3239 m) in **half an hour**. Accommodation can be arranged here. The trail beyond to Gosainkunda has already been described.

SYABRUBENSI TO TRISULI

To head directly back to Trisuli from Syabrubensi, cross the Langtang Khola on the suspension bridge, and head downstream on the east (L) bank of the Bhote Kosi through chir pine forest. Follow the river, then climb to join the outgoing trail beyond **Bharku** (6125 ft, 1867 m) in **2½ hours**. The outward trail from this point has already been described.

8 NORTH OF POKHARA

(Map No. 3, Page 171)

> *If there be a Paradise on earth, it is now, it is now, it is now!*
>
> Wilfred Noyce describing the area above
> NagDAADa in *Climbing the Fish's Tail*

Pokhara, a very scenic spot itself, can be the starting point for at least five treks described in this book. The three described in this chapter are: the traditional trek to Thak Khola, Jomosom, and Muktinath; the trek to Manang starting at Dumre east of Pokhara; and the trip to the Annapurna Sanctuary. It is possible to combine all three in a circuit of the Annapurna massif with a visit to the so-called sanctuary. Such a trek combines spectacular mountain scenery with incredible ethnic and cultural diversity, and traverses through very different ecological life zones. This is justifiably a classic trek, among the world's best.

Many people take shorter journeys from Pokhara, for example going to GhoDapani and returning via Tatopani and Beni (allow a week), or a two-day trip to NagDAADa via Suikhet, returning via Sarangkot and Phewa Tal. Another fine choice is a week-long trek to Ghandrung via NagDAADa and return via Dhampus.

Two other treks starting from Pokhara, to Dhorpatan and Kathmandu, are described in Chapter 11.

To Thak Khola and Muktinath

The trek from Pokhara to Jomosom on the Kali Gandaki, or the Thak Khola, as the river is called in its northern portions, is perhaps one of the easiest, most comfortable, and most popular treks in Nepal. There is relatively little climbing; cooked food and lodging are easily available along the entire route; and the terrain is more varied than on any other trek of comparable length. Although the route passes among some of the highest mountains in the world, the scenery is not as exciting as in, say, Khumbu. There are, however, several side trips that take the trekker up and out of the valleys and closer to the main Himalaya. Muktinath, a Hindu and Buddhist pilgrimage site, is a day's walk north of Jomosom.

Unless you plan a side trip to one of the uninhabited areas, there is no need to take food or shelter. *BhaTTI*, local inns, can provide *daal bhaat* and rooms to sleep in. Hotels in many villages offer food and accommodations that are more "Western" in style. These places are run by the *Newar, Thakali, Gurung*, and *Magar* ethnic groups.

Transportation from Kathmandu to Pokhara is available daily by air (RNAC) and by road, and from India by road. A walking route from Kathmandu is described in Chapter 11. You could take a plane to or from Jomosom to avoid backtracking, but this is not worth doing, since backtracking will increase your understanding and enjoyment of the area. Furthermore, it is difficult to count on getting a seat on

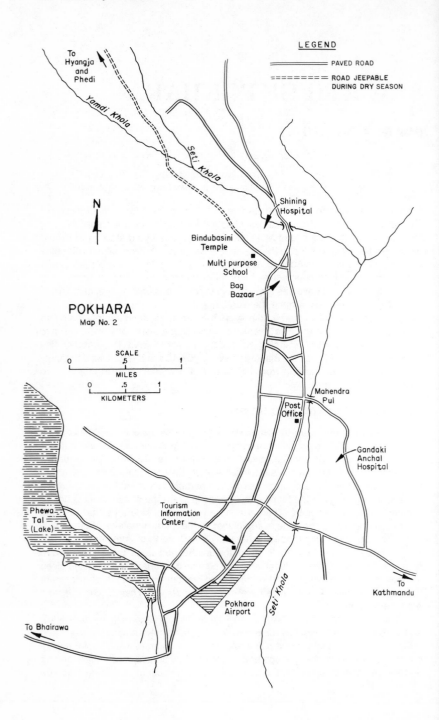

LEGEND

PAVED ROAD

ROAD JEEPABLE
DURING DRY SEASON

To
Hyangja
and
Phedi

Yamdi Khola

Seti Khola

N

Shining
Hospital

Bindubasini
Temple

Multi purpose
School

Bag
Bazaar

POKHARA
Map No. 2

SCALE

0   .5   1

MILES

0   .5   1

KILOMETERS

Post
Office

Mahendra
Pul

Gandaki
Anchal
Hospital

Phewa
Tal
(Lake)

Tourism
Information
Center

Seti Khola

Pokhara
Airport

To
Kathmandu

To Bhairawa

a scheduled flight to or from Jomosom. Flights are often canceled due to bad weather and the high winds.

As more roads are built, the question of using them arises. You can hire a jeep to take you up the Yamdi Khola Valley to Phedi, saving at least three hours of walking. If you prefer to walk but don't want to share the road with heavily laden jeeps, take the trail to NagDAADa from Phewa Tal, the lake at Pokhara. See page 184 for a description of the route in the reverse direction. My first trek in 1969 began from the airstrip in Pokhara because there was no road.

From the **Pokhara** airstrip (2686 ft, 819 m) you can now board a bus or taxi to Mahendra Pul in the downtown area. The bus from Kathmandu also brings you here. From Mahendra Pul take a bus or taxi to the Shining Hospital. Or you can walk. To do so, continue up to the upper end of the bazaar where the road descends a short hill. Near its bottom, an hour from the airstrip, turn left and head toward the Multi-Purpose High School and the Shining Hospital (the quonset huts in the field to your right). The first such nongovernmental facility established in Nepal, Shining Hospital has now merged with the Gandaki Anchal Hospital, which lies off the road to the south of Mahendra Pul. You can hire a jeep to Phedi at this field. If walking, continue north above the right fork of the Seti Khola, and after passing a river junction, cross the tributary Yamdi Khola to its left bank (3075 ft, 937 m). A Chinese hydroelectric project is under construction here. After passing through the small settlement of Yamdi, ascend to the Hyangja Tibetan Camp (3325 ft, 1013 m) **one hour** from the Shining Hospital. Food and lodging are available, and the handicraft center is well worth visiting. If you haven't seen a carpet factory in action, be sure to see the one here. The trail heads on to the town of **Hyangja** (3600 ft, 1097 m) in **forty minutes**, then enters the long, wide Yamdi Khola Valley, the floor of which is a series of irrigated rice paddies. Depending on the season, the route either goes through the paddies or follows the small irrigation ditch on the northeast side of the valley. **Suikhet** (meaning "irrigated fields") is the name given to the small settlement where the valley, after narrowing, opens up (3650 ft, 1113 m) to a few tea shops. **Phedi** (meaning "foot of hill") is at the bottom of the hill to the south (3700 ft, 1128 m). Reached just after crossing the Yamdi Khola, this area is at the western end of the paddies about **one hour** from Hyangja. Climb the hill through sal forest to the south and reach **NagDAADa** (4675 ft, 1425 m) on the ridge 1½ **hours** from Suikhet. The trail then goes west along the ridge. Phewa Tal, the lake at Pokhara, is visible to the southeast. There are stunning views of Machhapuchhre and the Annapurna range. Either on the way out or on the return trip, spend a night near here or near Chandrakot to get clear morning views of the range. NagDAADa, meaning "sharp ridge like a nose," is an appropriate name for this town. NauDAADa, usually spelled Naudanda by Westerners, means "nine ridges" and is clearly not the correct name. NauDAADa is a village on the road south of Pokhara. But the incorrect name is the common one here.

About five to ten minutes west of where you reach the ridge, and 125 ft (38 m) higher, the trail to Kusma forks left. Keep close to the ridge on the main trail and bear northwest through countryside reminiscent of Scottish highlands. Pass through **Paundur** (5650 ft, 1722 m) to the village of **KAAre** (5700 ft, 1737 m), which is in a pass. Continue through Jaljala (5275 ft, 1608 m) and **Lumle** (5300 ft, 1615 m) to **Chandrakot** (5250 ft, 1600 m) at the west end of the ridge. Reach KAAre in 1½ **hours** from NagDAADa, Lumle in another **forty-five minutes**, and Chandrakot in another **half hour**. Lumle is the site of a British agricultural development project where former Gurkha soldiers are trained in farming. It has one of the highest rainfalls in Nepal.

The views from Chandrakot, as from NagDAADa, are unforgettable. You will cross the Modi Khola, which flows south between the peaks Annapurna South and Machhapuchhre shortly. The Annapurna Sanctuary, which lies up river inside the gate formed by Machhapuchhre and Hiunchuli, the peak east of Annapurna South, is a worthwhile side trip.

The trail descends to the Modi Khola, follows its east (L) bank southward a short distance to a suspension bridge, and crosses to the prosperous town of **Birethanti** (3600 ft, 1097 m) **1¼ hours** from Chandrakot. This is a good place to stock up on supplies, because prices go up the farther you get from Pokhara. From here, one trail heads up the Modi Khola on its west (R) bank toward the Annapurna Sanctuary. The trail to Thak Khola heads west. Just up from the town by a picturesque waterfall is a cool pool on the Bhurungdi Khola. If you swim here, be sure to wear clothing in order not to offend the Nepalis. Follow the Bhurungdi Khola westward through forests at first. Stay on its northeast (L) bank, passing a steel suspension bridge. Cross several tributaries, then pass through two settlements, Lamthali and Sudame. In times of low water the trail may even cross the main river to avoid steep areas. Do what the locals are doing, but stay on the northeast (L) bank except for these short diversions. **Hille** (5000 ft, 1524 m) is reached in **two hours**, and shortly beyond is **TirkheDUgaa** (5175 ft, 1577 m). Farther on the branches of the Bhurungdi Khola are crossed on several bridges (5075 ft, 1547 m). The steepest climb so far, up to **Ulleri** (6800 ft, 2073 m), takes **two hours** from Hille.

If you want to pace the climb, there are 3767 steps to ascend to Ulleri; trekker Lance Hart counted them! Note the handsome slate roofs on the village houses. Near the last house is the new stone commemorating the death of a Dutch trekker. Higher up, at a *chautaara* on the left, is a worn rock tablet faintly inscribed as follows: "Once, sweet, bright joy, like their lost children, an Ulleri child." It is a memorial to 18-month-old Ben, the son of anthropologist John Hitchcock. Ben died here in 1961 while his father was doing field work.

From Ulleri, the trail climbs steadily, enters lush oak forest, and crosses numerous small streams. It is a great place for bird watching. An hour above Ulleri you come to Banthanti (7775 ft, 2307 m), meaning "a place in the forest," and an hour and a half later to Nayathanti (8550 ft, 2606 m), literally meaning "new place." New lodges in both villages cater to the great numbers of trekkers passing through in recent years. Lone trekkers have been attacked in this forest. If by yourself, hire a porter or join up with others. This caution applies all the way to Chitre. The trail emerges at **GhoDapani** (9350 ft, 2850 m), a cluster of hotels below the pass some **three hours** from Ulleri. GhoDapani, meaning "horse water," is now a far cry from the one building I saw on my first trek in Nepal in 1969. Then it truly was a watering place for the horse caravans that traveled between Pokhara and Mustang. There are more hotels at the pass, GhoDapani Deorali, which is 250 ft (76 m) higher than the town. Trekkers should make certain they catch the views, either from below the pass to the north, from the pass itself, which is now considerably deforested, or from the view tower at Poon Hill, which is 875 ft (267 m) higher than the pass on the ridge to the west. Reach the hill in less than an hour. Signs point the way to Poon Hill from GhoDapani and from the pass. Views of Dhaulagiri and the Kali Gandaki gorge are best in the early morning. From the pass, a trail follows the ridge to the east to link with the trail from Ghandrung. The views to the east along the ridge are very impressive too.

To continue to Thak Khola, descend through rhododendron forest, then prickly-leaved oak, to cultivated areas. Pass through the villages of **Chitre** (7600 ft,

JOINS MAP NO. 6

JOINS MAP NO. 9

LEGEND

Major Ridges and Passes
Rivers and Lakes
Road (Under Construction)
Trails
Air Strip

2316 m) and **Phalate** (7400 ft, 2256 m) before reaching **Sikha** (6300 ft, 1920 m) **two hours** from the pass. An unforgettable descent offers views of the immense south face of Dhaulagiri to the north. Descend, crossing a tributary and then some land-slides, to **Ghara** (5550 ft, 1692 m) **less than an hour** from Sikha.

Several large, dangerous landslides above and below the village of Sikha were triggered by a combination of natural forces (young mountains, steep terrain, loose wet soils) and man's activity (overgrazing and deforestation). Nepal faces a serious environmental crisis, but recently the government has joined up with inter-national donor agencies in an attempt to control the physical decimation of Nepal's forests, soil, and water. Along some trails you'll find newly built forest nurseries and vast tracts of recently planted tree seedlings.

Continue through a notch with a tea shop and descend to the south (L) bank of the Ghar Khola. Cross it on a wooden bridge (3850 ft, 1173 m) and reach the few houses called Ghar Khola above the junction of the Ghar Khola and the Kali Gan-daki. The trail to Beni crosses the Ghar Khola here to continue south on the east (L) bank of the Kali Gandaki. But you should head upstream, cross the Kali Gan-daki on a suspension bridge, and go on to **Tatopani** (4000 ft, 1219 m) **1½ hours** from Ghara.

The police check post is in the south end of town, off the west side of the trail. Several lodge keepers here have installed bio-gas plants to operate their stoves and lights, as much an energy-conservation measure as an economic one. Another has installed a hydro-generator to power the electric lights in his hotel.

Tatopani, a prosperous *Thakali* town, takes its name (literally "hot water") from the hot springs located along the banks of the river. One, near the middle of town, has been modified considerably from the simple pool I enjoyed on my first trip. Now the walls are cemented and the hot water piped in. The spring still soothes aching muscles, but it is not as clean as it used to be. Don't foul the water with soap. Wash in the river below the spring, rinse and then soak in the hot water. Another more primitive hot spring is on the other side of the river north of town. Cross the river on a temporary bamboo bridge five minutes beyond the town and walk back to the spring.

Head north from Tatopani, pass the few houses of Jaltal, and note the junc-tion of the Miristi Khola and the Kali Gandaki. If you venture from Lete to the north Annapurna Base Camp, you will reach this river in its upper portions. It could well be impossible to go upstream from here; there is no record of anyone having done so. Beyond, the trail actually tunnels through the hillside to a few more houses called Phuite. Stay on the west (R) bank of the Kali Gandaki and pass through Suki Bagar to reach **Dana** (4600 ft, 1402 m) after crossing a tributary, the Gatte Khola. This stretched-out town with a police check post is reached in about **1½ hours** from Tatopani. Farther north, don't cross the main river on the suspension bridge unless you are traveling during the monsoon. Instead, continue on the west (R) bank to Titre, then climb to the few houses of Rupse Chhaharo (5350 ft, 1631 m), named after the waterfall just beyond. Rupse Chhaharo is reached in **1¼ hours** from Dana.

There are two route choices beyond, taking the east (L) or west (R) bank. The east-side trail is probably safer in the monsoon, but inquire locally about conditions. Most trekkers take the more spectacular west-side route, rebuilt in 1982. It takes you higher, offers better views, and is wider and easier on the feet. Despite recent repairs, large rock- and earthfalls continue to create very dangerous conditions.

On the west-side route, climb above the tea houses of Rupse Chhaharo to reach **Kabre** (5600 ft, 1707 m) in less than **half an hour**. Kabre is the northernmost village inhabited by hill castes in the Kali Gandaki Valley. From Kabre, continue north along the steep cliffside to where the valley narrows spectacularly and the cascading river torrent resounds across the canyon walls. Probably the world's steepest and deepest large gorge, the gradient to the summit of Dhaulagiri is more than 1 mile (1.6 km) vertical to 1 mile (1.6 km) horizontal (1:1.05 to be exact). Just beyond the main gorge you can see the old trail, cut like a three-sided tunnel into the wall. Above it are older pilgrimage routes. Pilgrims traveled this dangerous trail to Muktinath as long ago as 300 B.C.

Beyond the most impressive narrow section, the trail crosses a boulder-strewn flat and reaches a *chautaara* where the east-side trail rejoins it a few minutes south of Ghasa (6700 ft, 2040 m). **Ghasa** is less than **two hours** from Kabre. It takes a half hour to get through this sprawling, flat-roofed Thakali village.

During the monsoon, follow the east-side trail between Rupse Chhaharo and Ghasa. From Rupse Chhaharo heading north, take the right fork and cross the Kali Gandaki on a wooden bridge. Climb **twenty minutes** to Kopche Pani, a small cluster of tea houses. A further **forty-five minute** steep climb on a scree-boulder trail brings you to a similar spot, Pahiro Tabla (meaning "landslide place"). As you go along, look for the old trail on the west side and the ancient pilgrim trails above it. Along the way, you may see monkeys in the forests. In **2¼ hours**, reach the bridge and trail junction (6600 ft, 2012 m) a few minutes below Ghasa.

Note how remarkably the land has changed over this short stretch, as the climate becomes colder and drier. To the south, you may see lizards throughout the year, but from here northward none are seen in the cold season. Similarly, as you head north, you will encounter more pine forests and fewer broad-leaved trees. The houses beyond here have flat roofs because there is less rainfall. The changes will be even more dramatic farther along.

To continue north from Ghasa, cross a tributary, and pass through Kalku and the few houses of Gumaaune (literally "walking around") to a cement suspension bridge over the Lete Khola (8000 ft, 2438 m), a tributary from the west. Cross it to some bamboo teahouses. **Lete** (8100 ft, 2469 m), some thirty minutes beyond, is two hours from Ghasa. There is a trail coming in from the southwest before you cross the Lete Khola. It offers a high route over the south shoulder of Dhaulagiri to Beni. Annapurna I, the first 8000-m peak ever climbed, can be seen to the east from Lete. Again, note the change in ecology. Lete gets 124 mm (49 inches) of rain a year while a mere half day to the north, Tukche gets only 20 mm (8 inches).

Heading north, pass through the spread-out village of Lete, which blends into **Kalopani** (8300 ft, 2530 m). Sunsets from Kalopani and Lete are memorable. West of here is one of the world's biggest open-book geological formations. Cross a tributary north of town to a good suspension bridge over the Kali Gandaki. Cross it in the dry season if there is a good temporary bridge to cross back over the Kali Gandaki farther upstream. Check what others are doing. If you cross to the east (L) bank here, the trail passes through Dhampu and Kokethani before crossing a suspension bridge back to the west (R) bank just below **Larjung** (8400 ft, 2560 m) **two hours** from Kalopani. In the monsoon, or if you wish to reach the area below the southeast Dhaulagiri icefall, stay on the west (R) bank and cross a river delta with its alluvial fan to reach the few houses of Chatang in half an hour. Just beyond is a *chautaara* with a plaque commemorating the 1969 Dhaulagiri tragedy, in which seven members of an American expedition were killed in an ice avalanche. The trail to the icefall cuts off left just to the north. If continuing on to Larjung, cross another tributary, enter a pine and juniper forest, then cross the broad delta of the Ghatte Khola, wading where necessary, to rejoin the forest. Larjung is just beyond, perhaps **1¾ hours** from Kalopani. To the west is the incredibly fore-shortened summit of Dhaulagiri, almost 3.5 mi (5.5 km) higher.

From Larjung, head north, cross a tributary, and in a few minutes enter the fascinating town of **Khobang** (8400 ft, 2560 m). The trail passes through a tunnel, and doors to the houses open off it. The village is thus protected from the strong winds that blow up the valley almost every afternoon. **Khobang** is getting electricity. Khobang is called Kanti in the northern portion. **Tukche** (8500 ft, 2591 m), a historically important town is an **hour** beyond.

Tukche was once an important center for the trade of Nepali grain for Tibetan salt through the valley of the Thak Khola. *Thakali Subbha,* or customs contractors, controlled it and exacted taxes at Tukche in the summer and at Dana in the winter. By the middle of this century competition had reduced this trade, and the enterprising *Thakali* turned their attention south and became more involved in business ventures around Pokhara and in the Tarai. Their spread throughout many of the trade routes in Nepal resulted in the establishment of many *bhaTTi,* even before trekking became popular. With the coming of foreigners, the *Thakali* developed hotel facilities for them. I urge you to try to find a traditional *bhaTTI* and sample a good Nepali meal of *daal bhaat tarkaari* (lentils, rice, and vegetables). The *Thakali* prosper in whatever they turn to. In comparing my visits to this region almost ten years apart, I find the improvements impressive—water systems, latrines, more schools, indeed functioning schools, better trails, more varieties of crops, and cleaner homes. Of course, all is relative. If this region strikes you as destitute and dirty, what would you think of the poor areas of Nepal? *Thakali* have always exhibited a strong ethnic group consciousness, and Thak Khola is their homeland. Tukche and the next two major towns, Marpha and Jomosom, have recently been electrified through the installation of a mini hydroelectric generator. It produces 200 kw and is located across from Khobang.

A strong wind blows from the south up the valley, beginning in the late morning and lasting most of the day. This is probably caused when the air mass over the plateau to the north warms, rises, and creates a pressure difference. The best time to head south is in the early morning when the wind is from the north. As you go up the valley from Tukche, notice there is relatively little vegetation on the valley floor itself, but there are trees and forests on the walls. The valley floor is in a rain shadow due to the strong winds. When the wind is blowing, you may notice that there are no clouds over the center of the valley, but clouds do hang on the sides.

A trail to Dhampus Pass (described later) goes up the hill to the west of the *gomba* at Tukche. The next town upstream is **Marpha** (8750 ft, 2667 m), some **1½ hours** away. Marpha, a charming town, has a fine sewer system — a series of canals flowing down the streets. About ten minutes before Marpha, pass by the Government Agricultural Station, which has introduced new crops into the area. You may be able to purchase fresh fruit and vegetables in season at the most reasonable prices in the area. Marpha's inhabitants call themselves *PaunchgaaUle,* people ethnically similar to the *Thakali.* Some of the hotels in Marpha, and also in Jomosom, advertise pony rides as far as Muktinath. The foot-weary trekker may welcome the opportunity to change his mode of travel. Dhampus Pass can also be reached from Marpha. To continue upstream, leave the town through the *chorten* and cross first a tributary, then another alluvial fan from the west, the Pongkyu Khola. Along the trail you will see willow plantations, part of a reforestation project. The town of Syang is beyond, and its monastery is up the hill a bit farther.

On certain days during late October to early December, monks stage dance

Masked Tibetan Buddhist Lama dancing at Tukche Gomba. (Donald Messerschmidt)

festivals in the *gomba* of Marpha, Syang, and Tukche. Somewhat similar to the Mani-rimdu festivals of Solu-Khumbu, they are definitely worth seeing. The Nepali name for such a festival is *dyokyapsi*.

Cross a tributary farther up the valley, and reach **Jomosom** (8900 ft, 2713 m), the center for Mustang District, 1½ **hours** from Marpha. There is a STOL airstrip here with scheduled service to Kathmandu. But because of the winds, service is rather unreliable. Winter winds regularly reach 30-40 knots with gusts to 70! Other facilities include banks, a hospital, radio service, rather luxurious food and accommodations with solar water heaters, and, of course, a police check post. This town has prospered immensely over the years and now has a large number of government employees who must be fed. Many of the pony caravans bring food to Jomosom.

The countryside to the north is very arid, not unlike the Tibetan Plateau farther north. To the south, Dhaulagiri impressively guards the Thak Khola Valley. It is much less foreshortened than at Larjung. To the east, across the river on a shelf of land, is the town of Thinigaon (9500 ft, 2897 m), reached in half an hour from Jomosom. The inhabitants are technically not Buddhists (though they may say otherwise) but followers of Bon-po, the ancient religion that antedated Tibetan Buddhism. Up the valley east of Thinigaon is Tilicho Pass and Tilicho Tal. The latter, at 16,140 ft (4919 m), is one of the highest, most spectacular lakes in the world. Once open to trekking, this area has recently been closed to access from Jomosom because of a Nepali army camp this side of the pass. The ban may someday be lifted. It takes at least two days to reach the lake from the valley floor, and caution must be exercised because of the rapid ascent.

To continue on to Kagbeni and Muktinath, head northeast on the west (R) side of the Kali Gandaki (you could also take the east (L) side, but this would probably require more river fording). Stay on the valley floor close to the river. In 1¼ **hours** reach a wooden cantilever bridge over the Kali Gandaki (9000 ft, 2743 m). You may need to wade some rivulets here. Once on the east (L) bank, head upstream for **ten minutes** to the trail junction of Chyancha-Lhrenba (9050 ft, 2758 m). This place is known locally as Eklai BhaTTi, meaning "lonely inn." The left fork continues up the river to **Kagbeni** (9200 ft, 2804 m) in **half an hour,** while the right ascends out of the valley and heads more directly to Muktinath. The right fork reaches the junction (10,350 ft, 3155 m) of the trail from Kagbeni to Muktinath in 1½ **hours**. The name Kagbeni aptly reflects the town's character—*kak* means blockade in the local dialect, and *beni* means junction of two rivers. And this citadel does effectively block the valley. River junctions are especially sacred to the local people. Since the town is at the confluence of trails from the north, south, east, and west, the ancient king who sat here could control and tax the exchange of grain from the south and wool and salt from the north. The ruins of his palace, which can still be seen, are a reminder of the ancient kingdoms that predated the unification of Nepal. Some scholars believe the family that ruled here was related to the ancient kings of Jumla. The Sakyapa monastery here is rundown, but worth a visit. You may see two large terra-cotta images of the protector deities of the town—a male at the north end and a female at the south. This mingling of old animistic beliefs with those of the more developed religions is common in Nepal. People here call themselves *Gurung,* but are clearly not the same as the *Gurung* to the south. People from Tibet who have settled in Nepal often call themselves *Gurung* to facilitate assimilation. This practice has continued with the recent immigration of Tibetan refugees in the 1980s.

The impressive folding of the cliffs west of town illustrates the powerful forces of orogeny. You can just make out the crest of the Thorong La Pass up the valley to the east of town. Try to make out Kagbeni from the pass. The trail to Mustang and the Kingdom of Lo crosses the Kali Gandaki here and heads up the west (R) bank. There is a police check post in Kagbeni, currently the northern limit for trekkers.

To go to Muktinath from Kagbeni cross the Dzong Khola, the tributary to the east, and head east through terraces to the trail's junction (10,350 ft, 3155 m) with the trail from Chyancha-Lhrenba in 1½ **hours.** Continue east, noting the caves on the north side of the valley. So ancient are these caves that no one remembers if they were used by hermits or troglodytes. On a clear day, the walk can be ethereal, as the dry valley sparkles and the north wall seems suspended close to you. Contour above the town of Khyenghar (Khingar on some maps) to **Jharkot** (11,850 ft,

3612 m), an impressive fortress perched on a ridge 1½ **hours** from the trail junction above Kagbeni. Jharkot, called Dzar by Tibetans, is believed to have been the home of the ruling house of this valley. Note how some houses around the ruins of the fort are made of blocks of earth.

Continue climbing and contouring, often staying near an irrigation trough. Along the trail there are little piles of stones made by pilgrims returning from Muktinath in hopes of obtaining a better reincarnation. Go on to Ranipauwa (12,225 ft, 3726 m), a large tin-roofed building in disrepair, surrounded by a village of sorts. It is **forty minutes** from Jharkot. Across the valley you can see the extensive ruins of Dzong ("castle" in Tibetan) and the town built around it, the original seat of the king of this valley. **Muktinath** (12,475 ft, 3802 m) is less than **ten minutes** farther. Dhaulagiri looms impressively to the south.

Muktinath, located in a poplar grove, is a sacred shrine and pilgrimage site for Hindus and Buddhists. The Mahabharata, the ancient Hindu epic written about 300 BC, mentions Muktinath as Shaligrama because of its ammonite fossils called 'shaligrams'. Brahma, the creator, made an offering here by lighting a fire on water. You can see this miracle (burning natural gas) in a small Buddhist shrine *(gomba)* below the main Hindu temple *(mandir)*.

Hindus named the site Muktichhetra, meaning "place of salvation," because they believed that bathing there gives salvation after death. Springs are piped into 108 water spouts in the shape of boars' heads near the temple dedicated to Vishnu, the focal point for Hindus. Because Buddha is the eighth incarnation of Vishnu, the Hindus tolerate the Buddhists here. The Buddhists consider the image of Vishnu in this typically *Newari* style temple as the Bodhisatva, Avalokiteshwara. Vishnu is in the shape of an icon as well as a large ammonite fossil. The same fossil image is worshipped by Buddhists as Gawa Jogpa, the "serpent deity."

The miraculous fire revered by Buddhists and Hindus burns on water, stones, and earth and is inside the Jwala Mai Temple, south of the police check post. Natural gas jets burn in small recesses curtained under the altar to Avalokiteshwara. On the left the earth burns, in the middle water burns, and on the right the stone burns. One flame has died out; only two remain lighted. Your Sherpas and other Buddhist porters may ask you for a bottle to take some of the "water that burns" with them. Be sure to leave an offering of money for temple upkeep.

Padmasambhava, who brought Buddhism to Tibet in the eighth century, is believed to have meditated here. His "footprints" are on a rock in the northwest corner of this sacred place. On their way to Tibet, the eighty-four *siddha* (or great magicians) left their pilgrim staffs, which grew into the poplars at the site. You will find many old *chorten* and temples cared for by Nyingmapa nuns or old women from the nearby villages. A full moon is an especially auspicious time to visit Muktinath. In the full moon of August-September, thousands of pilgrims arrive for the main religious festival. At about the same time, local Tibetan villagers of the valley hold a great horse festival called *Yartung* — a time of horse racing, gambling, and general merriment.

Many people from Mustang and other areas come to sell handicrafts to the pilgrims. Some sell the *shaligram,* a mollusk fossil called an ammonite from a period roughly 140 to 165 million years ago. These objects, treasured for worship by Hindus, are said to represent several deities, principally those associated with Vishnu, the Lord of Salvation. You are apt to find them along the flats north of Jomosom.

To the east is the Thorong La Pass (17,650 ft, 5380 m) leading to Manang.

A trading caravan on the upper Thak Khola. (Donald Messerschmidt)

Crossing the pass from Muktinath to Manang is more difficult than crossing in the other direction, for in the dry season there are few if any suitable campsites with water on this side of the pass. It is a very long day to ascend from Muktinath to the pass and then to descend to the first campsite on the other side. Altitude illness may jeopardize those who are unacclimatized. Crossing from Manang, on the other hand, is easier because of the comparatively long time spent at high altitudes before approaching the pass, and because of the higher campsites below the east side of the pass. The pass is often crossed from Muktinath, but it certainly is more difficult and hazardous. Under no condition should you ascend from either direction unless the entire party, including porters, is well equipped to camp in snow should a storm arise. The trail descriptions for the Manang to Muktinath crossing are given with the Manang section later in this chapter.

On the return journey, consider some variations such as: returning to Marpha via Thinigaon, approaching from Jomosom on the east (L) bank of the river; crossing to the east (L) bank near Larjung and Khobang and following this side to Dhamphu opposite Kalopani; following the east (L) bank through the narrow gorge between Ghasa and Dana; returning to Pokhara by following the Kali Gandaki south from Tatopani past Beni, Baglung, Kusma, and east to Pokhara. This last variation is described in greater detail later, but first some side trips out of the Thak Khola Valley are described. All are strenuous trips to substantial altitudes where food, fuel, and shelter must be carried. At certain times of the year, snow can make the trips almost impossible. Parties should be prepared for cold at any time of the year. It is always best to have someone along who is familiar with the route. You could climb out of the valley at other points and get good views of the mountains.

Cumulative trekking times (walking time only, does not include rests or stops) from Shining Hospital to:

Phedi	2¾	hours	Kabre	25	hours
Suikhet	4¼	"	Tukche	30	"
Chandrakot	7	"	Jomosom	33	"
Ulleri	12¼	"	Kagbeni	35	"
GhoDapani	15¼	"	Muktinath	39	"
Tatopani	19¾	"			

DHAMPUS PASS

Dhampus Pass (17,000 ft, 5184 m) connects the valley of the Thak Khola with Hidden Valley. It lies beyond the tree line and is often snowed in. Huts used for pasturing yaks can be used for shelter and cooking en route to the pass. There are no facilities at the pass. Carry food, fuel, and shelter. Temperatures below freezing can always be expected and in the winter months the temperature drops below 0° F (– 18° C). A trip to the pass is ideal for those who want a more intense experience with the mountains. Reach it from Tukche or Marpha by going to some yak huts (13,000 ft, 3962 m) the first day, and to the pass the next. This may be too rapid an ascent for many people. If you are unprepared to spend a night at the pass, you could go up and return to the yak huts in a day.

To trek from Tukche to Dhampus Pass, go to the large open field at the north end of the village. Just behind the village, to the east, is a steep earth cliff. Follow a plainly defined switchback trail to the top and continue along the ridge behind the cliff. You pass through scattered apricot trees and horse pasturage for a mile to arrive at the base of a high rock cliff. Keeping well to the east, the trail ascends this steep, but not technically difficult cliff, and comes out just above where the ridge plunges down to the Kali Gandaki far below. You are now on the end of the ridge defining the north side of the Dhampus Khola. There are fantastic views up the Kali Gandaki toward Mustang, and a panorama from Tilicho Peak in the east round through the Nilgiris, the Annapurnas, and Dhaulagiri to Tukche Peak in the southwest.

Up to this point, the trail is fairly well defined. But on the ridge it degenerates into myriad cow and yak trails, and you are pretty much on your own. Continue up the north side of the ridge for about two hours until you come to a low point (relatively speaking), then cross the south (Dhampus Khola) side of the ridge. Looking up the Dhampus Khola Valley, you can see a large rock ridge going off your ridge and dropping steeply into the Khola. It is perpendicular to your line of travel. Traverse upward slightly toward this ridge to a wide trail, which takes you around and behind the ridge. This is the main trail to the upper portion of the Dhampus Khola Valley, and is used by local herders taking their yaks up to graze druing the summer. Yak yogurt is delicious and during the warm season you should try to buy some at the herders' huts along the way.

After crossing the rock ridge, climb obliquely upward by obvious routes to Dhampus Pass, which is not visible at this point. If there is any possibility of cloudy weather, hire a local man from Tukche as a guide. Once clouds settle in, it is very easy to get lost. If fog becomes a problem, don't descend to the Dhampus Khola to escape, since the Khola is impassable due to rock cliffs in its lower portions. If you become confused in a fog, stay up high and traverse eastward back toward Marpha or Tukche. Again, be sure to descend if severe symptoms of altitude sickness come on.

Beyond the pass, you can descend into the upper (southern) end of Hidden Valley for excellent views of Dhaulagiri's north face and the glaciated pass called French Pass, which lies between Dhaulagiri and its sister peak to the west, Dhaula Himal. You may see the remains of a plane near the pass, the Swiss Pilatus Porter that crashed in 1961 while ferrying people and loads from Pokhara for the Dhaulagiri Expedition. You may encounter semi-wild yak herds, snow leopards, and mountain sheep in Hidden Valley.

DHAULAGIRI ICEFALL

The area below the east Dhaulagiri icefall abounds with yak pastures and was the location of the 1969 American Base Camp. At a lower altitude than Dhampus Pass, it has correspondingly less severe conditions. The views of the mountains are excellent, possibly better than at Dhampus Pass.

To reach this area, proceed from the trail junction north of the few houses of Chatang between Kalopani and Larjung. The trail leaves the valley near a *chautaara* with a plaque commemorating the seven members of the 1969 American Expedition to Dhaulagiri who died in an ice avalanche. Again, it is best to hire a local guide. The area below the icefall (12,400 ft, 3780 m) can be reached in a day from the Kali Gandaki. Beware of avalanches in the vicinity of the icefall.

NORTH ANNAPURNA BASE CAMP

The route to the original Annapurna Base Camp was discovered by the 1950 French Expedition to Annapurna led by Maurice Herzog. The French first tried to climb Dhaulagiri, but found it beyond their capabilities, and instead tried to find a way to the base of Annapurna. They had difficulty getting there from the Kali Gandaki, and the route still has a bad reputation. It is seldom used except by shepherds and mountaineering expeditions. However, in the relatively snow-free early fall and late spring, the route is neither very difficult nor dangerous. The trail is often indistinct and traverses steep grassy slopes. Porters do not like this trail, but it is certainly no worse than little-used trails in many other areas of mountain wilderness.

The views along the way are spectacular. As the trail climbs steeply out of the Kali Gandaki Valley, the incredible gorge becomes more and more impressive. The views of Dhaulagiri and Annapurna from the crest of the ridge separating the Kali Gandaki from the Miristi Khola are breathtaking. Only from this perch (14,000 ft, 4267 m), some 7000 ft (2134 m) above the valley floor, can you appreciate just how high these mountains are. It is hard to believe that Dhaulagiri is the sixth highest mountain in the world from the foreshortened view from Kalopani. If you venture beyond the base camp toward Camp One on the north side of Annapurna, you can appreciate the impressive features of that side of the mountain.

There are neither villages nor shelter from Chhoya onward, so you must be self-sufficient for at least five days. It is best to hire someone from Chhoya to show the way. In times of high water, it may be impossible to cross the Miristi Khola and reach the base camp without building a bridge, an undertaking most trekkers prefer to avoid. But with the increasing number of expeditions to Annapurna, the chance of finding a usable bridge is good. Check beforehand to find out if there has been a recent expedition. In low water the river can be forded with some difficulty downstream. If there is no bridge, consider at least climbing to the height of land for the spectacular views.

If you are coming from the south, turn off the regular trail just after crossing the Lete Khola on a new suspension bridge. Keep close to the Kali Gandaki for some **ten minutes** before crossing the tumultuous river on a wooden bridge to reach Chhoya (8000 ft, 2484 m). If you are coming from the north, take a left fork a **few minutes** before reaching Lete and after passing through Upala Lete (8150 ft, 2484 m). This left fork takes you through a beautiful pine forest before you descend slightly in **ten minutes** to the same wooden bridge to Chhoya. You can get provisions in Chhoya or in Lete. From Chhoya, cross the delta of the Polje Khola and ascend to the few houses of Polijedanda (8175 ft, 2492 m). Then turn right and head southeast to the few more houses of Deorali (8275 ft, 2522 m) **half an hour** from Chhoya. This is the last village on the route. Here the trail forks left and you contour above fields to enter the valley of the Tangdung or Bhutra Khola, a little more than **half an hour** later. Contour below a small waterfall of a tributary to the main river (8075 ft, 2461 m) after a short, steep descent through forest. The river is 1¼ **hours** from Deorali. There should be a wooden bridge here unless it has been washed out during the monsoon. Fill up all your water containers as you may not get another chance during the next day.

The next section of the trail ascends 6000 ft (1829 m) and is unrelentingly steep. There are few suitable camping sites until near the end of the climb. After crossing to the southeast (L) bank, ascend a cliff and enter a mixed broad-leaved forest. The trail is easy to follow and the forest is pleasant. There are occasional vistas to inspire the weary. In the upper reaches you find areas of bamboo, then rhododendron, fir, and birch forests. In 2½ **hours**, reach a saddle called Kal Ghiu (11,000 ft, 3383 m). Some trekking groups call this place Jungle Camp. Camping is possible here if you can find water down the other side of the saddle. Keep close to the crest of the ridge as you pass several notches. Enjoy the rhododendrons in bloom in the spring. After keeping to the southeast side of the ridge and leaving the forest, the trail becomes fainter, reaches a minor ridge crest (12,600 ft, 3840 m), and crosses over to the northwest side. Keep climbing to a prominent notch with a *chorten* (13,350 ft, 4069 m) some **two hours** from Kal Ghiu. The views of Dhaulagiri are unforgettable.

The slope eases off now, and continues over more moderate grazing slopes to a place near a ridge crest called Sano Bugin (13,950 ft, 4252 m) where herders stay during the monsoon. There are rock walls here that the herders convert to shelters with the use of bamboo mats. If there is no snow to melt, water may be difficult to obtain. The gigantic west face of Annapurna, a challenge for rock climbers of the future, is before you. Head north along the ridge crest, or on the west side. The trail is marked with slabs of rock standing on end. In an **hour,** reach another ridge crest (14,375 ft, 4382 m) and cross to the southeast side of the ridge. This may be the "passage du avril 27" that Herzog's expedition discovered in order to get to the base of Annapurna. You are now in the drainage area of the Miristi Khola, the river that enters the Kali Gandaki above Tatopani.

Continue contouring for a **few minutes** to Thulo Bugin (14,300 ft, 4359 m) where herders stay. There is a small shrine here. Contour, crossing several tributaries of the Hum Khola, a tributary of the Miristi. The last stream (13,375 ft, 4077 m), reached in **half an hour,** is a little tricky to cross. Climb on, at first gradually, then more steeply, to reach a flat area sometimes called Bal Khola (14,650 ft, 4465 m) in **1¾ hours.** Camp here, for there are few other suitable places until the river is reached. The west face of Annapurna looms before you. Local people do not venture much beyond here in their tending of sheep and goats.

Descend and round a ridge crest to the canyon of the Miristi Khola proper. The river is almost a mile below you, yet its roar can be heard. Continue on steep grassy slopes and pass an overhanging rock (14,075 ft, 4290 m) suitable for camping **forty-five minutes** from the high point. Descend more steeply on grass, cross a stream, and go down into shrubbery until it appears that a 1000 ft (300 m) cliff will block the way to the valley floor. The trail heads west to a break in the rock wall, and descends through the break to the river (11,500 ft, 3505 m) **1½ hours** from the overhanging rock. The gorge at the bottom is most impressive and gives a feeling of relative isolation. Head upstream on the northwest (R) bank. The dense shrubs may make travel difficult. There are campsites by some sand near a widening in the river (11,575 ft, 3528 m) where it may be possible to ford in low water. Otherwise, head upstream for **ten minutes** to a narrowing where there may be a bridge. Cross the river, if possible, and camp on the other side if it is late.

Once on the southeast (L) bank of the Miristi Khola, follow the trail upstream. The vegetation soon disappears as altitude and erosion increase. The trail becomes indistinct in the moraine. As the valley opens up, bear right to the east and leave the river bottom to climb the moraine to a vague shelf. Continue beyond to a small glacial lake in the terminal moraine of the North Annapurna Glacier. Cross its outflow to the right and climb the lateral moraine to the left. There are views of the Nilgiris to the west. The base camp for the various attempts to climb Annapurna from the north is on a flat shelf of land (14,300 ft, 4359 m) to the north of the glacier. There is a steep drop-off to the glacier valley to the south and east. The base camp is reached in **three to four hours** from the crossing of the Miristi Khola.

The view of Annapurna I from the base camp is minimal. Better views can be obtained by contouring and climbing to the east to a grassy knoll from which much of the north face can be seen. You could also proceed toward Camp I by dropping from the shelf and climbing along the lateral moraine of the glacier to 16,000 ft (4877 m). Exploratory and climbing journeys will suggest themselves to those with experience. The Great Barrier, an impressive wall of mountains to the north, separates you from Tilicho Tal. Be sure to take enough food to stay awhile and enjoy this unforgettable area.

TILICHO TAL

To reach Tilicho Tal from Thak Khola proceed up the trail from Thinigaon (9500 ft, 2895 m). The trail winds up the north side of the valley leading to the pass to the east. There is little or no water along the lower part of the route. Pass through rhododendron, fir, and birch forests to reach alpine vegetation. Soon after crossing two tributaries, the trail leads to a *goTh* (14,000 ft, 2468 m) some **six hours** from Thinigaon. Another **day** takes you over the Tilicho Pass (16,730 ft, 5100 m) to the majestic ice walls beyond. The pass itself is not clearly seen from the *goTh*. It is glaciated, so those who are not equipped for ice climbing may prefer to head up one of the gullies north of the pass. The climb is higher, up to 17,500 ft (5334 m) or so, but the route is preferable for most parties. A trip to the lake and climbs of nearby summits are rewarding. The lake is often frozen. Trekkers attempting to climb up to the lake from the valley in two days must be especially watchful for signs and symptoms of altitude sickness. They should descend at the first signs of severe symptoms. You can also reach the lake from the east, heading up from Khangsar in Manang.

TATOPANI TO POKHARA VIA BENI

The return to Pokhara from Tatopani via Beni mentioned earlier involves less climbing and does not necessarily take more time. It is not advisable to go this way in late spring as it is much hotter than on the higher route. To proceed from Tatopani, cross the suspension bridge to the east (L) bank of the Kali Gandaki and cross the wooden bridge over the Ghar Khola to its south (L) bank to rejoin the Kali Gandaki. Proceed south on its east (L) bank.

After several hours on the trail, which in places is carved into the rock cliff and passes through subtropical valley forests, cross to the west (R) bank at Tiplyang (3400 ft, 1037 m) and climb high up the west (R) bank. Eventually descend to **Ranipauwa** (3900 ft, 1189 m), also called Galeshwar, and cross the tributary RahughaT Khola. Ranipauwa, some **six hours** from Tatopani, is the site of the annual *mela* (fair) that is usually in mid-November or early December.

An **hour** after crossing the tributary, come to a suspension bridge over the

Village men carrying suspension bridge cables to the construction site on the Kali Gandaki. (Donald Messerschmidt)

Kali Gandaki, just before **Beni** (2700 ft, 823 m), the administrative center for Mayagdi District. If spending the night in Beni, it is preferable to stay near the bridge (Kali Pul), where the breeze will keep mosquitoes away and there may be less noise. If you cross the bridge to the left bank, you will bypass the important administrative and market town of Baglung (3200 ft, 975 m). Allow **three hours** to walk the trail to Khaniyaghat below and on the side of the river opposite Baglung. The view of the south face of Dhaulagiri from Baglung is quite incredible. Alternatively, by staying on the west (R) bank, and crossing the Mayagdi Khola at Beni, you can reach **Baglung** high above the river in **three hours.** Descending and crossing the Kali Gandaki to its east (L) bank, you can reach **Khaniyaghat** (2725 ft, 831 m) in **half an hour.** In winter and spring this area is a paper-making center, producing paper for UNICEF greeting cards. Bark from the Dafne tree, a large shrub that grows up in the hills west and north of Baglung, is made into pulp and then paper, using simple screens. By proceeding to Balewa, three hours south of Baglung, you could reach an airstrip with regular RNAC service to Kathmandu.

From Khaniyaghat, continue south through sal forest to reach **Shastradara** (2550 ft, 777 m) in an **hour.** The trail follows close to the river to reach **Armadi** (2575 ft, 785 m) in **forty-five minutes.** Then climb a ridge to enter a wet subtropical forest leading to **Chamalgai** (3050 ft, 914 m) in another **forty-five minutes.** The cobbled path continues to Kusma (3000 ft, 914 m), the district center of Parbat District, in **half an hour.**

From Kusma there are two routes to Pokhara. One, which reaches the road south of Pokhara, is shorter and involves less climbing than the route described here. But it is much less scenic. This route is described going the other direction to Dhorpatan in Chapter 10.

For the other route, take the left fork at the east end of Kusma. Contour to the east and descend after **forty-five minutes** to a suspension bridge over the Modi Khola (2500 ft, 702 m). Three rivers meet here. Ascend up the valley of the middle one, the Rati Khola, to Dobila (3000 ft, 914 m). Don't confuse this town with the Dobila east of Baglung. Back in wet subtropical forest, the trail ascends to **Tilhar** (3600 ft, 1097 m) and **Saliyan.** It reaches the Bhaudari Deorali Pass (5500 ft, 1676 m) in about **four hours** from the Modi Khola. From the pass, the trail contours below the village of Paundur (5500 ft, 1676 m) to NagDAADa (4782 ft, 1458 m) in another **four hours.** This town should not be confused with the Naudanda southwest of Pokhara.

There are two routes from NagDAADa to Pokhara. One, the route of ascent from the Yamdi Khola via Suikhet, enters Pokhara from the north. The other goes along the ridge crest east of NagDAADa to the town of Sarangkot (5200 ft, 1585 m). About **half an hour** east of NagDAADa, you reach a point on the ridge crest from which all the peaks from Dhaulagiri to Manaslu and Himalchuli can be seen. Soon after, descend to the west end of Phewa Tal (2500 ft, 762 m) and follow its north shore to the airstrip. Sometimes you can hire a dugout to ferry you across. It takes about **four hours** to reach the lake from NagDAADa and another **hour** to walk to the airstrip. There is also a trail from Sarangkot to the north end of Pokhara, reaching the main trail just north of Shining Hospital, near the Bindubasini temple.

The Modi Khola and the Annapurna Sanctuary

Walking the uphill staircases in Gurung country is a mantra.

Trekker Anne Outwater

The term Annapurna Sanctuary, coined by outsiders, denotes the high basin southwest of Annapurna and the headwaters of the Modi Khola. This vast amphitheatre, surrounded by Himalayan giants, was explored by Jimmy Roberts in 1956 and brought to the attention of the western world by the British Expedition to Machhapuchhre in 1957. The gigantic mountains named for the goddesses Annapurna and Gangapurna, important figures in Hindu myth and folklore, justify calling it a sanctuary. Its gate, the deep gorge between the peaks Hiunchuli and Machhapuchhre, marks a natural division between the dense rain forest and bamboo jungle of the narrow Modi Khola river valley and the scattered summits and immense walls of the mountain fortress inside. This area is also referred to as the Annapurna Base Camp and the Machhapuchhre Base Camp.

Trekking possibilities are varied. Those without time to head up to Thak Khola can make a circuit from Pokhara into the Sanctuary, in less than ten days, with little backtracking. However, to enjoy the route and the sanctuary itself without feeling rushed, plan to take two weeks. This area can be easily combined with the entire Annapurna circuit or with a trek to Jomosom that offers various link-up possibilities.

The route up the Modi Khola has always had a reputation among porters for being slippery and difficult. Indeed, back in 1969, on my first journey there, I had to chase after my porter, who ran ahead three hours towards Pokhara, rather than risk the possibility of going up the Modi Khola. Of course, when I had asked him previously about going up there, he said nothing in order to not disappoint me! While primitive lodges and inns that cater to the trekker now exist outside the inhabited areas, the trail hasn't changed much. It is always wet, and in the steep and slippery places a fall could be disastrous. But the trail doesn't live up to its old reputation; the route to the North Annapurna Base Camp is a much more serious undertaking.

Until recently, parties had to be self-sufficient north of Chomro. As mentioned, now you can hope to find cooked food and lodging. However, during peak traffic times in the autumn and spring, the inns may run out of food, while shelter space is quickly filled by the multitude of trekkers who must retrace their route on the upper Modi Khola. Prudence suggests carrying shelter and food at these times. During winter months, snowfall may make the trip difficult or impossible, and avalanche hazard can increase the risk. When there is little traffic, you can't count on the innkeepers being there, so ask at Chomro before venturing forth.

For those traveling from Pokhara, one access route to the Sanctuary leaves the trail (described on page 170) at Chandrakot. Routes from Phedi and KAAre will be described in the opposite direction as part of the circuit from Pokhara. If coming from the Thak Khola region you could leave the route at GhoDapani, Chitre, TirkheDUgaa, or Birethanti. These options will be described in the Chomro to Suikhet section, along with a new shortcut from the Sanctuary to Pokhara.

CHANDRAKOT TO ANNAPURNA SANCTUARY

Begin at the *chautaara* at **Chandrakot** (5250 ft, 1600 m) but instead of descending, contour north by some fields. Some **twelve minutes** later, pass through a fault in the rock. Reach a *chautaara* in **eighteen minutes** and take the left fork into an oak forest, reaching another fork **twenty-five minutes** later. The right branch heads over the ridge to Dhampus. Instead, go straight and descend to the few houses of Pathalikhet (4750 ft, 1448 m) **five minutes** beyond. Continue and cross a suspension bridge over a tributary valley and climb up the other side to contour past more homes. Then descend into a larger tributary valley with considerable erosion. Cross the river on rocks or a cantilever bridge in poor repair (4600 ft, 1402 m) **twenty-two minutes** from the previous bridge. Climb up and pass through the scattered houses of WAAD. At the junction **a half hour** beyond the previous bridge (4700 ft, 1432 m), take the left fork. Here you appear to leave the main trail, a series of steps that go to Landrung and another route to the Sanctuary. I recommend that you take the left fork and go via Ghandrung, an impressive *Gurung* village, and bypass Ghandrung on the return. The left fork contours a bit, then drops to the valley floor in an oak-forested tributary valley. Reach a suspension bridge over the Modi Khola (3875 ft, 1181 m) in **twenty minutes.** Cross it to the true right to the few houses of **Ghandruk Besi** (meaning foot of Ghandruk). If coming from Birethanti, keep close to the river and, passing fields and forests, reach this point in an **hour.**

Head upstream, cross a suspension bridge over a tributary (4125 ft, 1257 m), and begin a long climb along a remarkable staircase to reach **Thamle** (5600 ft, 1707 m) in **one hour and ten minutes** from the Modi Khola. There are a few hotels here in this entrance to Gurung country. Another **fifteen minutes** beyond are the few houses of Kimche (5775 ft, 1760 m). A trail forks left here to TirkheDUgaa in the headwaters of the Bhurungdi Khola, on the way to GhoDapani. Along the way, you would pass through the villages of Moriya, Dhansing, and Sabet, taking some **four hours** to reach TirkheDUgaa. You could travel from Thak Khola by this route instead of one of the other trails from GhoDapani or Chitre.

Cross a tributary by a suspension bridge a few minutes later and continue on these magnificent steps. Imagine the effort it took to construct them! Those coming from Landrung will join this trail just beyond a *chautaara* and by a *goTh* on the right side (6300 ft, 1920 m) **thirty minutes** beyond Kimche. Ahead is the large, affluent *Gurung* village of Ghandrung (also called Ghandruk). Their wealth comes from handsome pensions provided to *Gurungs* who have served as Gurkhas in the British Army. This income was one of several factors that changed their primary livelihood from herding and hunting to sedentary farming.

Reach **Ghandrung** (6600 ft, 2012 m) in **forty minutes** from Kimche. At the southern end of Ghandrung, the trail leads to Banthante and GhoDapani at least a day's walk. You can also join this trail by heading upstream by Kimrong Khola in the next major tributary valley to the north. Although usually wet, the trail has been recently improved and food and shelter may sometimes be obtained at Banthante. It takes **fifteen minutes** to pass through Ghandrung, and along the way you may be upset or pleased to hear the whistle of progress — a diesel-powered rice mill, an example of private enterprise. Sometimes, *Gurung* dancing and singing can be staged for trekkers willing to pay.

Leave the town, cross a tributary and mostly contour through fields and oak forest in a side draw to reach Kimrong Danda (7400 ft, 2255 m), a prominent notch with houses and lodges an **hour** beyond Ghandrung. Descend into the valley of the Kimrong Khola (also called Kymnu, Kyumnu, Kimnu) on a trail much improved over the one I got lost on in 1969. Just below the crest of the ridge take the right fork and descend steeply to reach the river in **forty-five minutes** (6050 ft, 1844 m). You can cross on a log or suspension bridge to reach the small settlement of Kimrong

Khola. An enterprising innkeeper posts a map sign outside his lodge with various destinations and trail times listed.

A trail heads upstream in this tributary valley to reach GhoDapani and Chitre. It joins the trail from Ghandrung below Banthante, reached in **four hours** (7200 ft, 2194 m). Food and lodging may be available here in peak season. Beyond, the trail climbs to the ridge (Deorali) and descends to GhoDapani (9600 ft, 2926 m) in **three hours.** Although more often used now, the trail is still indistinct, and a local guide may be helpful. From the ridge, (Deurali) you can descend to Chitre in **three hours.**

To continue to the Sanctuary, take the right fork near a *chautaara* and climb steeply in an oak forest, leveling out at 7250 ft (2210 m) after an **hour.** Contour to enter the main Modi Khola valley.

Here, by a house above the trail, with a *bhaTTi* below, there is an important junction (7175 ft, 2187 m), reached in 1¼ **hours** from Kimrong Khola. To define it, look down below you in the Modi Khola Valley and you will see what appears to be a terraced spur of land jutting out into the main valley. On the return you can take the right fork here and descend to this spur, cross the river beyond, and reach Landrung directly. This pleasant, direct route from Pokhara is now possible thanks to a new bridge over the Modi Khola.

But to head to Chomro, contour and climb to enter the tributary valley draining the south side of Annapurna South (left) and Hiunchuli (right), the major peaks before you. Descend to **Chomro** (also called Chomrong), a prosperous *Gurung* village (6725 ft, 2050 m) reached in **half an hour** from the trail junction. Pass the school 400 ft (122 m) above the center of town.

As mentioned before, there are lodges beyond that cater to the independent trekker during the peak season. These are usually simple bamboo, stone, and thatch structures that may or may not be functioning when you are there. Crowds may deplete the space and food. I mention current names of lodges in this area because they are used as place names too. Ask in Chomro for current information. Also, be aware that lodge locations may change as well. It is best to carry some food and shelter.

This trail has been littered beyond belief. When I first journeyed up there in 1969, not a single shred of litter could be found. Now you'll find much detritus — soggy toilet paper festooning branches, food wrappers, cans, tampons — all despoiling the area and the experience. Yet behind you, where Nepalis use the trails, the litter is much less apparent. Why? Clearly the Nepalis must be picking up after careless trekkers because few Nepalis journey into the sanctuary on their own. Do all you can to clean up litter: collect trash, build a fire and burn it, and carry out the remainder. Try to help preserve the area's sanctity.

From Chomro descend northward to cross the main tributary on a new suspension bridge (6200 ft, 1890 m) **twenty minutes** beyond. Climb through terraces and the few houses of Kilche (6700 ft, 2042 m) to contour and enter the main Modi Khola Valley, which you will follow for the next **two days.** The trail was previously used only by shepherds who drove their flocks of sheep and goats up during the monsoon to browse in the forests and the shrubbery above treeline.

You reach a *goTh* upon entering the main valley (7625 ft, 2324 m) 1½ **hours** beyond the suspension bridge. This place may sometimes offer food and shelter. Contour along a reasonable trail in an oak-rhododendron forest, reaching growths of bamboo as you go further up the valley. Tibesa (8050 ft, 2454 m), **forty-five minutes** beyond, may provide services. Reach Kuldi (8200 ft, 2499 m) in **twenty-five minutes** as you go through increasingly dense forest. In 1969, there was an empty stone hut here, the only such structure on the entire route. Now there is a simple inn. The trail drops slightly from here and then appears transformed into the stone staircases of the *Gurung* villages to the south, but with the addition of drainage ditches!

Above the main trail, reached by two feeder trails, is the former site of a British experimental sheep breeding project that functioned for about ten years. The handsome, sturdy buildings in this most picturesque setting may be converted to tourist hotels in the future.

The main mountain visible at the head of the valley is Annapurna III; Machhapuchhre, the "fish-tail" mountain whose name has been obvious for several days now, is off to the right. After you leave this improved trail, descend over a series of slabs, which require care to negotiate. Enter a dense bamboo rain forest. The area around Pokhara and south of the main Himalaya receives considerably more rainfall than almost any place in Nepal. South of Pokhara, the Mahabharat Lekh, the range of hills above the Tarai, is lower and doesn't block the northerly flow of moisture. The trail is always wet in this jungle.

Reach a clearing and another hut (not occupied in the autumn of 1982) in **thirty-five minutes** (7700 ft, 2347 m). Cross several substantial tributaries. The third has an overhanging rock upstream that could serve as a shelter in a pinch. Eventually, you reach Dovan (8550 ft, 2606 m), another inn in **one hour and twenty minutes**. The rhododendrons festooned with moss in the forest beyond are gigantic. There are hemlocks too but, because of excess rainfall, not as many as elsewhere at this elevation.

The Modi Khola seems much closer as you wend your way through the jungle. Across the valley, some thirty to forty minutes later, you'll see streams of water plunging thousands of feet into the river. At a very slight rise at the neck of the gorge, called Deorali (8950 ft, 2728 m), thirty-five minutes after Dovan, you'll find a small rock shrine (Panchenin Barha) and strips of colored cloth. Local custom dictates prohibiting buffalo, chicken, eggs, or pork north of here, or else risking the anger of the mountain gods, whose revenge will be sickness and death in your party. Nepalis explain the misfortune that has befallen some trekking groups and mountaineering expeditions in the Sanctuary by breach of this custom. Just beyond is a spot where you can stand closer to the center of the valley to see the torrent rushing below you and the weeping wall across from you. Shortly beyond, the forest opens slightly and again, by venturing closer to the river from the main trail, you'll see a hundred-foot waterfall thundering down this canyon.

Continue to a clearing and another inn (Himalaya Lodge) (9425 ft, 2873 m) **an hour** beyond Dovan. After another stretch of dense forest, the valley begins to open up. In **forty-five minutes** reach Hinko (10,300 ft, 3139 m), a large overhanging rock that can provide shelter and is sometimes used as an inn. If empty, please don't use it as a latrine.

The next hour or more of trail is subject to avalanches. You may find the remains of some near the trail. After heavy snowfall above, which may be rain along the trail, the safest course may be to wait a few days for the slopes to clear. Since none of the avalanche slopes can be easily seen from the valley floor, it is difficult to be sure when it is safe to proceed. If up in the Sanctuary, wait a few days if food supplies allow. Be aware that trekkers have been buried by avalanches along here.

Cross several streams and reach another Deorali (10,600 ft, 3231 m) **thirty-five minutes** from Hinko where there may be another inn. Notice the beautiful birch forests across the valley. Most of the trees have been cut on this side. You come to the inn at Bagara (10,825 ft, 3300 m) in **thirty minutes**. As you proceed along, you can admire before you the triangular snow and rock face of Gangapurna, which

On route to Annapurna Base Camp. (Stephen Bezruchka)

has actually been climbed.

Suddenly, you cross the imaginary gates and are inside the Sanctuary! A stream flows in from the west and a large grass-covered moraine is ahead of you, with more grassy slopes beyond. Reach a shelf with several inns, so-called Machhapuchhre Base Camp (12,150 ft, 3703 m) in 1¼ **hours**. There has not been a legally sanctioned expedition to Machhapuchhre since 1957, and that one stopped short of the summit. The west face of Machhapuchhre looms above you, but the other views are limited to Annapurna South to the west.

Be cognizant of the rapid gain in altitude, but if conditions permit, try and stay higher, to gain better views. The trail heads west in a trough between the morraine and the north slopes of Hiunchuli. In an **hour**, the half-way point to the Annapurna Base Camp is reached, a stone hut (12,925 ft, 3939 m) with food usually available. The views are much better from here, but are even more spectacular further on, at the Annapurna Base Camp, where food and shelter may be available. This flat area (13,550 ft, 4130 m) was first used by the British in their climb of the South Face of Annapurna in 1970. It is the coldest and windiest of all places to stay, but is well worth it if you are acclimatized and suitably equipped. Venture beyond to the crest of the moraine to gaze upon the awesome mountain walls. From left to right they are: Hiunchuli, Annapurna South, Fang, Annapurna, Annapurna III, and Machhapuchhre. Tent Peak and Fluted Peak, rising above the hills to the north, complete the unforgettable panorama. Wander around and feel at peace with the earth.

People with time and equipment may want to venture across the rubble-covered glacier to the north and explore further.

Cumulative trekking times (walking time only, does not include rests or stops) from Chandrakot to:

Ghandruk Besi	2	hours
Kimche	3½	"
Ghandrung	4¾	"
Kimrong Khola	8	"
Chomro	8½	"
Kuldi	11¾	"
Dovan	14¾	"
Machhapuchhre Base Camp	17¾	"

CHOMRO TO SUIKHET

This route avoids some backtracking and is now feasible because a new bridge has been constructed over the Modi Khola. It could be followed in reverse as a direct route to the Sanctuary.

From **Chomro** (6725 ft, 2050 m) climb back the way you came, passing the school to reach a *chautaara* at 7350 ft (2240 m) where you take the left fork, to contour and reach the trail junction as outlined before. This place (7175 ft, 2187 m), some **thirty-five minutes** from Chomro, is on the short section between the two tributary valleys. Below to the east is a spur of mostly terraced land that appears to jut out into the Modi Khola Valley. There is a house above the trail and a *bhaTTi* below. Take the left fork that descends steeply, going around and through terraced fields of millet. Take the steepest choice at trail forks. Near the spur of land, which is just a shoulder of the Kimrong Khola Valley, cross a fence to keep to the crest of the spur. Reach the few houses of Jinu (5775 ft, 1760 m), **forty minutes** from the junction. This is a settlement of Jaishi Brahmans.

Beyond, the trail drops on the south side of the spur, heading towards the Kimrong Khola. Just before reaching it, fork left to a log bridge (5250 ft, 1600 m), some **fifteen minutes** from Jinu. Cross the tributary and climb up the south bank, pass a few houses, and then return to the Modi Khola Valley at around 5425 ft (1653 m). Reach forest and go almost all the way around a small side valley before dropping down to the few tea shops of Himalkyo (5050 ft, 1539 m) some **thirty-five minutes** from the previous bridge. Drop another 75 ft (23 m) to the new suspension bridge over the Modi Khola and cross the river to the left bank. You are back in subtropical deciduous forest. Pass through some fields and the few houses of ChiURe, near a beautiful high waterfall. The trail keeps to the river until at 4725 ft (1440 m), a **half hour** from Himalkyo, it begins to climb. Pass another waterfall and continue climbing and contouring, reaching terraces. An **hour** from Himalkyo, reach a suspension bridge over a tributary (5175 ft, 1577 m). Some **five or ten minutes** beyond, reach the main trail from Landrung to Ghandrung (5325 ft, 1623 m). A short climb brings you to **Landrung** (also called Landruk), a large *Gurung* settlement. At a fork in the middle of town (5575 ft, 1699 m) take the right branch to contour southward.

Leave Landrung, crossing a tributary (5625 ft, 1714 m) a **few minutes** beyond, and enter a side valley a **half hour** later. Reach a stream and log bridge by a mill (5725 ft, 1745 m). Don't cross; instead, go upstream on the right bank for fifty feet to cross on a suspension bridge. Climb onto an open area, Medi (5950 ft, 1813 m), with a few tea shops, **thirty-five minutes** from Landrung. Fork left to climb and, **six minutes** later, take the left fork again to climb rather than stay level. **Ten minutes** beyond Medi, round a ridge to Naga (6100 ft, 1859 m) where there are a few tea shops.

Contour across an impressive slide to the shops of Tolka (5975 ft, 1821 m), **ten minutes** beyond. The trail now contours into a major tributary valley, that of the Ghirsung Khola. Reach a suspension bridge (6000 ft, 1829 m) twenty minutes from Tolka in this magnificent oak forest. Cross it and climb steeply at first, then less so for **an hour** to a *chautaara* (7075 ft, 2156 m) located in a small pass. Several trails emanate from here. You want the one that continues in the same direction you have been walking and crosses to the opposite side of the ridge. Contour the ridge (7175 ft, 2187 m) for about **ten minutes**, then descend close to the crest of the ridge, still remaining in the forest. Meet a trail coming in from the right, in a small open area, some **twenty-five minutes** from the *chautaara* (6750 ft, 2057 m). Descend slightly to the lodges and tea shops at Potana (6675 ft, 2034 m) **ten minutes** below the junction. Shortly beyond, the trail forks. The right fork, which goes through forest to KAAre, comes out at the pass just to the west. This route may be a useful link, depending on your plans.

To return to Pokhara, descend, reaching fields on the north side of a ridge in the Indi Khola Valley in **half an hour**. The village of **Dhampus** is spread out farther along this ridge. Reach the far end of town by the water tank (5700 ft, 1737 m) in an **hour** from Potana. The views of the giants to the north are worth waiting for if the weather is bad. One can continue along the ridge to Dhital, Henjakot, and Astam before descending to Suikhet at a narrowing in the Yamdi Khola Valley. Those wishing longer views along the ridge will enjoy taking this route.

Most trekkers will want to descend, following the stairs below the water tank at Dhampus, joining trails coming in from the right. Keep close to the crest of the hill, sometimes crossing terraces if that is what locals are doing. Reach a *chautaara* thirty-five minutes below (4575 ft, 1394 m) and descend into forests of chilaune trees. *Chilaune* means itch in Nepali, and if you rub sap of this tree on your skin, you will learn how it got its name. As you drop down to the Yamdi Khola Valley floor, you'll be impressed with this uncut forest so close to Pokhara. The people of Dhampus protect this forest. Reach the valley floor (3750 ft, 1143 m) and cross the stream, heading east (downstream). Phedi is an **hour** from Dhampus.

If taking this trail in reverse, look for the small (50-foot, 15-m) waterfall on the north side of the valley, near the start of the climb. The trail begins a few minutes beyond. Reach Phedi (3700 ft, 1128 m), the foot of the climb to NagDAADa, in ten minutes. You can walk to Pokhara or take a jeep, if one is available.

Cumulative trekking times (walking time only, does not include rests or stops) from Chomro to:

Landrung	3¼ hours	
Potana	6½	"
Phedi	7½	"

GHODAPANI TO GHANDRUNG OR KIMRONG KHOLA

Those trekkers combining a trip to Thak Khola (Jomosom, etc.) with a visit to the Annapurna Sanctuary can take a more direct route to or from the Sanctuary (depending on your direction of travel) than the one described above. The trail, however, is rugged and can be slick and treacherous when wet.

From GhoDapani (9600 ft, 2926 m) at the pass itself, follow the ridge east for about 1½ **hours** to another pass (Deorali—10,100 ft, 3078 m). There may be a tea shop here. The views along the way are magnificent. Some prefer this view area to Poon Hill. You may also reach this pass directly from Chitre without going to GhoDapani. Look for monkeys in the forest.

From Deorali, drop very steeply through forest eastward to Banthani or Thanti, meaning "clearing in forest," (7200 ft, 2194 m) in 1½ hours. Sometimes there is a hotel here. Climb 150 ft (46 m), then descend steeply for 1000 ft (305 m) and climb another 1000 ft to DAADapani, some 2½ hours beyond Banthanti, where there may be a tea shop. From here you can head east to Ghandrung in two hours or head northeast to the Kimrong Khola, which is crossed and followed downstream on the left bank to reach the trail junction already described in 2½ hours.

To Manang and Over the Thorong La

The Manang area was only recently opened to trekkers. It offers many of the same attractions of a trek to Jomosom via Thak Khola, except that the Marsyangdi Khola valley lacks the strong winds and associated dry vegetation near the river. Furthermore, the area does not abound with *Thakali bhaTTi*, and the clang-clong of horse bells of long caravans won't be heard. On the other hand, the Manangba, the people of Manang, are a most worldly ethnic group and some of the men may have traveled farther on the globe than you. The mountain scenery is perhaps more breathtaking than on the other side, if only because the peaks in the open Manang Valley are closer.

Enjoy it all. Cross the Thorong La Pass and circle the Annapurna massif. It is a walk of over 150 mi (330 km), but the rewards certainly compensate for the effort. The circuit takes at least three weeks, perhaps a week more than just walking to Manang and then retracing your steps, but this includes time for some diversions. To do the circuit, your entire party, including porters, should be totally self-sufficient for three or four days in order to cross the pass. There are now primitive *bhaTTi* temporarily set up on both sides of the pass so it is possible to cross without being self-sufficient. But the increasing popularity of this trek makes it difficult to be sure of finding space and getting food. Storms may also make it difficult to reach the *bhaTTi*. A number of trekkers have died because they pushed on in storms when not adequately prepared with food, clothing, and shelter. Otherwise, cooked food and shelter can be obtained over most of the route. Staples for the crossing can usually be purchased in Manang village. Crossings can be difficult or impossible if there is deep, soft snow on the pass. Such conditions can be expected from January to March, and often longer. Storms can threaten the party at any time, and it is prudent to wait them out or turn back rather than risk lives. Needless deaths have occurred here.

The route is described from Dumre on the Kathmandu-Pokhara Road. You could begin by walking directly from Pokhara to intersect the trail described here at either Khudi or near Tarkughat. The Khudi to Pokhara route is described briefly here, while the Tarkughat to Pokhara route is part of the Pokhara-Kathmandu trek described in Chapter 11.

Dumre (1500 ft, 457 m) is reached in some **five hours** by bus from Kathmandu, or 2½ hours from Pokhara (more or less, depending on road conditions). Board the bus in Pokhara at Mahendra Pul or at the main bus terminal at Chhaina Chowk just east of the town-airport road junction, on the south side of the Kathmandu-Pokhara road. In Kathmandu the staging area is near the post office at Sundhara, where buses leave early in the morning, or at the main bus terminal just east of the Tundikhel. (The bus terminals are often called *bas parak*, "bus park.")

Dumre is one of the many towns that have sprung up along the road to serve the needs of travelers, traders, and villagers. It is a principal staging area for people arriving and departing for the hinterland of the Marsyangdi Khola. This is a

Machhapuchhre from just north of Pokhara. (Stephen Bezruchka)

place to purchase a range of provisions at reasonable prices, although more and more, goods can be bought at main towns along the dry-weather feeder road that parallels the Marsyangdi Khola (west bank). As of this writing, the road goes as far as Bhote Wodar, but it is expected to reach Besisahar soon. Porters can be hired at Dumre or at the terminus of the feeder road, and sometimes a guide may also be engaged. The feeder road is passable by four-wheel vehicles from October to May or June, depending on weather conditions. Jeeps may be hired on a "reserve" basis (expensive) or you can pay by the seat (crowded but inexpensive). There is usually a nominal charge for baggage, in addition to the seat charge.

Those wishing to trek the entire way (and avoid the road) should get off the bus at Bimalnagar, east of Dumre. Cross the suspension bridge and walk up the east side of the Marsyangdi Khola. You can rejoin the trail described here at either Tarkughat, PhalenksAAghu, or Besisahar, or you can stay on the east side all the way to Syang. Bimalnagar to PhalenksAAghu takes about eight hours.

From **Dumre** head north and, just beyond the town, cross a small river by a series of rocks to the north (L) bank and follow the feeder road uphill. The trail follows the road except for shortcuts, which provide pleasant relief. In **fifteen minutes** turn right, off the road, and enter a subtropical deciduous forest. Then climb to the first few houses of **Bhansar** (1800 ft, 549 m) in **ten minutes**. Continue past dwellings until you reach a *chautaara* in the center of town and go on **for some fifteen minutes** to reach an oil mill (fuel-driven, it whistles when operating). Turn right here toward the Marsyangdi Khola, which you will continue to follow for many days. The trail stays well above the west (R) bank and reaches the small town of Barabise (1650 ft, 504 m) in **twenty minutes**. Reach Chambas (1759 ft, 533 m) in **forty-five minutes**, then **Turture** (1725 ft, 526 m) in another **forty-five minutes**. Turture sits above a suspension bridge over the Marsyangdi Khola. The Palungtar airstrip (RNAC's Gorkha field), directly across the river, is no longer served by scheduled flights.

Walk through Turture bazaar and descend at the north end to cross the Paundi Khola; continue north along the west (R) bank of the Marsyangdi Khola. Just north of the Paundi Khola, on the banks of the Marsyangdi Khola, is a large sandy beach, good for tent camping. Tenters are advised to be cautious along this route (and on many others); there are many reported cases of robberies (principally by slitting tents during the night and extracting rucksacks, cameras, money, clothes, shoes, and other items).

North of Turture the trail passes through many small hamlets, including Tharpani (1875 ft, 556 m) in **an hour**. Beyond there are fewer settlements and more farmland until an **hour** later you come to the new town of Kalimati. Below and across from you, on the east (L) bank of the Marsyangdi Khola, you can see the town of Tarkughat.

To go to Manang, continue north following the feeder road and in **half an hour** cross a suspension bridge over a tributary, the Paundi Khola (same name as the river near Turture). Climb up to reach **Paundi Dhik** (1900 ft, 579 m) a **few minutes** later. There is a good swimming place under the bridge (*paundi* means "swim"). If you are returning from Manang and wish to head directly to Pokhara, you could do so from here by following in reverse the Pokhara-Kathmandu route description in Chapter 11. The road goes out across the fields. Stay on the trail through this small town. Don't take the left fork at the top end of the few shops, but continue north along the west edge of the fields. The trail soon rejoins the road, sometimes staying with it, sometimes avoiding it on shortcuts. The large tributary, the Dardi Khola, that you will see joining the Marsyangdi Khola on the east (L) bank, is reached in **fifty minutes**. An **hour** farther, cross another tributary to **Udipur** (2450 ft, 747 m) **five minutes** beyond. The forests that remain are tropical sal, but have been cut extensively. Continue on to the rapidly growing village of **Bhote Wodar** (also called Suidibar). In **half an hour** the trail reaches **PhalenksAAghu** (spelled "Phaliya Sangu" on one hotel signpost). Follow the road through the high (new) part of this town, unless you want to cross the Marsyangdi Khola here, whereupon you should descend into the old town by the bridge. The name PhalenksAAghu comes from the English word "plank" and the Nepali word for a rather primitive bridge, *sAAghu*. There was once a plank bridge here, and the name stuck. Such combinations of Nepali and English words can often cause difficulty when they are pronounced with a Nepali accent or spelled in the local script. (I can well remember a patient asking me for a "satipicket." It took some time to figure out that he wanted a certificate!) Another name for this town is Dalal, meaning "black market," a reference to activities of an earlier time.

An alternative trail here crosses the bridge and ascends the east (L) bank of the river to rejoin the other trail above Bhulbhule. This east (L) bank route is slightly shorter than the west (R) bank route and has more spectacular views. In the winter, many Manangba camp and trade on this side of the river. Trekkers who want to use the well-supplied shops at Besisahar might consider a combination route, following the west (R) bank to Besisahar, crossing the river there and taking the left-hand fork to join the east (L) bank route; or, following the east (L) bank trail from PahlenksAAghu, crossing back to the west (R) bank at Besisahar. The west (R) bank trail may be preferable, however, because the road is being built on this side, where there are more eating and lodging places. The east (L) bank trail is decribed as an alternative following the west (R) bank description. Another variation, or even a side trip, is to cross the Marsyangdi Khola here and climb to the lakes on the Baahra Pokhari Lekh for fine views of Manaslu, Peak 29, and Himalchuli. You could even head north from the lakes to rejoin the main riverside route a day beyond. The route from PhalenksAAghu to Baahra Pokhara takes about **two days** of steady climbing.

If you don't cross the suspension bridge at PhalenksAAghu, continue on up the west (R) bank through stands of wet subtropical forest (good birding, and even a squirrel or two may be seen, especially on early mornings). The trail on to Besisahar generally follows the feeder road. Reach a small town, Nadiwal (2650 ft, 808 m) in **forty-five minutes**. Take the shortcut right, down and across a small stream, then continue along the wide road bed to Bakunde (2675 ft, 815 m) in another **half hour**. You will see the large buildings and roofs of Besisahar in the distance. Descend to cross a tributary stream in **forty-five minutes**, then ascend to **Besisahar** (2700 ft, 823 m)—mistakenly called Bensisahar and Lamjung on some trekking maps—**fifteen minutes** beyond. The old Lamjung Darbar, a palace fortress, once the center of a princely state, is high on the ridge west of the town. Besisahar has two sections; the main part of town is **five minutes** beyond, across a small stream. This major town, situated on a shelf of land above the Marsyangdi Khola, is the Lamjung District headquarters and the site of a police check post, where you might be asked to show your trekking permit. The town also has a district hospital, prison, high school, government offices, shops, and lodges. It is a real "boom town" in every sense, with new construction visible on all sides of the old bazaar.

The bridge across the Marsyangdi Khola to the east (L) bank is reached by a trail that turns off near the south end of the main old bazaar, near the hospital. It can be used by those taking the east (L) bank trail from PhalenksAAghu, or by going to Bhulbhule on the east (L) side of the valley. If you are staying on the west (R) bank, continue north through town to the end of the wide roadbed. Descend from the shelf and cross the tributary stream some **fifteen minutes** later. Climb steeply up and continue contouring in wet subtropical forest and rice fields to Tanaute (2650 ft, 808 m) in **fifteen minutes**. Over half an hour later, the trail crosses a slide, and in another **half hour**, a tributary, the Balam Khola (2500 ft, 762 m). The bridge over the Balam Khola has been washed out for several years, and crossing during the rainy season may be difficult. Continue north above the Marsyangdi Khola to the Khudi Khola (2600 ft, 792 m), a main tributary stream that drains the east end of the Lamjung Himal. Ascend upstream about a quarter mile (0.4 km) to cross a new suspension bridge. Remants of an older bridge may be seen below, near old Khudi. A "new Khudi" (Naya Khudi) is developing at the new bridge site. Cross the bridge to the east (L) bank of the Khudi Khola, and turn right to rejoin the Marsyangdi River trail. The Marsyangdi Valley turns, narrows, and changes character now. Himalchuli is the major summit to the east.

If returning from Manang, you might consider walking directly to Pokhara from Khudi and avoiding Dumre. This route takes three days. The trail goes from Khudi to Baglung Pani, through Lamagaon, across the Badam Khola to Nalma, and across the Midam Khola, passing Kala Pattar to Begnas Tal, the lake in the eastern part of the Pokhara Valley. Most of the villages passed are inhabited by people of the *Gurung* ethnic group who farm the high hills and raise sheep. Trekkers wishing to meet few other foreigners should consider this route.

To reach Manang from Khudi, continue up the Marsyangdi north bank (R) eastward, past the Khudi school and tree nursery, and reach a tributary (2700 ft, 823 m) in **fifteen minutes**. Continue along the Marsyangdi Khola another **twenty minutes** to a long suspension bridge (2775 ft, 846 m). Cross to the south (L) bank to reach Bhulbhule.

To take the alternative route from PhalenksAAghu to Bhulbhule, cross the bridge at PhalenksAAghu and climb the hill for **ten minutes** to the fields above. The trail winds its way through fields, sometimes diverging into several trails. The villages are pleasant and the sights lovely. In mid-winter, you may see a temporary potters' encampment here, Newars from Kathmandu Valley who have come for generations to sites like this in the middle hills to extract clay and make pots for sale in the surrounding villages.

After **1½ hours**, the trail drops down into a steep ravine with a stone staircase leading in and out on both sides. Then it traverses along a steeper slope with fine views across the valley to the high mountains beyond. **Twenty minutes** from the ravine is the bridge crossing the Marsyangdi Khola to Besisahar. Several trails drop down to the river; take the one that traverses the slope and continue to another lookout (Deskadanda) **twenty minutes** beyond. It is another **1¼ hours** to the big pipal tree and small village of Simbachaur, and an additional **one hour and twenty minutes** to Bhulbhule. The trail from the opposite north bank (R) joins here at the bridge, which enters the middle part of Bhulbhule. There are a few shops in Bhulbhule, and also the first lodges operated by Manangbas, who have moved down here from the upper Marsyangdi Valley.

The most well-traveled route now continues eastward out of Bhulbhule along the south (L) bank of the Marsyangdi Khola; later it turns northward again. Continue upstream from Bhulbhule and in **ten minutes** pass a beautiful thin waterfall on your right, the first of many handsome waterfalls along the way to Manang. Below it is a fine pool for bathing, much better than the main river. A **half hour** later reach **Ngadi** (3050 ft, 930 m), on the banks of a small tributary stream. Beyond, enter a major tributary valley to the east, that of the Musi Khola. Descend to a suspension bridge (3125 ft, 953 m) in **forty-five minutes**. Cross it to the north (R) bank of the Musi Khola. Continue up the Musi Khola, pass another bridge, and climb out of the Musi Khola valley to reenter the valley of the Marsyangdi Khola. The trail contours and climbs in a pleasant little valley of terraces and forests to the settlement of **Bahundanda** (literally meaning "Brahman hill") on the right of a prominent brow at a saddle (4300 ft, 1311 m), **1½ hours** from the crossing of the Musi Khola. There are good views to the north if the weather is clear. On the high hills all around are *Gurung* ethnic settlements. There is an undeveloped hot springs (*tato paani*) at the edge of the Marsyangdi Khola, below the knob of Bahundanda hill, but it is a steep descent (and return ascent) and takes some time and effort to find. Ask locally for the way. There are shops in the town.

Descend into an equally pleasant tributary valley and in **forty-five minutes** cross its river on a cantilever bridge (3700 ft, 1128 m). Ascend to the main river valley and follow the trail beautifully carved out of the rock wall of the valley. Pass the houses of Khanegaon (3900 ft, 1189 m) in **forty-five minutes**, and contour to Ghermu on the edge of a shelf above the river in **half an hour**. Do not ascend toward the cliff to the northeast, but from Ghermu descend to a suspension bridge over the Marsyangdi (3650 ft, 1113 m) and cross it to the west (R) bank in **ten minutes** to **Syang** (3725 ft, 1136 m) by the river.

There is an undeveloped alternate route from Bhulbhule to Syang on the west (R) bank of the Marsyangdi Khola. You are not likely to meet many people on this trail, and you will also miss some good views. The route is slightly shorter because it avoids the high climb over Bahundanda Hill. If you are coming from Khudi, up the right bank of the Marsyangdi Khola, do not cross at Bhulbhule. If you are in Bhulbhule, cross to the north (R) bank, and turn right, upstream. Stay on this side all the way to Syang. The trail goes through fields and along the bottom of the brushy hillside approximately **a half hour** to the small riverside hamlet of Arkhale. Cross the tributary Phle Khola and continue on another **thirty minutes** to Gopte, across a small stream by the same name. Above the hamlet of Gopte avoid the riverside trail, but take the left fork and ascend gradually for about **forty-five minutes** to the village of Chapedanda. You cross the bottom of a very large landslide shortly before Chapedanda. It is another **hour** on to Syang, where the main track from Bahundanda crosses the suspension bridge. The main track on into Manang now continues up the west (R) bank of the Marsyangdi Khola.

The tall waterfall that you may have admired from the other side of the river provides the water for the next tributary that you cross just beyond Syang. The gorge becomes narrower and the trail rises and falls. There are overhanging rocks such as the one you pass in **half an hour** (3800 ft, 1158 m). These rocks can provide campsites. A lone house is passed in **ten minutes**, then the trail continues **fifty minutes** to the village of **Jagat** (4400 ft, 1341 m)—also called Gadi Jagat or Chote—situated in a saddle in the forest. This used to be an old customs post for the salt trade with Tibet.

Continue through broad-leaved forest and pass by another overhang suitable for a campsite. Cross a small tributary (4400 ft, 1341 m) and admire the spectacular waterfalls on the other side of the river. An **hour** beyond Jagat, reach the small settlement of **Chamje** (4700 ft, 1433 m). There are many changes in the people, architecture, and vegetation as you head upstream. Houses are now built of rocks, the vegetation is less tropical, and the culture is more Tibetan-like.

Just beyond the town, the gorge is very impressive. Descend for **less than ten minutes** and cross to the east (L) bank of the Marsyangdi Khola on a suspension bridge (4625 ft, 1410 m). The forests around you are of oak. Continue upstream, usually high above the river, for almost 1½ **hours** until you emerge from the gorge with its torrent below. An ancient landslide from the mountain to the east filled the gorge here, creating a lake that has become silted in above. The river itself flows buried beneath the rubble and is heard but not seen. Enter a broad, pleasant, flat valley with a somewhat quieter river. En route are impressive falls on both sides of the valley. The first house in the flat valley is Tale. There is a suspension bridge across the river, but don't take it. A sign indicates that you have entered Manang District. Continue ahead to the houses of **Tal** in the center of the flat valley (5600 ft, 1707 m) in **ten minutes**. *Tal*, meaning "lake" in Nepali, refers to the prehistoric one. East of Tal is another spectacular waterfall. Try to spend a night here, for there is nowhere else along the trek quite like it. The area of Manang to the north is called Gyasumdo, meaning "meeting place of the three highways." It is inhabited partly by *BhoTiya* who are primarily agro-pastoralists. These people were the real trans-Himalayan traders of the region until 1959 or 1960 when the trade closed after the Chinese takeover of Tibet. Nareshwar Jang Gurung wrote an interesting survey on Manang (see Recommended Reading).

The trail to Manang proper crosses the small tributary beyond Tal on a log bridge and ascends upstream in the valley that again narrows. In 1½ **hours** pass by an older suspension bridge made of steel and bamboo, but with only cables to walk on. Don't cross it, but continue upstream on the east (L) bank to reach another overhang in **twenty minutes**. Then cross a new suspension bridge over the Marsyangdi Khola (6250 ft, 1905 m) to the west (R) bank and reach **Dharapani** (6375 ft, 1943 m) in **five minutes**. There is a police check post here. Continue on upstream and note the valley coming in from the northeast some **ten minutes** beyond. It comes down from the Larkya Pass and leads north of Manaslu to the Buri Gandaki. The village of Thonje lies at the confluence of the Dudh Khola and the Marsyangdi Khola. Thonje in *Gurung* means "pine trees growing on a flat place." Don't cross the wooden cantilever bridge over the Marsyangdi Khola upstream of the river junction. Some **ten minutes** beyond the confluence, take the lower fork—the upper leads to some higher villages. Take the upper trail at the next two forks a **few minutes** beyond.

A pleasant **half-hour's** walk brings you around the corner to the town of **Bagarchap** (7100 ft, 2164 m)—meaning "butcher's place." This town has flat-roofed houses, indicating that rainfall is less here because the monsoon clouds have unloaded some of their water to the south. The waterworks flowing through the town are quite interesting—you will see nothing remotely similar until you reach Marpha in the Thak Khola across the Annapurna range to the west. The Nyingmapa sect has built a small new *gomba* here with handsome frescoes on its walls. There are views of the Annapurnas and part of Lamjung Himal. Just beyond the town, take the left fork. Do not go down to the cantilever bridge crossing the Marsyangdi Khola. Admire the views of Manaslu behind you. Continue in pine forest and in **forty minutes**, cross a tributary (7550 ft, 2301 m) coming down from the Namun Bhanjyang, a high pass crossing the Himalayan barrier east of Lamjung Himal. Once heavily traveled, this pass is now only occasionally used by *Gurung* shepherds who pasture their sheep and goats on the high slopes. The newly constructed trail along the Marsyangdi Khola has replaced the dangerous old route that people avoided by taking the strenuous high route. Beyond the bridge, take the right fork. The left fork heads up to high pastures and the Namun Pass. It provides an alternative route, used formerly, that has a fine campsite at Timung Meadows. Lodging is available there too. The main trail, described here, is rejoined at Koto. On the main trail, continue a short way to the rushing Syalkyu waterfall (7625 ft, 2324 m) with a wooden cantilever bridge in front of it. You may see four light-colored diamond shapes on the rock to the left, near the middle part of this waterfall. Local legend holds that a lama painted these auspicious symbols centuries ago. Beyond, the path, which is carved out of the cliffs, rises on steps and continues in lush oak forests to cross another tributary (7775 ft, 2370 m) in **fifteen minutes**. Unlike similar valleys in eastern Nepal, there are not many rhododendron trees along the trail. Continue to a clearing and the new settlement of Lattemarang (8050 ft, 2454 m)—also called Tanzah Bishe—in **half an hour**.

The trail in this pleasant part of the valley continues along the south side and crosses another tributary on a wooden bridge (8225 ft, 2507 m) **twenty minutes** later. Just beyond is another house. **Fifteen minutes** after the bridge takes the lower fork (8375 ft, 2553 m), the trail continues in blue pine and spruce forests. Don't cross any of the three wooden bridges over the Marsyangdi Khola that you pass in the next few minutes, but continue and cross a tributary on a wooden bridge (8625 ft, 2629 m) **forty minutes** later. Cross another small stream and reach the few houses of **Koto** (or Kotoje) in a pretty clearing (8625 ft, 2629 m) in less than **ten minutes**. Police may check your trekking permit here. The prominent tributary valley heading north is the Nar Khola, which drains the region called Nar Phu. The inhabitants are traditionally pastoralists.

To continue to Manang, cross a tributary, then another, and enter **Chame** (8900 ft, 2713 m) in less than **half an hour**. This government town is the Jilla Panchayat, the district center for Manang. It has a bank and a police check post. The non-governmental people live at the west end of town where there is a *gomba*. At the far end of town, first cross a tributary from the south, then the main Marsyangdi Khola on a wooden cartilever bridge (8890 ft, 2710 m) to the north (L) bank. There are more houses here and some hot springs right at the river's edge about 200 yards south of the bridge over the Marsyangdi Khola on the north (L) bank. As you go up the valley into pine forest, the trail is not as well built or maintained as it has been up to now. Continue along the pleasant trail to reach the new houses of Taleku (9200 ft, 2804 m) in **half an hour**. Like the other towns since Dharapani, this one has an entrance *chorten* and an exit *chorten*. The trail continues close to the river, even cut out of the clay hillside in places. Above you is an impressive canyon. The Marsyangdi Valley is almost unrelentingly narrow.

Continue along for **half an hour** to the first of four successive tall waterfalls, opposite you on the south (R) side of the valley. Another **half hour** brings you to a wide wooden cantilever bridge (9575 ft, 2919 m) that crosses to the south (R) bank of the Marsyangdi Khola. Previously this bridge was covered, and you can still see the remnants of a gate. There is a lodge on the north side of the bridge. The former *Khampa* settlement of **Bhratang** is just beyond. The gate on the bridge was the *Khampa* way of maintaining control of traffic in the valley. Climb up for **five minutes** to the village of Bhratang. The *Khampa*, Tibetan refugee warriors, were all resettled in 1975 and the town is abandoned save for a few people. One building in this town is remarkable—a large open room that must have been used for meetings. Just west of the town is another wooden cantilever bridge (9650 ft, 2941 m) to the north (L) bank. Annapurna II can be seen to the south—you may have wondered along the way what peak it was, for it looks distinctly different from the north than the view from Pokhara. Enter a fir and spruce forest. Cross again to the south (R) bank in **thirty-five minutes** on another wooden bridge (10,050 ft, 3063 m), then climb into a serene pine forest. After the days in the gorge, you can appreciate the beauty and silence of the next **forty-five minutes**. A clearing with some *chorten* (10,450 ft, 3185 m) is next, and beyond some meadows and a small lake. Soon you leave the forest and in **fifty minutes**, reach a bridge over the Marsyangdi Khola to the north (L) bank (10,375 ft, 3162 m). It is also possible to stay on the south (R) bank as far as lower Pisang. Look back and admire the incredible slabs above the river valley on the east side. If you think you see a building on the ridge, you are right—it is a Buddhist shrine.

You are now in the dry, arid region of Manang called Nyesyang. Since it is in the rain shadow of the Himalaya, which act as a barrier to the wet monsoon clouds from the south, the area gets little rain in the summer. Snow falls here in the winter and remains on the ground much of the time. The men are traders and part-time farmers, and the women are full-time farmers. There is comparatively little animal husbandry. You may meet many young men with considerable facility in English who have traveled far and wide in Asia. They may try to sell or trade almost anything. The people of Nyesyang were granted special trading privileges by the King about 180 years ago. This included passports and import and export facilities. These privileges have been extended to all the people of Manang District. Initially they traded local items for manufactured goods, usually in India and Burma, but more recently they have begun using hard currency from export of expensive items to import machines and other manufactured goods from most South Asian countries. The resultant seasonal migration means less development of agriculture and animal husbandry. So you won't see many herds of yak, sheep, or goats at the higher elevations. These people are thus quite dependent on food imports.

From the bridge there are basically two routes, which join up in the valley below the village of Braga. The direct route keeps to the valley floor, staying mostly on the south (R) side. If you keep close to the river, you come to lower **Pisang** (10,450 ft, 3185 m) in less than **half an hour**. The other trail ascends on the north side of the valley to reach the rather spectacular town of upper Pisang (10,800 ft, 3292 m) in **half an hour**. The view of Annapurna II from here is unforgettable. From upper Pisang, you can descend to lower Pisang and continue along the lower valley route, or you can take a higher route that climbs to several villages on the north (L) side of the valley. The views of the mountains from this route are more impressive than from the other, and the villages are quite interesting, but it takes perhaps two hours more to reach Braga.

To take the lower direct route, cross the Marsyangdi Khola to its south (R) bank at lower Pisang. Cross a tributary from the south and ascend into pleasant pine and juniper forests. Climb to the upper valley floor beyond a narrowing. Ongre (10,900 ft, 3322 m), a flat area with a few houses, is reached in 1½ **hours**. There is a police check post here and an airstrip to link this remote area with Kathmandu. Foreign aid from Yugoslavia is supporting a mountaineering school. A **half hour** beyond Ongre, south of the trail, is the Trekker's Aid Post of the Himalayan Rescue

Association. It is staffed in the autumn and spring. A hydroelectric station is also planned to provide electricity for upper Manang Valley. Continue along, crossing another major tributary from the south, and head over toward the Marsyangdi Khola to cross it (11,250 ft, 3429 m) in another **hour**. Ascend along the north (L) bank to a small town, Munchi (11,425 ft, 3482 m), where the high north side route joins the main valley route. Don't cross the wooden bridge some **fifteen minutes** beyond, but round a ridge a **few minutes** later and reach the entrance *chorten* below **Braga** (11,500 ft, 3505 m).

The high north side route begins in upper Pisang. Like many villages here, the town is constructed using flat roofs. The roof of one house serves as the yard or open area of the house above it. There is a long handsome wall of prayer wheels in an open space below a little-used *gomba*. To head up the valley on the north side, take the trail leaving town to the west. Pass through the entrance *chorten*, descend slightly, cross a tributary (10,800 ft, 3292 m), and contour in a pleasant pine and juniper forest. Pass above a small green lake, and contour to a long *mani* wall. Then descend to cross a tributary (10,775 ft, 3284 m) a little over **half an hour** from Pisang. Take the upper fork and begin a steep climb for an hour to **Ghyaru** (12,050 ft, 3673 m). Spectacular views of Annapurnas II and III and Gangapurna are the main attractions, along with the dark, tunnel-like streets of the town. Contour out of the town to the west, cross a tributary (12,075 ft, 3680 m), and reach a ridge crest (12,375 ft, 3772 m) some 100 ft (30 m) above some ruins, perhaps of an old fort, in **1²/₃ hours**. Rest here and enjoy the views of Gangapurna, Glacier Dome, and Tilicho Peak to the west. North of Tilicho Peak lies the "great frozen lake," named by Herzog, although it is out of view from here. If you cross the Thorong La Pass, you will eventually return to Pokhara by heading well north and then west of this peak.

Continue contouring, cross a tributary, and pass three trails joining yours on the left. Cross another tributary to **Ngawal** (11,975 ft, 3650 m) **forty-five minutes** from Ghyaru. Descend to cross a tributary in a **few minutes**, then continue descending, avoiding a left fork (11,625 ft, 3543 m) **ten minutes** beyond town. Descend to the valley floor (11,325 ft, 3452 m) and in about an **hour**, reach the few houses of Munchi (11,425 ft, 3482 m). Here the trail meets the main lower trail from Pisang. **Braga** (11,500 ft, 3505 m) is less than **half an hour** away.

Braga, a large and interesting village, is the seat of the oldest monastery in the area. The *gomba* is perhaps 500 years old, and belongs to the Kargyupa sect of Tibetan Buddhism. Like most of the *gomba* in this region, it is not very active, but is well worth a visit, for it contains some unique works of art. The main temple holds 108 terra-cotta statues, each about two ft (60 cm) high, arranged in rows along three of the four walls. They represent much of the Buddhist Pantheon. There is another three-story temple above this main building. The temple is described in detail in David Snellgrove's *Himalayan Pilgrimage* (see Recommended Reading).

The village of **Manang** (11,650 ft, 3351 m) is **half an hour** beyond Braga. In between two tributaries along the way, on a ridge to the north, lies the Bod-zo *gomba*. It is perhaps the most active institution around. The beautiful wall paintings that Snellgrove admired in his book have been poorly repainted. Reach this *gomba* by climbing upstream before crossing the second of the series of tributaries. Head up the valley for **half an hour** to the ridge crest (11,750 ft, 3581 m). You can most likely restock your provisions in Manang, although prices are quite high. Perhaps you may see an archery contest or a horse race! Manang itself is spectacularly perched across from a glacial lake formed by water from Gangapurna and Anna-purna III. To the west is the village of Khangsar, the last habitation before Tilicho Tal (lake). And beyond is the impressive north face of Tilicho Peak. An approach to the lake has been described from the Kali Gandaki side. It can also be reached from Khangsar in **two days**. Someone familiar with the route could be hired here. In bad weather it can be difficult to find the lake from the east. It is frozen in winter, and periods of thaw vary from year to year.

If you are planning to cross the Thorong La and reach the Kali Gandaki (river) to the west, it is important to spend a day or two acclimatizing here before pro-ceeding. If you have flown to Manang, you should spend at least three or four days in this region before attempting to cross the pass. Those who have walked up should spend one or two days at 12,000 ft (3658 m) or so. Acclimatization days are best spent being active and climbing to high elevations for views, but returning to lower altitudes to sleep. There are many suitable hikes on both sides of the valley.

To proceed from Manang over the Thorong La, the high pass leading to Muktinath and the Kali Gandaki Valley, cross a tributary below a falls beyond Manang and reach **Tengi** (11,950 ft, 3642 m) in **half an hour**. This is the last perma-nent settlement below the pass. Climb for **half an hour** beyond Tengi to a fork. Take the right fork—the left descends to cross the river to Khangsar—and reach some *goTh* called Kosang (12,725 ft, 3879 m) shortly beyond. **Ten minutes** farther is a higher settlement of *goTh* called Khöra. The trail has now turned northwest up the tributary valley of the Jargeng Khola. To the southwest you can see the sum-mit of Roc Noir, part of the Great Barrier. The countryside around you is quite dry and alpine, with occasional birch groves. Pass some *goTh*, cross small tributaries, and contour along pleasant meadows. If you are here early in the morning or late in the afternoon, look for herds of blue sheep, which may descend for water. Reach Leder, a *goTh* (13,700 ft, 4176 m) **2½ hours** from Tengi. Some supplies may occasionally be available here. This may be the last shelter before the pass, though there are plenty of suitable campsites. Farther on, the Manangi people may have set up *bhaTTi* to cater to trekkers during peak season. But do not count on sufficient shelter and food for all travelers. Bring your own tent and some food. Do not attempt to cross the pass unless all of the party, including the porters, are equipped for cold and bad weather. If the weather is threatening, and everyone cannot be housed in tents in case of a snowstorm, do not proceed. Lives have been needlessly lost on this pass because parties proceeded in bad weather. Recently, many people have been crossing the pass wearing running shoes. If you do not carry proper boots, at least recognize that there is risk of frostbite should a storm occur.

From Leder, climb, contour, and then descend to the river by a covered wooden cantilever bridge (14,000 ft, 4267 m) in **forty minutes**. Tall people should watch their heads on this bridge! Cross to the west (R) bank of the Jargeng Khola, where suitable campsites can be found. This narrow valley is being severely eroded. Climb and contour upstream, crossing some scree (14,325 ft, 4366 m) to reach the riverbed and, just beyond, a campsite (14,450 ft, 4404 m) called Phedi—meaning "foot of hill"—an **hour** from the bridge. There may be a *bhaTTi* here dur-ing the trekking season. As already mentioned, the available shelter may be full when you arrive, and you may not get food. Be prepared to camp if necessary. I feel it is preferable to do so. Poorly prepared parties may spend a miserable night here. Some parties have been unable to continue up and were forced to turn back. The trail now leaves the river valley, which continues northwest, and ascends west. In dry weather, water can be scarce the next day, so fill up. There are two high campsites (14,675 ft, 4473 m and 14,875 ft, 4534 m) **ten to fifteen minutes** apart along the trail. The campsites may not have any water. There are no good campsites with water beyond the pass unless you camp on snow in the appropriate season.

From Phedi, ascend to a notch (15,725 ft, 4793 m) in 1¼ **hours** and head left (west), traversing to the base of a prominent lateral moraine (15,900 ft, 4846 m) in **half an hour**. Reach its crest (16,050 ft, 4892 m) **a few minutes** later and continue west along less steep terrain. After many false crests, reach the Thorong La Pass (17,650 ft, 5380 m) in **two hours** if you are adequately acclimatized. A large cairn marks the pass, but it may be almost entirely covered with snow. There is an impressive glaciated peak to the south. It is not very difficult to ascend if you have the requisite skills, experience, and equipment, and if you are well acclimatized. Thorongse, the peak to the north, requires some technical rock climbing. The pass is exhilarating in that it is an abrupt transition from one major Himalayan valley to another, but views from the pass are probably less impressive than those on either side. Far below you to the west is the Kali Gandaki. Those with sharp eyes and binoculars can pick out the green oasis of Kagbeni.

The descent from the pass is gradual at first and follows the middle of the valley for the first hour. It becomes considerably steeper and keeps to the south side of the valley on scree. The first campsites (14,150 ft, 4313 m) are some **two hours** down from the pass just after crossing a tributary to the right. In the dry season, after and just before the monsoon when all the snow has melted, there is no water available, necessitating a descent to near Muktinath. Reach a *goTh* in **ten minutes** where there may be a tea shop and space for lodging. The same provisos regarding food and shelter apply here as well as for the eastern side of the pass. Cross a tributary (which may be dry) to the left (it flows from the south) and descend to a major tributary in the valley floor (12,650 ft, 3856 m) 2½ hours from the pass. Cross it to the south (L) bank and ascend a bit to continue down the main valley. Reach **Muktinath** (12,475 ft, 3802 m) after rounding a corner some **fifteen minutes** later.

To continue, reverse the trail descriptions given earlier for the trek from Pokhara to Muktinath.

Cumulative trekking times (walking time only, does not include rests or stops) from Dumre to:

Kalimati	4¾ hours	Bagarchap	25¾ hours
Besisahar	10 "	Chame	29¼ "
Khudi Khola	12¼ "	Pisang	33 "
Bhulbhule	13 "	Braga	36 "
Bahundanda	16 "	Manang	36½ "
Chamje	21 "	Leder	39¼ "
Tal	23 "		

9 SOLU-KHUMBU
(The Everest Region)

Because it is there.
Replied George Mallory, one of the first climbers to attempt Everest, when asked why he wanted to climb it. He disappeared into a cloud near the summit in 1924.

There are several possible ways of reaching Solu-Khumbu District of Nepal. The classical way to Khumbu, the northernmost part of the district, is to walk from Kathmandu. But since roads continue to be built ever closer to Khumbu, this route, beginning at Kathmandu, is never used. Someday a road may reach Namche Bazaar! Lamosangu or Dolalghat on the Kathmandu-Kodari road were the traditional staging areas until recently. A road has now been built to Jiri from Lamosangu. Most trekkers walking in will take the road as far as possible. Begin trekking from Lamosangu to enjoy the manifold variety of hill Nepal.

There are STOL airstrips in several places along the way, and aircraft charters can be arranged. The airstrips are at Jiri, some three days' walk from Kathmandu; at Phaphlu in Solu, a week's walk; and finally at Lukla, a day's walk from Namche Bazaar. There are now regularly scheduled flights by Royal Nepal Airlines to Lukla. In addition, a strip has been constructed above Namche Bazaar. It is called Shyangboche and was used by visitors to the luxury Everest View Hotel in Khumjung, and to a certain extent by trekkers. But with the closure of the hotel in 1983, flights have been cancelled.

As mentioned earlier, rapid ascent to high altitudes can be dangerous, even fatal. For some people, rapid ascent to even 10,000 ft (3100 m) has been disastrous. Lukla is at 9275 ft (2827 m) and the airstrip at Shyangboche is at 12,435 ft (3790 m). Hence it is best to walk to Khumbu and arrange to fly out, if you want to fly part way. If you must fly in, fly to Phaphlu or Lukla and ascend gradually. In winter, few landings are made at Lukla or Shyangboche because of snow. Often it is difficult to arrive at Lukla and get a flight out, sometimes even with a confirmed reservation! Thus most trekkers flying one leg tend to fly in to Lukla and accept the added risk of altitude illness.

If you are walking both ways, the journey from Kathmandu to Khumbu can be combined with the trek from Khumbu to Ilam District in eastern Nepal, followed by air transportation to Kathmandu. Or you can go by jeep and train to Darjeeling. This is described in Chapter 11. You can also reach and leave the Khumbu region via Rolwaling to the east by crossing a high glaciated pass, the Trashi Labsta. This long crossing is somewhat hazardous and requires some mountaineering skills and equipment and considerable stamina. The route is described in Chapter 11.

To Solu-Khumbu
(Map No. 4, Page 205)

Although there are few close views of the mountains until you get to Khumbu, the walk from Lamosangu to Khumbu is recommended as an introduction to the

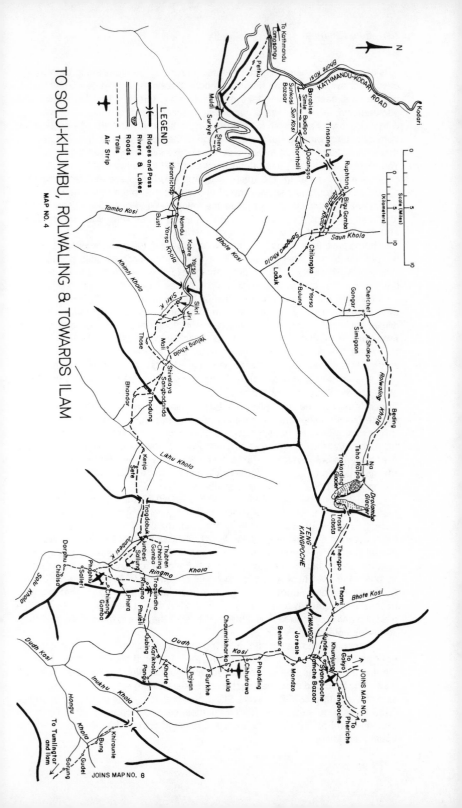

hills of Nepal and their inhabitants. A few pleasant diversions along the way are described. Average walking time to Namche Bazaar is ten to twelve days. Local people have been known to take much less time, but they traveled all day and sometimes at night. After all, a curvilinear distance of eighty miles is involved, but with switchbacks and diversions in the trail, it is about 150 miles of walking from Lamosangu to Namche Bazaar. Furthermore, the trip involves a series of ascents that total 35,200 ft (10,724 m) and a series of descents that total 26,100 ft (7954 m). You more than climb Everest along the way, but it is well worth it.

Generally speaking, the main rivers run south and are separated by high ridges, so the route is a succession of ups and downs, often following tributaries flowing east and west. Compared to the trek between Pokhara and Kathmandu, also going against the grain of the land, the ridges and valleys are much higher and the climbs and descents are more strenuous.

In the past, *bhaTTi* and tea shops were rare along the route except near Khumbu, but this is no longer the case since the trail has become quite popular with Westerners. There is usually no difficulty in obtaining cooked food along the way, but it is wise to carry some food with you. Shelter should also pose no problem.

Take the bus heading to Barabise on the Kathmandu-Kodari Road. It leaves every few hours from the staging area north of the Kathmandu City Hall, east of Tundikhel. The bus to Lamosangu—which means "long bridge"—takes some **three to five hours**. You could go by bus only as far as Dolalghat (2080 ft, 634 m) and walk from there. This adds a day to the journey, but avoids a long climb at the beginning if starting from Lamosangu. Better to have the extra day to spend in Khumbu.

A new road is complete from Lamosangu to Jiri, built as part of the Swiss Multipurpose Development Project. Sections of the road can be used as trails for the early part of the trek. Also, minibus transportation is available from Lamosangu. The road shortens the trekking time considerably. A question often asked is how much vehicular transportation should be used to shorten treks. The Everest trek originally started from the Kathmandu Valley; now the starting point is moving ever closer to Solu-Khumbu. Trekkers who want to experience the hills as well as the mountains may choose not to use all the available roads, or they may choose a trek in which those options aren't available.

The Jiri road begins across the Sun Kosi (river), about 1½ mi (3.3 km) west of Lamosangu. Here, there is a large hydroelectric generating station built by the Chinese. It is not worthwhile to walk up the road; the usual foot trail is more direct. From the road at Lamosangu (2430 ft, 741 m) cross the Sun Kosi on a sturdy suspension bridge, and, after passing through the village, climb steeply to the southeast through chilaune forest to gain a ridge. Follow it to the village of **Kaping** (4300 ft, 1219 m) in 1¾ **hours**. Another 1¼ **hours** brings you to **Petku** (5450 ft, 1661 m). Continue climbing through terraced farms, interspersed with thatch-roofed houses and eventually reach a ridge (6850 ft, 2088 m) and the village of Pakhar. The road and trail soon intersect, and the route follows the road to **Muldi** (8350 ft, 2540 m) some **five hours** from Petku.

From Muldi the trail continues along the ridge, passes the settlement of Ningale, and begins to descend. Just before the descent, there are distant views extending from Annapurna in the west to the Khumbu Himal in the east. The path leaves the road and descends east for 1½ **hours** before crossing to the south (R) side of a tributary (5875 ft, 1791 m). Shortly beyond, it reaches the village of **Surkye** (5750 ft, 1735 m). In another **fifteen minutes**, cross to the north (L) bank of the Chandrawati Khola (5175 ft, 1577 m), and reach Shera (4750 ft, 1448 m) some 2½ **hours** after Muldi.

Mani *stones in Khumbu. (Dave Hardenbergh)*

Directly beyond Shera, take a suspension bridge over another tributary from the north and continue on the north (L) side of the valley, at times walking in pleasant chir pine forests, but soon returning to the ubiquitous terracing to reach **Kirantichap** (4325 ft, 1320 m) some **four hours** after Shera. You are now in the area covered by the *Tamba Kosi Likhu Khola* map of the Research Scheme Nepal Himalaya. The map is quite useful for the next five days' walk. Intersect the road at Kirantichap, but keep to the more direct footpath.

From Kirantichap descend for an **hour** through pleasant chir pine forests to a sturdy suspension bridge over the beautiful blue waters of the Bhote Kosi (2800 ft, 853 m). This is one of many fine bridges built by Scottish engineers. The village of Busti lies on the opposite side of the river, a suburb of the larger town downstream. Climb up the east (L) bank to the ridge and follow its south side to the village of **Namdu** (4900 ft, 1493 m), reaching its lower part **two hours** after crossing the river. You intersect the road along the way, and local conditions dictate whether to follow it. Pass by a small pagoda dedicated to Lord Shiva. His symbol, the trident, is quite conspicuous here. **Kabre** (6025 ft, 1836 m) is reached in 1¾ **hours** from Namdu. The trail descends slightly to cross the Yarsa Khola before reaching **Yarsa** (6475 ft, 1974 m) in another **hour**. You are now in *Jirel* country, an area surrounding Jiri populated by a hill ethnic group whose language is related to that of the Sherpas.

From Yarsa the trail rises through oak and chir pine forests, past a small town, **Chisapani**, towards a notch in the ridge you are contouring. Beyond Chisapani and before the pass, you can fork right and go directly to Those, avoiding Jiri. But Jiri is too interesting to pass up. The pass (8280 ft, 2523 m) is reached in less than **two hours** from Yarsa and provides distant views of Rolwaling Himal. Almost due north is the high ridge, crested with a black tower called Chobo Bamare (19,550 ft, 5959 m), that you may have seen for several days now. The road heads north, while you descend east through pleasant forests and terraces to the Sikri Khola (6250 ft, 1905 m) and the town of **Sikri**, which is reached in **little more than an hour**.

There are two choices from here, depending on whether you want to visit Jiri, where there is a hospital, a STOL airstrip, and a dairy and agricultural project originally financed with Swiss aid. The route that avoids Jiri passes through the Those bazaar.

To go to Jiri, cross the two tributaries of the Sikri Khola before they join and climb through chir pine forests to round a ridge (7000 ft, 2134 m) where there is a market every Saturday. Beyond that, descend to **Jiri** (6250 ft, 1905 m) about 1¾ **hours** beyond the Sikri Khola.

From Jiri there are again two choices. One route passes through Those, a *Newar* bazaar and a town with many shops where you can replenish your supplies. The other route ascends higher and offers distant views of mountains.

The route from Jiri through Those follows the west (R) bank of the Jiri Khola south to about 6125 ft (1867 m), crosses to the east (L) bank, and ascends, passing near the village of Kune (6775 ft, 2064 m) to join the trail from Sikri Khola that avoids Jiri. The trail continues to a notch marked with *chorten* (6800 ft, 2070 m) in a chir pine and oak forest and then descends, passing the settlement of Kattike to the south, to the Khimti Khola (5750 ft, 1753 m), which is followed on its west (R) bank to a suspension bridge. Cross it and follow the river north to **Those** (5775 ft, 1760 m). From Jiri to Those takes 2½ **to three hours**.

To take the high route from Jiri, climb the east side of the Jiri Valley in a rhododendron forest to reach a pass (7875 ft, 2400 m) after 1½ **hours**. Then descend to a bridge over the Yelung Khola. I assume the bridge has been rebuilt since it washed out a day before I was to cross it in the monsoon of 1982. Cross it to the northeast (L) bank and go on to a suspension bridge over the Khimti Khola. **Shivalaya** (5900 ft, 1800 m), the village on the other side, is 1½ **hours** from the pass.

To avoid Jiri and go through Those, follow the east (L) bank of the Sikri Khola to near its junction with the Jiri Khola to the south. Cross the Jiri Khola to its east (L) bank and climb up the side of the valley to join the trail from Jiri at 6775 ft (2064 m). Follow this trail to Those as already described. From the first turnoff to Jiri, it takes 2½ **to three hours** to Those. From Those, follow the river on its east (L) bank, walking upstream for 1½ **hours to Shivalaya** (5900 ft, 1800 m).

All the route choices end up at Shivalaya. From here the trail climbs steeply up the ridge to the scattered village of **Sangbadanda** with its schoolhouse (7350 ft, 2240 m) in 1¾ **hours**. Just up from the schoolhouse, the trail branches. If you take the right fork, shortly beyond is Kasourbas and the beginnings of Sherpa settlement. The left branch heads up past the village of **Buldanda** (8200 ft, 2500 m) to the cheese factory at **Thodung** (10,140 ft, 3091 m) about 2¾ hours from Sangbadanda. Besides buying cheese here, you can get a good view of Gaurishankar to the north. This peak (23,459 ft, 7150 m) was once thought to be the highest in the world since it was visible from afar. Thodung is definitely a worthwhile detour. There is a monastery half an hour south of the cheese factory. To rejoin the regular route, head south along the ridge to the pass (8900 ft, 2713 m), reaching it in an hour.

The direct trail to the pass, the right fork, continues along the north side of the valley of the Mohabir Khola, crossing numerous tributaries and entering a rhododendron and broad-leaved forest until the pass (8900 ft, 2713 m) is reached. It takes 1¾ **hours** to reach the pass from Sangbadanda. There are now tea shops run by Sherpas at the pass, and also one of the largest collections of *mani* walls in Nepal. From the pass, take the left fork. The trail descends into the beautiful, lush valley to the east and heads toward the two large *stupas* by a small *gomba* at the town of **Bhandar** (7200 ft, 2194 m), which is called Changma by Sherpas. This walk takes an **hour** and brings you into the area populated by Sherpas.

From the scattered village of Bhandar, descend the fertile plateau towards a notch to cross a river (6600 ft, 2012 m) on a covered bridge. Just beyond, take the fork to the far left. Then go on through forests and terraces to cross the Surma Khola (5100 ft, 1555 m) to its north (L) bank. Continue to the Likhu Khola and cross it on the second suspension bridge (5060 ft, 1543 m) to its east (L) bank. It takes

two hours to reach the river from Bhandar, then **less than an hour** walking up-stream along its east (L) bank through broadleaf forest to reach the Kenja Khola, which is crossed to **Kenja** (5360 ft, 1634 m).

The biggest climb of the journey so far, up to the Lamjura Pass (11,580 ft, 3530 m), begins behind the town and follows a ridge more or less on its south side through oak forest to the small settlement of **Sete** (8450 ft, 2575 m), which has a small *gomba* above it. Be sure to obtain water from the streams crossing the trail below Sete, as there is little until you have descended the other side of the pass. It takes **2¼ to three hours** to reach Sete from Kenja. Beyond, the trail continues along the ridge in a prickly-leaved oak forest. Reach the few houses of Dakchu (9350 ft, 2850 m) an **hour** beyond. A recently installed water-supply system may be functioning here. Goyun (10,350 ft, 3155 m) is a small cluster of tea shops an **hour** beyond. The trail passes through impressive stands of fir. The ridge you have been following meets the main ridge striking north-south, and you fork left at a *mani* wall (11,300 ft, 3444 m). Contour in a splendid rhododendron grove to reach the pass. During the monsoon, people use makeshift shelters along the way to churn milk into butter or *ghiu*. The pass (11,582 ft, 3530 m) is **three to four hours** from Sete. Despite the height of the pass, there is no view of the mountains, but those with time and energy can climb the peak north of the pass (13,159 ft, 4010 m) for views in good weather.

From the Lamjura Pass, the trail descends through a fir-rhododendron forest and emerges at **Tragdobuk**, also called Taktor (9380 ft, 2860 m) in **1½ hours**. Continue on the north side of the valley, round a notch, and drop down to the town of **Junbesi** (8775 ft, 2675 m) in an **hour**. The Serlo Monastery above the village is quite active. The monks print ancient Buddhist texts from woodblocks.

About 1½ hours off the main trail to the north of Junbesi lies Thubten Chhol-ing Gomba, an active monastery with 150 monks. The abbot there, Tulshig Rim-poche, was formerly at the Rongbuk Monastery on the northern slopes of Mount Everest in Tibet. It is a rare privilege to have an audience with this eclectic being. The small *gomba* is exquisitely painted and definitely worth seeing. To reach it, head north from Junbesi past some *chorten* and *mani* walls to a bridge (9000 ft, 2743 m) over the main Junbesi Khola, 30 minutes from town. Continue up the east (L) bank until you spot the monastery on a shelf above you to the east. Follow the main trail past fine Sherpa homes until you are just about under the *gomba* and head directly up to it. The town of Mobung is nearby. The *gomba* is one to 1½ hours from Junbesi. *Rhythms of a Himalayan Village* is a most informative book about this area.

From Junbesi you can also head south to the major Solu towns of Salleri and Phaphlu and to a Tibetan resettlement center at Chialsa. This area is described later in this chapter. The *Shorong/Hinku* map of the Research Scheme Nepal Him-alaya covers the trek from here to Namche Bazaar.

To continue to Namche Bazaar from Junbesi, cross the Junbesi Khola on a log bridge below the stupas (8700 ft, 2552 m) and take the extreme left or upper trail up the valley to the south. The trail passes through blue pine forest to rhododen-dron and prickly-leaved oak forest typical of the western midland forest described in Chapter 12. Such forests are often found on south-facing slopes in this region. After reaching open country, round the crest (10,000 ft, 3048 m) of the Sallung ridge, from which you can see Mount Everest on a clear day! Head north up the valley of the Ringmo Khola to the town of Sallung (9700 ft, 2953 m), about **two hours** from Junbesi.

From here, the trail descends through oak forests to cross two tributaries, then the main river of the Ringmo Khola (8525 ft, 2599 m). The trail then ascends to the few houses of **Ringmo** (9200 ft, 2805 m) 1½ **hours** from Sallung. Here, enter-prising Sherpas may serve you apple juice. En route, the trail branches after cross-ing the river. The right branch heads south to Phaphlu. This region is described later. From Ringmo, the wide trail ascends east through juniper woods past some rectangular *mani* walls to Tragsindho La pass (10,075 ft, 3071 m) with *chorten*, *mani* walls, prayer flags, and hotels. To the south, 450 ft (137 m) below, there is a cheese factory on the west side of the river. You probably will have seen signs pointing the way there. To the east is the valley of the Dudh Kosi, which you follow north to Khumbu. Meanwhile, 460 ft, (140 m) below you is Tragsindho Monastery. To reach it, take the left branch of the trail at the junction 100 ft (30 m) below the pass on the east side. The other trail passes above the monastery and rejoins the monastery trail 100 ft (30 m) below the *gomba*. It takes **forty-five minutes** to reach the pass from Ringmo and another **fifteen minutes** to reach the Gelugpa monas-tery, which is considerably enlarged and much more active than during my first visit in 1969.

From Tragsindho, the trail descends to the southeast, passes through forests, and emerges at the Sherpa village of **Manidingma** (Nuntale) (7200 ft, 2194 m) in 1½ **hours**. Beyond, descend past terraces into oak forests to emerge at a bridge over the Dudh Kosi (4900 ft, 1493 m) 1½ **hours** from Manidingma.

The trail crosses the river to the east (L) bank and heads north to reach Nam-che Bazaar in three days. Sometimes the trail is over a mile above the river, which falls through a steep gorge. This part of Solu-Khumbu is called Pharak. There have been many improvements in agriculture in Pharak over the years. You may notice fruit trees and many varieties of vegetables. The main trail north of here is being continuously improved and may vary from the descriptions in this book. Ask local-ly for the latest routes.

Follow the river for a while through forests, then climb through terraces to reach the *Rai* village of **Jubing** (5500 ft, 1676 m) in **forty minutes**. This is your only opportunity along this trek to see a settlement of these people who populate so much of eastern Nepal. The British found the *Rai* to be excellent soldiers and ac-tively recruited them as Gurkhas. Climb through the village, round a ridge, and aim for the prominent notch in front of you. From the notch (6900 ft, 2103 m), contour to the village of **Karikhola** (6575 ft, 2004 m) inhabited by Sherpas, *Rai*, and *Magar*. Karikhola is 1½ **hours** from Jubing. The *Magar* hail from western Nepal, settling here generations ago. They no longer speak their native language.

Cross the bridge over the Kari Khola, take the right fork, and ascend its north (R) bank through the scattered settlement of Kharte. The trail continues to climb through this tributary valley into prickly-leaved oak and rhododendron forest, where langur monkeys may be occasionally seen. The ridge crest, Khari La (10,100 ft, 3078 m), is **three hours** from Karikhola. At this point, you are almost a mile above the Dudh Kosi. Unlike the gorge of the Kali Gandaki, in central Nepal, you pass well above the steep slopes.

The next tributary valley to the north has to be traversed. Descend 1000 ft (305 m) and cross the tributary after an **hour**. Continue on the north side of the valley to reach **Poiyan** (9175 ft, 2796 m) in **half an hour.** Again, continue to the crest of a ridge, Chutok La (9662 ft, 2945 m), leading down to the Dudh Kosi and again enter the valley of another tributary. Shortly after beginning a steep descent, you can see the STOL landing strip at Lukla, almost due north, as well as the sacred mountain Khumbiyula at the head of the valley. The village of **Surkhe** (7525 ft, 2293 m) at the bridge crossing the tributary below is **two hours** from Poiyan.

The trail now leaves this tributary valley and heads more directly north toward the town of Chaumrikharka, another scattered village. Along the way, pass the fork to Lukla (7850 ft, 2393 m), a **half hour** beyond Surkhe. This junction is just before the main trail crosses a stream on a small cantilever bridge. The STOL field (9350 ft, 2850 m) is reached in an **hour** from here. Before ascending to Chaumrikharka (8500 ft, 2591 m, to 8900 ft, 2713 m) the main trail crosses a spectacular deep gorge with a high waterfall (7900 ft, 2408 m). Upper **Chaumrikharka** (8700 ft, 2652 m), with three large *stupas* and a *gomba*, is 1¾ **hours** from Surkhe. From here on, the going is easier; the major climbs are over. The trail from Chaumrikharka (which means pastures for yak-cow cross-breeds) passes through pleasant fields and ascends to a small ridge (8775 ft, 2674 m), where the trail to the north from Lukla joins the main trail up the Dudh Kosi valley. **Choplung**, a newly built town is a **half hour** from Chaumrikharka.

Lukla (9350 ft, 2850 m) has become a major trekking center over the years. The name Lukla means "place with many goats and sheep," but clearly things have changed! In addition to the airstrip nestled among spectacular mountains, there are now many hotels featuring food and accommodations varying from slightly more expensive than the cheapest in nearby places, to quite luxurious and, of course, expensive. Many trekkers try to fly into Lukla, tour Khumbu, and fly out. There never seem to be enough flights out of Lukla to prevent bottlenecks, and bad weather can cause delays of several days or even a week or more. Sometimes several hundred trekkers of many nationalities may find themselves stranded at Lukla. Many of them have come to Nepal to escape the pressures of their jobs and homes. Yet when they find themselves missing flights to Kathmandu to return to their jobs and homes, they can become very difficult to contend with. Patience wears thin and tempers flare. Although it may be comical to those who remain calm, such displays project an unfortunate image of the visitors to the rather re-laxed natives. These problems can be prevented by avoiding Lukla as a point of pickup by air. Shyangboche farther north is certainly no better, for there are no scheduled flights. However, Phaphlu, an airstrip perhaps two days farther from Khumbu, has fewer logistical problems, and the prosperous area of Solu visited en route is quite pleasant. The airstrip at Phaphlu is being enlarged to enable Twin Otter aircraft to land, which may lessen the crowd problems at Lukla. Walking out towards Lamosangu on the Kathmandu-Kodari Highway is time consuming, but especially worthwhile if you have never traveled this route before. Walking out to the south is another possibility. Flights back to Kathmandu can be arranged from the STOL strips at Lamidanda and Rumjatar, two towns near the route. You can also continue south to the Tarai and either link up with the East-West Highway and go to Kathmandu, or fly from major towns such as Janakpur. Or you could go southeast to Dharan or Ilam. This route is described in Chapter 11. Finally you could walk out of Khumbu by crossing the high and potentially dangerous Trashi Labsta, a pass to the west of Thami, and return to Kathmandu via Rolwaling. Only well-equipped parties of experienced mountaineers should attempt this route.

To proceed from Lukla to Khumbu, head north and join the main trail at Choplung. All trekkers heading to Khumbu, whether on foot from Kathmandu, or by

Kwangde and other summits to the east of Namche Bazaar. (Dave Hardenbergh)

plane, will end up at **Choplung**. To proceed from there, head north, crossing another tributary (8850 ft, 2698 m), with a beautiful peak at its head. Soon, come to a bridge over the Dudh Kosi, with the village of Ghat (8350 ft, 2545 m) on both banks. There are hotels here. Proceed on the east (L) bank through to Phakding (8700 ft, 2652 m), now expanded to both sides of the river. Phakding is 1½ **hours** from Choplung and 2½ hours from Lukla. Here, cross to the west (R) bank (8600 ft, 2621 m) of the Dudh Kosi. Continue through blue pine and rhododendron forests to the village of **Benkar** (8875 ft, 2905 m), which is reached in an **hour** from Phakding. Watch for large, hanging, tongue-like beehives just beyond a waterfall on the east (L) bank cliffs opposite you in this steep-walled canyon. In a short while, cross to the east (L) bank and climb up through Chumowa. Here you may notice extensive vegetable farms as well as a Japanese hotel. The vegetables grown here are excellent. A kerosene depot is planned to alleviate the fuel pressures on Khumbu's forests. Cross another tributary, the Kyangshar Khola (9100 ft, 2773 m), before climbing up a cleft in the canyon wall to Mondzo (9300 ft, 2835 m) about **forty-five minutes** from Benkar. The trail then descends in a cleft to the left of a huge rock, and crosses to the west (R) bank of the Dudh Kosi on a large suspension bridge to reach **Jorsale** (9100 ft, 2774 m) in **forty-five minutes**. This is the last village before Namche Bazaar. Enter Sagarmatha (Everest) National Park here and pay the entrance fee. You can see the route on the *Khumbu Himal* map of the Research Scheme Nepal Himalaya. Jorsale is called Thumbug on this map.

Continue up the west bank through blue pine forests to reach the confluence of the Bhote Kosi from the west and the Dudh Kosi from the east. The west fork is crossed (9325 ft, 2843 m) to its east (L) bank and the climb to Namche Bazaar begins. Some 500 ft (152 m) up the crest of the prow, Everest can be seen behind the Lhotse-Nuptse ridge. Water has even been piped to this point. **Namche Bazaar** (11,300 ft, 3446 m) is **two or 2½ hours** from Jorsale. You are now in Khumbu. Sherpas run the stores, hotels, and restaurants. Prices are high but most staples are available. Old expedition food and equipment are available in the shops. The headquarters of Sagarmatha National Park is in Namche, with an excellent museum on the hill to the east. General regulations of the national parks are discussed in Chapter 3. You and your party must carry and use only non-wood fuel during your stay in the park.

Namche Bazaar is a remarkable town. In the autumn of 1983, a small hydro-electric generating station built on the stream flowing out of town began producing electricity for lighting and a few other services. As the administrative center for Khumbu, Namche Bazaar has many officials and offices, including a police check post. Many of the officials are lowlanders who would rather be elsewhere, though they do enjoy the good things about Namche Bazaar—the clean air, good water, and impressive views. Namche Bazaar used to be a trading center where grain from the south was exchanged for salt from Tibet, and it remains a trading center even though the salt trade has ended. The weekly market held on Saturday is colorful and well worth seeing, and there are lots of interesting shops. Enterprising Sherpas have set up hotels with hot showers and a variety of foods. It is a good place to rejuvenate after the rigors of the heights. If you find Namche too commercial, stay in Kunde or Khumjung. But spend at least one night in Namche to become acclimated.

Cumulative trekking times (walking time only, does not include rests or stops) from Lamosangu to:

Muldi	8	hours	Junbesi	45	hours
Shera	10½	"	Tragsindho Monastery	49½	"
Kirantichap	14½	"	Jubing	53¼	"
Kabre	19¼	"	Karikhola	54¼	"
Sikri	23½	"	Poiyan	61¼	"
Shivalaya	29	"	Choplung	63½	"
Kenja	36½	"	Jorsale	67½	"
Sete	42½	"	Namche Bazaar	70	"

Khumbu

(Map No. 5, Page 215)

> *To arrive by foot in Sherpa country is to gain some insight into what it was like for the Israelites to reach the promised land.*

Mike Thompson, anthropologist and climber

You should not regard Namche Bazaar or Tengboche as the turnaround point on the trek. There are enough things to do in Khumbu to occupy two or three weeks. Four main river valleys can be explored, each with spectacular mountain scenery. You can visit two monasteries and at least three village *gomba*. And perhaps most appealing are the Sherpa people and their culture. If you have employed a Sherpa whose home is in Khumbu, you will most likely be given the hospitality of his home. Those fortunate enough to be in Khumbu during the full moon in May or November-December may see Mani-rimdu, the Sherpa drama festival depicting the victory of Buddhism over Bon. The May production is usually at the Thami Monastery and the November-December one at the Tengboche Monastery. Several of the trips possible in Khumbu are described here.

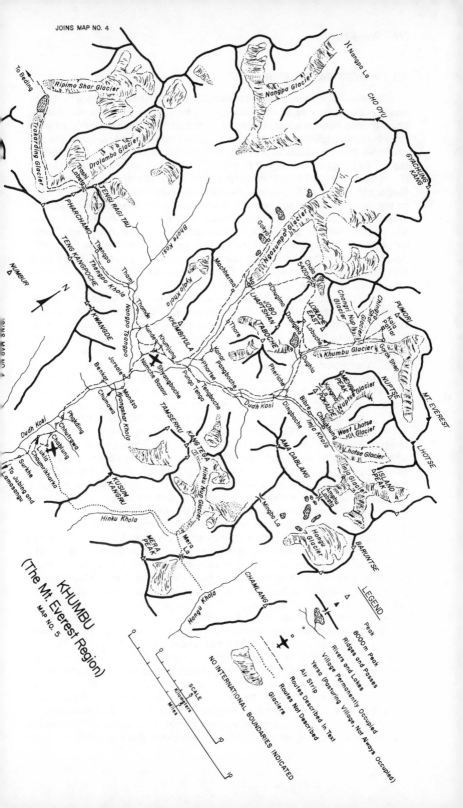

KHUMBU
(The Mt. Everest Region)

MAP NO. 5

LEGEND

△ Peak
▲ 8000 m Peak
Ridges and Passes
Rivers and Lakes
✕ Village Permanently Occupied
Yersa (Pasturing Village, Not Always Occupied)
✈ Air Strip
Routes Described In Text
Routes Not Described
Glaciers

NO INTERNATIONAL BOUNDARIES INDICATED

SCALE
Kilometers
Miles

To Beding
Ripimo Shar Glacier
Trakarding Glacier
Drolambo Glacier
Tashi Labsta
TENGI RAGI TAU
PHARCHAMO
Thengpo
Thengpo Khola
TENG KANGPOCHE
Thami
Thame
Thamo
Nangpo Tsangpo
KWANGDE
NUMBUR
N
Bhote Kosi
Kyajo Khola
Kunde
Khumjung
KHUMBYULA
Nangpa Glacier
Nangpa La
CHO OYU
GYACHUNG KANG
Nangozumpa Glacier
Gokyo
Machhermo
Thore
Chugima
Dzongla
Cholo 5420?
JOBO LHAPTSHAN
TABOCHE
Phortse
Konar
Pangboche
Pheriche
Dughla
Lobuche
LOBUCHE EAST
Changri Nup Glacier
Chimgard Shar
Kala Pattar
PUMORI
Gorak Shep
Khumbu Glacier
NW
MT EVEREST
LHOTSE
West Lhotse Glacier
Lhotse Glacier
NUPTSE
Nuptse Glacier
MERA PEAK
AMPHU LAPCHE
Chukhung
Imja Khola
Dingboche
ISLAND PEAK
Imja Glacier
Ama Chosa
BARUNTSE
Hongu Glacier
Mingbo La
AMA DABLANG
Dudh Kosi
Tengboche
Pungo Tenga
Benkar
Mondzo
Kyongshar Khola
Jorsale
Namche Bazaar
Shyangboche
TAMSERKU
KANG TEGA
Hinku Nup Glacier
Phakding
Chhutrawa
Chablung
Lukla
Chaunrikharko
KUSUM KANGRU
Chumowa
Surkhe
To Jubing and Lamosangu
Dudh Kosi
Hinku Khola
MERA PEAK
Mera La
Hongu Khola
CHAMLANG
Hongu Glacier

TO EVEREST BASE CAMP

From Namche Bazaar the trail rises to the saddle to the east where the Sagarmatha National Park museum (11,550 ft, 3520 m) sits. You can head northwest to Shyangboche from here. Instead, contour high above the Dudh Kosi until, by some large boulders (11,800 ft, 3597 m), this trail joins the one from Khumjung. The trail continues through forests of blue pine and rhododendron, passing below the village of Trashinga and through the houses of Levishasa and the forest nursery to the Dudh Kosi (10,650 ft, 3247 m), where there is a small settlement called **Pungo Tenga**, with several mills, a series of water-driven prayer wheels, and some hotels on the far left bank. It is **two hours** from Namche Bazaar. The trail climbs past the prayer wheels through very pleasant forest, with occasional impressive views of Kangtega, to **Tengboche** (12,687 ft, 3867 m), about **two hours** from the river. The forest of pine, fir, black juniper, and rhododendron en route is remarkable. Early in the morning or late in the afternoon, if you are quiet, you may be able to spot a musk deer along here. Across the valley to the south, there are silver birch forests, which grow well on the colder north slopes.

Look for blood pheasants feeding near Tengboche in the morning. As from so many places in Khumbu, the views from Tengboche are spectacular. What a place for a monastery! It was founded in 1923, but the main temple was destroyed in the 1934 earthquake. The monks follow the Nyingmapa sect of Buddhism. The Tengboche *gomba* can be visited, and sometimes respects can be paid to the venerable abbot. When visiting the abbot, be sure to offer him a ceremonial scarf or *kata* obtained from another monk. A donation from each visitor is appreciated. The abbot has built a Sherpa cultural center. There are several choices for food and lodging. The park maintains guest houses for trekkers and also latrines or *chaarpi*.

From Tengboche the trail heads east and descends slightly past the nunnery at Deboche (12,325 ft, 3757 m) and the few houses at Milingo, all the while in a fine forest of rhododendrons that are spectacular in bloom. These trees are festooned with moss lower down. Pass immense trunks of juniper, which bespeak the extensive forests that once existed here. Continue to the river, the Imja Khola, and cross it at a narrowing on a suspension bridge (12,400 ft, 3780 m) from which you get a spectacular view of Ama Dablang. Cross to the north (R) bank. Some **five or ten minutes** beyond, near some *mani* stones, the trail forks. The left (higher) fork ascends to the Pangboche Gomba (13,075 ft, 3985 m), while the right goes directly to the village of **Pangboche** (12,800 ft, 3901 m) some 1½ **hours** from Tengboche. The *gomba*, the oldest in Khumbu, was built some 300 years ago at the time that Buddhism is said to have been introduced into Khumbu. According to legend, a venerable old lama tore out his hair and cast it around the *gomba*. The large black juniper trees surrounding it sprouted from those hairs. They are so large because it is forbidden to cut them. The *gomba* contains some yeti relics—a scalp and some bones—which you can see for a few rupees.

Continue northeast from either the village itself or from the *gomba*, and reach a trail fork at a *mani* wall (13,725 ft, 4183 m) 1½ **hours** beyond Pangboche. The right fork goes toward Dingboche, while the left, slightly less prominent fork climbs past one hut to the crest of a small ridge (14,050 ft, 4282 m) from which Pheriche can be seen. Descend a short distance to the bridge over the Khumbu Khola (13,875 ft, 4229 m) and cross it to the west (L) bank to reach **Pheriche** (13,950 ft, 4252 m) in some **two or three hours** from Pangboche, depending on acclimatization.

Pheriche, once a *yersa* or temporary yak herding area, is now settled throughout the winter—entirely because of the trekking traffic. It is a very different place

Tengboche and the Gokyo Valley to the north. (Dave Hardenbergh)

from the one I encountered on my first visit in 1969. There are hotels built from blocks of sod, a garbage dump, and some latrines. Pheriche is usually crowded with people, although solitude can be found nearby. There is a Trekkers' Aid Post, which was set up by the Himalayan Rescue Association in 1973. The post does research on altitude illness as well as providing medical care to trekkers and porters. A pressure chamber is currently being tested here to treat altitude illness. Of course, it is even better to prevent it by slow acclimatization. Every party should spend two nights, or at least a complete day and night, at Pheriche. During the day spent here, an ascent or hike is an especially good idea. You could spend this day going to Dingboche and farther east up the Imja Khola as described later. Or you could climb the ridge to the northeast to as high as 17,000 ft (5030 m) for views of Makalu to the east and of nearby summits. There is a hermitage on the way. You could also recross the Khumbu Khola and climb up on the shoulders of Taboche to the west. Or simply do the next day's walk, but return to Pheriche for the night. If you are already bothered by the altitude, it may be best to walk along the valley floor or just rest! Check the section on altitude illness in Chapter 5.

To go on to the foot of Everest, continue north from Pheriche along the flats past the *yersa* of Phuling Karpo, then turn northeast up a grassy lateral moraine of the Khumbu Glacier. The route crosses its crest, descends to cross a glacial stream emerging from the snout of the glacier, which is covered by the moraine

(15,025 ft, 4579 m), and ascends to the huts of **Dughla** (15,075 ft, 4593 m). It takes 1½ **hours** to reach Dughla from Pheriche. Climb to pass to the right of stone memorials on a ridge crest. These are built for climbers killed on expeditions to nearby summits, mostly Everest. There were none here when I first walked up this valley in 1969! The trail then contours on the other side of the glacier after crossing another stream of melted water. The trail heads northeast to the tea shops of **Lobuche** (16,175 ft, 4930 m), situated below the terminal moraine of a tributary glacier. Lobuche is about 1½ **hours** from Dughla. A climb to the ridge crest to the west provides fine views, especially at sunset.

There is shelter beyond Lobuche. Several stone huts at Gorak Shep cater to trekkers in the autumn and spring. It is possible to use Lobuche as a base to climb to Kala Pattar for views and to return the same day. This is advisable to avoid altitude problems. If you plan to sleep at Gorak Shep, it is best to have your own tents since space in the drafty huts can't be counted on.

To the southeast of Lobuche lies a pass, the Kongma La (18,135 ft, 5527 m). A good side trip is to cross the Khumbu Glacier, ascend the pass, and head south to Bibre as described later. This trip takes a very long, strenuous day, and requires confidence on rock. Pokalde Peak, south of the pass, could also be climbed.

Beyond Lobuche the trail follows a trough beside the Khumbu Glacier, then climbs through the terminal moraine of another tributary glacier. From a high point here, the rubble-covered hill of **Kala Pattar** in front of Pumori can be seen, and at its base, a lake that is often frozen. Those planning to go to Gorak Shep at the northeast end of the lake should descend to the sands and contour the lake on its northeast shore to the rock monuments to persons who have died nearby. Gorak Shep (17,000 ft, 5184 m) is reached in 2¼ **to three hours** from Lobuche. You can no doubt see Tibetan snow cocks here and approach them quite closely.

The cairn of upper Kala Pattar (18,450 ft, 5623 m) to the north of the rounded hill that is the surveyed point of Kala Pattar can be reached in 1½ **hours** from Gorak Shep by ascending directly and keeping slightly to the northeast. You can see the South Col of Everest from here, as well as the immense west and south faces. This is certainly one of the most majestic mountain viewpoints in the world. Alternatively, by proceeding from the terminal moraine, you can head directly up to Kala Pattar without going to Gorak Shep. It may be difficult to find the "trail" through the moraine, especially if there has been a recent snowfall. Trail sense is an asset, though small cairns mark the way.

The world's highest mountain was named after Sir George Everest, the head of the Survey of India from 1823 to 1843. Sherpas use its Tibetan name, Chomolongma, which means "Goddess of the Wind." Sagarmatha, its Nepali name, means "Churning Stick of the Ocean of Existence." It was first climbed in 1953 by Sir Edmund Hillary and Tenzing Norgay.

The sites of the various base camps used for climbing Everest are close to the foot of the Khumbu icefall (17,575 ft, 5357 m) and can be reached from Gorak Shep in a few hours by venturing over the rubble-covered surface of the Khumbu Glacier. As you approach the first evidence of base-camp garbage, note that recent base camps are an hour or so beyond, right at the foot of the Khumbu icefall. If you are here when no expedition is climbing Everest, it may be tedious and time consuming to find the exact location. It is possible to visit the base camps from Lobuche and return the same long day. There are not good views from the base camps and little reason to go if visiting this area is not important to you. If time is limited, it is better to ascend to Kala Pattar.

Better views of the Khumbu icefall and the other side of the Lhotse-Nuptse

Wall can be obtained by climbing up the southeast ridge of Pumori. This ridge is reached by going part way to the base camps and turning northwest. Do not go out on the Khumbu Glacier to reach the ridge; stay on the lateral moraine. You will be able to see the North Col of Everest before encountering technical difficulties. Lhotse can also be seen. The view of the massive hunk of Everest is not as good from here as from Kala Pattar. Gorak Shep is the best base for this trip.

You can vary your return trip in several ways. Crossing the Chugima pass offers one route. You can also take a trail on the left side of the Imja Khola, crossing it below where the Khumbu (or Pheriche) Khola enters. Cross back before Pangboche, or continue on the south side to meet the trail to Tengboche.

The times given for the journey beyond Namche Bazaar are quite variable. They depend upon the weather conditions as well as the fitness and acclimatization of the party. Allow at least five days to reach Kala Pattar from Tengboche. Hire local porters to carry your loads since they can handle the altitude much better than you. If you are going to high altitudes, be prepared for cold winds and snow. It is most important to heed the warning signs of altitude sickness described in Chapter 5. Many trekkers have died in this region because they did not do so. And they continue to die!

UP THE IMJA KHOLA

Reach **Dingboche** as already described or climb up the ridge (14,250 ft, 4343 m) behind Pheriche and descend to it in **half an hour**. You can take a shortcut from Lobuche by crossing the stream emanating from the snout of the Khumbu Glacier and climbing up the lateral moraine. Then follow a trail that contours to the south, passing the small temporary village of Dusa before dropping down to Dingboche. This third possibility is the quickest route from Lobuche.

From a little west of Dingboche you can climb up to Nangkartshang Gomba (15,430 ft, 4703 m) in 1½ **hours** for fine views of Makalu to the east. This is a detour if you are going to Chhukhung, but you could then head east to join the trail coming from Dingboche at **Bibre** (15,000 ft, 4571 m). Bibre is reached in 1½ **hours** from Dingboche by the direct route. The trail continues east, crossing numerous streams that flow from the Nuptse and Lhotse Glaciers, to a number of yak huts or *yersa* at **Chhukhung** (15,535 ft, 4734 m) perhaps 1½ **hours** after Bibre.

You can now see Ama Dablang's east face. It is worthwhile to spend a day or two traveling around to the east and to the northeast for close views of the incredible Lhotse-Nuptse Wall. Either the *Khumbu Himal* or the *Mahalungar Himal* map is very useful here and suggests many hikes. Imja Tse (Island Peak), a trekking summit, is northeast of Chhukhung.

KHUMJUNG AND KUNDE

The STOL strip called Shyangboche (12,205 ft, 3720 m) is carved out of a shelf of land. Reach it less than an hour from Namche Bazaar, taking the trail that climbs past the *gomba*. There are hotels and restaurants here. The government yak breeding farm five to ten minutes to the northwest is recognized by an impressive fence enclosing it. Often the yaks and naks (females) may be pastured much higher. The farm is attempting to preserve and maintain good genetic stocks necessary for the cross-breeding programs in which hearth *chAUmri* (cross between cow and yak) are developed. You can proceed past the preserve to the northwest, climbing to a crest (12,700 ft, 3871 m) in peaceful juniper forests and descending to **Kunde** (12,600 ft, 3841 m). The north end of this town is the site of

Kunde Hospital, built by the Himalayan Trust established by Sir Edmund Hillary.

To reach Khumjung, the "sister city" of Kunde, you can either traverse east from Kunde, or go directly from Shyangboche by climbing northeast from the airstrip past a large *chorten* in a blue pine forest. Descend past the Himalayan Trust school to the potato fields below **Khumjung** (12,400 ft, 3780 m). A village *gomba* in a juniper grove to the north contains yeti relics that can be seen for a donation. The yeti scalp has been sent around the world for a test of its authenticity. Read *High in the Thin Cold Air* by Sir Edmund Hillary and Desmond Doig (Garden City, New York: Doubleday, 1962) for details. The famed Sherpa artist Kappa Pasang lives in Khumjung.

Of final interest is the now closed Everest View Hotel, beautifully situated on a shelf (12,700 ft, 3870 m). It can be reached in half an hour or less from the airstrip by following the well-graded path beginning at the lower end of the airstrip. Or you can reach it from the stupa at the eastern end of the potato fields of Khumjung.

Much has changed in this area since my first visit. Immediately noticeable are the new houses with Western-style windows, corrugated tin roofs, and chimneys. Water systems have been constructed, making it somewhat easier to get water. People are much more cautious with their use of firewood since it is so time consuming to search for it. Communal fires are much smaller than at, say, Phortse, where wood is more plentiful. Families have a greater variety of Western goods. Mountaineering equipment and clothes are often used rather than the traditional items. Indeed the school bell at Khumjung is an old oxygen cylinder. Wealth is more often measured in terms of equipment and money rather than traditionally in the size of yak and sheep herds. Indeed, with children going off to school, it is difficult to find laborers to tend the animals. Of course the general level of education is quite good, and there are many Sherpas who are fluent in English. The population pressures have turned potato fields into homes below Khumjung. And it is not uncommon to find widows caring for children and looking after homes. Mountaineering expeditions take their toll and the Sherpas as an ethnic group were never large in number. The monasteries are perhaps less well supported now. It was traditional for a family to send the youngest child to the monastery, but now such practices are less common. Some of the changes are for the good, and some are questionable. No matter how we perceive it, the Sherpas feel their lot is better now.

TO GOKYO

The trip up the Dudh Kosi from Khumjung takes you to summer yak-grazing country, to beautiful small lakes, and to the foot of Cho Oyu and Gyachung Kang peaks. The trail goes northeast of the stupa at the east end of Khumjung and climbs along the side of Khumbiyula crossing a rocky prominence to a crest of a ridge (13,000 ft, 3992 m) where there is a stupa. This takes **two hours** from Khumjung. Above you on the slopes of Khumbiyula watch for a herd of Himalayan tahr (called *goral* by locals). Phortse is across the river. The trail descends steeply to near the river (11,950 ft, 3643 m). Take the left fork at junctions, as those to the right descend and cross the river to Phortse. The trail heads north and, after an **hour** or so, Cho Oyu is visible. You cross many spectacular waterfalls that are frozen in winter. Many landslides have occurred on both sides of this steep valley. After emerging from the woods, the trail passes several summer yak herding huts, or *yersa*, including Tongba (13,175 ft, 4015 m), **Gyele**, and Dole (13,400 ft, 4084 m). It takes **2¾ hours** from the stupa on the ridge crest to **Gyele**. The next *yersa* at Lhabarma is far from water, but it is available at the one after that, Luza. Because

Ama Dablang from Khumjung. (Stephen Bezruchka)

this valley has not developed traditional resting points, such as Pheriche on the way to the foot of Everest, people are ascending too rapidly. Serious altitude illness is occurring more often here, while the incidence on the way to Everest has declined. Be prudent and take the time to rest a day or two.

From Gyele, **Lhabarma** (14,200 ft, 4328 m) is reached in **less than an hour** and **Luza** (14,400 ft, 4390 m) is another **hour.** In the next tributary valley is **Machherma** (14,650 ft, 4465 m), another **forty-five minutes** away. Go on for an **hour** to **Pangka** (14,925 ft, 4548 m), but here again, there is no water near. From Pangka, descend slightly, following one of the melted glacial rivers that flow down the west side of the Ngozumpa Glacier, which is to the east now. The trail crosses this river at a narrowing and soon emerges at the first of several small lakes (15,450 ft, 4709 m) **1½ hours** beyond Pangka. Another **forty-five minutes** brings you to the next lake, or *tsho*, with the *yersa* Longpanga at its northern end. There is no good shelter here, so continue for another **half hour** to the third lake (sometimes called Dudh Pokhari) and the *yersa* of **Gokyo** (15,720 ft, 4791 m) on its east shore.

From Gokyo, Cho Oyu looms to the north. There are several places to go for views. Currently the most popular is to ascend the ridge to the northwest to a small summit (17,990 ft, 5483 m). This climb takes **two to three hours** for those well acclimatized and provides an excellent panorama from Cho Oyu, to Everest, to Lhotse, and all the way to Makalu. Some trekkers consider the vew from this Kala Pattar, as it is called, better than from the one above Gorak Shep. Alternatively, you can follow the trail north between the lateral moraine of the glacier and the hills to the west until you reach the next lake (16,150 ft, 4923 m) where, near its east shore, there are some roofless huts, about **1½ hours** from Gokyo. A climb of a few hundred feet up the hill to the north of the lake provides fine views. You could also continue another **1½ hours** to the last lake. The *Khumbu Himal* map may suggest many other hikes. You could return from Gokyo by following the east side of the valley, reaching it from below the snout of the glacier at Pangka. Or you could cross the glacier directly east of Gokyo. Alternatively, you could follow the route described below in reverse to reach the Khumbu Glacier and the foot of Everest.

Most of the *yersa* settlements in Khumbu belong to the people in the permanent villages to the south. They are usually locked up when no one is there. If you employ a local Sherpa, he can very likely get permission for you to use those owned by his family or acquaintances. You should pay a few rupees a night to use them. During much of the popular trekking season, hotels operate out of most settlements all the way to Gokyo.

PASS 5420 METERS (CHUGIMA)

For people who want to combine visits to the Everest Base Camp region with one to the upper reaches of the Dudh Kosi beneath Cho Oyu without extensive backtracking, this pass is a scenic and enjoyable route. It does involve a short glacier crossing for which a rope and ice axe are advisable; however, there are no serious dangers or technical difficulties. In the process, you circumnavigate Jobo Lhaptshan (21,128 ft, 6440 m) and Taboche (20,889 ft, 6367 m) for excellent views of Cho Oyu to the north.

Be aware that fresh snowfall on the pass seriously increases the difficulty and the risk of frostbite. If you do not have enough experience to be sure that the new snow will not cause problems, consider skipping the pass. In the autumn of 1982, snowfall resulted in at least five trip-ending cases of frostbite, and some trekkers suffered permanent damage. At that time, renowned mountaineer Reinhold

Messner assessed the conditions and elected to avoid the pass and go around via Phortse!

To descend from the Everest Base Camp area, follow the trail down below Lobuche some **fifteen to thirty minutes** as far as the stream crossing on the lateral moraine (16,000 ft, 4877 m), but instead of crossing it, contour along a trail on the side of the valley eventually turning northwest into the valley of the pass. You can thus stay at a high elevation and instead of descending to the shores of the lake below you (Tshola Tsho), cross the main stream that feeds into the lake higher up. Pick the trail up again near the stream crossing if it has been lost. The trail ascends to the *yersa* of Dzonglha (15,889 ft, 4843 m), beautifully situated on a shelf of land with fine views in every direction. It is about 2½ **hours or more** from Lobuche. This is a very good spot to camp, either in tents or in the huts. The feeling of sitting under the north face of Jobo Lhaptshan is unforgettable.

Alternatively, if approaching this area from the south, go to Dughla and follow the trail slightly below it before bearing west to the small trail skirting the end of the Tshola Glacier moraine, which has almost blocked the valley and formed the Tshola Tsho (lake) above it. Reach the end of the lake (14,804 ft, 4512 m)—it is ice-covered in November—in **half an hour.** The best camping spot for spectacular views is near here, but the only huts are some distance farther on. The trail follows the north shore of the lake and rises gradually until it reaches Tsholo Og (15,306 ft, 4665 m), a *yersa* of three huts, in **forty-five minutes.** All are unoccupied and locked in winter. Water must be carried from a stream **ten minutes** farther on. Dzonglha is another **hour** up the faint trail Above this *yersa*, the trail is less distinct, and although there is no further shelter, there are signs of people using the pass.

Cross a small crest just above Dzonglha and descend slightly into the gentle valley coming down from the glacier in the pass to the northwest. The pass, sometimes called Chugima or Chola by locals, is the 17,783-ft (5420-m) crossing marked on the Schneider *Khumbu Himal* map. There is a small trail aiming for the glacier-smoothed rock to the east of the glacier itself. The moraine at the head of the valley is reached in an **hour** from Dzonglha. Ascend to the right of the glacier, sometimes on loose rock, sometimes on large slabs with handsome graining, until you reach a small valley or moat between the rock and the glacier. En route you may find the remnants of a meteorological survey station and a bench mark (E9/GEN). Eventually, gain the glacier around 17,350 ft (5285 m). Keep to its south side and ascend steeply at first (30°) on the snow-covered surface. Watch for crevasses. During the monsoon the surface may be bare ice and require crampons. The glacier levels out and the pass (17,783 ft, 5420 m) is reached in perhaps 2½ **hours** from Dzonglha. A new valley and new vistas open up before you. From the pass there are no views of the giants, but an opportunity to appreciate the lesser, often more beautiful, mountains. Those with experience and equipment may want to scramble up the snow to the minor summit to the south.

The descent on the west side of the pass is initially down steep, hard snow, then onto variegated talus heading south. Beware of ice avalanches and loose rock from the hanging glacier on the peak marked 5666 m on the Schneider map. Reach the valley floor with its boulders and hummocks. If heading to Gokyo, you can bear west without losing much altitude, then descend to cross the Ngozumpa Glacier. If heading south, continue along the trail through the boulders and hummocks near the main stream in the rather flat valley. Near the end of the shelf, there are caves by the stone fences of Chugimo (16,175 ft, 4930 m). They are suitable for shelter or camping. Reach them in **two to three hours** from the pass. As you leave the flats, follow the trail on the north (L) side of the stream and reach

Yaks grazing near the Tengboche Monastery, with Everest barely visible over the Lhotse-Nuptse ridge to the left and Ama Dablang on the right. (Ane Haaland)

Dragnag, a beautiful *yersa* (15,100 ft, 4602 m) within sight of the terminal moraine of the Ngozumpa Glacier, in **forty-five minutes**. Cross the river on a rock bridge to the south (L) bank. The river may be concealed beneath it. Don't descend, but contour **fifteen minutes** to a *yersa* called Tsom (15,000 ft, 4572 m), labeled Gonglha on the *Khumbu Himal* map. Alternatively, you could descend from Dragnag to Na (14,435 ft, 4400 m), labeled Tsoshung on the map, which is below the tongue of the glacier. From here, you can join the route described earlier on the west (R) bank of the Dudh Kosi by crossing the stream west of Na and contouring gently up to the south to reach the shelf above the river in **half an hour**. Before you proceed, note the view of the impressive south face of Cho Oyu to the north.

   To head south to Phortse on the east side of the valley, continue contouring below Tsom, crossing a tributary to reach Thare (14,250 ft, 4343 m) in **forty-five minutes**. Another **half hour** of climbing brings you to Thore (14,435 ft, 4400 m), which is probably the spot marked Thare on the Schneider *Khumbul Himal* map. Names do get confusing in Khumbu, especially since names on the Schneider map are Tibetan for the most part, while the inhabitants are Sherpa, and the initial survey-ors were Indian! Fortunately the route is completely straightforward. After a couple of tributaries, the *yersa* of Konar (13,425 ft, 4092 m) near another tributary is reached in **1½ hours**. There is no permanent habitation along this valley before Phortse. All of the huts along the route are in excellent condition, and the area is very beautiful—perhaps there is a relationship to the paucity of trekkers.

Continue into a handsome juniper and birch forest to a tributary that is the source of the Phortse water supply. Continue through rhododendrons to upper **Phortse** (12,140 ft, 3700 m), some **forty-five minutes** from Konar. Phortse is the impressively perched village you have probably seen from the south. It dominates the entrance to the valley you have descended. To leave Phortse, descend through the fine forest to the west to the Dudh Kosi (11,200 ft, 3414 m) in **half an hour** and ascend to meet the trail from Khumjung to Gokyo that has already been described in another **half hour.**

TO THAMI

The trail to Thami begins at Namche Bazaar and heads west without going behind the *gomba* as the other trail does. You can also take the trail heading west from Shyangboche before the descent to Namche Bazaar. The trail contours the Nangpo Tsangpo Valley, passing Phurte (11,400 ft, 3475 m), then crossing the main tributary from the north, the Kyajo Khola (11,200 ft, 3414 m) at the small town of Kyajo. Continue on to **Thamo** (11,300 ft, 3444 m) **1½ hours** from Namche Bazaar, or less from Shyangboche. To the north above the trail is the town of Mende where there is a new monastery with an English-speaking *Rinpoche* (reincarnate abbot). Westerners sometimes study there. Proceed to **Thomde** (11,500 ft, 3505 m) where a miniature hydroelectric project is being planned to provide electricity to Khumbu. The trail continues to follow the river and crosses it (11,550 ft, 3520 m) some **forty-five minutes** beyond Thamo to ascend on its south (R) bank. Pass through pleasant forests and reach the Thengpo Khola flowing east from the Trashi Labsta pass. Cross it to the north (L) bank (12,075 ft, 3680 m) and ascend a small hill to the north to the valley flats and the town of **Thami** (12,400 ft, 3780 m) an **hour** from Thomde. There is a small hill just to the north of Thami beyond which you are not permitted to go. To the north up the main riverbed lies the Nangpa La (18,753 ft, 5716 m), an important pass into Tibet that was once the popular trading route. To the west of Thami, where the hill behind the town terminates at the base of a cliff, is a monastery (12,925 ft, 3940 m) worth visiting. Farther to the east at the head of the valley is the Trashi Labsta, a high pass (18,885 ft, 5755 m) leading west to the Rolwaling Valley. It is described in Chapter 11.

Solu

(Map No. 4, Page 205)

Those with sufficient time should consider visiting the towns of southern Solu. This region is inhabited by Sherpas who have migrated south from Khumbu and settled where it is much easier to farm and live. They are generally wealthier than their northern counterparts, and signs of this wealth are readily apparent. Another attraction of this area is a successful Tibetan camp at Chialsa.

People who are heading to Khumbu, but who wish to detour to this region, must leave the regular route at Junbesi, while those returning to Kathmandu should turn off from Ringmo, or possibly from Phuleli. There is a high route from Ghat west over the ridge and south to Ringmo, but it is not practical except in the dry season if there has not been any snow at higher elevations.

From **Junbesi**, cross the bridge below the stupa and take the right fork of the level trail that follows above the northeast (L) bank of the Junbesi Khola. In **less than half an hour** you come to **Khamje** (8525 ft, 2599 m). Continue along the river until it flows in the Dudhkunda Khola, also called the Solu Khola, and cross this river (7725 ft, 2355 m) to its east (L) bank. Head south, following close to the river for the most part, until a shack (7480 ft, 2250 m) is reached. The trail rises beyond the shack and soon joins the main north-south trail higher on the east bank at a magnificent house with a private *gomba* (8100 ft, 2469 m) in **Phaphlu**. This walk takes about **two hours** from Khamje. The impressive forests are mostly prickly-leaved oak. A hospital has been built here by Sir Edmund Hillary. Head south for about **forty-five minutes to Salleri** (7700 ft, 2347 m), the district center of Solu-Khumbu. Along the way, pass the Phaphlu airstrip (7775 ft, 2370 m). From a distance Salleri is reminiscent of a Wild West town. The name Salleri means "pine forest." Another **fifteen minutes** to the south is **Dorphu** (7500 ft, 2256 m), where a colorful market is held every Saturday. To visit the Tibetan camp at **Chialsa**, follow the trail to the southeast from Dorphu for a **little over an hour**. It continues climbing above most of the houses to the camp (9000 ft, 2743 m). Be sure to visit the carpet manufacturing center.

Another attraction of the area is **Chiwong Gomba** (9700 ft, 2953 m), a monastery spectacularly situated high on a cliff overlooking Phaphlu and Salleri. It can be reached by heading north from Chialsa for some **three to four hours**. Trekkers heading south from Ringmo can get to it more directly. It could also be reached from the bridge over the Dudhkunda from which a trail heads directly up to join the main north-south trail on the east side of the valley at 8200 ft (2500 m). From here, head south and shortly take the fork to the left heading to Chiwong. The *gomba* is well described in *Buddhist Himalaya* (see Recommended Reading). The Mani-rimdu dance/drama festival is staged here in the autumn.

To reach this area on your return from Khumbu, head south from **Ringmo**. The trail branches left from the one to Sallung at 9050 ft (2758 m) just below the town, and goes south on a wide path. After contouring through a forest, the trail passes through the attractive town of **Phera** (8300 ft, 2530 m) 1¾ **hours** from Ringmo. Beyond, take the left branch, since the right descends to the river and then to Junbesi. Continue on the main trail, passing the turnoff to the left to Chiwong Gomba and reaching **Phaphlu** in **two hours**. The rest of the route has been described. There is also a route heading directly over the ridge from Phuleli to Chialsa.

10 WESTERN NEPAL

The Promised Land always lies on the other side of a wilderness.
Havelock Ellis, English psychologist

Western Nepal, the region west of the Kali Gandaki river, offers interesting country and people to the trekker who has done the popular treks. But it is more difficult to travel here than in the more frequented east. Except for the trek to Dhorpatan, food and accommodations generally cannot be obtained. Very few people in the area speak English, trails tend to be more difficult, and the country seems more rugged. Furthermore, the Himalayan scenery in this part of Nepal is less impressive than in the east. It is very difficult to get the feeling of being in the mountains that Khumbu, Rolwaling, and Langtang provide. However, there are many other attractions. For the person wishing to see impressive forests, rugged and generally high terrain, and interesting peoples, the west has much to offer.

Two areas are described. The first is visited on a circuit from Pokhara to Dhorpatan with the return via Tansen. There are few logistic problems here compared to those encountered in the second area, which is seen on a circuit from Jumla to RaRa Lake.

Dhorpatan-Tansen Circuit
(Maps No. 3, Page 171 and No. 6, Page 228)

A circuit from Pokhara to Dhorpatan with the return through Tansen offers a pleasant trek through mixed country and includes views of impressive mountains. The Dhorpatan Valley is most unusual for its spaciousness in this tangled country. There are many interesting side trips. In the winter, when snow can make the crossing of the Jaljala Pass into Dhorpatan difficult if not impossible, there is another lower pass providing access. Unfortunately, it is necessary to make the decision to go via the more spectacular higher pass. Lodging is available along most of the trek and would only be a concern if the last day into Dhorpatan dragged on.

There are several options for starting this trek. You could fly to Balewa south of Baglung on regular RNAC flights and walk from there. There is also a STOL strip in Dhorpatan, but as yet no regular flights, though a charter could be arranged. Starting from Pokhara, there are two choices. You could walk to NagDAADa to the northwest and then to Bhaudar i Deorali, Tilhar, Dobila, and Kusma as has been described in reverse in Chapter 8. Alternatively, you could board a bus toward Butwal on the Siddhartha Rajmarg at Mahendra Pul in Pokhara and get off at the village called NauDAADa about **one to 1½ hours'** ride to the south. Don't confuse this town with NagDAADa, on the way to GhoDapani. Finally, you could take the same bus all the way to Tansen, and reverse the descriptions.

POKHARA TO DHORPATAN VIA JALJALA

Take the bus to NauDAADa as already described. From **NauDAADa** (3600 ft, 1097 m), head west and contour, then descend to the south to a tributary from the

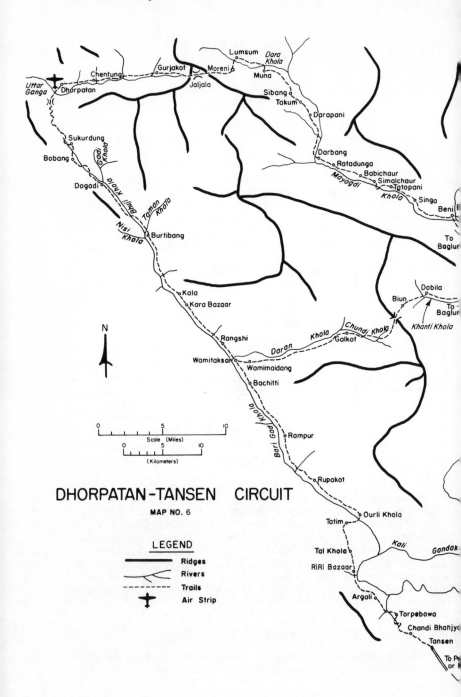

DHORPATAN-TANSEN CIRCUIT

MAP NO. 6

LEGEND

————— Ridges

Rivers

- - - - - Trails

✈ Air Strip

north. It can be crossed directly, or in high water, **ten minutes** upstream at a suspension bridge. On the east (R) bank, reach **Seti Dovan** (2950 ft, 900 m), a large bazaar town **forty-five minutes** from NauDAADa. The uncleared areas are wet subtropical forest. Continue west above the north (L) bank of the Andhi Khola to **Rangatani** (3100 ft, 945 m) in **half an hour.** Cross the suspension bridge here and follow the south (R) bank during high water. Either bank can be followed in low water. Continue upstream to **Chilaunabati** (3600 ft, 1097 m) in 1½ **hours**, then to **Phedi** (3850 ft, 1173 m) in another 1½ **hours**. There are usually three fords of the river at places that depend on the river level. This is a main route and the trail is easy to find. Beyond Phedi, begin a steep ascent over a good trail with steps part of the way. The pass and the town of **Karkineta** (5350 ft, 1631 m) are reached in 1½ **to two hours**.

The descent to the Modi Khola now begins. Head southwest from the pass and descend through Potebar (4400 ft, 1341 m) in **half an hour,** Phedi (3225 ft, 983 m) in **half an hour,** and **Yamdi** (3000 ft, 914 m) in another **half an hour.** Stay on the east (L) bank of the river for **half an hour** to reach a tea shop. Ford the river to its west (R) bank. Contour the rice paddies and ascend a small bamboo-forested gully. Continue past a large, well-built, three-story white cement and stucco modern-style house. All this takes only **fifteen minutes**. Beyond, keep to the right and descend a few stairs to emerge by three houses. Continue to the town of Ghandichaur (2875 ft, 876 m) in another **ten minutes**. The trail then passes through pleasant mixed forests and terraces, and ascends to a large suspension bridge over the Modi Khola (2400 ft, 732 m) in **half an hour.** Cross to the west (R) bank and ascend for **half an hour** to **Kusma** (3000 ft, 914 m), a large town that is the administrative center for Parbat District. The alternative trail starting at NauDAADa north of Pokhara joins here. The forests are of sal.

Continue north along a cobbled trail to the small town of **Chamalgai** (3050 ft, 930 m) in **half an hour.** Descend for **half an hour** to Armadi (2575 ft, 785 m), with a few houses. The trail now follows the east (L) bank of the Kali Gandaki, passing through **Shastradara** (2500 ft, 777 m) in **forty-five minutes** and reaching **Khaniyaghat** (2725 ft, 831 m) at a suspension bridge in an **hour.**

There are now two basic routes. One generally heads north to Beni, then west and northwest to cross a pass (11,200 ft, 3414 m) into the Dhorpatan Valley. The other heads west of Baglung, crosses over to the Bari Gad Khola at Wamitaksar, and follows it northwest over a pass (9600 ft, 2926 m) into Dhorpatan. The former is quicker and much more scenic, but in the winter, when snows block the pass, it may be impassable for many days. The other route is almost always feasible. The Baglung to Wamitaksar variation is described later.

In traveling to Beni, there are two options depending on whether you want to pass through Baglung, a district center. To avoid Baglung, continue upstream from Khaniyaghat on the east (L) bank, passing through Parse and Parbeni just across the river from Beni. Cross the Kali Gandaki on a suspension bridge just north of Beni (2700 ft, 823 m) and enter the town, which is on the west (R) bank of the Kali Gandaki at the junction with the Mayagdi Khola, which flows in from the west. Beni is reached in **three hours** from Khaniyaghat. It is the administrative center of Mayagdi District.

To take the other route through Baglung, cross the river at Khaniyaghat and climb up to **Baglung** (3200 ft, 975 m) in **half an hour.** This town, pleasantly situated on a shelf above the river, is the administrative center for Baglung District. Dhorpatan lies in the northwest corner of this district. From Baglung, one trail heads west to Wamitaksar. It is described later. To continue to Beni, head north and de-

Building a house in the hills. (Donald Messerschmidt)

scend from the plateau to the Kali Gandaki. There is another direct route from the bridge crossing at Khaniyaghat that stays close to the river and does not climb to Baglung. Either way, continue north up the west (R) bank of the Kali Gandaki, passing a tributary and a few tea shops to reach Beni in **three hours**.

Those flying to the Baglung airstrip land at **Balewa** (3425 ft, 1044 m), which is situated on a shelf above the west (R) bank of the Kali Gandaki **three hours'** walk south of Baglung. A little over **two hours** north of Balewa, descend to cross the Khanti Khola (2800 ft, 853 m) to its north (L) bank and ascend to Baglung in another **half hour**.

To proceed from Beni head west above the north (L) bank of the Mayagdi Khola. Reach **Bagua** (2875 ft, 876 m) in an **hour**, Singhi (3000 ft, 1044 m) in another **forty-five minutes**, Raksho in another **half hour**, and the large town of **Tatopani** (3075 ft, 937 m) in another **fifteen minutes**. Just before you reach Tatopani are some hot springs closer to the river than the town. The forests along here are mimosa and alder. About **twenty minutes** farther upstream, cross the river on a suspension bridge, then shortly recross it to the north (L) bank (3100 ft, 945 m). The town of **Simalchaur** (3175 ft, 968 m) is just beyond. An **hour** brings you to **Babichaur** (3350 ft, 1021 m), another large town. Continue through Shastradura (3475 ft, 1059 m), Baloti, and past an impressive landslide on the south (R) bank to reach **Ratadunga** (3475 ft, 1059 m) in **1 ¼ hours**. Do not cross the suspension bridge here, but continue west through Dhakarka to **Darbang** (3650 ft, 1113 m) in a **little over an hour**. This large town has a police check post.

Cross the river on a suspension bridge and proceed up its south (R) bank past a landslide to a tributary from the west, the Danga Khola, in **less than an hour.** Cross the tributary to its north (L) bank (3750 ft, 1143 m) and begin a steep ascent up the crest of the ridge. To your left is a chir pine forest, while to your right where there is more moisture, the usual wet subtropical forest. In **1½ hours** reach **Darapani** (5125 ft, 1562 m) high above the west (R) bank of the Mayagdi Khola. Contour to the west to **Takum** (5500 ft, 1676 m) in another **hour.** Another **half hour** of level walking brings you to **Sibang** (5750 ft, 1753 m). After a short climb of **forty-five minutes**, you reach a fine viewpoint north into the Dhaulagiri range. Below is the junction of the Dara Khola, flowing from the west, and the Mayagdi Khola, draining the Dhaulagiris to the north. Continue contouring, pass above the town of Phaldigaon, and reach **Muna** (6350 ft, 1935 m) in **1½ hours.** Across the valley lies the spectacularly perched village of Dara.

From Muna, descend to the river, the Dara Khola, and cross it on a suspension bridge (6100 ft, 1859 m) after **fifteen minutes.** Enter a dry oak forest. Climb, then contour for **two hours**, crossing a tributary from the north, and descend to **Lumsum** (7150 ft, 2179 m). There are only a few houses here, but one offers food and lodging. Except during the late spring, summer, and early fall, there is no food or lodging available beyond until Dhorpatan, a full day's walk ahead in good weather.

To continue from Lumsum, head upstream a short distance on the north (L) bank, then cross the Dara Khola on a suspension bridge (7250 ft, 2210 m). A steep **one-hour** climb follows to the few houses of **Moreni** (8500 ft, 2591 m), and another **fifteen minutes** brings you to a *goTh* (8750 ft, 2667 m) where food is obtainable in season. Leave the typical, terraced hill and ascend into an oak, hemlock, and rhododendron forest for **2½ hours.** Near the top, where oak and hemlock are replaced by fir and birch, pass a small *chorten* on the left and emerge into a broad open plateau (11,200 ft, 3414 m) near a *chautaara*. This area is called Jaljala and is the highest point, but not the watershed. The actual watershed between the Gandaki and the Bheri-Karnali river systems is some distance ahead and is easily missed.

The views from here are excellent. From west to east, you can see Putha Hiunchuli, Churen Himal, Gurja Himal, which is very near you; then Dhaulagiri, the Nilgiris, Annapurna, Annapurna South, Machhapuchhre, Baudha Himal, and Himalchuli. It is worthwhile to camp here for views in the morning. Water can be obtained at a spring a short distance back on the trail to the east.

To continue to Dhorpatan, keep to the south side of the plateau and after **forty-five minutes** pass a large stone *goTh* on the left and descend to cross a tributary. Ascend briefly to a plateau (10,900 ft, 3322 m) and at its western end, drop 300 ft (110 m) to cross a small river on a log bridge. This river, the Uttar Ganga, is reached some **one to 1½ hours** after Jaljala. The trail now follows the north (R) bank of the river for **3½ to four hours** to Dhorpatan. The forests are of blue pine and black juniper. In an **hour**, reach some stone *goTh* at **Gurjakot** (9900 ft, 3018 m), where food can be obtained except in the cold season. The river here, the Simudar Khola, is crossed at three points, and in another **half hour**, the Gur Gad River is reached. It can be crossed on rocks, or, in high water, on the bridge **ten minutes** upstream. Continue west, reaching a broad flat area that can be wet and boggy. In this case, bypass it to the north below a *gomba*. This monastery is of the Bon-Po sect, a forerunner of Tibetan Buddhism. Pass some *goTh* and cross a river to **Chentung** (9600 ft, 2926 m), the first permanent habitation since Moreni, an **hour** from the Gur Gad. This village, and the one at the west end of the valley an **hour** beyond, are inhabited by Tibetan refugees who settled here in 1960. **Half an hour** beyond

Chentung, cross a tributary from the north and continue another **half hour** past more Tibetan houses to **Giraund** (9325 ft, 2842 m), the site of an airstrip.

Cumulative trekking times (walking time only, does not include rests or stops) from NauDAADa to:

Karkineta	6	hours	Darbang	21½	hours
Kusma	9¾	"	Muna	27¾	"
Khaniyaghat	12½	"	Lumsum	30	"
Beni	15½	"	Jaljala	34	"
			Dhorpatan	39	"

NEAR DHORPATAN

Dhorpatan is the name of the area, an unusually broad, flat valley in this rugged hill country. It was probably once a lake that was later filled in. Many Nepalis from villages to the east, south, and west live here during the summer months when they grow potatoes and pasture animals. Their settlements are seen along the perimeter of the valley, especially on its southern aspect.

These Magar girls from Taka have stuffed cigaret wrappers in their ear lobes to stretch them as a sign of beauty. (Stephen Bezruchka)

Although there are few views from the valley floor (Annapurna South can be seen some thirty-five miles to the east), easy climbs of the surrounding hills provide unparalleled views. You can travel a few days to the north into blue sheep country, or up into the snows and glaciers of the western Dhaulagiri range. The base camps of the various expeditions at the head of the Ghustung Khola are worth visiting. You could continue on across Chalike Pahar to the Dogadi Khola, and across to the Seng Khola and the Jangla Bhanjyang trail, which could then be followed back to Dhorpatan. Food and shelter must be carried for all these trips to the north.

To the west and northwest live the *Kham Magar*, an ethnic group with many animistic and shamanistic traditions. Food and shelter are difficult to obtain in this area and are best carried. A four- to five-day circuit through this region can be most interesting. After a long day down the Uttar Ganga, you can reach the villages of Taka and Shera where the flat-roofed houses are reminiscent of Thak Khola, or of areas farther west. Cross the ridge up the tributary valley to the north, and descend to Hukum (Hugaon), or go beyond to Maikot on the north side of the Pelma Khola, in a day. The third day takes you through Puchhargaon and Yamakar to Pelma. Or you could continue across the Ghustung Khola and camp in the meadows of Thankur. A long day across the Phagune Danda Pass (13,100 ft, 3993 m) brings you back to Dhorpatan.

Those with less time should at least walk up one of the hills surrounding the valley for a view. The ridge crest directly south of the airstrip is the easiest viewpoint, and takes less than two hours via one of its north facing spurs. The view from here in clear weather extends to beyond Langtang in the east! The hill to the north of the valley (13,600 ft, 4145 m) can be reached in three to four hours from the airstrip. Surtibang, "the writing, desk hill" to the southwest, is an excellent viewpoint. Reach it by heading west for half an hour as the valley narrows to a bridge over the Uttar Ganga. Cross and ascend to the top (13,300 ft, 4054 m) in four hours from the airstrip. Hiunchuli Patan is visible to the west. Finally, the highest of the peaks surrounding the valley, Phagune Dhuri (15,500 ft, 4724 m), lying to the northwest, can be reached from the pass to the east. The round trip usually takes longer than a day.

From Dhorpatan, you could retrace your steps, worthwhile if bad weather has prevented good views. Otherwise, heading southeast to Tansen provides an interesting contrast. Although there are essentially no mountain views until Tansen, the trail passes through pleasant typical hill country. The time required is similar for both routes.

DHORPATAN TO TANSEN

To head south to Tansen from the Giraund airstrip, go south across the valley toward the obvious pass. Depending on the year, there may be small bridges over the Uttar Ganga, but it is often necessary to wade. Pick up the trail from the east and reach the pass (9625 ft, 2934 m) in **half an hour.** Descend to a stream, and at 9300 ft (2835 m), begin crossing a series of six small bridges over the stream for the next 600 ft (185 m) through a rhododendron, oak, and hemlock forest. Continue descending on the northeast (L) bank of the Bhuji Khola to reach Dowal (7600 ft, 2316 m) in **one to 1½ hours** from the pass. This is the first permanent settlement. Typical terraced Nepali country lies ahead. The forest is of prickly-leaved oak. In an **hour,** cross and recross the river and ascend slightly to **Sukurdung** (6700 ft, 2042 m), where there is a post box. Beyond the large schoolhouse, the trail crosses to the southwest (R) bank of the Bhuji Khola and descends slightly to **Bobang** (5800 ft, 1768 m) in **forty-five minutes**. Continue descending after a level stretch, and cross to the east (L) bank (5200 ft, 1585 m) of the Bhuji Khola in **half an hour**. In **fifteen minutes**, reach another suspension bridge (5052 ft, 1532 m) and cross to the west (R) bank. You are in wet subtropical forest. In another **fifteen minutes**, reach a covered bridge at **Dogadi** (4775 ft, 1455 m). Bypass another covered bridge and a suspension bridge, then cross to the east (L) bank on a suspension bridge (4250 ft, 1295 m) in **forty-five mintues**. Reach another suspension bridge (3600 ft, 1158 m) over the Taman Khola, a tributary to the east, and cross it to **Burtibang**, a large town with a police check post reached in an **hour**. From here the trail keeps to the east (L) bank for almost **two days**.

Continue along the Bhuji Khola, climbing somewhat through Renam to the small town of **Bingetti** (3400 ft, 1036 m) **two hours** beyond Burtibang. Cross a tributary from the east, the Bing Khola, on a suspension bridge (3100 ft, 945 m) and reach **Kala** (2950 ft, 900 m), a large town, in another **half hour**. Keep on the east (L) side of the river and enter **Kara Bazaar** (2850 ft, 869 m) in an **hour**. Pass through Balua (2700 ft, 823 m) in another **forty-five minutes** and **twenty minutes** later, cross the Labdi Khola, another tributary. Climb through a sal forest before descending to **Rangshi** (2575 ft, 785 m) in an **hour**. The main river is now called the Bari Gad Khola. Another **half hour** brings you to the log bridge (2500 ft, 762 m) crossing the Daran Khola from the east. Just beyond, a left fork ascends to Wamitaksar. Baglung can be reached in a very long day. The route from Baglung to here is described later.

To continue to Tansen, pass through the few houses of Sutti and reach **Bachitti** (2325 ft, 709 m) in 1½ **hours**. The trail continues along rice paddies through Laureshimal, Jorkale, and Abachor, crosses a tributary from the east, and reaches **Rampur** (2150 ft, 655 m), a large bazaar, in 2¼ **hours**. Continue through **Mojua**, cross a tributary, pass through Rupakot, Churkati, and Dhab, and cross a large slide on a tributary from the east to reach **Ourli Khola** (2075 ft, 632 m) in 3¼ **hours**. Cross the main river to its southwest (R) bank on a large suspension bridge, then climb up steeply for 1¼ **hours** to **Tatim** (3700 ft, 1128 m).

Keep climbing, take the left fork after passing through the town, and round a ridge jutting to the east (4475 ft, 1364 m). Dhaulagiri and Churen Himal can be seen from here. Enter chir pine forests, then drop slightly to a saddle and the town of **Ghiubesi** (4300 ft, 1311 m) an hour from Tatim. Enter a small, beautiful valley and go left through Chautaara (4500 ft, 1372 m) in **twenty minutes**. There is an impressive three-story house at the pass. Descend to the west, pass through **Pataunje Pani** (4400 ft, 1341 m), and drop steeply into a widening valley to reach the town and river of **Tal Khola** (2500 ft, 762 m) in **forty-five minutes**. Continue dropping down on the west (R) side of the valley to 2275 ft (693 m) before climbing out of the valley and heading downstream above the west (R) bank. Drop into the valley of the Kali Gandaki and descend to the large town of **RiRi Bazaar** (1550 ft, 472 m) 1¾ **hours** from Tal Khola.

Go through the town, cross the RiRi Khola to its south (R) bank, and climb above the west (R) bank of the Kali Gandaki river through Oruan Pokhari and Sattari Pokhari to reach **Argana** (2350 ft, 716 m) in **forty-five minutes**. Descend into another valley to reach **Argali** (2175 ft, 663 m) in **half an hour**. There is a side trail heading off to the left of the fountain and *chautaara* in this village. It leads to a palace built in 1947 as a retirement home for then Prime Minister Juddha Shumshere J.B. Rana. It is worth a detour.

Continue shortly beyond Argali to the Gurung Khola (2025 ft, 617 m). Cross to the south (R) bank and follow the river upstream. Pass through Torpebowa (2400 ft,

732 m) in **half an hour,** then cross to the east (L) bank and climb for **fifteen minutes** to Tirap (2625 ft, 815 m). Cross the river three times and reach Rossuas (3625 ft, 1105 m) in an **hour.** The town of **Gurung Khola** (4325 ft, 1318 m) is **half an hour** beyond. Soon you see a pipe and a tunnel through the hill, but keep climbing for **fifteen minutes** to **Chandi Bhanjyang** (4625 ft, 1410 m). Enter a new valley and turn right (west) to contour the Shrinagar ridge on a wide trail. The trail passes through a few small settlements before it crosses the ridge to the south and drops into Tansen (4650 ft, 1417 m), the district center for Palpa, in an **hour.** The head of the road is at the lower end of town. Buses leave for Pokhara in the morning. It is also possible to take a bus south to Butwal and Bhairawa. Be sure to catch the view of the mountains from the ridge behind Tansen. There are also many interesting temples in Tansen.

Cumulative trekking times (walking time only, does not include rests or stops) from Giraund to:

Bobang	3½ hours	Tal Khola	23½ hours
Burtibang	6 "	Tansen	28¼ "
Rampur	16 "		

BAGLUNG TO DHORPATAN, AVOIDING JALJALA

An alternate, less scenic route from Baglung to Dhorpatan is suitable when snow blocks the route over Jaljala. From Baglung, walk west on the main street. Leave the town and contour close to the Khanti Khola. Reach Khare (3450 ft, 1052 m) in an **hour.** Pass, but do not cross, a suspension bridge to reach the bazaar of **Dobila** (3525 ft, 1074 m) in **half an hour.** Cross to the west (R) bank of a tributary to the northwest. The trail climbs a bit as if toward the main river, then forks after a **few minutes.** Take the right (upper) fork to leave the valley floor. The trail ascends a ridge, passing through scattered settlements, most of which are part of **Biun.** Reach Tarakasi (4600 ft, 1402 m) in **forty-five minutes.** From here there are views of Machhapuchhre, Annapurnas II and IV, Dhaulagiri, Himalchuli, and Annapurna South. Reach the part of Biun containing a red post box (5800 ft, 1768 m) in **forty-five minutes.** In another **forty-five minutes** pass through Dokapani on the south side of the ridge and climb for **half an hour** to a notch (7100 ft, 2164 m) in the oak forest. Take the left fork, which drops a bit, then contour to **Ragini** (7000 ft, 2134 m) in a notch in **fifteen minutes.** To reach the valley to the west, take the left fork and drop along the crest of a ridge to the west. Reach Gasgas (5575 ft, 1700 m), a few houses, in **forty-five minutes.** Shortly beyond is a school. Reach a suspension bridge (4650 ft, 1417 m) over the Chundi Khola in **half an hour.** Cross it to the north (R) bank and head downstream for **fifteen minutes** to **Narethanti** (4425 ft, 1364 m), a small town by a suspension bridge that is not crossed. Cross the next suspension bridge to the south (L) bank. The trail follows close to the river to reach the large bazaar of **Galkot HaTiya** (4075 ft, 1242 m) in an **hour.**

Shortly beyond the bazaar, cross a suspension bridge to the north (R) bank (3950 ft, 1204 m) and reach the small bazaar of Banyan (4050 ft, 1234 m) in **half an hour.** Cross a small tributary from the north to reach Bas Khola (3850 ft, 1173 m) in another **half hour.** In **fifteen minutes** cross again to the south (L) bank on a suspension bridge (3675 ft, 1120 m). Cross another tributary to Potsua (3675 ft, 1120 m). Do not cross either of the next two suspension bridges over the river, now called the Daran Khola. Reach Kanebas (3400 ft, 1036 m) in **half an hour.** The trail ascends a bit to **Wamiukaalo** (3775 ft, 1151 m) in 1½ **hours.** There is a trail that keeps closer to the river, but it is more difficult. Continue climbing for **half an hour** to a notch in the ridge at **Wamimaidang** (4550 ft, 1387 m). The trail then descends the south side of the ridge into the valley of the Bari Gad Khola. In **forty-five minutes,** just beyond a few houses, the trail forks and the right branch descends north to the large town of **Wamitaksar** (2900 ft, 884 m) in **fifteen minutes**. Pass through the town and descend for **half an hour** to the crossing of the Daran Khola on the Dhorpatan to Tansen trail. The rest of the route has already been described. Dhorpatan can be reached from here in **two days**.

Jumla–RaRa Lake Circuit

(Map No. 7, Page 237)

At the southern edge of Mugu District at an altitude of almost 10,000 ft (3050 m) lies RaRa, the largest lake in Nepal. It has a circumference of almost eight miles (13 km) and is nestled between heavily-forested steep-sided ridges that thrust up from the fault lines that riddle this section of the foot of the Himalaya.

RaRa can sometimes be reached directly by chartered STOL aircraft. Enquiries should be directed to RNAC or to the National Parks and Wildlife Office in Bijuswari, Kathmandu. Otherwise RNAC operates scheduled flights to Jumla (7700 ft, 2347 m), the Zonal Headquarters of Karnali Zone, which is situated in a broad valley three days' walk south of RaRa. It is possible to trek to Jumla from Pokhara, more than a two-week trip, but most people fly there.

First the usual route from Jumla to RaRa is described. There are two variations. Most people do well to take the longer route—at least if traveling without a guide familiar with the shorter *lekh* route. The return route described follows a little-used trail to Sinja, an interesting historical town. From here, a former trade and communication route leads to Jumla. Some food must be carried no matter which route you take.

Rice, wheat, potatoes, or beans may sometimes be available in the bazaar in Jumla, but food shortages are a recurring problem in this whole area. As far as possible, all supplies required for trekking should be brought from Kathmandu. Porters can be hired locally, but English-speaking ones are very rare. It is almost essential to carry a tent when trekking in this area. Most of the people along this trek are *Thakuri*, the king's caste. They are loathe to allow anyone below their caste to enter or stay in their homes.

As mentioned, there are regular flights to Jumla by RNAC, but it is difficult to arrange return flights, either in Kathmandu or in Jumla. Once you arrive in Jumla, see the RNAC representative immediately to confirm your return flight. If you are stuck in Jumla, and unable to make direct connections to Kathmandu, consider taking one of the frequent flights to Nepalganj and connecting from there to Kathmandu. It is also possible to walk seven days south to Surkhet and fly from there.

JUMLA TO RARA LAKE

Looking north from the Jumla Bazaar, you can see most of the trail to the top of Danphe Lekh. The trail goes just to the left of the highest point of this *lekh*.

Heading out of the main bazaar from Jumla, the trail forks almost immediately. Take the left fork and pass close to the hospital as you follow the trail along the bank of the stream heading north out of the valley. In **less than an hour,** cross to the east (R) bank on a small wooden bridge. Begin the ascent from the valley floor, climbing toward the right. The trail rises through a series of cultivated fields, passes close to a few scattered houses, and ascends steadily for **over an hour.** While still well below the main treeline, the trail rises steeply for about **fifteen**

JUMLA & RARA LAKE

MAP NO. 7

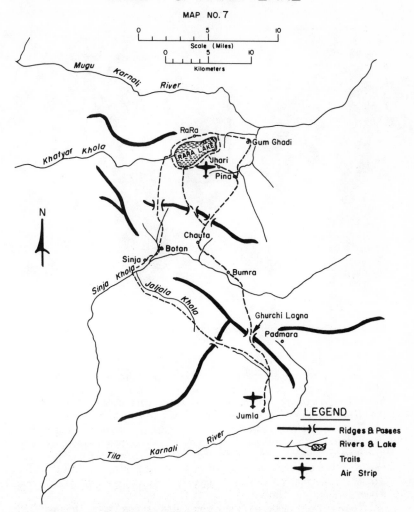

minutes, crosses a small stream, and enters one of the few clusters of blue pine trees on the open stretch of hillside. Near this spot—above the trail and slightly off to the right—is a campsite with a fresh-water spring (9000 ft, 2743 m), a good place to rest and cook your morning meal. This is the last water before the pass.

Ascending out of the trees, the trail opens out onto wide meadows rising gently to the north. **Fifteen minutes** beyond the trees, the trail forks near some stone huts. Take the less obvious right fork and shortly reenter the forest. The left fork is a more level main route to Sinja. The trail emerges into high meadows, visible earlier from below, in 1½ **hours** from the fork. Another **hour** on increasingly difficult rocky terrain brings you to the pass, the Danphe Lekh (12,100 ft, 3688 m). The

Much effort goes into cutting and hauling fodder for water buffaloes. (Ane Haaland)

summit is marked with a small *chorten*. There is a small peak to your left (13,715 ft, 4180 m), and another to your right (13,857 ft, 4224 m). From this point you should have a fine view back down over the Jumla Valley to the 15,000 ft (4500 m) ridges to the south. There is no northern view until you cross the top of the pass.

From the *chorten*, follow the trail across the top of the ridge, winding through patchy forest to the north, before dropping again into open meadows. Note carefully the spot where you emerge from the trees. If you come back this way, it is very easy to miss the opening. If you climb straight on over these meadows, you reach a different pass that leads to the village of Padmara to the southeast, and a much longer walk back to Jumla.

Leaving the meadows and crossing a small stream, follow the trail into the trees and descend rapidly through dense mixed forest for **two hours**. Notice the magnificent birch trees, the bark of which is collected for use as paper. And keep your eyes open for a DAAphe—the multi-colored national bird of Nepal.

Near the end of the descent, the trail drops very steeply to the Sinja Khola, which is immediately crossed by a substantial log bridge (8900 ft, 2713 m). Turning west, proceed along the north (R) bank of the river. Within the next hour, choose any suitable campsite along the valley floor by the river.

Approximately an **hour** from the bridge, the trail rises from the riverbed to pass near the village of **Bumra** (9350 ft, 2850 m). An alternative campsite could be in the vicinity of the village. Supplies such as eggs or firewood can sometimes be procured.

From Bumra continue along the side of the hill, proceeding about 500 ft (150 m) above the river. Pass just above another small village within **fifteen minutes**. After another **fifteen minutes**, descend steeply to cross a small stream entering the main river from the north. On the valley floor, pass an unused schoolhouse, cross the main stream (9250 ft, 2819 m), and immediately climb steeply again for **half an hour** to regain your former altitude. Within another **hour**, descend again to cross another stream entering from the north. At the foot of this descent, huddled beneath the steep rock walls on the far side of the stream, stand the two houses comprising the village of **Chauta** (9000 ft, 2743 m). Each of these houses is a "hotel," though sometimes neither food nor accommodation is available. Splendid clay *chilim* (pipes) are made in this area, and are sometimes sold at one of the hotels.

From Chauta, head north, following the trail gently uphill and crisscrossing the stream, the Chauta Khola, in a steep narrow valley. A pleasant walk through groves of large walnut trees takes you to a small *dharmsala* or resting place with a good clear-flowing spring. Reach some isolated cultivated fields in an **hour**. In another **fifteen minutes** the trail passes out of the trees and, leaving the course of the stream, swings left onto the high open pastures. You are now climbing again to the pass of Ghurchi Lagna.

The wide trail proceeds almost directly westward, rising across a broad grassy valley which runs almost at right angles to the final ridge. After you pass groups of large boulders for **half an hour**, the valley you are following splits into two distinct valleys. One heads northwest, and the other, containing the main trail, goes slightly northeast. The main trail heads up the right valley, climbing more or less north to the pass of the Ghurchi Lagna (11,300 ft, 3444 m), which is marked by a small stone *chorten*. The pass is some **three hours** from Chauta.

From the junction of the two valleys below the final approach to the pass, a lesser trail into the valley that heads northwest leads directly to RaRa in **five or six hours** along a high ridge trail. Though it offers spectacular views and a much shorter route to the lake, this trail should not be attempted by inexperienced trekkers, or when snow or monsoon clouds threaten to impair vision. In places, the trail is less than 18 in (45 cm) wide, often passing near the edge of high rock cliffs. Attempt it only with a guide.

If taking this alternative less-used trail, follow the bed of a small stream in the valley and rise gradually through a birch forest for **half an hour**. The trail breaks to the right (north) to follow a valley of scrub vegetation. When it wears thin in coarse grassland, there is no alternative but an **hour** of rough scrambling to the top of the ridge. Follow the ridge to the northwest, trying to stay as close as possible to the crest. Within 1½ **hours** you should reach a small *chorten* (13,300 ft, 4054 m) and see the lake far below. From the *chorten*, follow the ridge as it descends about 200 ft (60 m) across the rocky terrain. Then traverse, climb, and descend again for **ten minutes** or so before reaching a trail breaking off to the right. It drops quickly through rhododendron scrub into the dense forest slopes and leads down to the lake. Continue descending steeply through the trees, emerging in 1½ **to two hours** on the southern shores of the lake.

On the regular trail from the Ghurchi Lagna Pass, descend north again into forest. Some **five minutes** below the top is a *dharmsala* near a small stream. From here the trail is difficult, dropping very steeply away from the stream over a series of rocky outcrops. It descends in and out of belts of trees and emerges almost **two hours** later. Traverse for another **half hour** to the village of **Pina** (8000 ft, 2438 m). Pass a water source and suitable camping sites on the way to the village. About **five minutes** before the village, you pass Pina's only hotel, an isolated house directly on the main trail. If you are lucky, it may be open for business. The hotel is open only about half the year, generally during the spring and monsoon.

The village of Pina is grouped into upper and lower clusters connected by an intricate maze of paths through the fields. The main trail from lower Pina proceeds in the direction of the river below, reaching Gum Ghadi (6500 ft, 1981 m) in about three hours. This is the government headquarters and police check post for Mugu District. One trail from Gum Ghadi cuts back, ascending steeply to the northern ridge of RaRa. The other trail from the village continues dropping steeply to the Mugu Karnali river, the gateway to the trails into Humla and Mugu.

To proceed most directly to RaRa from Pina, take the new trail that splits from the main trail about **ten minutes** above the hotel. It passes through upper Pina after beginning on the side of a valley at the edge of the village. To find the trail when descending from the Ghurchi Lagna Pass, take the left fork at the first stream you come to after leaving the pass a **few minutes** outside of Pina. Bearing to the left, the trail traverses the side of this westward heading valley, passes through cultivated fields for **half an hour** and gradually meets the valley floor and a stream at the end of the traverse. Cross this small stream by a mill (7500 ft, 2286 m) and climb again for **fifteen minutes** before dropping almost immediately to the main valley stream. Follow the stream for another **half hour** through more fields in an ever narrowing valley. Cross the stream on a substantial wooden bridge and climb steeply to the north for **half an hour** to the village of **Jhari** (8350 ft, 2530 m). Continue up through the village to the north, pass some huge cedars, climb again through the forest, and emerge after about **two hours** onto high open pasture. Cross the easily gained summit (10,050 ft, 3063 m) and emerge at the "airstrip" on the south side of **RaRa Lake** (9800 ft, 2987 m). The airstrip is the only flat area around the shores of the lake. Directly across toward the northwestern side of the lake is the village of Chhabru, then the newer building of the national park headquarters, and farthest to the northeast, the village of RaRa. In late 1978, the residents of Chhabru and RaRa were resettled in the Tarai.

Cumulative trekking times (walking time only, does not include rests or stops) from Jumla Bazaar to:

Danphe Lekh Pass	5 hours	Pina	14¾ hours
Bumra	8 "	RaRa Lake (airstrip)	19 "
Ghurchi Lagna Pass	13 "		

RARA

The area surrounding the lake, which was designated as a national park in 1975, offers spectacular scenery, although views of snow-capped peaks are limited. Magnificent examples of fir, pine, spruce, juniper, cedar, birch, and rhododendron are found in the forest. Wildlife, including bears, cats, wolves, and deer, have been observed in the area. Around the shores of the lake are some fine "Malla Stones"—pillars of rock bearing Devanagari inscriptions and figures of the sun and moon. The inscriptions probably date from the Malla kings who reigned over much of the western Himalayan region in the twelfth century.

The best camping areas are on the lake's south side, which has much more diverse topography and vegetation than the north side. Meadow lands, virgin spruce forest, and some streams on the southwest corner of the lake make for ideal camping.

Legend and folklore provide the bulk of knowledge about RaRa Lake. The villagers believe it is at least 1800 ft (550 m) deep. They feel it is fed from

An old temple of the ancient Malla Kingdom at Dullu in western Nepal. (Johan Reinhard)

underground springs flowing from the Mugu Karnali river, which is located about 1800 ft (550 m) downhill from the lake on the other side of the north *lekh*. Given its size and location near one of the main trade routes to Tibet, it is surprising that the lake does not have greater historical or religious significance. Unlike many Himalayan lakes, it is not a pilgrimage site. An annual festival in July and August commemorates the intervention of the great god, Thakur, who changed the direction of the outlet of the lake. Firing an arrow to the west, he opened the western hill to form the present outlet, and taking huge quantities of earth, he filled in the eastern outlet and stamped it firmly with his great feet. His footprints, embedded in a rock, are visible to this day at the eastern end of the lake. They are the festival's main objects of interest—other than the attractive dancers and the local brew.

The lake's inaccessible location has kept many of its secrets undiscovered. The potential for discovery may be one of the most exciting aspects of this trek.

RARA TO JUMLA VIA SINJA

You can return by taking a less-traveled longer route through Sinja, the historical summer capital of the Malla Kingdom (twelfth to fourteenth centuries). Food, shelter, and a good map or a local guide familiar with the route are necessary.

From the village remains of RaRa (9900 ft, 3018 m), take the shore trail southwest to the lake outlet, the Khatyar Khola (9780 ft, 2981 m)—also called the

Nisha Khola—in **forty-five minutes**. Do not cross the bridge here, but continue down the north (R) bank for **half an hour**, then cross the stream on a log bridge. One trail continues west on the south (L) bank of the *khola* after ascending a 100 ft (30 m) knoll. Instead, take the left fork (heading south) up a small valley. Climb through the woods on a sometimes indefinite trail that keeps to the western side of the valley. Reach a meadow with a *goTh* (10,740 ft, 3274 m) on a crest in an **hour**.

Continue south, climbing steeply through oak, then birch, then rhododendron forests to reach an alpine ridge (12,500 ft, 3810 m) in **2½ hours**. Above to the left is Chuchuemara Danda. Traverse on its west shoulder for **fifteen minutes** and come out on a saddle above the Ghatta Khola. Descend 500 ft (150 m) to the headwaters of the river and continue down through the valley for an **hour** to Ghorasain, site of the national park's guard quarters (10,500 ft, 3200 m), in 1½ **hours**. Here the stream turns southwest. This is an appropriate and beautiful place to camp.

From here it is possible to reach Sinja by climbing to the southwest to 11,500 ft (3505 m) and descending to Lum (9500 ft, 2896 m) before following the Mindrabali Khola to Sinja. This trip would take a short day. The other route proceeds to the southeast, down the left side of the glacial valley of the Ghatta Khola for 1½ **hours**. Reach the terminal moraine and descend it for 300 ft (90 m). Continue down the valley another 1½ **hours** to a bridge (8700 ft, 2652 m) underneath the town of **Botan** lying to your left. Cross the log bridge and head downstream, meeting the Sinja Khola. Continue on its north (R) bank past some scattered houses to reach **Sinja** (8000 ft, 2438 m) in **two hours**.

Sinja lies in a highly cultivated valley. To the south on a prominent knoll are the remains of the former capital of this area. It is presently the site of a temple, Kankasundri. This area is well worth visiting by climbing the 400 ft (120 m) to the top of the knoll.

To return to Jumla, follow the historical route between Sinja and Kalanga, the old name for Jumla. The two-day route through beautiful forests ascends a river valley to a *lekh* and descends to Jumla. A camp roughly halfway on the crest of the *lekh* (11,500 ft, 3505 m) is ideal.

From Sinja ascend the Jaljala Khola to the southeast, keeping to the south (L) bank on a very good, clear trail for **six hours**. On the far watershed, the trail descends through forests and pastures south to **Jumla** (7700 ft, 2347 m). The 25 mi (40 km) of this stretch take about **ten hours**.

Cumulative trekking times (walking time, does not include rests or stops) from the village remains at RaRa to:

Ghorasain	6	hours
Sinja	10	"
Jumla	26	"

11 OTHER TREKS

Two roads diverged in a wood, and I—
I took the one less travelled by,
And that has made all the difference.

Robert Frost

Four other treks are described in this chapter. The first is an exit from Khumbu to Rolwaling and on to Kathmandu. The second is another exit from the Khumbu region, going southeast to Ilam from where you can proceed by road and train to Darjeeling. The third is the route from Pokhara to Kathmandu, a pleasant introduction to hill Nepal. In addition, several brief treks in and around the Kathmandu Valley are described. Finally there is a trip through the Tarai to Chitwan National Park, home of much interesting wildlife.

Thami to Rolwaling and Barabise via the Trashi Labsta
(Maps No. 4, Page 205 and No. 5, Page 215)

This is a spectacular high route that leaves Khumbu via a glaciated pass and reaches the Rolwaling Valley to the east and its major settlement, Beding, in a minimum of four days. There are no villages or shelters along the way and the route is dangerous even in the best of conditions. Only experienced mountaineers should attempt it and then, only with a party that includes some Sherpas who have been over it before. The entire party, including all the porters, should be equipped for severe conditions of cold and high altitude. Since it is necessary to camp on ice, parties should carry tents and fuel for everyone as well as ice climbing equipment (ice axe, rope, crampons, and ice screws). Under ideal conditions the crossing need not require technical climbing, but such conditions cannot be counted on. Storms are to be expected and food for at least five days should be carried in order to be able to wait out bad weather. Temperatures below freezing are always encountered. Crossings have been made at all times of the year, but the best time is probably April to early December. Falling rock is the danger most often encountered. Ice avalanches are also possible. Many people have died attempting this crossing, but competent, well-equipped parties should have little trouble. Sherpas even take yaks over it! You must be very aware of the hazards of rapid ascent to altitude and of hypothermia. There are no quick escape routes, especially on the Rolwaling side of the pass, should altitude illness become serious.

The route is described from Thami to Rolwaling, thus offering a route out of Khumbu that avoids the traffic jams at Lukla. This direction is also preferable because parties attempting the crossing have usually acclimatized first in Khumbu. Furthermore, if altitude problems strike on the ascent, it is easier to retreat to lower altitudes from this side than from the other side where technically difficult terrain and long glaciers must be negotiated.

From **Thami** (12,500 ft, 3810 m), described in Chapter 9, head west, passing below the monastery to reach a *yersa*, Kure (13,875 ft, 4229 m), in **seventy minutes.**

The next *yersa* (14,050 ft, 4282 m) is **ten minutes** beyond. Proceed as the valley of the Thami or Thengpo Khola opens up and admire the peaks on its south side, especially the north face of Teng Kangpoche. The extensive *yersa* of Thengpo (14,175 ft, 4321 m) is reached in **twenty-five minutes.** Climb through the various fenced-in fields of this *yersa* and continue up the north side of the valley. Traverse a rock slide from the north to the end of the slide (15,465 ft, 4714 m) **1⅓ hours** from lower Thengpo. The best views east, including the west face of Makalu behind Ama Dablang, are along here. Continue on a grassy slope, then begin climbing a loose moraine to reach a flat area suitable for camping (15,910 ft, 4849 m) in **half an hour.** Climb the moraine for an **hour** to Ngole (16,745 ft, 5104 m) below an icefall to the north. Ngole, which has tent sites and overhanging rocks for shelter, is protected from the icefall and is a good place to camp below the pass. In order to avoid rockfall off the southern slopes of Tengi Ragi Tau, the peak to the north, it is wisest to ascend beyond here in the early morning. There is another possible campsite (17,150 ft, 5227 m) **half an hour** beyond. Below and to the south a lake lies in the moraine.

Continue climbing beyond this last site on snow or rock as the season dictates to another level area (17,700 ft, 5395 m) in **half an hour.** Some **fifteen minutes** more climbing, closer to the face of Tengi Ragi Tau, brings you to yet another small campsite (17,850 ft, 5441 m). These last two campsites are not entirely protected from rockfall, a hazard that varies with the time of year. Be on the lookout for serious symptoms of altitude illness, and descend if they occur.

The icefall before you, which has been visible for some time, is from the Trashi Labsta Pass. Ascend a scree slope to the northeast of the icefall and traverse to a sheltered spot (18,250 ft, 5563 m) under the rock face of Tengi Ragi Tau in another **half hour.** The times taken, of course, depend on the acclimatization of the party. If coming from Rolwaling, this sheltered spot could be an appropriate place to pitch a tent and camp. It is safer to camp lower, but you should not descend late in the day if much rock is falling. To proceed over the pass, climb on snow east of the icefall to a long, more gradual slope. There are sheltered spots under overhanging rocks under the face of Tengi Ragi Tau, but it is not a good idea to camp this high, because the risk of altitude illness is greater. Better to sleep low and climb high. Proceed west to the height of land and the Trashi Labsta Pass (18,882 ft, 5755 m)—the name means "luck bringing prayer flags"—in another **forty-five minutes.** There is a cairn with prayer flags at the pass. The times listed here are actual traveling times, and most parties take at least **half a day** from Ngole to here when rests are included. New vistas open up to the west, but the views to the east are limited to Teng Kangpoche. Directly south is the peak Pharchamo (20,582 ft, 6273 m), a trekking summit.

The descent is over a snow-covered moderately steep glacier with crevasses, and requires roped travel and the ability to do crevasse rescues. Reach the Drolambo Glacier (17,850 ft, 5440 m) in perhaps **forty-five minutes.** Parties wishing to explore further can get plenty of ideas from the Schneider map. Note that the route marked on Schneider's *Rolwaling Himal* map is not the one described here, as the marked route is no longer in use. The route described here is less hazardous. The route in use when you cross could be different. Thus it is advisable to have along a Sherpa familiar with the current way. Head south along the Drolambo, proceeding near a medial moraine. It is safest to camp above the icefall that lies at the snout of the Drolambo, which in turn lies above the Trakarding Glacier. Camping here will minimize the danger that rocks from the medial moraines might melt out of the ice on the stretch above the Trakarding Glacier and tumble down. A campsite (17,750 ft, 5410 m) can be found in about **half an hour** after reaching the valley glacier. Unlike the narrow upper part of the eastern side of the Trashi Labsta, the country here is open.

Continue descending the Drolambo, staying east of the first medial moraine and of an icefall that you pass in **half an hour**. Most likely you can travel in a trough that is easy and quite safe, providing you have made an early start and the sun hasn't hit you. Late in the day everything here is usually quite loose and you may feel like a target in a shooting gallery in the middle of a waterfall! In the usual trough, there is one steep ice step, perhaps 40 to 50 ft (15 m) high, where it is best to belay the party down. Crampons, ice axes, rope, and ice screws are usually necessary and helpful to all. Descend carefully on snow and ice-covered rock, keeping close to the rock face to the right to avoid falling rocks and ice. In **2½ to three hours** from the camp above, reach a spectacular rocky spur (16,950 ft, 5166 m) below the icefall on the Drolambo, but still considerably above the Trakarding Glacier below. There are plenty of campsites here that are safe from falling rock and ice. If ascending to the pass from Rolwaling, it would be prudent to camp here if you arrive late in the day, unless it is very cold and the rocks are frozen in place. If there is no sound of falling rock when you stop here on the way to the pass, it is probably fairly safe to continue.

The Trakarding Glacier is the long rubble-covered ice river flowing northwest below you. It is reached in **half an hour** from the spur (16,125 ft, 4915 m). Rock overhangs that provide shelter should be apparent. Traverse northwest under the icefall of the Drolambo Glacier to a campsite called Thakar (16,075 ft, 4900 m) in **fifteen minutes.** There are few if any good camping sites on the extensive moraine of the glacier until the lake is passed. Finding water is also a problem. Keep close to the northwest side of the glacier, following an indistinct trail marked with cairns. There is sometimes falling rock from the northwest, so be cautious. The going is slow along this moraine. Occasional rock overhangs are passed that would make possible campsites if water could be found.

As you near the big lake, Tsho Rolpa or Chu Pokhari, keep to the south of the extensive lateral moraine on the northeast side of the glacier. Along this moraine there is a hazard from falling rock and fine dust is constantly being blown along. In recent years the looseness of this moraine has made it even more dangerous. Parties sometimes traverse on the south side of the lake. Check with someone familiar with the current route. After traversing about one-third of the way along the lake, make a steep ascent northeast to meet the rock, then traverse an avalanche chute off Tsoboje—be quick here—and descend a scree slope on the other side of it. Continue in the trench between the wall to the southwest surrounding the lake and the steep walls to the northeast. Contour a snow cone from an avalanche chute to a large sandy area (15,050 ft, 4587 m). It takes some 3½ **to four hours** to get here from Thakar. There is a good campsite here some two-thirds to three-fourths of the way along the lake, but water may be hard to find. There may be a small stream here (often frozen), or you might have to climb over the moraine to the lake, which may be frozen. An ice axe is helpful in getting water.

Continue along the trail, contouring around the terminal moraine at the end of the lake in **half and hour** and continuing around the terminal moraine of the Ripimo Shar Glacier, which comes down from the northeast. In **fifteen minutes,** pass through a small *yersa* of unroofed frames, Sangma (14,175 ft, 4321 m), and descend to cross the outflow (13,900 ft, 4237 m) of the lake to the left a **few minutes** later. Descend the broad valley, enjoying the fragrant shrubs. In **half an hour** cross to the north (R) bank of the Rolwaling Khola (13,725 ft, 4163 m). There is a route to the

Bhatti *innkeeper. (Donald Messerschmidt)*

south over the ridge via the Yalung La, a pass to the Khare Khola. But continuing on the usual route, reach the west end of the settlement of Na and the limit of the glaciated valley. Downstream, the Rolwaling Valley is a sharp river-worn V. Na is a large *yersa* at the base of an impressive peak to the north. It is occupied by Beding people part of the year, depending on the potato harvest. The Sherpas of Rolwaling believe that their valley was formed by the sweep of a giant horse and plow guided by Padmasamblava, who brought Buddhism to Tibet from India. According to one source, *rolwa* means a furrow while *ling* is a country. Another meaning for *Rolwaling* is "the place where the *dakini* play." They also feel it is one of the eight *beyul*, or hidden valleys in the Himalaya. Because of this, they do not allow anyone to kill animals in the valley.

Descend 125 ft (38 m) to the lower part of Na and in an **hour**, reach rhododendron and juniper forests, a pleasant contrast to the barren landscape above the lake. Pass through another *yersa*, Dokare (12,575 ft, 3833 m) **fifteen minutes** later and continue to **Beding** (12,120 ft, 3694 m) **1½ hours** from Na. This is the main settlement for the Sherpa inhabitants of the Rolwaling Valley. It is located in a narrow gorge and gets little direct sunlight. There is no farmland or mountain view, save that of Gaurishankar before you reach the village. The *gomba* here is impressively located and worth visiting to see the fine paintings. There is a school built by Sir Edmund Hillary and some interesting flour mills. People wishing to take a side trip with a view of spectacular Menlungtse (Jobo Garu on the Schneider map) can ascend to the Manlung La in 1½ days from Beding, if they are already acclimatized. There is some trade to Palbugthang and Thumphug over this pass during the summer, mostly rice exchanged for Tibetan salt.

Leave Beding and pass through a *yersa* (11,975 ft, 3650 m) in **ten minutes.** Then cross a tributary (11,875 ft, 3584 m) in another **ten minutes.** This river, the Gaurishankar Khola, has eroded a gap in the wall, allowing a pretty waterfall to cascade through. Just beyond is a *yersa*, Chumigalgya, and there are two more in **five and ten minutes** respectively (the last at 11,700 ft, 3566 m). The trail continues into a pleasant fir, rhododendron, and birch forest and descends in **twenty minutes** to a small sanctuary (11,275 ft, 3437 m) to the Nepali deities Sita Mahadev and Kanchi Mahadev. A cantilever bridge here to the south (L) bank of the Rolwaling Kola is the beginning of a trail that leads to the Daldung La. It offers a higher route out of the Rolwaling Valley to use in the monsoon when the main route may be too wet. Don't take it unless so advised by the locals. Continue in forest for **thirty-five minutes** until you cross a tributary from the north. Here there is a good, but very foreshortened view, of Gaurishankar to the north. Some **ten minutes** beyond, come to a covered bridge crossing the Rolwaling Khola (10,200 ft, 3108 m). Cross to the south (L) bank and keep to the south side of the narrow valley. Notice how everything is much greener and lusher here, perhaps because this north facing slope receives less direct sun. In addition to the deciduous vegetation, there are impressive fir trees.

Continue on the south side above the valley floor and enter a burned area (9350 ft, 2850 m) in **thirty-five minutes.** Some **twenty minutes** beyond reach some steep slabs (9150 ft, 2789 m). Leave the riverbed and ascend the slabs along an impressive locally-made ramp. Reach a clearing in **half an hour**—you are still in the burn which has more growth the farther west you go. **Ten minutes** beyond is a campsite under an overhanging rock, and nearby is a fault cave. Continue high on the side of the valley to stands of oak. Pass under a swirling waterfall (9175 ft, 2797 m) an **hour** beyond the slabs. Continue contouring for **almost an hour** before descending to reach the few *goTh* of Shakpa (8700 ft, 2652 m). Descend in **less than an hour** to the village of **Simigaon** (6550 ft, 1996 m). Sherpas and hill Nepalis inhabit this lush oasis, which has interesting fruits and vegetables in addition to the predominant millet fields.

Descend steeply to the river, the Bhote Kosi, passing under some large rock overhangs. Cross to the east (R) bank on a suspension bridge (5000 ft, 1524 m) **forty-five minutes** from Simigaon. The trail rises above difficult stretches of an impressive gorge to the south. Traverse the few fields of Chetchet **fifteen minutes** beyond and admire the falls that tumble at least 300 ft (100 m) down the east (R) bank. Some **thirty-five minutes** beyond Chetchet, the trail forks. The lower fork keeps close to the river and is suitable during low water. The upper fork is for the monsoon. In **half an hour** the valley widens and in its floor ahead is the village of **Gongar** (4525 ft, 1410 m). Cross the Gongar Khola, a tributary from the west, to the trail fork beyond. The left fork keeps close to the river and goes to Charikot. You can take it to join the usual Everest Base Camp route from Lamosangu. The right fork ascends and heads to Barabise. This route is described here. Climb on a spur through terraces to a *chautaara* (5150 ft, 1570 m) **half an hour** from Gongar. Contour and cross two tributaries in **half an hour.** Climb another **twenty-five minutes** to a Shiva sanctuary (5825 ft, 1775 m) to the left of the trail. Surrounded by a rock wall, this sanctuary contains a few bells and innumerable tridents of iron in various shapes and sizes. Climb another **half hour** to **Thare** (6475 ft, 1974 m), a scattered

Tamang village. It is not marked on Schneider's *Lapchi Kang* map.

Continue contouring to **Dulang** (6225 ft, 1897 m), the next scattered village. Another **fifty minutes** brings you to the ridge where the Warang school (6600 ft, 2012 m) is located. Enjoy the views of Gaurishankar to the northeast. Pass through the settlement of **Yarsa** (6225 ft, 1897 m) **twenty-five minutes** beyond, then contour and descend for **twenty minutes** to cross the Warang Khola (5775 ft, 1760 m). Contour another **twenty-five minutes** to the scattered village of **Bulung** (5850 ft, 1783 m). Continue to a high clearing, the site of the local middle school (6335 ft, 1931 m), some **twenty-five minutes** beyond. You are now leaving the valley of the Bhote Kosi for the tributary valley of the Sangawa Khola. Contour for **forty-five minutes** to a stupa, then a *chautaara* with Tibetan-style religious paintings. Pass above the scattered village of Laduk and reach the school situated above it (6810 ft, 2075 m) in **twenty minutes.** Don't climb beyond, but take the lower fork and descend slightly. Cross a recent slide, then the Thuran Khola (6260 ft, 1908 m) in another **1¼ hours.** Above you is the town of Charsaba, but the main trail ascends and contours below it. Beyond a main ridge, the town of Chilangka (6310 ft, 1923 m) is reached in **sixty-five minutes.** Descend past another small slide and cross the Jorang Khola (5585 ft, 1702 m) in **twenty-five minutes.** Contour through chir pine forest to reach **Lading** (5835 ft, 1778 m) in **fifty minutes.**

Beyond there is a choice of routes. The left fork descends to the river, the Saun Khola, crosses it to the east (R) bank on a log bridge, ascends near a tributary, the Amatal Khola, and passes the village of Amatal to the few houses of Ruphthang (7670 ft, 2335 m) in approximately **four hours.** This route is more direct than the other, but it avoids the climb up to Bigu Gomba, one of the most fascinating Buddhist nunneries in Nepal.

To head to Bigu Gomba, also known locally as Tashi Gomba, don't descend the Saun or Sangawa Khola, but contour around a ridge and descend to the Samling Khola, a tributary from the north. Cross it on a cantilever bridge (5710 ft, 1710 m) to the west (R) bank in **forty-five minutes.** Begin climbing up to **Bigu Gomba.** The entire terraced hillside has numerous houses and is called Bigu. It takes **two hours** or more to reach the actual monastery (8235 ft, 2310 m) with its long white building, the home of the nuns, in front of the temple itself, which is set among juniper trees. This nunnery was built around 1933 and houses thirty-six nuns, most of them Sherpas. It is unusual because its east and west walls are lined with interlacing statues of Avalokiteswara, each with eleven heads and 1000 arms, hands, and eyes. You are not allowed to photograph the inside of the *gomba.* This convent of the Kargyupa sect is described by Christoph von Fürer-Haimendorf in "A Nunnery in Nepal" (see Recommended Reading).

To leave Bigu, traverse north on a high trail, then contour and drop to join a main trail west of the *gomba* near three stupas (7895 ft, 2406 m) in less than **half an hour.** Continue until you spot **Ruphtang,** one house on top of a small hill, and take a left fork to descend and cross a tributary from the north on a covered bridge by some mills (7460 ft, 2275 m). Climb the hill to Ruphtang (7660 ft, 2335 m) **half an hour** from the stupas. This may be the last habitation below the pass, the Tinsang La. Climb beyond, steeply at first, then more gradually in a forest of prickly-leaved oak. There is a tea shop (8740 ft, 2664 m) some **fifty-five minutes** above Ruphtang. Continue climbing in impressive fir forest with numerous camping sites. There is a *goTh* (10,240 ft, 3121 m) **two hours** from Ruphtang, and a pleasant stream some 500 ft (150 m) higher. The pass itself (10,890 ft, 3319 m), with several *goTh* nearby, is **half an hour** beyond. The view of the Himalaya, although somewhat distant, is breathtaking. The tower of Chobo Bamare is quite close.

From the pass, descend into rhododendron and fir forest that becomes almost pure rhododendron forest lower down, then blends again into prickly-leaved oak forest. A small *gomba* above **Dolangsa** (8165 ft, 2489 m) is reached in **sixty-five minutes** from the pass. There are many variations in the route down the Sun Kosi river to its junction with the Bhote Kosi below Barabise. You can head south through Nangarpa and cross the main river west of Gorthali before proceeding along its north (R) bank. Or you can keep to the north side of the valley, crossing tributaries and going below a pretty waterfall (7390 ft, 2252 m) **sixty-five minutes** beyond the *gomba*. Beyond, you can continue contouring, or you can descend closer to the river. If descending, reach **Kabre** (5265 ft, 1605 m) in **seventy minutes** from the waterfall. Continue west, crossing a tributary from the north on an old suspension bridge (3890 ft, 1185 m) in **thirty-five minutes.** Contour another **ten minutes** to the first stores of **Budipa** (3790 ft, 1155 m). The main trail continues contouring about 500 ft (150 m) above the main river and passes through the scattered houses of **Simle** (3550 ft, 1080 m) in **fifty-five minutes.** The solace and freedom from the noises of the twentieth century are almost over. Horns can soon be heard. The trail rounds a ridge to descend to **Barabise** (2690 ft, 820 m) on the west (L) bank of the Bhote Kosi in **forty-five minutes.** Buses leave this staging center for Kathmandu periodically during the day.

There is another high pass leading out of the upper Rolwaling Valley, the Yalung La (17,422 ft, 5310 m). The descent is made to the southwest to Suri Dhoban. Inquire at Beding for a guide.

An alternative route from Rolwaling branches from Simigaon, and instead of crossing to the west (R) bank of the Bhote Kosi, heads south on its east (L) bank, passing through Tashinam to Manthali (3450 ft, 1080 m), approximately one day from Simigaon. The Sieri Khola, a tributary from the east, is crossed en route. Continue on the east (L) bank of the main valley and cross the Suri (or Khare) Khola at Suri Dhoban (3215 ft, 980 m). Continue to Tyanku in a day. Cross the main river, the Tamba or Bhote Khosi, at Biguti (3150 ft, 960 m) and climb up to Dolakha (5580 ft, 1700 m), which has several interesting temples. Shortly beyond, reach Charikot (6560 ft, 2000 m) less than a day from Tyanku. The main trail to Solu-Khumbu is soon intersected and Lamosangu is 1½ days farther. This trail is somewhat shorter than the higher Tinsang La trail, but less scenic.

Cumulative trekking times (walking time only, does not include rests or stops) from Thami to:

Ngole	3½ hours		Simigaon	18 hours
Trashi Labsta Pass	5 "		Lading	25½ "
Beding	14 "		Barabise	34¼ "

Namche Bazaar to Ilam and Darjeeling
(Maps No. 4, Page 205 and No. 8, Page 250)

Of the various routes of return from the scenic splendor of Khumbu to areas where conventional motorized travel is possible, this is one of the best because it involves a minimum of backtracking and provides a fine terminal point after traversing the entire eastern section of Nepal. However, the route is somewhat longer (about two weeks is required) than retracing your steps to Barabise or Lamosangu, or going south via Salleri and Okhaldhunga to Janakpur. Also the trails are much less traveled by Westerners, making food and sleeping arrangements more difficult for those who don't speak Nepali. In addition, Westerners are unfortunately not

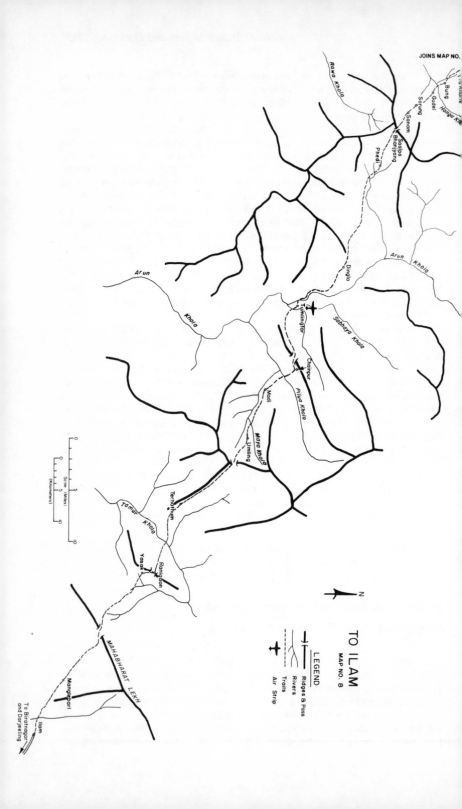

permitted at this time to cross the Indian-Nepali border directly from Ilam to Darjeeling. Instead, they must take a jeep south from Ilam to the East-West Highway and follow it east to cross the border into India.

It is wise to stock up on provisions in Namche Bazaar. There is always *daal bhaat tarkaari* available along the trail, but the shop in Chaumrikharka is the only one until you reach Dingla in almost a week. But if you leave Namche Bazaar a few days before the Saturday market, you meet hundreds of porters carrying goods to sell at the market, and you may be able to buy provisions from them. It is a good idea to hire a local guide for the stretch up to Dingla, as it is easy to get lost in some of the forests near the ridges. Beyond Dingla, there are weekly markets in several places, including Chainpur, Terhathum, Yasak, and Ilam.

Start the route by retracing steps for **1½ days** down the valley of the Dudh Kosi to **Kharte** (8400 ft, 2560 m), which is characterized by a single large white house near the top of the hill above Karikhola. From here, do not descend to Karikhola; instead, head southeast toward Pangu, which is visible from Kharte. It is about **three hours** away at a slightly higher elevation. The trail has several forks, but the ones that go more steeply downhill are correct. The trail makes a moderately successful attempt at contouring as it goes up and down to cross numerous streams. **Pangu** (9338 ft, 2864 m) is a Sherpa village characterized by *mani* walls and a *gomba*. From the village, proceed east for **half an hour** on a gentle trail up to the pass, the Pangkongma La (10,410 ft, 3173 m). From here you can see across the Inukhu Khola to the next ridge and to Nachi Dingma in a clearing two-thirds of the way up to the next pass. Follow the trail that goes left (north) out of the pass. It goes down gently for an **hour** to a ridge crest with some houses and fields. The trail now goes down the end of the ridge, becoming steeper until it drops by many nearly vertical switchbacks down to the Inukhu Khola (6090 ft, 1856 m) **two hours** from the pass.

Cross the river on a makeshift bridge and go slightly upstream across boulders and sand to where the trail begins again in dense growth. Climb up steeply to the terraces in **half an hour**, and continue up through terraces and poor houses for the next **hour**. Another **hour** through the forest finally brings you across a stream to **Nachi Dingma** (8531 ft, 2600 m), which has an abandoned open house. From the house, go left diagonally across the flat clearing to a stream in about **five minutes**, then up again through forests to a sharp, notched pass, the Surkie La (10,122 ft, 3085 m), in a **little more than an hour**. All the passes are exhilarating for the views, the sense of accomplishment, and the chance to rest.

Descend to reach a shelter with water in **ten minutes.** Then bear right and go down, sometimes steeply, sometimes less so, to **Khiraunle** (7875 ft, 2400 m) in an **hour**. This is a spread-out Sherpa village with an interesting stupa surrounded by trees. Continue down diagonally to the right (south) across numerous streams to reach a ridge crest in **half an hour**. Descend straight down through the large, spread-out *Rai* village of **Bung** (5250 ft, 1600 m) for an **hour**, then cross a small river to the north via a curvy bamboo bridge. Finally, go down the north (L) bank of the river to reach the Hongu Khola (4320 ft, 1316 m) in another **half hour**. There is a spectacular waterfall where the tributary joins the main stream, and also a good pool for bathing. After crossing the Hongu Khola on another temporary bridge, ascend steeply through rice fields for **1½ hours** to **Gudel** (6560 ft, 2000 m), a *Rai* village somewhat higher than Bung across the valley. Now the trail leaves the ridge crest and proceeds gently up along the right side to reach the Sherpa village of **Sorung** (8530 ft, 2600 m) in **two hours** and **Sanam** (8530 ft, 2600 m) in another **hour**. The prayer flags and solid houses have a more prosperous appearance here than in the *Rai* villages below.

The trail descends slightly for **half an hour** to meet a stream that earlier was far below the trail. There is a shelter here. Follow the stream for **half an hour** until the trail turns right along a small tributary, which is followed for **half an hour** to another shelter near the last water source before the pass, **Saalpa Bhanjyang** (10,990 ft, 3350 m), another **half hour** up.

The trail goes down rather gently to the east-southeast for **two hours,** but some luck is needed to keep on it. Finally, the trail goes diagonally left onto a ridge crest, then down steeply for an **hour** to the *Rai* village of **Phedi** just above a river. From here, Dingla can be reached in one day with the aid of moonlight.

The trail follows close to the river, predominantly on the south (R) bank, until a small shop by a bridge is reached in **three hours.** Now contour gently up (east) to reach a ridge crest in **1½ hours.** Then go west to cross a small stream before reaching the true ridge crest in another **hour.** When I was here, a strong aroma led us to a tree groaning with tangerines. Its owner gladly sold us eighty-seven for one rupee and probably laughed to think how we nearly broke our backs trying to carry them off. Dingla sits on the next ridge to the south. Reach it by going diagonally down and west, sometimes on a good trail, sometimes on paddy walls, to reach the stream in an **hour.** Beyond the bridge, the correct trail goes fairly directly up to **Dingla.** The town has a few shops, some eating places, a college, and a temple.

Two side trips start from Dingla: one goes up the Arun Khola and the other goes down it. The trek up takes you to the base of Makula and a Himalayan region that is much less visited than the Everest area. The trek down the river goes to Dhankuta and Dharan. It is a fast exit to a road. But to continue east, proceed southeast down the end of the ridge to reach the Arun Khola in **1½ hours**. As it is impossible to cross the river at this point, follow the west (R) bank south via a jungle trail to reach a bridge in **half an hour.** Once across the river, the trail ascends steeply up the bank for **ten minutes** to the **Tumlingtar** airstrip on an immense flat area. Follow the trail on the far east side of the airstrip for **half an hour** to a shop where excellent food and lodging can be obtained. Now descend from the flat area to a smaller river that must be waded before beginning the ascent to Chainpur. Go up to the left to reach the crest of the ridge at **Kerang** in **two hours.** Follow the broad level trail on the right side of the ridge for another **hour** to **Chainpur,** a large, pleasant bazaar town where the police check trekking permits. The town boasts a hotel that can provide separate rooms and good food.

Here again there is a choice of routes. You can go east to Taplejung in two days, then head south via Phidem to Ilam in three days. The second, more expedient choice is to go south to Terhathum in 1½ days, then on to Ilam in another 2½ days. A description of the latter route is given here.

Leaving Chainpur, the trail descends for **forty-five minutes** and crosses a stream, the Pilua Khola. Then it ascends for **1¼ hours** to **Madi** at about the same elevation as Chainpur. Now proceed on a level trail to the right to reach **Palomadi** in another **hour.** Another **hour** on level ground brings you to **Alimela,** from which it is only a short descent and climb to reach a crossing of the Maya Khola in **half an hour.** Then climb through the widely scattered village of **Umling** and eventually to the pass over Mungabori Lekh in **2½ hours.** The last part is through an extremely beautiful meadow and forest with a few tea shops **fifteen minutes** before the pass. Now the trail descends rather gradually and follows the long ridge stretching out to Terhathum. Pass through the pleasant village of **Jirikimpti** in **two hours** and keep fairly level on one side of the ridge or the other to reach **Terhathum** in another **hour.** This is a dense little bazaar town with three parallel streets, a Chinese book-store, and district offices.

A little-known temple in eastern Nepal. (Dave Hardenbergh)

The trail to Ilam now continues down the left side of the ridge to **Keorimi** in **1½ hours**. Beyond, it goes down more steeply on the end of the ridge into the furnace-hot valley of the Tamur Khola. The river is reached in **1½ hours**. Go upstream for **ten minutes** to where a man in a dugout boat can take you across the river for a small charge, or go **half an hour** farther upstream and walk across the bridge for free. From either place, there is a stiff climb of some **three hours** to **Ranigaon.** If you cross by the dugout, go to the small, extremely steep direct trail just opposite the landing place of the boat. It becomes somewhat cooler after a **one-hour** climb. From the saddle at Ranigaon, it is **half an hour** up the left side of the ridge to **Yasak,** a small Brahman bazaar town.

Another **hour** of reasonably level going brings you to **Milkrode.** Its high school is visible from afar. **Two more hours** of traversing the left side of the hill eventually bring you to a stream. Once across the stream, the trail finally goes steeply up through a village to the barren crest of the Mahabharat Lekh in **two hours.** Follow this crest to the left for an **hour,** taking the right fork at the base of a small hill shortly after a tea shop. The bazaar town of **Manglebari** is visible across a valley. Descend to the stream and follow it until the trail gradually goes diagonally up and crosses various streams and ridges to reach the town in **four hours.** It is now only **four hours** to **Ilam.** Along the way, descend to a small stream, then climb slightly before descending a long way to the stream at the base of the Ilam hill an **hour** from the town.

For the first time in many weeks, you will see jeeps. From Ilam, take a jeep south to Sanishari, a **day's** journey. Then continue by jeep for another hour to the junction with the East-West Highway. To return to Kathmandu by bus or plane, go either to Biratnagar, where there are daily flights, or to Bhadrapur, where there are fewer air connections. It is possible to motor directly to Kathmandu in **two days.** But to proceed to Darjeeling, take a bus east to Kakarbhitta on the border. Pass through customs and take a one-hour jeep ride to Siliguri. From Siliguri, you can take a train, a jeep, or a bus to Darjeeling, or you can go by a jeep or bus to Kalimpong, or to Gantok, Sikkim. Most vehicles leave early in the morning or around noon.

Cumulative trekking times (walking time only, does not include rests or stops) from Kharte to:

Khiraunle	7½ hours		Terhathum	25	hours
Sanam	11	"	Yasak	30	"
Phedi	12½	"	Manglebari	34¾	"
Tumlingtar (airstrip)	17	"	Ilam	39	"

Pokhara to Kathmandu
(Maps No. 2, Page 168; No. 3, Page 171; and No. 9, Page 255)

The swiftest traveller is he that goes afoot.

Thoreau

Despite the road between Pokhara and Kathmandu, and the availability of regular flights, it is still worthwhile to walk this stretch in order to see typical hill villages and learn much about local life and customs. Besides, there are good views of Himalchuli, Peak 29, Manaslu, Ganesh Himal, and the Annapurnas along the way. As with trails heading east from Kathmandu, the route goes against the grain of the land, but in contrast with those trails, the difference in altitude be-

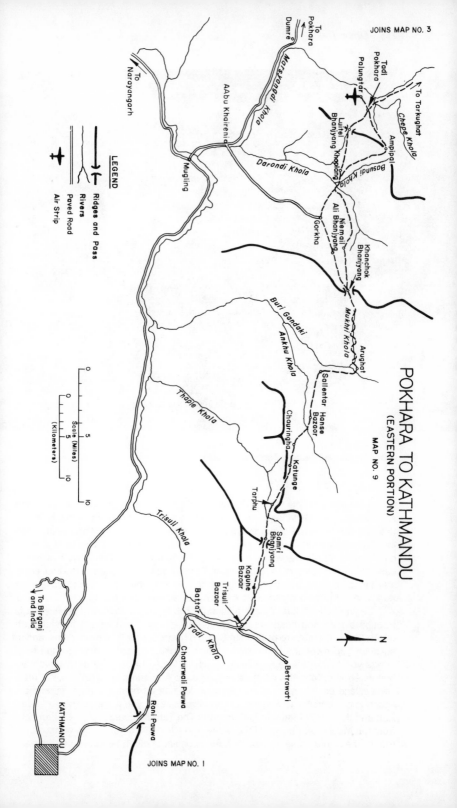

POKHARA TO KATHMANDU
(EASTERN PORTION)
MAP NO. 9

JOINS MAP NO. 3

LEGEND

Ridges and Pass
Rivers
Paved Road
Air Strip

Scale
0 5 10 (Miles)
0 5 10 (Kilometers)

N

To Pokhara

To Narayangarh

Marsyangdi Khola

Aabu Khaireni

Mugling

Darondi Khola

Tadi Pokhara
Palungtar

Luitel
Bhanjyang Khoplang

Niemail
Ali Bhanjyang

Gorkha

Chepe Khola

To Tarkughat

Ampipal

Basundi Khola

Khanchok
Bhanjyang

Mukhi Khola

Arughat

Buri Gandaki

Ankhu Khola

Thaple Khola

Sallentar Hanse
Bazaar

Chauringha

Katunge

Tarphu

Samri
Bhanjyang

Kagune
Bazaar

Trisuli
Bazaar

Trisuli Khola

Betrawati

Bajjar

Tadi Khola

Chaturwali Pauwa

Rani Pauwa

KATHMANDU

To Birganj
and India

JOINS MAP NO. I

Ampipal village. (Donald Messerschmidt)

tween the hills and the valleys is less, which makes this trek much easier. There are numerous *Newar* villages en route where you can get cooked meals. Because this is a low, level trek through typical hill areas with good food and reasonable lodging available, it is an excellent introduction to trekking. Travel here is most comfortable during the winter months—December through February. The trek is described from Pokhara to Kathmandu. There is now a spur road to Gorkha, so by starting or ending there, a shortened trek is possible. This track leaves the Kathmandu-Pokhara Highway at AAbu Khaireni, west of Mugling.

Begin at the Pokhara airstrip (2686 ft, 819 m) by crossing the runway. Pass through a gate and head across the narrow gorge of the almost invisible Seti Khola. The valley suburb of **Pinchin Camp** or **Ram Bazaar** is soon reached, and in an **hour**, you meet the main road from the Pokhara Bazaar. Another **half hour** brings you to the Bijayapur Khola, which is forded or crossed on a temporary bridge. Another **forty-five minutes** brings you to **Arghaumpauwa** (2550 ft, 777 m), a large village on the valley floor. Continue for **half an hour** around a hill and descend into the valley to **Sisuwa**. In **forty-five minutes** you come to the far end of Kuti and then to **Sat Muni** in **half an hour**. The Tal Khola, reached in **half an hour** from Sat Muni, is at the end of the valley, and a trail leads from it to a village at the foot of the Deorali ridge in **half an hour**. A **one-hour** climb brings you to the pass and the big village of **Deorali** (3000 ft, 913 m). There are sal forests along the valleys and wet subtropical forests on the ridges.

From Deorali, head northeast and drop to the base of the ridge after **forty-five minutes** to a stream that you follow to near the Madi Khola. Follow either the streambed or a trail up on its north (L) bank to reach several seasonal houses by the stream in an **hour.** The trail then keeps to the south (R) bank for another **hour** before turning right (southeast) to reach the village of **Sisaghat** (1300 ft, 396 m) on the Madi Khola in **half an hour.** The river is crossed by a ferry that is best hailed from high on the west (R) bank. This process is time consuming and you must bargain with the ferryman. Expect to be held up for at least an hour.

Once on the east (L) bank, follow it downstream for **fifteen minutes** until you reach the entrance of a tributary valley to the east. Head up this valley, staying above the north (R) bank of the river, for 1½ **hours** to **Suti Pasal.** Then head up to the pass at the head of the valley, following the stream closely most of the way. It becomes very steep just below the pass. **Kunchha** (2800 ft, 853 m) is reached some two hours after Suti Pasal.

From Kunchha, go west, cross a stream, and head down the valley for an **hour** to a village called **Turi Pasal** or **Naya Bazaar.** Another **hour** brings you to a large town called **Mani Chauk.** Cross the stream at the lower end of the town and follow the north (L) bank of the Poundi Khola, passing the village of **Sundar Bazaar** (2100 ft, 640 m) in **forty-five minutes.** Cross the Poundi Khola to its south (R) bank on a suspension bridge (1700 ft, 518 m) about **forty-five minutes** beyond Sundar. The trail then heads south along the west (R) bank of the Marsyangdi Khola, keeping close to the telephone line until it crosses a massive suspension bridge to reach the large town of **Tarkughat** (1650 ft, 503 m) on the east (L) bank in **half an hour.**

From Tarkughat the trail heads south on a shoulder (1950 ft, 594 m) above the east bank of the Marsyangdi. It is shaded by many banyan and pipul tree *chautaara* and is very pleasant. The Chepe Khola appears to the east, and after 1½ **hours** you descend to cross it on a good suspension bridge by a few houses (1550 ft, 573 m). The trail continues up the south (L) bank to reach a plateau and town called **Tadi Pokhari** (2025 ft, 617 m) in **half an hour.** Continue southeast for **half an hour** to **Barapilki Bazaar** (2050 ft, 625 m), then another **forty-five minutes** to **Luitel Bhanjyang** (2350 ft, 713 m) in a small pass.

There is a United Mission hospital and a primary school at **Ampipal** (4000 ft, 1219 m) on the ridge north of **Luitel Bhanjyang.** You can reach it by heading north from Tadi Pokhari and asking the way. This walk will take some **two to three hours.** Another route starts east of Luitel at the Darondi Khola near Chor Kuta, goes part of the way up the Basundi Khola, and continues on its southwest (R) bank past Simpani to Ampipal Bhanjyang. Again, it is necessary to ask the way. From the Darondi Khola, it takes two to three hours. A third route proceeds north from Luitel Bhanjyang, while a fourth begins from the east (L) bank of the Chepe Khola and takes the uphill (L) route.

From Luitel Bhanjyang, the trail descends and heads east to a ridge separating the Basundi Khola Valley to the north from that of the river flowing east from the pass at Luitel. The town of **Khoplang** (2100 ft, 640 m) is situated on this ridge 1½ **hours** from Luitel. From Khoplang, the trail descends into the tributary valley of the Basundi Khola, passes a small town called **Basundi** (1600 ft, 488 m), and reaches the Darondi Khola (1450 ft, 442 m), another large river, in 1½ **hours** from Khoplang. The river usually has to be forded.

There are two routes from here, depending on whether you wish to detour to Gorkha, home of the founder king of Nepal, Prithvinarayan Shah. To go to Gorkha, go south from the east (L) bank of the Darondi Khola for **fifteen minutes** past a tributary valley on your left to a *chautaara* at the base of a hill. The main trail to Gorkha begins here and goes up through forests and fields to reach **Gorkha** (4000 ft, 1219 m) from the west in 2½ **hours.** This large town with many shops and temples is reminiscent of Kathmandu, but is smaller, and has very few tourists. The new spur road to Gorkha leaves the Kathmandu-Pokhara highway at AAbu Khaireni.

The Shah family of Gorkha was simply one of many important family alliances in Nepal until Prithvinarayan Shah became master of the House of Gorkha at the age of twenty in 1743. Following a dream of which he never lost sight, Prithvinarayan Shah took twenty-six years, from 1744 to 1769, to conquer the Kathmandu Valley. He managed the near impossible task of building a powerful army out of the small population of Gorkha and maintaining its morale through two generations of fighting. He even retained the vital support of the small peasant and subsistence population of Gorkha. These people bore the brunt of feeding a large standing army over an extended period. Finally, the Gorkha army under Prithvinarayan Shah succeeded in uniting Nepal in the face of numerous and more powerful adversaries by engaging in surprise attacks rather than in large battles, and by keeping its enemies so divided that they were never able to unite in successful opposition to the conquerors.

The home of the founders of Nepal is still very much characterized by its fascinating history. By far the most spectacular site is the old palace of Prithvinarayan Shah, now a very holy shrine. The palace is situated amid terracing and gardens looking out on a panoramic view of the Himalaya. Reach it by climbing 1000 ft (304 m) up a beautiful stone staircase from Gorkha Bazaar. The palace is well guarded, and only a special caste of Brahmans, who serve the gods within the palace shrine, are allowed to go beyond the courtyard. It is believed that if any ordinary person looks at the gods, he or she will die. All the stonework in Gorkha is unique and beautifully crafted, but the palace and surrounding area are outstanding in Nepal.

About 30 ft (10 m) below the palace is the cave where the hermit Gorkhanath once lived. Gorkha received his name from this famous saint, and the cave, which is presently filled with statues, is an extremely holy place.

To head on toward Kathmandu, descend to the north side of the main ridge from the notch near the shrine and go east to reach a town called **Koke** or **Ali Bhanjyang** (3800 ft, 1158 m) in 1¾ **hours.** There are some shops here. Continue to the east, climbing along beautiful open ridges, and pass through a Brahman village called **Tapli** (4800 ft, 1463 m) an **hour** beyond. There are good views of Himalchuli, Baudha, Peak 29, Manaslu, and Ganesh Himal from this ridge. Descend from the ridge to **Khanchok Bhanjyang** (3600 ft, 1098 m) in 1¼ **hours.** The forests are of chir pine and chilaune.

To bypass Gorkha, ford the Darondi Khola and head upstream to the valley of the Khanchok Khola—also called the Masel Khola—1½ **hours** to the east. There is a town called **Niemail** or **Sikhar** to the southeast near the junction of the two rivers. Follow the Khanchok Khola for **three hours** to **Khanchok Bhanjyang** to join the route passing through Gorkha.

From Khanchok Bhanjyang climb northeast for 300 ft (91 m) to Sano Khanchok **half an hour** beyond. Shortly, begin the descent of the Mukhti Khola, which flows east to join the Buri Gandaki at Arughat. Spend some **three hours** in this valley, crossing and recrossing the river on an ill-defined trail. You are back in wet subtropical forest. After the first 2¼ **hours,** the trail keeps to the south (R) bank until it crosses the river on a twisting cantilever bridge. Cross the suspension bridge over the Buri Gandaki just beyond at **Arughat** (1600 ft, 488 m).

Once on the east (L) bank of this river, head south, keeping quite close to the river for almost **two hours** until you climb slightly to reach the Sallentar Plateau and the town of **Sallentar** (2000 ft, 609 m). From Sallentar the trail heads east, descending to the Ankhu Khola (1550 ft, 473 m). Follow the river on its north (R) bank to the town of **Hanse Bazaar** (1550 ft, 473 m) an **hour** beyond Sallentar. Continue along the north (R) bank, avoiding the log and mud bridge east of town. Continue past some Brahman villages until you come to a steel suspension bridge in an **hour.** Cross to the south (L) bank and enter the small village of **Ankhugursanger** (1700 ft, 518 m).

The trail continues east over a small saddle and ascends to **Thasoranpheri** (2000 ft, 609 m) in **forty-five minutes.** Beyond, the trail ascends on an ill-defined ridge past the town of **Chauringha** (3000 ft, 913 m) to a notch in the ridge with a tree on a *chautaara* (4200 ft, 1281 m) in 1¾ **hours.** It then contours the south side of the ridge, passing **Katunge** (4450 ft, 1356 m), several intervening hamlets, and **Bundi** (4450 ft, 1356 m) **half an hour** past the notch. The trail winds along up a ridge with commanding views of the mountains in good weather. The forest is again chir pine and chilaune. Descend past several clusters of houses, Bhotini, and reach a prominent notch in the ridge called **Tarphu** (4200 ft, 1281 m) **two hours** beyond Bundi. The telephone line again makes its appearance along this section.

From Tarphu, descend 1000 ft (304 m) and cross the Barang Khola in **half an hour.** As along many parts of the trail from Pokhara, there are dry and wet weather sections. Except during the monsoon, the river is crossed by a temporary log bridge near a few mills. In the monsoon, however, use a steel suspension bridge a little upstream. Follow the valley upstream, passing the towns of **Tarksank** (3250 ft, 990 m) and **Kirichowa** (3650 ft, 1112 m), to **Samri Bhanjyang** (4250 ft, 1296 m) 1½ **hours** beyohd Tarphu.

The trail now descends the valley of the Samri Khola to Trisuli. The forest again becomes wet and subtropical. For **over an hour** the trail keeps to the south (R) bank, passing **Kapri Bas** (3600 ft, 1097 m), Ulangaro (2660 ft, 808 m), and **Kagune Bazaar** (2375 ft, 724 m) before crossing to the north (L) bank of the river to **Morwah Bazaar.** A little over **two hours** after Samri you should reach the outskirts of Trisuli. Go through the upper part of the town past the Indian Aid Compound responsible for an electrical generation project that produces large amounts of power. From the project's penstocks, you can see down to the Trisuli Khola and **Trisuli Bazaar,** located by a bridge (1766 ft, 538 m). Regular bus service to Kathmandu is available from here. The trip takes four to five hours. Buses leave between 7 A.M. and 8 A.M. and between noon and 1 P.M.

The **two-hour** climb from Trisuli Bazaar to Nuwakot, a famous historical fort, is a worthwhile side trip. From the bus stop in Trisuli Bazaar, go back to the east (L) bank of the river. Take the first stony path going up to the left immediately after the bridge, and climb to where it joins the main road. Follow the main road north for a **few minutes** until you reach a three-story red brick house on the left. Take the stone path going upward across the road from this house, and climb for approximately 1½ **hours** to the old city of Nuwakot.

Signs of change—a smokeless chulo for cooking. (Donald Messerschmidt)

This strategic town was captured in 1744 by Prithvinarayan Shah, the first king of a united Nepal. Its capture was a major victory in his twenty-six-year campaign to conquer the Kathmandu Valley. He later built a seven-story palace in the fortified town. It is still in excellent condition and can be visited simply by requesting the police who guard the area to open it for you. The seventh story commands a view in every direction. Looking out from the highest point, you can easily imagine the following historic battle.

In 1792 the Chinese army, which, until that time, had been making a largely successful incursion into Nepal, made the colossal blunder at Nuwakot of attacking uphill against the skilled Nepali mountain troops. The Chinese were thrown into confusion by a hail of boulders, logs, and every kind of missile. As they retreated in panic, they were halted at the bridge by their own generals, who refused to accept the possibility of retreat. Cut down by the famous Gurkha *khukuri* (curved knives), or drowned in the monsoon-swollen river, the Chinese army was routed in this decisive battle.

To go on to Kathmandu on foot from Trisuli, cross the bridge to the east (L) bank of the river and follow the automobile road south to the village of **Battar** in **forty-five minutes**. Then turn east around the foot of the mountain on which the fort of Nuwakot stands. Go through a low pass and down to the Tadi Khola which joins the Trisuli Khola to the south. Cross a steel suspension bridge **half an hour** upstream from Battar. After the crossing, follow a smaller stream up to the town of **Chaturwali Pauwa** (3400 ft, 1037 m) about **three hours** beyond the Tadi Khola. You have now begun the climb to the rim of the Kathmandu Valley. Continue for another **half hour** to **Barmandi** (4000 ft, 1219 m), a village consisting of a group of large farm houses on a level stretch. Another 1½ **to two hours** of climbing brings you to **Tungi Pauwa.** Along the way, pass through the village of **Tarpu Gaon,** distinguished by a huge tree growing on a level stretch. Reach the village of **Ranipauwa** and the automobile road in **half an hour.** The road has taken quite a detour compared to this direct trail, but, of course, it rises much less steeply.

The hill you have been climbing is popularly known as the five *maanaa* climb, since it is said that a loaded porter needs to eat five *maanaa* of rice to climb it. Alas, most cargo now goes by truck! From Ranipauwa it is easier to continue along the road to the pass, Kaulatana Bhanjyang (6000 ft, 1829 m).

The remaining forests are oak. The pass is reached in about **forty-five minutes.** The auto road then descends gradually for about three miles until the main walking trail cuts off to the side of the ridge and descends to the rim of the Kathmandu Valley. On the right side of the rim, the remains of a monument of five mounds to represent the five *maanaa* of rice can still be seen. A short descent brings you to **Jitpui Phedi** (4600 ft, 1402 m) and a police check post. Shortly beyond is Balaju with a swimming pool and twenty-two fountains. Expect to spend 1½ **to two days** covering the journey from Trisuli to Kathmandu.

Cumulative trekking times (walking time only, does not include rests or stops) from Pokhara airstrip to:

Deorali	3¼ hours	Arughat	22¾ hours
Kunchha	7½ "	Ankhugursanger	24¾ "
Tarkughat	9¾ "	Tarphu	27½ "
Luitel Bhanjyang	11½ "	Samri Bhanjyang	28½ "
Darondi Khola River	14½ "	Trisuli Bazaar	30 "
Khanchok Bhanjyang	21 "		

Kathmandu Valley Treks
(Map No. 10, Page 263)

The following section has been kindly contributed by Binney van Bergen, a Canadian who has been living in Kathmandu for the past few years.

One of the most accessible but neglected trekking areas in Nepal is the Kathmandu valley and rim. One can experience all the joys of trekking in Nepal without embarking on an extended journey into the more remote regions of the country. The Kathmandu valley and surrounding area boasts superb and varied scenery, encompassing views of the rugged Himalaya as well as peaceful rural countryside.

Along the trails, one is bound to encounter Nepalis of diverse occupations and ethnic groups, some of whom have never even visited the city of Kathmandu. Most trails pass through tiny rural settlements where the trekker can witness the daily life of rural Nepalis: planting and harvesting wheat and rice; building new homes, collecting firewood and fodder for animals; threshing grains; grinding corn, millet, and wheat; weaving baskets and corn-husk mats; as well as doing household chores such as preparing meals and caring for children. Tea shops along the way differ from those found on major trekking routes only in that the visit of a western trekker is a welcome surprise to the owner, and often many villagers will gather around and try to speak with you. The arrival of a trekker is always greeted by small children as a major event, and they inevitably will try out their English on you.

Along with enjoying Nepal's spectacular scenery and meeting the gay, friendly people, absorbing the spiritual culture of the valley is one of the rewarding aspects of trekking near Kathmandu. Hundreds of temples, shrines, sacred places, and monasteries dot the valley, and most of the treks described here include a visit to at least one. Often while trekking in the valley, there is an opportunity to observe devout Hindus and Buddhists in some form of religious worship, be it chanting, meditating, performing a special *pujaa* (offering), bathing in sacred rivers, or making a pilgrimage. On my first visit to Gokarneswar, I had the good fortune to witness a Hindu sacred thread ceremony, whereby young boys become real Hindus. Visiting these sites will enable the trekker to gain more of an insight into the spiritual life and history of Nepal.

A recommended trekking aid in the valley is the Schneider map, which is available in all the local bookstores. This excellent 1:50,000 contour map accurately shows trails, towns, and rivers. I find it indispensable for trekking, especially for routes not described in a guidebook. Although the map is on the pricey side, it is well worth it, not only for route finding, but for identifying landmarks visible from some of the viewpoints, and for determining the elevation of the routes. All the treks described in this book, except for parts of the Dhulikhel to Panauti and the Namo Buddha treks, are in the area covered by the Schneider map.

One way in which trekking in and around the valley differs from that on the more popular routes is that there are literally hundreds of criss-crossing trails used by locals. It is often difficult to follow exactly a route described in a trekking guide, but this is usually of little consequence. If you know generally where you are headed and the name of your destination, it will be difficult to get lost. Nepalis are very helpful and will always assist you in finding the route, even if the only Nepali word you know is the name of your destination. It is, however, important to know generally where you are headed. Nepalis rarely walk for pleasure and will

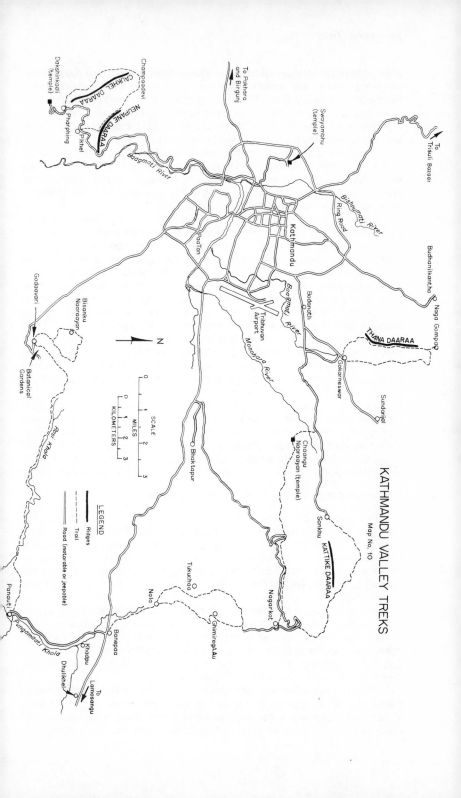

KATHMANDU VALLEY TREKS

Map No. 10

often point you to the main road to a destination and will discourage you from taking perhaps a more scenic route. It is also not uncommon for a Nepali to point out the direction he feels you should be headed in, even if he hasn't the slightest clue of where it is you want to be going. One of the pleasures of walking in the valley is that there are trails everywhere. You need only use your imagination, choose an area on the map where you would like to walk, and set off.

I recommend bringing a picnic lunch. Although you can usually find a tea shop or private home that will prepare you a Nepali meal, cooking it can often take several hours, which may not give you enough time to reach your destination by dark. Always carry purified water or bring iodine or water purification tablets to treat any water you may need along the way.

All the treks described here can be completed in one day, returning to Kathmandu before dark. For the more adventurous trekker, with limited time, a pleasant variation would be to combine some of the walks described into a trek of two days or more. Generally, you should plan the overnight stops for Nagarkot and Dhulikhel. Although all of the larger towns will have overnight accommodations, Nagarkot and Dhulikhel have lodges that cater specifically to trekkers. Most of the treks described here begin or end in the vicinity of these two towns, and planning an overnight trek is simply a matter of connecting a few of these treks. Use your imagination to design a trek to meet your interests and available time.

A recommended route would be to leave from Bhaktapur and spend the first night in one of the many trekkers' lodges in Nagarkot. One could walk to Nagarkot via Chaangu Naaraayan (described here as a walk from Nagarkot to Chaangu Naaraayan) or by following the paved road north of Bhaktapur to Nagarkot. If you decide on the latter route, leave the paved road at a clump of bamboo, half an hour's walk past Bhaktapur, and follow the straight path along the water pipe in the valley to the right of the road. After an hour's walk along the pipe, the trail climbs steeply through a pine-reforestation area and rejoins the road to Nagarkot. From Nagarkot walk to Sankhu to the north or Banepaa to the south. From Banepaa, catch a bus to Dhulikhel and spend the second night here. Trek to Panauti and/or Namo Buddha the next day, depending on your interests and available time.

GOKARNESWAR TO NAGA GOMPA AND BACK

This moderate trek starts at the old temple in Gokarneswar and follows the top of the Thana DAARaa ridge to the Naga Gompa (Buddhist monastery) above Budhanilkantha. The trail along the ridge passes through lovely pine forests and has excellent views of the valleys on both sides. From the monastery two return routes are available; one to Budhanilkantha, and the other through the bottom of the cultivated valley back to Gokarneswar. The entire trek takes about four hours to complete.

This trek starts in the town of Gokarneswar. To reach Gokarneswar by car, follow the road past Bodanath and take the first dirt road to your left, which goes to Sundarijal. Follow this road for about two miles past Bodanath and park near the temple complex in Gokarneswar. To reach Gokarneswar by bus, take a mini-bus to Bodanath from the west side of Ratna Park; from Bodanath take another mini bus to Sundarijal but get off at Gokarneswar.

At Gokarneswar, the Mahadev temple is worth a visit. This temple, situated beside a small, local gorge, on the bank of the Bagmati River, is an impressive three-roofed structure dedicated to Shiva. It was built in 1582 and has been recently restored. Most of the carved wood roof struts have been replaced in the restoration. There is also a fine eighth century stone image of the goddess Parvati in a small shrine between the temple and the road.

The trek starts on the dirt road directly opposite the temple complex entrance. Follow this road to the west, through a new reforestation area, to the top of the ridge. Take the right, high fork in the road soon after the start. There are beautiful views of the valley to the southwest, including the shining spire of the Bodanath stupa. Fifteen minutes from the beginning of the trek, the road crosses the ridge near an antenna tower, heads north, and continues level on the east (R) side of the ridge. In another ten minutes the trail passes another saddle, marked by a large *pipal* tree and a few houses.

Ignore the level road, which continues to the right, past the saddle, and take the higher of the two trails on the left, which climbs about 100 meters to the top of the Thana DAARaa ridge. Follow the top of this ridge north, through pine forests, and enjoy the rewarding views on both sides. There are also many grassy picnic or resting areas along the top of the ridge. The monastery that is your destination is visible at the end of the ridge, about two miles ahead. It is easily recognized by the many surrounding prayer flags dancing in the breeze.

After an hour and a half you will reach an old stone fence below the monastery. Cross through an opening in the fence and immediately turn to the left and climb an obscure trail to the monastery. Ignore the level trail to the right. After half an hour of climbing, you will reach the large dirt road that traverses the hill below the monastery.

The trail to the Naga Gompa monastery follows the road to the left for 100 yards and then climbs the hill again for another fifteen minutes. The Naga Gompa is rather scattered, with several buildings for the monastery and also a nunnery occupied by about twenty very friendly nuns. The views from here are excellent.

There are two options for continuing the trek. The one described here returns to Gokarneswar via a main trail in the bottom of the valley, below the ridge you followed initially. An alternate route follows the road west, taking advantage of the many little shortcuts, to the town of Budhanilkantha, about a mile away. Budhanilkantha is the site of the famous sleeping Vishnu statue. Buses and taxis back to Kathmandu are available from the center of town.

To return to Gokarneswar along the valley, follow the road below the monastery to the east, past a school building, reaching cultivated fields after ten minutes. Watch for a large path leading from the road through a fence, down to the valley below. Follow this trail, which reaches a village about 200 yards below the road. Pass through the village on the trail that bears to the right. The main trail leads back to the ridge along which you came, as the locals consider this the best route, so you must be careful to follow a smaller trail which leads down into the valley. This trail is reached five minutes beyond the village, just past a large new *chorten,* where the main trail traverses on a level to the ridge. Do not take this trail, but take the left fork, which descends steeply. After half an hour of descending, you will cross a stream and join the main trail at the bottom of the valley. Follow this level trail south through pleasant cultivated fields until you reach Gokarneswar forty-five minutes later.

NAGARKOT

Nagarkot is a small village perched on a ridge famous for its views of the Himalaya. To reach Nagarkot, follow the road to the west of Bhaktapur all the way to the top of the ridge or, alternatively, take a bus to Bhaktapur from the Bagh

Cleaning wool for a Radi carpet, a traditional Nepali, rather than a Tibetan, design. (Dave Hardenbergh)

Bazaar bus stop in Kathmandu, and at Bhaktapur catch a minibus to Nagarkot.

There are several lodges in Nagarkot. A popular outing is to spend a night there, awake early to watch the sun rise over the Himalaya, and then do a day trek. Most of the lodges are for trekkers (bring your own sleeping bag), and one, the Terra Goan, has electricity and hot running water. Reservations made through the Terra Goan Hotel near Bodnath are required. A morning jaunt to the lookout tower, a half an hour walk up the road from the army barracks, will reward you with a 360-degree panorama of the Himalaya and Kathmandu Valley.

NAGARKOT TO SANKHU

This moderate trek begins at Nagarkot and follows a fairly level trail north along the top of the Kattike DAARaa ridge. This trail has excellent views of the Himalaya on one side and of the Kathmandu Valley on the other. The route then descends gradually through a pleasant forest to the valley and follows a road back to Sankhu. A worthwhile side trip is to visit the famous temple of Bajra Jogini located on the side of the hill above Sankhu. The entire trek takes four hours to complete.

This trek begins where the main road up to Nagarkot first reaches the top of the ridge, just beyond the sharp hairpin turn. You can clearly see the turn on the Schneider map. There are several signs for lodges here, including the "Nagarkot Lodge – Restaurant at the End of the Universe." If you have taken the bus up, get off at the bus stop, at the army barracks, and walk back down the road, heading north, for fifteen minutes to the starting point of the trek.

Follow the dirt road leading east off the paved road at the starting point. Pass several lodges and after a few minutes take the right fork, which descends to the three new cheese factory buildings, about half a mile away. You can visit this factory and buy cheese if you wish. The trek follows the left fork and passes the Nagarkot lodge within ten minutes. Five minutes past the lodge, the trail forks again. Follow the right fork, which is the main trail. The views from this part of the trail are spectacular. Five minutes past the fork, the trail enters an open area with several trails leading from it. Take the left trail towards the Kattike DAARaa ridge. The trail is deeply eroded and descends quickly. After fifteen minutes of descending, the trail levels out again. Ahead is a terraced knoll with two trees on top. Keep to the left of the knoll. The trail descends again into a small settlement. Follow the trail through the settlement and after seven minutes you will arrive at a saddle in the ridge. On the ridge to the north you may notice a road that has badly eroded the hillside. This is the direction in which you will be heading.

At the end of the saddle the main trail contours around to the left. Leave the main trail and climb directly up the ridge. The trail is obscure but just climb straight up. After a five-minute climb you will arrive at a "T" junction. Follow the left trail up and at each fork take the upper trail. After a few minutes, the trail peters out into an open grassy area. Climb up to the top of the ridge to your right and follow the ridge top for twenty minutes. Anywhere along this ridge is a great spot to rest and admire the view. The ridge dips down into a saddle and then climbs up again. Head towards the right, in the direction of the road on the far ridge to the north. The trail forks again ten minutes from the last saddle. Keep right on the deeply eroded trail, which forks again after five minutes. Again take the right fork. This short stretch is a little treacherous so walk cautiously. In five minutes you will reach an open area in another saddle. To your right you can see the road. At this point you have a choice of two routes.

First, you may follow the dirt road down (west) for **forty-five minutes** until it enters a town, where the routes join. Second, the alternate route, which is described here, descends steeply on the north side of the Kattike DAARaa ridge. It passes through a pleasant forested area, with many clumps of bamboo, and follows a large stream, with several waterfalls. There are many lovely picnic sites along the way. From the clearing take the trail to the left (west) of the ridge and follow the stream, staying on the right bank. Twenty minutes from the clearing the trail forks. Take the left trail, which passes through dense vegetation and follows the stream down. Along the trail are several small paths leading to the stream. You will find nice lunch stops by the stream if you follow any of these side trails. Soon you will see the road to Sankhu, in the base of the valley ahead of you. Descend more steeply here, through an old pine forest, and after half an hour reach a town where the trail joins the alternate route along the road.

Go down through the town and watch for a lane to the left that leads to a suspension bridge over the river. Cross the bridge and follow the road to the left, which leads to Sankhu. After twenty minutes walking, look up to your right to see the golden roofs of the Bajra Jogini temple peeking through the dense forest. Thirty-five minutes after crossing the bridge, you will reach the town of Sankhu, a post on the old trading route from Kathmandu to Lhasa. Sankhu has many fine old *Newari* houses, with elaborately carved window frames. There is also an old temple with several shrines along the main road at the north entrance to the town. Just before this small temple complex, there is a trail to the right along a brick wall. This trail leads to the temple of Bajra Jogini, which is about a thirty-minute walk from this point. The temple complex is an ancient, sacred site dedicated to the Tantric goddess Bajra Jogini. The main temple is a seventeenth century, three-tiered structure with a golden *torana* (arch above the entrance) depicting the goddess.

To reach the bus stop in Sankhu, follow the road into town. After five minutes reach a square and take the first road to the right, reaching the bus stop in ten minutes.

NAGARKOT TO BANEPAA VIA GHIMIREGAAU

This moderate trail is mostly downhill, at some points descending rather steeply. Ridges are followed all the way to Nala and provide continuous views into the valley. The trail passes through GhimiregAAu, a large rural village. Nala is a small town with two beautiful temples. We took the route in February and even then some of the trails were a bit muddy and slippery. The entire trek takes five to six hours to complete.

The trail begins on the paved road at Nagarkot just below the army barracks. Follow this road south. Thirty-five minutes from the barracks there is a trail to the right marked with a sign "shortcut to top". The mud steps of this trail rise steeply. Take this trail, which crosses the road again after ten minutes. There is a small weather station on the hill to the left and a lookout tower on the hill to the right. The trail you will follow is across the road to the left of the lookout tower and to the right of a small stone house with red roof and green doors.

Take the detour to the lookout tower and enjoy the fantastic panorama. The Himalaya stretches from the west to north to east. The Kathmandu Valley lies to the west and southwest. The summit of Pulchowki is visible to the southwest and is recognizable by the tall skinny radio tower perched on top. Nargarjun is the rounded, forested hill to the west, and the Shivapuri ridge is visible to the northwest.

The route you will follow is to the south into the valley directly below.

GhimiregAAu lies just behind the closest, short ridge, which ends in steeply descending terraces. From GhimiregAAu the route follows the top of the next forested ridge, which curves into the flat green valley. Nala lies on the valley floor, just behind the end of this ridge.

Leave the tower by the same trail. Back at the road, take the trail descending directly south, below the lookout tower. Five minutes from the road the trail forks. Take the lower fork, which heads for the ridge stretching into the valley. The trail is quite clear. It descends through a badly eroded area where efforts at reforestation are quite evident.

Thirty minutes from the road, the houses of GhimiregAAu are visible to the right. Cross the barbed wire fence, which is intended to keep animals out of the reforestation area, and enter the town. The trail descends through the town, and in places is very steep and eroded.

In twenty minutes reach a "T" in the trail, where there is a water spout on the left. Follow the left trail towards the ridge leading south into the valley. The trail contours along through terraced fields. This is a well traveled route, and the trail is clearly marked.

In ten minutes cross a stream and follow the lower trail on the same contour. This narrow trail follows an irrigation canal. After thirty minutes, the trail cuts sharply to the left down an eroded gully and after another five minutes cuts right again past a few houses and onto the ridge. (The trail down the gully descends to the east of the ridge) A lunch stop can easily be found by taking one of the many little wood cutter's trails off the main trail into a small clearing.

After thirty-five minutes, reach the butt of the ridge and see Nala directly below. Notice the Buddhist shrine of Lokeshwar, called Karunamaya, on the road entering the town to the right. In the center of town, slightly to the left, is the splendid four-tiered Nala Bhagvati temple. Both of these temples are worth a visit.

Walk through the town to the main road, which leads in a southerly direction to Banepaa. Follow this road for forty minutes until you reach the town of Banepaa. Continue straight to the main highway and then turn left to reach the bus stop. Although a major fire some twenty-five years ago destroyed many of its buildings, Banepaa remains an economically important trading center for the surrounding area.

NAGARKOT TO BANEPAA

This walk is a slight variation of the walk described above. Rather than travel via GhimiregAAu, the route contours along the side of the ridge on the west side of the valley, through the town of Tukuchaa. This is an easier walk because the trails do not descend as steeply as those described on the previous trek. The entire trek takes three to four hours to complete.

Begin the trail as described in the previous trek, but from the lookout tower continue west along the main road. At the end of the road take the path leading to the left. The right trail descends steeply to a small square pond.

Continue along this trail through the reforestation area until you reach a fork, ten minutes beyond the end of the road. Take the middle trail, which descends south along the ridge in front of you. The upper trail leads to Bhaktapur.

In thirty minutes reach a small town. To the west, Bhaktapur and the villages of Sural and Tathali are visible. Across the valley to the east, the white houses of the town of GhimiregAAu are seen. Nala lies south-southeast in the valley below.

Pass through a small rhododendron forest and in thirty minutes reach the town of Tukuchaa, where the trail winds among the houses, even passing through an occasional front yard of a home. There are always people about who will be pleased to point out the way to Nala.

Twenty minutes past the town you will reach a large stream. Some of the large rocks in the middle of the stream offer a pleasant lunch stop.

Follow the trail along the river for another twenty-five minutes to reach the town of Nala. Here there is a large Buddhist temple to Lokeshwar, called Karuna-maya. The main entrance is in the courtyard. Notice the pots and pans attached to the high roof. Inside is an unusual statue of Buddha.

From this point the trail follows the road to Banepaa, as described in the previous trek description.

NAGARKOT TO CHAANGU NAARAAYAN

This very easy trek, with little climbing, takes three to four hours to complete. It descends west along a long ridge leading from Nagarkot to Chaangu Naaraayan. The views from the ridge are excellent. The trek ends at the superb temple complex of Chaangu Naaraayan, north of Bhaktapur.

The trek begins at the terrace of the Tarra Goan lodge, located on the west side of the Nagarkot ridge. A red and white sign on top of the ridge, where the bus stops, points out the direction of the lodge. From the terrace, look in a westerly direction to see the long hill extending into the valley. At the end of the hill the gilded roofs of Chaangu Naaraayan should be visible. The route you will take follows this ridge.

From the terrace, descend west along the large path, staying near the top of the ridge. The path crosses the road several times but after an hour of walking you will come to a point where the road reaches a saddle in the ridge. Look for a trail that climbs up from the saddle, through a pine plantation, onto the ridge. Climb gradually for half an hour, after which time the trail becomes level. Enjoy the gorgeous view of the valley and Himalaya beyond. The town of Chaangu is reached about two hours from the top of the ridge.

The origins of Chaangu Naaraayan date back to the fourth century. The temple courtyard contains many beautiful stone carvings. It would be well worth bringing a guidebook that describes the various carvings and statues. (See Appendix C, The Art of Nepal, by Lydia Aran.)

There are two ways to return to Kathmandu. The quickest way back is to leave the temple complex by the western doorway. Below to the northwest is the Monohara River and beyond the river is the road from Sankhu to Kathmandu. Head toward the small group of houses on the road. A path leads through the forest to the river. Cross the river and walk along rice paddy walls to the small town, from where a bus to Kathmandu can be flagged down.

A longer route returns via Bhaktapur. Either descend south from Chaangu Naaraayan and follow small trails through the rice paddies to Bhaktapur or follow the motorable road on the east side of the village all the way back to Bhaktapur. Either route should take about two hours.

VALLEY NORTH OF BOTANICAL GARDENS IN GODAAVARI

The botanical gardens in Godaavari are reached by following the road leading south from the ring road at PaaTan. To go by bus take the Langankhel bus from the northeast corner of Ratna Park in Kathmandu to the Lagankhel bus stop in PaaTan. From here take the bus to Godaavari.

This easy-to-moderate trek takes you on a loop in the horseshoe-shaped valley north of the botanical gardens in Godaavari. It involves only moderate climbing for short distances. The entire valley is quite prosperous due to the fertile farming land on the valley floor. Although the villages in the valley are very traditional, modernization is making its impact, as indicated by the occasional corrugated metal roof and the power lines. The locals are very friendly, and the occasional cry of "bye bye one rupee" is simply a game the children play. This trek is a pleasant one to introduce visitors to rural Nepal. It takes three to four hours to complete.

Enter the Botanical Gardens and follow the main road through the gardens to the gate at the opposite end. Cross the bridge to the right and bear right on the road through the small village. The road leads to a river, which you follow downstream for a few meters to a small dam, where the controls for the irrigation canals of the valley are located. Cross this dam, then stay on the right side of the irrigation canal. Notice a water-powered mill housed in a little hut on the other side of the bridge.

The trail branches at this point: one branch leads into the valley; the other is a stone path that leads up to a trail that contours around the rim of the valley. Take the upper trail. Notice the shape of the valley, and the trails that contour along halfway up the side of the encircling hills. You can practically see the whole route you will take. Notice directly to the north a pronounced dip in the hills enclosing the valley. This is the site of Bisanku Naaraayan, your probable lunch stop. If at any time you think you have lost the route, simply follow trails leading in the direction you wish to go. You cannot get lost unless you climb to the top of the ridge and descend the other side, which would be very unlikely.

Follow the main trail along the side of the valley. Avoid the many branching trails, which lead to houses. You will not see rugged mountain scenery from this part of the trail but you will find peaceful rural scenes and get a sense of how the non-city dweller lives.

About forty-five minutes from the Botanical Gardens gate, you'll arrive at an open area with a small duck pond, where one trail leads up into the bush and the other leads slightly downhill. Take the downhill trail, passing a carved stone platform with three water spouts, like several others you will have passed along the way. Beyond these spouts the trail forks again. Take the upper trail, which leads into the bush. Climb steeply for about five minutes, until you reach a junction with a level trail that runs at a right angle to the trail you are on. Turn left on this trail and follow it for about ten minutes. This trail forms the bottom of the horseshoe.

You soon encounter another fork in the trail. Notice ahead of you the cleft in the ridge where Bisanku Naaraayan is located. Take the trail that descends steeply to the left. After another ten minutes or so, you come across another open area with water spouts. Cross the stream past these water spouts and follow the main trail. Continue on this trail along the side of the ridge. Eventually the trail will run just below the barbed wire fence enclosing the reforestation project on the upper part of the ridge. If at any time you are unsure of your route, simply ask a local to direct you to Bisanku Naaraayan. Any one of them will happily point out the way.

Approximately 2 to 2½ hours from beginning the trek, you will arrive at Bisanku Naaraayan, at the dip in the ridge. This is a wide-open area with a few shelters for pilgrims and several large trees, as well as a new government health post. From this point there are excellent views of the Kathmandu Valley and the beautiful snow-capped mountains in the distance. This site is one of the celebrated Vishnu shrines that devotees of the god must visit at some point in their lives.

Water systems such as this one have high priority among development projects in Nepal. Some enterprising villagers have even piped water to their houses. (Stephen Bezruchka)

"A steep, narrow stairway cut into the rock leads to a wooden platform in front of a tiny opening to the cave, where freeformed stones are usually protected by a lattice of metal links. The connection to Vishnu is through a legend: Shiva once hid here from the demon Bhasmasur, who had obtained from him the power to turn all living things into ashes and dust by a touch of the hand. Vishnu convinced the demon to touch his own forehead, and the demon turned himself to dust. The hillock adjacent to the cave is said to be made from the ashes of Bhasmasur." (Insight Guide: *Nepal*)

Climb the steep stone steps to the top of the holy site. A short walk along the north (L) side of the ridge will reward you with even better views. This is a good spot for a lunch break.

To return, descend the stone steps and continue along the trail you arrived on (turn right at the health post). Eventually you will cross the rice paddies in the bottom of the valley and return to the irrigation dam. Your destination is the point where the far ridge meets the valley floor, just below the Godaavari quarry. Follow the trail past a large concrete school and continue down the wide path to the floor of the valley. A small log bridge crosses a stream and leads to the main path through the rice paddies. This path leads back to houses at the other side of the valley, the point at which you began.

Cross the irrigation dam again and bear left through the village. Cross the bridge and go through the gate to the left, the entrance to the botanical gardens. If you have the time and energy, a wander through the gardens is worthwhile. In the building to the right of the main gate, plants from the gardens are for sale.

GODAAVARI TO PANAUTI

This moderate walk initially involves 600 feet of climbing, but the trail is good and only an hour should be enough to reach the top. The trek then follows a ridge with beautiful views of the Kathmandu Valley and the Himalaya. From the ridge, the route descends into the Rosi Khola river valley and follows a level trail through small villages and farming land all the way to Panauti, an all-*Newar* town located at the confluence of two rivers. Panauti is religiously significant, renowned for its temples, and worth exploring if time allows. The entire trek takes five to six hours to complete.

Begin the trek at the botanical gardens parking lot (see previous trek for directions). Enter the gardens and follow the main road. Just past a white building on the right, 100 yards from the entrance, a narrow trail leading steeply uphill is marked by a black sign saying, "Terrain Garden Nepalese Style." Follow this trail and turn right when you reach the phone lines one minute later. At the fork take the upper trail, which joins a stone path. Follow this stone path, which climbs steadily but not steeply, to the top of the ridge. The many square ponds that form the fish hatchery are visible below. The large white building below the rock quarry is the St. Xavier's school. About forty-five minutes from the beginning of the trek you will reach the top of the ridge. Just before that point, directly opposite the rock quarry, a small path bears right, off the main trail. Follow this path, which runs along a barbed wire fence on the left, then crosses it a few yards beyond.

For the next hour, climb gently along the top of the ridge. Whenever you encounter a fork in the trail, take the upper trail. Just remember to stay on top of the ridge, which curves to the right. From here the views of the Himalaya are spectacular. The ridge on which you are standing forms the rim of the valley I described in the previous trek description. The cleft in the next ridge is the site of Bisanku Naaraayan.

Fifteen minutes after first crossing the barbed wire fence, past a small muddy ravine, you will come across a fork in the trail. Take the upper fork up the ridge. The trail passes through a large open meadow, past which you can see the ridge along which you will walk. Notice how it curves to the right. You will follow the ridge until the large cleft and then descend the other side. The mountain to your right with the tower on top is Pulchowki, the highest mountain in the Kathmandu Valley rim. A few minutes past the meadow, the trail forks again into three trails. Take the upper trail, keeping the barbed wire fence on the left.

After another half hour, the trail climbs again, contouring around the right side of a knoll, which forms the back of the horseshoe surrounding the botanical gardens. Twenty-five minutes from this point, the trail bears left and crosses to the left side of the ridge. These are the last views of the Godaavari Valley on this trek.

Walk along the left side of the ridge for about ten minutes, during which time you are looking straight at the valley into which you will descend. You can see the trail along the right side of the Rosi Khola river in the bottom of the valley. Although we stopped for lunch in the valley, the top of this ridge is also a good choice for a lunch stop. From this point head straight down. Do not take either of the two trails to the left. One minute later, reach a main trail. Go left for a few yards and then steeply right as you descend down the right side of the valley.

The trail leads through a village. Then, thirty minutes past the top of the ridge, the trail forks. Take the left trail, down into the valley. As you descend, the trail forks again. Take the trail leading down and to your right. The water pipe descending the ridge on the opposite side of the valley is a good landmark because your trail is directly opposite this pipe. Rather steep and sprinkled with loose rocks, the trail reaches the bottom of the valley in about twenty minutes. At the bottom of the valley, cross the stream on the right, near another water pipe.

Thirty-five minutes from the stream, you should notice an old moss-covered stupa to your left. Shortly after passing the stupa, the trail forks. Take the right fork through fields and cross two log bridges. You can stop for lunch on the bank of this river. After crossing the last bridge, head left through the town and back to the Rosi Khola.

Follow this wide trail for another forty-five minutes until it intersects a main trail right across from a shop. At this point turn right, away from the river. There are a few tea shops here that provide a pleasant rest stop. Twenty minutes past the tea shops, you will pass through another town. Ten minutes past the town, cross the river on a bridge and follow the road along the left bank. This road leads directly to Panauti, which becomes visible at the top of a rise twenty minutes after crossing the river. Panauti is reached thirty minutes later.

Considered one of the finest all-*Newar* settlements in the region, Panauti is predominantly an agricultural town, and before the development of Banepaa, it was an important trade center. The main street leads to a walled open space containing the three-tiered Indreshwar Mahadev Temple, built in the fifteenth century, and the Naaraayan Shrine. Both are being restored. The Indreshwar Mahadev Temple is architecturally and historically one of the most important temples associated with the *Newari* culture of the Kathmandu valley. Across the Pungamaati River stands the famous seventeenth century Brahmayani Temple, which has undergone a major renovation. Fine examples of *Newari* painting are found inside this temple.

Your transport (your own or a bus) will be waiting at the bus stop in Panauti.

Children playing in Taplejung. (Ane Haaland)

The route back to Kathmandu follows the dirt road to Banepaa, and then the paved road passing by Bhaktapur. The trip back takes about one hour by car.

DHULIKHEL

Dhulikhel is another town often visited by trekkers looking for spectacular Himalayan views. The old Dhulikhel lodge is located in the town, which is set slightly off the main highway. To reach the lodge, follow the road leading from the highway to the town and turn right onto the main road in the town of Dhulikhel. It is a favorite place to stay to get away from the bustle of Kathmandu, meet other trekkers, or to take Nepali lessons from the owner, Mr. B. P. Shrestha. Should you decide to stay overnight at the lodge, you will be rewarded by a Himalayan sunrise if you awake early and climb to the small Bhagvati Temple. To reach this temple follow the road to the southern end of town and continue on upwards on the large trail, which cuts off the many switchbacks in the road. After thirty minutes' climb, you will reach a stone arch and a set of steep stone stairs leading off the road to the left. Climb these steps to the temple, from where the whole Himalayan panorama extends for 180 degrees in front of you.

To reach Dhulikhel by car, follow the main road to Bhaktapur but continue past the south side of Bhaktapur, through the town of Banepaa and up a steep ridge to Dhulikhel, an hour's drive from Kathmandu. Alternatively, you can catch a bus for Dhulikhel at the main bus stop on Durbar Marg, across from Ratna Park.

DHULIKHEL TO PANAUTI

This easy trail, with relatively little climbing, takes about four hours to complete. It passes through the town of a Dhulikhel, follows a fertile valley and then follows the Pungamaati (Punyamaata on Schneider map) Khola to the sacred town of Panauti.

The trek begins at the point where the main road reaches the center of town. Continue straight across the main street and follow the road west for ten minutes, until you reach a river. Turn right and follow the trail along the river. In twenty-five minutes you will reach the trail that leads out of the valley to the town of Chauket. Follow this trail into the town and take the road to the left, fifteen minutes from the trail that left the river. Pass a small mill and, before the tea shop, take the trail to the right, which winds along the right side of the valley. In thirty minutes you will reach the Pungamaati Khola. Follow the left bank southwest for another ten minutes and then cross the bridge to the road on the right bank of the river. This road reaches Panauti after another thirty minutes.

Once in Panauti, take the main road to the left and reach the temples at the confluence of the river in ten minutes. The temples are briefly described in the Godaavari to Panauti trek. A peaceful lunch spot can be found past the temples, on the boulders in the river.

To return to Dhulikhel, follow the same trail to Chauket and descend to the river valley. Rather than going left, cross the valley and follow the trail up the other side, ending up on the west side of Dhulikhel. At the main temple in Dhulikhel turn right and follow the road back to the main road into town. Just before reaching the starting point you will pass the Dhulikhel lodge, a nice spot for tea or a cold drink.

An alternate return route follows the road from Panauti until it branches right to the town of Khadpu. From Khadpu descend into the valley and across to the trail leading up to Dhulikhel.

PANAUTI TO DHULIKHEL VIA NAMO BUDDHA

Although this trek is easy, involving only limited climbing, it is quite long, requiring five to six hours to complete. The trek follows the Pungamaati (Punyamaata on Schneider map) Khola through rice paddies and small villages. It then climbs steeply to the Namo Buddha monastery, from where there are excellent views of the Himalaya. From Namo Buddha the route follows a motorable road all the way back to Dhulikhel.

The trek begins in Panauti at the Brahmayani temple on the north side of the Pungamaati Khola. Follow the main street in Panauti to the temple complexes and cross the suspension bridge to the north side of the river.

Follow the path along the river past the temple, keeping the river on your right. In ten minutes reach a fork and take the left trail along the river. In twenty minutes you climb a small hill and pass through a village. Five minutes past the town, at the top of the ridge, you come to another fork. Again take the left trail. Walk through the rice paddies and in twenty minutes cross a small river on a concrete bridge. Turn left after the bridge and after the first house of the settlement take a right turn. In five minutes you will reach a town. In another ten minutes cross another stream and reach another town after ten minutes. Past this town the trail forks again. Take the main trail to the right and begin to climb. After fifteen minutes of climbing look up and notice the prayer flags which mark Namo Buddha, a Buddhist monastery and retreat. In another twenty minutes you will come across stairs leading to a stupa. Go up these stairs to the stupa and small town. The trail resumes just beyond the rightmost house of the town, at the edge of the ridge. The trail is narrow and steep. Look back and see the Himalaya stretching across the horizon. Fifteen minutes beyond the town the trail forks. Take the left trail, which rises steeply, and reach Namo Buddha in another five minutes.

On the hill top you first come across a beautiful stone carving of Buddha, a tigress, and her cubs. Legend has it that Buddha was walking and came across the tigress and her cubs. The tigress was starving and hence could not feed her hungry cubs. Buddha felt great compassion for the family and began to feed the tigress the limbs from his own body in order that she and her cubs would not starve to death.

A good lunch stop is at the top of the stupa, just past the carving. The monastery is located beyond this stupa. This monastery is a retreat for Buddhist monks. When I last visited, there were eight monks and one western nun staying there permanently. You may visit the inside of the *gomba* and often you will see monks going about their chores, such as making prayer flags.

The trail resumes behind the monastery. Follow this trail for ten minutes until you reach the road. Turn left on the road and follow it back all the way to Dhulikhel. In an hour and twenty minutes you will reach the town of Kabre. Forty minutes from here you will pass some steps on your right that lead to the Shiva temple. This is where trekkers staying overnight in Dhulikhel come to watch the sunrise. From these steps a shortcut crosses the road and heads straight down to Dhulikhel, which you will reach in another ten minutes. Walk through the town and reach the Dhulikhel Lodge in twenty minutes.

PHARPHING TO CHAMPAADEVI AND BACK

This moderate to difficult trek takes about five hours to complete. It begins at Pharphing, a town located along the Dakshinkaali road. It follows a wide path in the valley leading north for about forty-five minutes until a small settlement is reached. From this settlement, the trek climbs steadily for 1¾ hours, until it reaches Champaadevi. From Champaadevi the views are beautiful in all directions, with the snow-capped Himalaya to the north and east and the Kathmandu Valley below. Champaadevi itself is on a ridge that forms part of the Kathmandu Valley rim. From the summit of Champaadevi, the trail descends back into the valley along the top of the Neupane DAARaa ridge. The ridge is covered with an open pine forest and is blanketed with pine needles. Views of the Himalaya and the Kathmandu Valley are seen along the entire ridge. The trek ends at Pikhel, a small town along the Dakshinkaali road. Buses leading back to Pharphing where you may have parked, or to Kathmandu, stop here and one in either direction can be stopped.

The Dakshinkaali road leads off the ring road just west of Kalimati and goes south past Kirtipur and Chobar. Follow this road for about twenty minutes until you reach Pharphing. The paved road turns steeply to the left, and a dirt road leads straight from the paved road into town. This is the bus stop and a good place to park your car.

Walk along the dirt road into the town of Pharphing and take the first right. This road passes by two Buddhist monasteries (*gomba*); one close to the road and another higher on the ridge. Southeast of the higher one is the seventeenth century Bajra Jogini temple. Above the higher monastery is the Gokarnath cave, marked by prayer flags. If time allows these are worth a visit.

The trail forks not far beyond the lower monastery. The fork is marked by a large *pipal* tree. The lower fork leads into the valley, whereas the higher one contours around the ridge. Take the higher fork, which continues in a northwesterly direction on the left side of the Caukhel DAARaa ridge. This trail is being widened in preparation for motor traffic, but already the signs of erosion of the road are significant.

Forty-five minutes from the beginning of the trail you will reach a small village with a pond for ducks and buffaloes. The water spout in this town is the last water available on this trek. From this town proceed straight up the ridge in a northerly direction. There are many criss-crossing eroded trails, some obscured by the rocky terrain. Simply head straight up along the top of the ridge. After about one hour of climbing a small summit of the ridge will be reached.

From here your destination is the high point on the ridge to the northeast. This is Champaadevi. Find the main trail, which heads to the right for a short distance and ends in a "T" junction. At this junction turn left and follow the trail up to the top of the Champaadevi ridge. Ten minutes beyond the junction, the trail forks. Take the upper fork leading to the high point on the ridge, which is reached thirty minutes later.

From the top of Champaadevi, the views in all directions are superb. Not only are the entire Himalayan ranges visible, but the entire Kathmandu Valley rim as well. Pulchowki, the highest point in the valley rim, is the summit on the ridge to the southeast. It can be identified by the tall radio tower on its summit. Shivapuri is the high point on the valley rim to the north-northeast. Nagurjun is the forested hill inside the rim and directly to the north. If you look to the south, you can see three distinct ridges leading from Champaadevi into the valley; the westerly one and shortest of the three is the one you climbed. The middle one is called the Caukhel DAARaa and the easterly one is the Neupane DAARaa. This trek descends along the easterly ridge.

Follow the ridge top to the east and in about twenty minutes reach the small Shiva shrine often locally refered to as Chapaadevi. Alternatively, you could follow the trail that leads down to the right. This trail eventually bears left and joins the trail from the shrine.

Pass the shrine and go to the edge of the knoll. Head right down the rocky path to the southeast. Here the trail joins the alternate route that bypassed the shrine. After thirty minutes, the trail forks again. Take the upper trail and stay on the top of the Neupane DAARaa ridge. Notice the gilded spire of Swayambhu in the valley below.

The trail leads into a large open pine grove. The area, blanketed with pine needles, feels quiet and peaceful. Apparently the only reason it is not more popular with Nepalis as a picnic spot is the lack of water on the ridge. After thirty minutes, the trail bears right (south) and leads back down to the road, towards the town of Pikhel. The whole slope is very eroded, and the trail in many places is obscure, but as long as you head down you will reach the road. At Pikhel, there are tea shops as well as a bus stop. Take the bus back to Kathmandu, or to Pharphing if you left your car there. The walk to Pharphing from Pikhel takes about forty minutes.

Chitwan National Park
(Map No. 11, Page 280)

Chitwan National Park, covering 360 square miles, some sixty miles south-west of Kathmandu, is perhaps the best place in Nepal to see jungle wildlife. Tours to the park can be arranged by several commercial agencies (see Addresses in Appendix A). The usual format includes round trip by air, elephant rides, stays at either a jungle lodge or a tent camp, hikes, boat rides, and animal observation. Rhinos are usually seen and occasionally a leopard or tiger. These tours are quite expensive, but for those who can afford them, well worth it.

But for the cost-conscious and adventuresome trekker-tourist, there is another way to see the park. Travel independently to Saura on the outskirts of the park and arrange it all yourself. For such a visit allow at least two days in the park and two days for round-trip travel from Kathmandu. If you start from Birjung, coming overland from India, the travel time can be shortened and made a part of your journey to Kathmandu. The best season to visit Chitwan is from October to April. From February onward is probably the best time to see wildlife.

Since the airport at Bharatpur has been closed, the usual way to reach the park from Kathmandu is by bus from Narayangarh. There is a new road from Mugling, on the Kathmandu-Pokhara Highway, to Narayangarh that shortens the travel time considerably. Then take a bus or truck east towards HetauDa along the East-West highway. Get off at TaDi Bazaar. Sometimes, buses leave Kathmandu for Birjung by way of Narayangarh. These are the most convenient because you can get off right at TaDi Bazaar and not have to change vehicles at Narayangarh.

From TaDi Bazaar you can walk south the four miles to Saura, or sometimes a ride can be arranged in a jeep or ox-cart. Several rivers must be crossed and the road is often impassable during the monsoon, though there are ferries for people.

A river-crossing in Chitwan. (Ane Haaland)

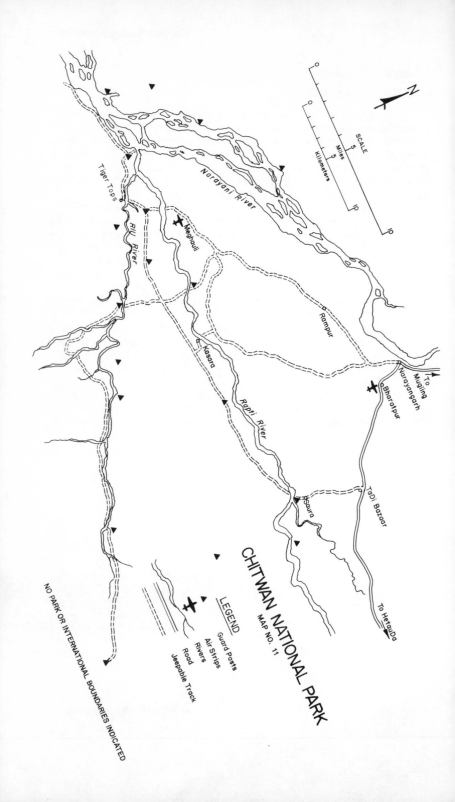

CHITWAN NATIONAL PARK

MAP NO. 11

LEGEND

Guard Posts
Air Strips
Rivers
Road
Jeepable Track

NO PARK OR INTERNATIONAL BOUNDARIES INDICATED

SCALE

Miles

Kilometers

N

Narayani River

Tiger Tops

Riu River

Meghauli

Rampur

Kasara

Rapti River

To
Mugling

Narayangarh

Bharatpur

Saura

Tadi Bazaar

To Hetauda

By this route it is easy to reach Saura in one day from Kathmandu. Those coming from Birjung should first go to HetauDa and then take a bus heading west towards Narayangarh. Get off at TaDi Bazaar.

It is also possible to reach the park by flying to Meghauli, but this town is far from Saura and offers little opportunity for independent travel. There is a road from Bharatpur to Meghauli, and buses leave Bharatpur early in the morning.

Saura, a small village located at the northeast corner of the park, is the starting point for visits. Simple accommodations, camping sites, and Nepali food are available. There are also several hotels and more emphasis is being placed on meeting the needs of the independent tourist. A modern campground has been constructed, and there is a small shelter. Water is available in the nearby Rapti River or from local wells. Although some wood may be available locally, campers are encouraged to bring their own stoves and fuel to help curb deforestation. In Saura there is a guard station, park offices, visitor's center, and museum. A permit must be obtained to enter the park. Payment of the entrance fee includes the services of a guide. You can also hire a private guide at Saura and observe wildlife outside the park.

Elephants can be rented at the park offices. Usually two or three people ride one elephant and the trip lasts 1½ hours. On such a ride in the park you may see rhinoceroses, spotted deer, sambar, rhesus monkeys, peafowl, and jungle fowl.

Another interesting adventure is to ride canoes down the Rapti River, which can be arranged at the Saura park office. The twelve-mile (20-k) trip down the river to Kasara, the park headquarters, takes about 3½ hours. A special permit is required. There are no hotel or dining facilities at the headquarters, but camping is allowed. There is a museum there as well as a gharial breeding project. A longer trip downstream, lasting five to six hours, brings you to within a one-hour walk of the Tiger Tops Hotel. The best time for this trip is late October to February. Along the way you see many interesting birds and crocodiles. You must walk back.

A popular trip is to go partway down the Rapti by canoe and make a side excursion east up a small stream where crocodiles are normally seen sleeping on the banks from mid-October to mid-March. At the Tiger Tops Hotel, you may be able to arrange elephant rides with the management. You might be able to hitch a ride back from the hotel in a jeep, but it is usually necessary to walk back to Saura, a very long day. This could be dangerous since you must walk through long stretches of grassland inhabited by rhinos. En route, pass two guard posts, then a sign pointing to the park headquarters and a small museum a quarter mile off to the left. Pass two more guard posts before reaching Saura. It could be necessary, or interesting, to spend a night at a guard post.

Several blinds (*machaan*) for observing animals have been constructed in the jungle, usually next to waterholes. Ask at the park office in Saura for a guide. They can be reached by elephant, or on foot. Consider spending a night at one to observe the active feeding times and to hear the nocturnal sounds of the jungle. The view is best during a full moon. Animals can be seen undisturbed rather than flushed out as when riding on elephants. Lucky trekkers have seen tigers and leopards, and most people observe rhinos, wild boar, deer, monkeys, and colorful birds.

Finally, you can walk in the jungle. It is not advisable to wander through dense jungle on foot without an experienced guide. Rhinos and sloth bear are the main hazards. Rhinos are quite common in forests, grasslands, and water. Their sight is poor, but their sense of smell is excellent. You can be on top of a rhino before noticing it. They do charge people, and are amazingly fast and agile. If a

One way to climb aboard an elephant. (Stephen Bezruchka)

rhino charges, climb the nearest tree immediately. If there are no trees, run in an arc, as rhinos usually charge in a straight line. Best of all, avoid walking in tall grasslands. To my knowledge, no tourist has yet been killed in the park from wandering around, but there have been several close calls.

Vegetation and Animals

Most of Chitwan National Park is covered with sal forests, the climax forest of the higher elevations in the park. There are small areas on the highest ridges where chir pine occurs, but sal predominates, becoming best developed below the

A gharial crocodile in Chitwan National Park. (Stephen Bezruchka)

base of the hills. Sal is a hard, heavy, slow-growing species, typically reaching eighty to 100 feet. It is valuable as the principal commercial species of southern Nepal.

Low regions of the park are subject to flooding and are dominated by tall grass species. There are over fifty species of grasses, and *Saccharum* and *Phragmites* are common. Stable tracts near the large rivers are covered by a distinct riverain forest characterized by the red silk cotton tree, or *simal (Bombax ceiba)*. The massive red flowers of this tree make a remarkable display in January and February. These trees, when young, have a thorny bark, while older ones grow large buttresses at their bases. Some of its common associates are *belar (Trewia nudiflora)*, *sissu (Dalbergia sissoo)*, and more occasionally, the Flame of the Forest, *palos (Butea frondosa)*, which provides beautiful floral displays in spring.

Vegetative cover is at a maximum just following the monsoon. By March and April, grazing, cutting, and burning have reduced the cover to a relative minimum until the rains bring growth again in late June. Thus, from February on is a good time to see wildlife.

Perhaps the greatest attraction of the Chitwan area is its wildlife. The one-horned rhinoceros is the most conspicuous of the large species. It is estimated that there are perhaps 350 rhinos in the area. Rhinos prefer riverine and grassland habitats, seeking the shelter of the forest during the hot months. In May and June they may often be seen in considerable congregations at wallows or waterholes, where they seek relief from the heat.

Another of the more famous species of the park is the royal Bengal tiger. While research being carried out in the area indicates that tigers may spend considerable time near areas of human activity, they are seldom observed except by careful effort or fortunate chance.

The large gaur is found in the hilly areas of the park. At least four species of deer, including chital, or spotted deer, hog deer, barking deer, and sambar, occur in the lower parts of the forest and grasslands. The hog deer stays near the short grass along the river banks. They are an important prey species of the tiger.

Other mammals that occur in the park include sloth bear, leopard, fishing cat, jungle cat, jackal, wild boar, otter, langur and rhesus macaque monkeys, several kinds of mongooses, and several species of civet cats. During periods of high water the gangetic dolphin is seen in the large rivers.

Reptiles include large crocodiles—the fish-eating gharial, common in the Narayani River, and the mugger, found in the Narayani and in ponds near the river. Numerous species of snake are found in the park including the king cobra, common krait, rat snake, and Indian python.

Birds are the most conspicuous fauna of the park with close to 300 visitor and resident species. Among the larger species are peafowl, red jungle fowl, Bengal florican, black partridge, giant hornbill, white-backed vulture, grey-headed fishing eagle, crested serpent eagle, and several species of stork and egret. Waterfowl, such as the brahminy duck and barheaded goose, come to winter along the rivers.

Many smaller birds occur as well. The most colorful and conspicuous are parakeets, kingfishers, woodpeckers, pigeons, and bee-eaters. Songbirds are common with the black-headed oriole among the best known. There are over 100 species of butterflies in the park, including some of the largest ones, as well as the largest recorded moth.

Heavy uncontrolled use of the park out of Saura is creating considerable pressure on the habitat. The same cautions regarding conservation of fragile alpine areas of Nepal apply here.

SECTION III
THE COUNTRY AND
THE PEOPLE

A small girl in front of a garuda, *the carrier of the Hindu god, Vishnu. (Ane Haaland)*

Top: *Common mongoose, occasionally spotted in the hills. (D. L. Golobitsh)*
Left: *The elusive red panda, photographed in Langtang by a lucky trekker. (D. L. Golobitsh)* Right: *Open-billed stork at Chitwan. (Stephen Bezruchka)*

12 NATURAL HISTORY

To a person uninstructed in natural history, his country or sea-side stroll is a walk through a gallery filled with wonderful works of art, nine-tenths of which have their faces turned to the wall.

Thomas Huxley

The flora and fauna of Nepal, its magnificent terrain, its people and their culture, are the great attractions of this remarkable country. In an effort to help the trekker interpret what he sees, a brief guide to the geology, climate, and ecological divisions is presented here with descriptions of the animals that might be encountered along a trek. The scientific study of Nepal's flora and fauna is still going on, so this chapter should not be taken as the final word. Instead, it should be considered a stepping stone to the more comprehensive references cited in Recommended Reading. The Tribhuvan Natural History Museum in Swayambhunath, Kathmandu, can provide some information, as can the Nepal Nature Conservation Society. The society can be contacted through the Kathmandu Guest House, Thamel, Kathmandu.

Geology

There appears to be some agreement that the origins of the Himalaya can be explained by the theories of plate tectonics and continental drift. Geologists believe that convection currents in the upper mantle of the earth are fueled by heat generated from radioactivity in the core. These currents move continents millimeters per year. Where there are ascending currents, the land mass on the earth's surface above the current thins out, stretches, and breaks apart. Where descending currents meet, initially the crust is pulled in to form a depression (geosyncline); then the land masses overlying very slowly crash together and strong compressive forces crumple the land, producing the folds we call mountains. Erosion and glaciation sculpt them to their present form.

Current theories on the formation of the Himalaya suggest that before the beginning of orogeny (mountain building) some seventy million years ago in the Mesozoic geologic era, there was a large ocean, caused by a geosyncline, separating the Asian from the Indian continent. The Mediterranean Sea is a remnant of this ancient ocean, called the Tethys Sea. The Tethys Sea was fed by rivers from the two continents, which deposited their sediments into it. The Asian continent from the north slowly moved into the Tethys Sea, whose sediments were folded into the Tibetan Marginal Range, the mountains south of the present Tibetan Plateau. This area lies on the Nepal-Tibet border today. After compression, the sediments rose up and the sea disappeared. The rivers originating in these mountains flowed north and south. The next phase occurred ten to fifteen million years ago in the Miocene period. The Indian continent began to overthrust itself against the Asian, resulting in the uplifting of the main Himalayan chain, called the Main Central Thrust. The Tibetan Marginal Range was also lifted higher, and the Tibetan

Plateau was formed by the stretching of the land mass to the north. The rivers flowing south were given a steeper gradient by the overthrusting of the Indian continent. Because of the increased precipitation on the southern parts, the rivers had enough force and water to cut through the mountains faster than they were being lifted up.

The third phase took place 600,000 years ago in the Pleistocene period, when further thrusting from the continental collision gave more uplift to the main Himalaya. Some of the rivers could not erode fast enough and were dammed into lakes such as Tilicho and RaRa.

The final phase during the later Pleistocene period was the rise of the Mahabharat Lekh, the outer foothills. This dammed some of the rivers flowing south, resulting in the formation of lakes such as the one in the prehistoric Kathmandu Valley. It dried up only some 200,000 years ago. Forced to run in longitudinal valleys, the rivers broke through the Mahabharat Lekh in three weak places—the Karnali at Chisapani in the west, the Gandaki at Deoghat in the middle, and the Kosi at Barahchhetra in the east.

The mountains of the Himalaya, the highest in the world, are unique among the great mountain ranges in that they themselves do not form the watershed. It lies almost one hundred miles to the north on the edge of the Tibetan Plateau. The result is the world's greatest gorges, through which the trans-Himalayan rivers penetrate the mountain barriers on their way to the Indian Ocean. The Himalayan mountains are the youngest in the world and may still be rising from the pressures of the collision of continents.

Today three main geological zones can be recognized in Nepal. The Tropical Plains and Foothills lie over Tertiary (twenty-five to seventy million years old) sediments composed of conglomerate sandstone, shale, and marine limestone. Many fossils are found in the Siwaliks or outer foothills including giraffe, hippopotamus, and mastodon. Minerals found here include placer gold and coal. The Middle Region, intensely folded, is made up primarily of Paleozoic (270 to 500 million years old) sediments composed of phyllite (derived from shale) and micaceous quartzite. There are limestone, dolomite, carbonaceous shale, slate, granite, and iron formations. Copper, lead, zinc, iron, cobalt, and nickel are some of the minerals found there. Few of these deposits are economically retrievable. The Himalaya is made of Mesozoic and more recent sediments consisting of metamorphic elements containing few minerals. In western and northeastern Nepal, there are granitic intrusions and hydrothermal activity. The hot springs, which trekkers enjoy, correspond to rupture lines in the terrestrial crust. They appear at low points of geological relief and are close to the Main Central Thrust. Indeed hot springs do not occur outside of this area. The Nepalis use the springs for certain rituals and pilgrimages as well as for bathing. The *BhoTiya* tend to ascribe therapeutic benefits to them.

Climate

Nepal has a monsoon climate. The heavy rains of the monsoon occur from June to September, and begin in the eastern parts. Two to three weeks can separate the onset of the monsoon in the east from that in the west. Similarly, more rain falls in the east, although local conditions are very important in determining the amount of percipitation. At high altitudes, above about 20,000 ft (6000 m), there is snow rather than rain. In addition, a less well-defined winter monsoon occurs from December to the end of March. This precipitation takes the form of snow at altitudes above about 8000 ft (2440 m).

The monsoon is caused by the movement of moist air north and west from the Bay of Bengal. As the moist air rises, it cools and condenses as rain. This precipitation falls on the southern side of the main Himalayan range. Generally there is less at higher altitudes since the clouds have already given up much moisture at the lower altitudes. When the resulting dry air mass crosses the Himalaya, it has very little moisture left to deposit on the northern sides. A rainscreen thus exists on the north sides of the Himalaya, producing the xerophytic conditions in Dolpo and Mustang.

The winter rains enable Nepalis to grow a second crop at lower altitudes. Generally, crops are grown up to the altitude at which clouds hang during the monsoon, as the clouds limit the amount of sun available. Local factors are immensely important in determining the rainfall and climate. Rain falling on north and west faces evaporates less, and more rain falls on steeper slopes, so there tends to be greater variety in the flora in these areas. Shady areas also have a more varied vegetation. While trekking, observe the changes in vegetation on different terrain, and try to predict local climatic factors that produce them.

Vegetation

Nepal's vegetation can be classified in several ways. Amateur botanist J.D.A. Stainton, author of *Forests of Nepal* (see Recommended Reading), characterized thirty-five different forest types or plant communities. They can be divided into four biomes determined by altitude: Tropical and Subtropical; Temperate and Alpine Broad-leaved; Temperate and Alpine Conifer; and Minor Temperate and Alpine Associations. There is usually a transition zone in which one biome gradually drops out and is replaced by the next. Thus perhaps 3500 ft (1070 m) is the limit of Tropical and Subtropical vegetation. Temperate and Alpine Broad-leaved forests are found above this up to 9000 ft (2800 m). Generally, the vegetation becomes more familiar to trekkers from temperate climates as they ascend. Temperate and Alpine Conifer forests begin above 7000 ft (2130 m) and are found to perhaps 12,000 ft (3600 m). Above the tree line, Minor Temperate and Alpine Associations, the familiar alpine plants, grow to about 16,000 ft (5000 m). These altitudes are only approximate and vary immensely with local conditions.

The country can also be divided into topographical divisions. Some forest types are denoted here by their indexing species. Botanical names are given with common names where possible. No descriptions of species are given, but the terminology should be general enough to identify some forest groups while trekking. Consult *Forests of Nepal* for a complete treatment. There is no comprehensive guide to the floral species of Nepal, but *Flowers of the Himalaya* is most useful, and *Himalayan Flowers and Trees* is of help too (see Recommended Reading).

The best way to learn about the plants of Nepal is to trek with someone who knows them. Treks organized by a few agencies include a naturalist who can interpret the vegetation for trekkers. The Department of Medicinal Plants has published floral lists for several regions of the Kathmandu Valley including Godaavri and Pulchowki. The amateur botanist can become familiar with many of Nepal's forest types by visiting these areas and comparing plants with the lists. The lists are available from the department's offices in Thapathali. Nepali names of plants and animals are given where known, in square brackets [ ]. These names may vary locally.

TARAI AND BHABAR

The Tarai, the flat region of Nepal that is the continuation of the Gangetic Plains of India has been substantially cleared for cultivation. The mosquitoes that carry malaria are found only in and around the large, impressive stands of sal forest in this area. The steady rise from the Tarai to the foothills is called the Bhabar. Again, sal forest [sakhuwaa] predominates in these flat regions.

DUN VALLEYS AND OUTER FOOTHILLS

The first outer foothills are termed the Siwalik or Churia hills. They rise to 4000 ft (1220 m) and parallel the Indian border. Then come the heavily forested Dun Valleys dropping to the same altitude as the Tarai. And farther north is the Mahabharat Lekh, rising to 9000 ft (2740 m). In western Nepal, sal and subtropical deciduous forests are found at the lowest altitudes, and forests of chir pine [khoTe sallaa] *(Pinus roxburghii),* with needles in bunches of three, occur from above 2000 ft (610 m) up to 6000 ft (1830 m). The upper regions are mostly oak forests [bAAjh] *(Quercus incana* and *Q. lanuginosa)* containing some rhododendrons. In eastern Nepal, sal and tropical evergreen forests predominate at the lower altitudes, followed by subtropical evergreen forests at midrange, and topped by temperate mixed broad-leaved forests in the upper altitudes.

MIDLANDS

Nepal's midlands, the large region between the outer foothills and the Himalaya, vary considerably in different areas of the country. The West Midlands is the region between the Kali Gandaki river and the western border. Chir pine forests occur in this area to about 6500 ft (1980 m), while the oaks [bAAjh] *(Quercus incana* and *Q. lanuginosa)* occur to 8000 ft (2440 m). At higher altitudes, forests of prickly-leaved oak [karsu] *(Q. semecarpifolia)* and fir [taalis patra] *(Abies spectabilis)* with large upright cones and no leaf stem, as well as birch [bhoj patra] *(Betula utilis)* are found, especially above 11,500 ft (3500 m). Rhododendron forests, so spectacular in eastern Nepal, are not to be found here to as great an extent. Coniferous forests up to the tree line include hemlock *(Tsuga dumosa)* with tiny cones hanging down and leaf scars on old twigs, and blue pine [sobre salla] *(Pinus excelsa)* with needles in bunches of five. In selected locations such as around Dhorpatan, black juniper [dhupi] *(Juniperus wallichiana)* grows. Forests generally resemble those found in Kumaon, India, to the west.

The East Midlands is the region between the Arun Kosi river system and the eastern border. The flora is eastern Himalayan in character. In the lower altitudes, the Bengal subtropical hill forest (also known as the wet subtropical forest) includes a kind of chestnut [Daalne kaTus] *(Castanopsis indica)* and [chilaune] *(Schima wallichi),* but has been much affected by habitation. There are areas with subtropical semi-evergreen hill forests containing tree ferns and screw pine *(Pandanus furcatus).* Lower temperate mixed broad-leaved forests occupy middle elevations, followed by evergreen forests. Rhododendron forests are common from middle elevations to tree line. On one species [laali gurAAs] *(Rhododendron arboreum),* the blooms become lighter as altitude increases.

The Central Midlands is the area between the Kali Gandaki and the Arun Kosi rivers, excepting the region south of Annapurna and Himal Chuli. It is a complex mixture of East and West Himalayan forest types. This is especially evident in that western forests occur on south slopes, while eastern forests are found on north slopes. In wet areas, alder [utis] (*Alnus nepalensis*) is common in erosion pockets and broken areas.

The area south of Annapurna and Himal Chuli differs from the midlands nearby in that it receives much more rainfall, mostly because the moisture-laden clouds from India have relatively low hills to cross before reaching it. At lower elevations, [chilaune] and *castanopsis* forests and subtropical semi-evergreen hill forests occur. At middle altitudes, lower temperate mixed broad-leaved forests are found on north and west faces. Slightly higher, oak [gogne] (*Q. lamellosa*) occurs on north and south faces. Due to the excess rainfall, coniferous forests are not predominant, even at the higher elevations. Upper temperate mixed broad-leaved or rhododendron forests predominate in the higher areas.

DRY RIVER VALLEYS

Impressive rivers cut through the Himalaya and produce remarkable gorges in their upper elevations before settling down in their lower courses. Strong prevailing winds usually blow upstream and create a rain shadow that extends several thousand feet up the valley. In the gorges, however, eastern slopes get little sun and tend to be quite damp. Above the damp regions close to the river itself, the next few thousand feet of the gorge may be quite dry. These dry areas are followed by wet slopes higher still. Instead of the usual vegetation succession due to altitude, the dry middle section may have pine forests topped by broad-leaved forests.

INNER VALLEYS

Valleys lying within the Himalayan ranges receive less rainfall than those lying south of the range. Valleys in the west receive even less rainfall at lower altitudes than those in the east. In the upper reaches of eastern valleys such as Khumbu, Rolwaling, and Langtang, the valley shape changes from a water-worn, heavy rainfall *V* to a glacier-worn *U*. Travel is easier in the broad, open, upper reaches of these valleys. Terminal moraines of glaciers become evident and the glaciers can be seen at work. There is extensive grazing in the upper valleys where temporary shelters are inhabited during the monsoon. The forests to tree line are not much different from forests at similar altitudes south of the main Himalaya. Above tree line, however, the predominant species of juniper [dhupi] changes from *Juniperus recurva* to *Juniperus wallichiana*, which at times grows as a small tree. In addition, the alpine shrubs are those found in more xerophilous (desert-type) areas of flora. Similarly, the herbs are those of the Trans-Himalaya rather than of monsoon country.

The upper Kali Gandaki or Thak Khola exhibits a tremendous change of climate and vegetation over a short distance. The valley begins below Ghasa in the monsoon vegetation of the midlands. Here there are subtropical rain forests with alder [Tunaa] (*Cedrella toona*) and mimosa (*Albizzia mollis*). This gives way to blue pine, cypress [raaj sallo] (*Cupressus torulosa*), hemlock, some horse chestnut [lekh pAAgraa or karu] (*Aesculus indica*), rhododendron, and yew [barme] (*Taxus spp.*). Beyond Kalopani are stands of fir, birch, and some cypress with steppe forests beyond. Above the valley floor are black juniper and cypress. The valley floor is quite dry, but the wetter slopes above have forests of fir, birch, and blue pine. Some spruce [jure sallaa] (*Picea smithiana*) grow in side valleys. Between Marpha and Jomosom the valley floor supports only xerophilous shrubs, which continue for several thousand feet above. Higher up are steppe forests, then dry alpine scrub, and finally wetter slopes. The prevailing upstream winds produce a rain shadow in the valley floor and for several thousand feet above it. Treeless steppe country continues into Mustang. There are no forests beyond until the Tibetan Plateau and the Takla Makan desert, a distance of over 1000 miles (1600 km.).

HUMLA-JUMLA AREA

The Humla-Jumla area is somewhat drier than might be expected due to a chain of *lekh* (hills) to the south, which intercept much of the rain. Here the Himalaya are not so impressive and, correspondingly, the countryside is more open and less deeply eroded. Cultivation generally extends to higher altitudes than in the midlands. Much of the area is covered with blue pine, especially on south facing slopes, while spruce is found on north and west facing slopes. Himalayan cedar [dewadaar] (*Cedrus deodara*) and cypress also occur. Apricots and walnuts sometimes grow wild. Generally the flora is west Himalayan in character.

ARID ZONE

North of the Dhaulagiri and Annapurna Himals, the country is generally treeless and the climate and vegetation are much like that of Tibet. Rainfall is minimal since the area lies in the rain shadow of the Himalaya. Few trees are found. The vegetation is that of a treeless steppe. Shrubs, grasses, and alpine flowers predominate.

ALPINE ZONE

The zone above tree line in Nepal is much the same as in most mountainous parts of the world. Plants grow to very high altitudes, even to 20,000 ft (6100 m), and bloom from April to October. First to bloom are the primulas and polygonums, followed by dwarf rhododendrons. Primulas, potentillas [chiniyaaphal] and other moisture-loving alpine species bloom during the monsoon. Also found are sandworts (*Arenaria*), edelweiss (*Leontopodium*), rock jasmines (*Androsace*), sage brush (*Artemisia*), and joint pines (*Ephedra*). Toward the end of the season, there are gentians, larkspurs (*Delphinium brunonianum*), *Allardia glabra*, and *Selimum cortioides*.

AROUND HABITATION

Deforestation for terracing and grazing is common in areas of habitation. Trees such as kafal, walnut, fig, tamarind, *Bassia butyracea*, [jaamun] (*Eugenia jambos*); *Ficus cunea*, and *Moringa pterygospermum* are grown for their food value. Trees and shrubs producing fodder such as camel's foot [koiraalo] (*Bauhinia variegata* and *B. purpurascens*), hackberry (*Celtis australis*), and mimosa (*Albizzia chinehsis*) are planted. [Gogan] *Sarauja nepalensis, Brassaiopsis hainla, B. aculeata, Grewia oppositifolia*, and oak are trimmed for fodder. The pipaal (*Ficus religiosa*), with pointed leaves, and banyan [bar] (*Ficus bengalensis*), with rounded leaves and branch roots, are usually planted together at *chautaara* to represent the male and female principles. Bamboo clumps are often planted near villages and are harvested to make baskets, trays, bridges, irrigation pipe, mats, swings, and for building construction. Bamboo occurs naturally on large rocky slabs with poor soil.

Most villages and terraces are built on south facing slopes in order to get sufficient sun for agriculture. By contrast, north facing slopes are usually forest and grazing lands.

Rice is grown in the hills up to 6500 ft (2000 m). It is planted before the monsoon, transplanted after the monsoon begins, and harvested in the autumn. Below 2100 ft (650 m), two crops can be grown. Rice straw is used for making mats, thatched roofs, and other items. Wheat is planted in late autumn in the rice fields, then harvested in the spring. In the dry northern areas, however, it is grown in the summer. Corn is planted in the spring and harvested during the monsoon. Millet is planted in the spring, then transplanted into corn fields before the corn is harvested. The millet is then harvested in the fall. Barley, a common high altitude crop, is planted in the spring and harvested in the fall. At lower elevations it is planted in the fall and harvested in the late spring. Buckwheat, another crop of the

Millet dries in the courtyard of this Magar house while pumpkins and corn are stored on the roof and eaves. The flax of the grasses below the pumpkins will be woven into clothing. (Stephen Bezruchka)

heights, is planted in late spring, and harvested in the autumn. At lower elevations, it is planted in the autumn and harvested in the early spring. Potatoes, often a staple at high altitudes, are planted in the spring and harvested in the fall.

Vegetables such as chilies, other spices, lentils, soybeans, mustard, turnips, radishes, pumpkins, and spinach are grown in small gardens surrounding houses. Fruit trees found in low lying areas include bananas, tangerines, papayas, and mangoes. Also many semi-cultivated plants such as nettles are eaten or used for making thread. Nearby forest trees have many uses. Sal is carved into many useful items and is used for house and bridge construction. Pine is used for shingles and timber. Oak makes good agricultural tools such as plough parts and hammers. Rhododendron wood is used for making wooden containers to hold yogurt because the wood enhances the flavor. Birch bark is used as wrapping paper.

Mammals

Zoogeographically, the world is divided into four realms, and each of these is then divided into regions and subregions. Characteristic species of animals are found in each. Nepal is strategically placed in the overlap zone of the Oriental Region (which includes most of India and much of Southeast Asia), and the Holarctic (or Palearctic) Region (which includes Europe, North Africa, and Northern Asia). The Oriental Region is found in the Tarai, while the Holarctic Region is represented in areas north of the Himalaya, especially Mustang, Dolpo, Manang, and Humla. Generally, where two zoogeographical regions meet, there is a broad intermediate zone in which both regions contribute species. The result is usually a diversity of animals.

But Graeme Caughley, who studied the animals of Nepal in the 1960s, has observed, "Nowhere else is the boundary between two faunas so abrupt. Over a distance of forty miles, one fauna gives way to another." Moreover, in this forty miles, the number of species of animals is surprisingly low. As in vegetation types, there is a characteristic eastern and western Himalayan pattern. Furthermore, species found to the east and west of Nepal do not seem to occur in the intervening area. Thus the red deer is found in Bhutan, and in Garhwal, but not in Nepal. Also, animals found in the western Himalaya, such as the ibex, markhor, wild goat, and urial, do not occur in Nepal. Similarly, animals found in the eastern Himalaya, such as the takin, are absent in Nepal. One might expect to find species unique to the Himalaya, but this is not the case, perhaps because the area is geologically so young.

Not only are few species encountered in the areas where most trekking takes place, but the population of these animals is low. This is most likely due to human habitations, which modify the vegetation. Superstition may also contribute to increased destructive pressure on certain species. The faunal zones in Nepal have been characterized by Caughley as follows:

In the **Tarai Zone**, Oriental Region fauna is typically found, with representations from both the Indian and Indo-Chinese subregions. Several areas have been set aside as wildlife sanctuaries and national parks. Wildlife reserves are planned at Sukhla Phanta, Karnali, and Koshi Tappu. There is a national park at Chitwan. The one-horned rhinoceros, tiger, swamp deer, wild buffalo, gaur, leopard, clouded leopard, sloth bear, wild boar, monkeys, and many small animals are found in the Tarai region.

The **Foothill Zone**, the area from the Tarai to the monsoon-affected tree line, was originally all forested, but is now often cleared for agriculture. Leopard, goral, serow, barking deer, sambar, musk deer, Himalayan black bear, wild boar, red panda, red fox, jackal, and the monkeys—common langur, common rhesus, and Assam rhesus—are found in the forested areas. Smaller animals include porcupine, yellow-throated marten, orange-bellied squirrel, civet, river otter, weasel, shrew, and Indian hare.

The **Himalayan Zone** is the area above the tree line within the monsoon region. Surprisingly few species are found there. The Himalayan mouse hare (pika) and the Himalayan tahr may be seen.

The **Northern Slope Zone** is the area in the rain shadow north of the Himalaya. The fauna are of the Holarctic Region. Lynx, wolf, brown bear, snow leopard, musk deer, fox, and blue sheep are found. There are areas, such as in Khumbu, where the Holarctic fauna penetrate south of the main Himalaya. Similarly, blue sheep are found north of Dhorpatan but south of the Himalaya, probably because the area receives less precipitation than other areas of the Himalayan Zone, and because the grass vegetation needed to support them grows above tree line.

Nepali names are given for some of the animals in the following list of mammals of the Foothill and Himalayan zones:

Barking deer [*mriga, ratuaa, rate*] are small reddish animals that make a barking sound when alarmed. These solitary deer live in forest and scrub to 8000 ft (2438 m).

Musk deer [*kasturi, mriga*] are hornless nocturnal animals with pronounced canine teeth. They live in rhododendron and birch forests near tree line, although they sometimes venture above it. They are poached for the musk pod found only in the male.

Serow [*thar*] are solitary goat-antelopes with mule-like ears. They live in thickly-wooded, inaccessible bamboo river valleys and may venture into open slopes at dawn or dusk.

Himalayan tahr [*jhaaral*] are hairy, goat-like mammals found throughout the mountains at around 12,000 ft (3650 m). They graze along the open patches of steep cliffs.

Goral [*ghoral*] are small goat-like animals that inhabit steep ravines and gullies at, or shortly above, tree line. They prefer grass and shrub-covered slopes near the shelter of rocks or forest, and are found in small groups in the morning and evening.

Blue sheep [*naaur*] are not really blue, but tan. These beautiful animals inhabit the grassland above tree line, usually near rocky areas. Herds sometimes venture close to forests in late winter and early spring. Look for them north of Dhorpatan and on the Manang side of the Thorong La.

Wild boar [*bAdel*] are large omnivorous pigs that live in forests at various altitudes and are known for rooting the ground and destroying crops.

Common langurs [*lAngur*] are large monkeys which can be seen in groups in dense forests and even open country above 12,000 ft (3650 m).

Rhesus monkeys [*bAAdar*] are smaller macaque monkeys which are found in open country, rocks and cliffs, and pine forests to 8000 ft (2450 m), as well as near villages.

Himalayan black bears [*himaali kaalo bhaalu*] are large, sometimes dangerous animals that live in steep, thick forests near tree line. They descend in winter.

Red pandas [*hobre, raato baa saano pADaa*] are secretive animals that live high in hemlock and fir forests near bamboo and brush. During the day, they sleep in trees.

Jackals [*shyaal*] are wide-ranging animals found near villages. They can steal poultry and attack small domestic animals. Their eerie howls are unforgettable.

Red foxes [*raato phaauro*] live singly or hunt in pairs. They are nocturnal and tend to be found in brush or cultivated areas up to elevations as high as 10,000 ft (3050 m).

Leopards [*chituwAA*] are found at or below timberline. These solitary cats attack many domestic animals.

Snow leopards [*him chituwAA*] are beautiful cats found in the heights. They are difficult to spot.

Common mongooses [*nyaauri muso*] may be seen running along roads or walls as they hunt.

Himalayan weasels are wide-ranging animals that can be seen in dense forests, dry sandy valleys, low swamps, or among rocks. They also lodge in holes in high pasture fences.

Beech or stone martens [*dhunge malsAApro*] are squirrel-cats that live in the high forests in holes or among rocks. They prey on small animals.

Common otters [*ot*] can sometimes be spotted playing near cold mountain streams and lakes.

Himalayan marmots live higher than any other animal in the world—up to 18,000 ft (5500 m). Although found in West Nepal and Sikkim, they are absent in between.

Himalayan mouse-hares [*muse khraayo*] are also small high altitude dwellers.

Birds [*Charo*]

Unlike mammals, for which there is a species gap between the Oriental and Holarctic regions, the number of bird species found in Nepal is overwhelming—over 800—half the number found in all of South Asia. In the Tarai, the birds are characteristically of the Indian subregion of the Oriental Region, while at high altitudes, and on the northern slopes, Eurasian (a subregion of the Holarctic Region) birds predominate. Besides the mixture in the midlands, Indo-Chinese (a subregion of the Oriental Region) birds are also common. Also, in the far west, some Mediterranean (a subregion of the Holarctic Region) birds occur. Many birds pass through Nepal on spring and fall migrations. In the winter, visitors from the north arrive, and in the summer, birds, like people, come from the Indian plains to the hills of Nepal.

Birds of Nepal (see Recommended Reading) is invaluable to those interested in the amazing diversity of Nepali birds. Good treks for birdwatching include Khumbu for its high altitude birds, Manang and north of Jomosom for Tibetan species, and Chitwan National Park for jungle birds. Kathmandu Valley itself is excellent. Some 430 species have been observed there. In order to see as many different species of birds as possible, go from low to high elevations.

The following descriptions of many of the bird families of Nepal illustrate some of the sights the birdwatcher may see.

Grebes are aquatic birds and are often seen in winter on the lakes of Pokhara or on RaRa Lake.

Herons are water feeders that can be seen along streams and open flooded fields, or feeding upon insects near pasturing bovines. Egrets are especially common in rice paddies.

Cranes may be seen in flocks during their migration. They often land in open. areas.

Ducks and geese are not native to Nepal, but they may occasionally be seen in winter flying overhead along the major rivers or over high altitude lakes.

Hawks, eagles, and vultures are winter visitors from Asia. They can be found at high altitudes near and above the tree line.

Pheasants, partridges, and quail are common throughout much of Nepal. The national bird of Nepal, the impeyan pheasant [DAAphe] is found in scrub and trees near tree line, especially in the spring. The snow cock may be seen running along hillsides in alpine scrub.

Pigeons and doves of many species are common. The trekker may be surprised to find the familiar city pigeon along rocky streams. The spotted dove is often heard around towns, while the rufous turtle dove is found in forests. The snow pigeon flies in flocks in higher regions.

Parakeets range over several elevations, and may often be encountered in noisy flocks.

Cuckoos are usually heard first, then sometimes spotted. These large, colorless birds are found in the higher hills.

Owls are often heard at night.

Barbets are chunky, colorful birds that have loud, monotonous calls and are found at low to middle elevations.

Woodpeckers thrive in the many forests throughout much of the country.

Larks are somewhat drab birds, but they are unforgettable when observed courting. They do this by singing and fluttering in circles at high altitudes.

Swifts, as they name implies, speed through much of Nepal. Indeed, the fastest bird in the world (white-rumped swift) is found in Nepal. Their flight is a fast flutter compared to the swallow's deep graceful wingbeats.

Swallows are found near habitations or nesting on cliffs.

Orioles are found at low and middle elevations.

Drongos are slim, black birds with scissor tails. They are found in various habitats, and often chase crows, kites, and other large birds.

Mynas, members of the starling family, are often found near man or on the outskirts of towns.

Crows, magpies, and jays of various species are found all over Nepal. House crows frequent the low and middle hills; the jungle crow, a larger, all-black bird, ranges into the high mountains. At the high altitudes, the Tibetan raven may be seen.

Bulbuls are crested birds that have a conspicuous call and perch near treetops or flowers.

Babblers are a large family of birds. They live in groups quite close to the ground and produce a variety of songs. Nepal is the only place where the spiny babbler is found.

Flycatchers are small birds that may be seen in clearings, darting about in search of insects.

Warblers are small, nondescript birds that live near the ground, in grassy areas, or in trees.

Thrushes are fine songsters found in various habitats—mountain streams, wooded ravines, low forests, and rooftops.

Titmice are small birds, many with conspicuous crests, found in oak forests at high elevations.

Nuthatches and tree creepers are small birds found moving up and down tree trunks and branches looking for insects in the bark. Nuthatches go down, while tree creepers go up!

Sunbirds and flowerpeckers are tiny birds with long curved bills. They are the Asian counterpart of hummingbirds. Look for them in oak and rhododendron forests in the spring.

Munias, sparrows, and weavers are common. The so-called house sparrow is common near settled areas; other species live in forests. The weaver builds long pendulous nests in ravines, grassy cliffs, and trees.

Finches and buntings of many species are found in the mountains.

Butterflies

Nepal has over 500 species of butterflies. They can be observed almost anytime. The following notes on their habitat are from Colin Smith, the resident authority on Nepal's butterflies.

Butterflies are attracted to flowers, both in gardens, and in flowering cultivated fields. Damp sand beside rivers, small streams, and water channels attracts butterflies. Areas where humans or animals have been are also attractive to them. Ridges, forested on both sides with a slight clearing at the top, or clear with a few trees near the ridge crest, are good places to find them. Butterflies often tend to return to a favorite spot. Some do not range much, while others go on very long migrations. Bamboo attracts a disproportionate number. Although butterflies like the sun, sometimes forests with sunlight bouncing through the trees are a favored habitat. The best time to see them is probably during the early monsoon, although just after the monsoon in the prime trekking time is also good.

Collections of butterflies may be seen at the Tribhuvan University Natural History Museum in Swayambhunath, or at the Prithvinarayan Campus in Pokhara.

Reptiles

The distribution of reptiles in Nepal is still poorly understood. Among the non-poisonous species encountered in the hills are the common wolf snake (*Lycodon aulicus*), the keelback (*Amphiesma platyceps*), the striped keelback (*Amphiesma stotala*), and the *dhaman,* or rat snake (*Ptyas mucosus*). The only poisonous species at all common in the hills is the mountain pit viper (*Trimeresurus monticola*), although the green pit viper (*Trimeresurus albolabris*) is sometimes found. The harmless common wolf snake is often mistaken for the poisonous common krait (*Bungarus caerulens*). To date, I do not know of any non-herpetologist trekker who has seen poisonous snakes, and have heard no reports of snake bites among trekkers. Fear not snakes, but too rapid ascent to altitude.

Domestic Animals

Domestic animals do not belong in a chapter on Natural History. But do you ever wonder why the water buffalo holds his head up high, searching all the time, and has so little hair? Kami Temba told me the reason. Once the water buffalo was hairy and was a good friend of the yak. They both loved salt, but there wasn't much around. The yak said he would go to Tibet to get some if the water buffalo would loan him his hair so he could survive in the cold. The water buffalo agreed. The yak went off and never returned. To this day, the water buffalo holds his head up, searching, awaiting the return of the yak with his hair and salt.

13 HILL AND MOUNTAIN PEOPLE OF NEPAL

by Donald A. Messerschmidt*

Nepal has always been a meeting ground for different people and cultures.

Dor Bahadur Bista, Nepali anthropologist

Nepal is a land of great diversity. Its social, cultural, religious, geographical, floral, and faunal varieties fascinate and challenge the imagination. The diversity across the land is quickly seen and felt by trekkers and travelers. In a relatively short distance (although it may be days of arduous walking) a trekker can leave the low, subtropical Tarai forests and ascend northward into the high alpine meadows, the *lekh* of the Himalaya. The scenery changes from elephant grass to rhododendron forests, from water buffalo wallows to yak pastures, from heavy rain clouds to the dark blue of a clear Tibetan sky. The *Tarai-wala* (a person of the Tarai) is left behind for the *PahAARi* (hillsman), the *Lekhali* (person of the high country), the *goThaalo* (alpine herdsman), and the *BhoTiya* (Tibetan) of the hills and mountains.

Variations in social and cultural expression seem to parallel the physical, geographic, and biotic changes associated with altitude and latitude. The trekker sees an ever-changing variety of farmsteads, villages, and bazaars; passes the shrines of Hindu, Buddhist, and animist; encounters farmer, trader, storekeeper, pilgrim, innkeeper, and herder; and notes changes in the architecture of homes and religious edifices. The colorfully diverse expressions of human adaptation to the Himalaya are unexpectedly fascinating for a land to which most visitors come expecting only spectacular mountains, smiling guides, yak herds, and pagoda-like temples.

The author of this chapter is an anthropologist who advised me on trekking before I first came to the Himalaya and who has continued to provide information on Nepal for subsequent editions of this book. His first experience in Nepal was with the Peace Corps in 1963; his involvement with the country has continued for more than twenty years. He has worked in community development, taught in the American school in Kathmandu, studied the Gurungs of west-central Nepal for his Ph.D. from the University of Oregon, led treks and study tours, conducted research (funded by the National Geographic Society and other institutions), and participated in scientific forums on the Himalaya. Most recently, he has worked as a social scientist on a natural-resource-conservation project in Nepal. "People," he says with conviction, "are the most important resource to work with when it comes to conserving and managing the Himalayan environment." Dr. Messerschmidt has published extensively on Nepal and is an executive member of the Nepal Studies Association. He holds a permanent position in the Department of Anthropology, Washington State University, Pullman, Washington. As one of the foremost authorities on Nepal, he has generously provided this chapter for the book. His hobbies include writing and photography. He also studies and breeds Tibetan mastiff dogs and is currently researching a book on the natural history of this noble Himalayan breed. The section on jewelry comes from the studies of Bronwen Bledsoe, whose interest in Nepal began on a college study tour led by Donald Messerschmidt.

Village life: carrying water (Ane Haaland), spinning wool (Stephen Bezruchka), weaving a carpet (Dave Hardenbergh)

Nepal has dozens of ethnic and caste groups, each differentiated by unique aspects of language, dress, locale, lifestyle, house style, economy, and religion. At one level of analysis, however, certain elements of uniformity tend to knit all the diversity together. Take language. It divides Nepalis into two major camps: those who speak Nepali as their mother tongue—primarily the caste groups; and those who speak languages identified by linguists as part of the Bodic division of Sino-Tibetan (sometimes called Tibeto-Burman), that is, the hill ethnic groups and those of close Tibetan affinities. At another level, however, language draws them together; most Nepalis, regardless of local dialect, speak Nepali in the public forums of trade, education, government, and daily encounters with outsiders. (In some places English has become the second major language of the land.)

Another of the more visible attributes of uniformity in Nepal is a marked association between cultural groups and the altitude/latitude where they tradition-ally live. Each distinct group can be identified in great part by the ecological niche it occupies. Each niche is characterized by similarities in dress, house style, religious expression, patterns of trade, and subsistence. Caste groups, for exam-ple, tend to occupy the lower valleys in dispersed settlements, where they raise rice on irrigated paddy fields. Ethnic groups tend to cluster in nucleated villages on higher, more northerly ridges, where they raise upland crops such as millet, corn, barley, and wheat. Each depends upon the other for exchange of produce and for other economic, social, and religious interaction. In addition, Nepal's rich cultural heritage has been heavily influenced and sometimes irrevocably changed by the recent influx of tourism, education, technology, mass communications, and other aspects of modernization.

In the brief anthropological description of Nepal that follows, the many ethnic and caste groups are described in terms of differences and similarities to one another. It is inevitable in a generalized discussion that much of the uniqueness of the people is blurred, and descriptions are given that do not fit all situations. The discussion focuses on those peoples most often met on trails in the hills and mountains. Because few trekkers travel in the Tarai valleys and plains adjacent to India, discussion of the peoples of that region is omitted. The intent here is to pro-vide the trekker with enough general information to better understand and appre-ciate the sights seen and the people met while trekking. An abbreviated list of hill and mountain peoples is provided, and some major festivals of Nepal are described at the end of the chapter.

Religion

Nepali religion is based on two "great" or "high" traditions—Hinduism and Buddhism—each undergirded by expressions of local "little" traditions of animism and shamanism. (Of course, practitioners of the latter do not necessarily see their religion in this way; the dichotomy is only for purposes of analysis.) Since only a very small percentage of Nepalis are Muslim, or "Musalman," they will not be considered here.

"Hinduism is not a religion, but a way of life," states ethnologist A.W. MacDonald. This seems evident from observing the devout in Nepal. Hinduism is rooted in the texts of the ancient Vedas dating to 2000 B.C. As it evolved, three main deities became focal: Brahma the creator, Vishnu the preserver, and Shiva the destroyer. In their varied manifestations they pervade daily ritual and sym-bolize the cycle of life. There are no basic dogmas, no qualities that define a Hin-du, except perhaps whether that person employs a Brahman as a priest. It is left to

Gaine *musicians performing near Pokhara. (Ane Haaland)*

each individual to decide the form of his or her worship. The caste system is a fundamental aspect of Hinduism. An individual who aspires to rebirth in a higher caste must live a proper life in his present caste. This precept has exerted a significant stabilizing effect on Indian and Nepali society. Caste etiquette was codified as law in Nepal in the Muluki Ain of 1854. Although this law has now been repealed, it still governs behavior.

Buddhism, on the other hand, is more a philosophy than a religion. Founded by the disciples of Siddhartha Gautama, born at Lumbini in Nepal's Tarai around 623 B.C., Buddhism is based on the four noble truths: Existence is suffering, craving and attachment cause suffering, the attainment of nirvana is an end to this suffering, and there is a path to nirvana, the eightfold way. These are: right views, right resolve, right speech, right action, right livelihood, right effort, right mindfulness and right concentration. Buddhism depends on the institution of a monastery and monks. The Buddhist community supports a monastery and derives strength from it. Meditation and observance of moral precepts are the foundations of Buddhist practice. To trekkers, the recitation of the esoteric mantra *Om mani padme hum,* and the spinning of prayer wheels, are examples of meditative practice observed by the common folk.

In Nepal, Hinduism is reflected both in the system of caste, which defines social status, and in a subsistence economy based on rice agriculture and a highly ritualized cattle culture (cow worship). Buddhism, principally the Mahayana ("Great Vehicle") Tibetan form, with strong tantric expression, is found among the

BhoTiya people of the northern border area. Vajrayana Buddhism is practiced by Buddhist *Newar* of Kathmandu Valley. Buddhism and Hinduism tend to blend in many settings, such as the Kathmandu Valley where indigenous *Newar* practice both religions, side by side and intermixed. The various local expressions of these two religions, and of animism and shamanism, are so conceptually interwoven that it would take much more than this short account to untangle and explain them accurately and clearly.

Animism and shamanism are concerned respectively with spirits that exist in nature and with the human condition, body and soul, alive or departed. Animistic beliefs and shamanic ritual permeate both of the "high" cultures of Buddhism and Hinduism. At virtually every wayside shrine, in almost every religious rite, in ceremonies performed by lay people as well as by Hindu temple priests (*pujaari*), Buddhist priests (*lama*), or village shaman (*jhAAkri*), you will see some form of worship (*pujaa*) focusing on both the animate and inanimate objects of nature. Funerals, rites of passage, and curing ceremonies are all richly ornamented with the animist's and shaman's concern for placating local spirits and natural forces. If you happen upon a religious ceremony, your presence may be offensive (your proximity to food preparation or to hallowed ground, for example, may be deemed ritually polluting). As you observe ritual events, be aware of the sensitivities of the officiants and participants. And open your senses to the fullness of their expression, especially to the sometimes awesome respect shown for nature—to the moon, earth, fire, water, and air; to cow dung and smoky incense; to cow's urine and curds; to the blood sacrifice of chickens, pigeons, goats, and buffalo. Therein you will begin to glimpse a very close association between villager and nature, a necessary relationship that many people, caught up in the frenetic pace of the modern world elsewhere, seem to have forgotten or have uncaringly abandoned.

History

The Himalaya has always been viewed, it seems, as a safe haven for immigrants and refugees. One large movement of peoples into Nepal dates from the twelfth to fifteenth centuries A.D. when many Hindus—particularly of Rajput origins—fled the Indian plains during the Moghul invasion. Some refugees settled in Kathmandu Valley, but great numbers remained more rural, populating the lower valleys and hills all across the land. The *PahAARi* people of the adjacent India hills (Kumaon and Garhwal, just west of Nepal) are culturally, physically, and linguistically the "cousin-brothers" of the Nepalese caste hillsmen who date from this refugee invasion.

The refugee arrivals were mostly *Brahman* (priest caste) and *Chhetri* (warrior caste, known as *Kshatriya* in India), along with low-caste craftspeople and menial laborers. They encountered a local population of *Khas* people and many ethnic groups, with whom they intermixed to various degrees—linguistically, economically, religiously, and socially. The caste Hindu migrants brought certain strong social and cultural traditions—a status hierarchy, language, religion, and a rice- and cattle-based economy that, blended with the local lifestyle and world view, formed what is today's unique Nepali national culture.

Nepali history until the Gorkha Conquest of the eighteenth century A.D. is one of petty principalities. These small hill kingdoms fell into two groups—the *baaisi raja*, or twenty-two kingdoms, of western Nepal, and the *chaubisi raja*, or twenty-four kingdoms, of central Nepal (between the Kali Gandaki and the Trisuli rivers). Many treks of central and western Nepal pass through these former kingdoms, and if you are observant you can see remnants of fortresses (*kot*) on many of the higher hilltops. The most famous fortress, now a sacred temple site, is the "Gorkha Darbar" (Gorkha palace) above Gorkha Bazaar in central Nepal. Others are found in high places along the Marsyangdi River trail (e.g., Lamjung Darbar, just west of Besisahar), near Pokhara (Kingdom of Kaski), and along the Kali Gandaki river just north of Beni (Rakhu). The famous Malla Kingdom of far west Nepal encompassed parts of western Tibet and was so strong that it influenced political events as far east as the upper Kali Gandaki Valley. The west Nepal Mallas (not to be confused with the later Malla rulers of Kathmandu's three city-states) ruled from about the twelfth to fourteenth centuries A.D. They were apparently related to the *Khas* people, an ancient group whose presence as a power in the region had profound effects on all of Nepal's subsequent social history. They ruled simultaneously with the arrival of the migrant Rajputs. The fighting forces for these Nepali kingdoms were conscripted from local ethnic populations, such as the *Magar* and the *Gurung*.

It should be noted that various kingdoms of western Tibet, Ladakh, and Kashmir also had their influence on northern Nepalese affairs, particularly in the region of Jumla (far northwest) and Mustang (north central). Many Tibetan fortresses (*dzong*) may be seen in the northern border areas. The history of these

Pressing mustard seeds for oil. (Steve Conlon)

regions is only now beginning to be rediscovered by scholars. The ancient alliances and influences of these many principalities, Nepali and Tibetan, are still felt in the internal political workings of the present day Kingdom of Nepal. And the silent and empty ruins speak to a rich and yet little-studied feudal past—part of its untapped socio-historic and archaeological heritage.

The small central hill kingdom of Gorkha eventually became the most famous under its eighteenth century leader Prithvi Narayan Shah. His grandiose plans were to unify the Himalaya into one great mountain state. In the 1760s he laid siege to the Malla *Newar* city-states of Kathmandu—PaaTan and BhatgaaU (Bhaktapur) and ultimately went on to control a vast territory from Bhutan on the east to Kashmir on the west, parts of southern Tibet on the north, and territories of the British East India Company on the south. By the early 1800s, however, this Gorkha conquest was halted by the British, and the Gorkha domain was cut back to approximately its present boundaries. The British were so impressed with the fighting abilities of the Gorkha hillsmen, however, that they chose not to subjugate the kingdom. Instead, they allowed it to remain independent and a source of the warriors of Gorkha, whom they called Gurkhas, for the British army. The present Shah kings of Nepal are the direct descendants of Prithvi Narayan Shah of Gorkha.

Nepali Cultures

The inhabitants of Nepal can be classified culturally into three general groups: Hindu castes, ethnic groups of the hills, and northern border people.

HINDU CASTES

The Hindu castes are called by the general term *PahAARi* (people of the hills). They inhabit the middle hills and lower valleys, generally below 6000 ft (1800 m). Each caste has an ascribed profession, but many people no longer follow the rules.

High Castes

Today this group includes peasant farmers, civil servants, money lenders, and school teachers, as well as people following the traditional caste occupations.

Bahun (Brahman)—the traditional priest caste. In former times, the Brahmans did not handle plows or eat certain prohibited foods (e.g., onions, tomatoes, certain kinds of meat) or drink alcohol. These days, however, many of these prohibitions are ignored, even the rule against drinking. Some of these rules are still followed in the more remote and traditional rural areas. Brahmans can be grouped into those from the east (*Purbiya*) and those from the west (*Kumaon*). Offspring of irregular unions among Brahmans are termed *Jaishi Bahun*.

Chhetri—the traditional warrior caste. It includes much the same occupations as the Brahmans as well as soldiers in the Gurkha armies. The King's family is Thakuri, a subcaste of *Chhetri*. The term *Matwali Chhetri* ("those who drink liquor") refers to western peoples who are not given the sacred thread characteristic of the "twice born" castes of Brahman and *Chhetri*.

Menial Castes

Many men and women of the three lower menial castes no longer pursue blacksmithing, shoemaking, or tailoring, but work as day laborers on the land of others or as porters for large trekking parties or merchant-traders.

Damai or *Darji*—tailors and musicians for Hindu weddings and festivals.

Kaami—ironworkers, toolmakers, and sometimes silversmiths and gold-smiths (*Sunar*).

Saarki—cobblers and leatherworkers.

(These are the main castes found in the Nepali hills. Many other caste groups are found among the *Newars*, below, and in the Terai regions.)

ETHNIC GROUPS OF THE HILLS

The ethnic groups of the hills have been in the Himalaya somewhat longer, it is thought, than the Hindu castes. They are descendants of several waves of migration from the north and northeast. These groups tend to cluster between 6000 ft (1800 m) and 9000 ft (2700 m).

Newar—merchants, civil servants, craftspeople and artists in wood, brass, and bronze, and farmers of the Kathmandu Valley and the hill bazaars. Many are hotel keepers. *Newar* society is stratified into numerous castes and subcastes modeled after the Hindu caste system. The *Newar* practice both Hinduism and Buddhism, and their communities typically have many well-endowed temples and monastic compounds.

Kiranti (*Rai* and *Limbu*)—peasant hill people of east Nepal. *Rai* villages are found as far west and north as Solu District on the Mount Everest trek. Some are Gurkha soldiers. *Limbu Kiranti* are also found in neighboring Darjeeling district in India, where they are employed on tea plantations.

Tamang—peasant farmers, day laborers, and porters of east and central Nepal. They are particularly numerous around the Kathmandu Valley and the upper Trisuli Valley, and are frequently seen carrying incredibly large loads on the trails of west-central Nepal. The *Tamang* are predominantly Buddhist.

Magar—peasant farmers of central and west Nepal. Some of their villages can be seen on the hillsides above the Kali Gandaki river in upper Myagdi District, and some live as far north as southern Dolpa and Mustang districts. *Magar* join the Gurkha armies, and are recruited to the oil fields of the Persian Gulf. *Magar* are much influenced by Hinduism.

Gurung—peasant farmers and shepherds of central Nepal. They generally live higher than their *Magar* neighbors. Many *Gurung* are Gurkha soldiers, and some have recently become successful business people in and around Pokhara, in central Nepal. They practice Buddhism (in the northernmost villages), Hinduism (in the lower villages), and their own ancient shamanism. *Gurung* are commonly seen in Lamjung, Parbat, and Kaski districts on the Manang, Jomosom, Ghandrung, and Annapurna Sanctuary treks. In Gorkha District live the *Ghale* people, a prominent *Gurung* clan.

Sunwar and *Jirel*—small groups of peasant farmers east of Kathmandu Valley.

Thakali—farmers and mountain herdspeople, traders, and business people of Thak Khola in central Nepal. They are often found trading or keeping inns and hotels in and around Pokhara and surrounding districts as far south as the Terai. They are aggressive entrepreneurs, the former salt merchants of the Kali Gandaki trade corridor to Tibet. This small group has made a large impact on the economy of central and north-central Nepal. They are strongly influenced by Tibetan Buddhism and their own ancient shamanism.

(*Gurung, Tamang,* and *Thakali* are closely interrelated linguistically and culturally but display different adaptations according to the local ecology and their own histories.)

Above: Plowing terraces. Below: Labor-intensive harvesting of rice. (Stephen Bezruchka)

NORTHERN BORDER PEOPLES OR BHOTIYA

Like the ethnic groups of the hills, these people came to Nepal from the north and northeast long before the arrival of the Hindu castes from the south. They inhabit the northern valleys and mountainsides, usually above 9000 ft (2700 m), and are the true "Himalayan highlanders." Their socio-cultural, linguistic, and religious affinities are clearly with Tibet. They are Buddhist and pursue economies such as high-altitude farming, long-distance trade, yak and sheep husbandry and, more recently, portering and guiding for trekking and mountaineering parties. In north-central Nepal, most of the pony-train drivers are *BhoTiya* villagers from upper Mustang District and around Muktinath. Since 1959, many Tibetan nationals have migrated as refugees into Nepal. They live in camps in the Kathmandu and Pokhara valleys and in east Nepal, and as traders and laborers in some of the northern border towns, especially in the Thak Khola region of Mustang District. Many of these newly arrived Tibetans have intermarried with local *BhoTiya* and are virtually indistinguishable from them.

BhoTiya ethnic names usually reflect the places where they live; the attached suffixes *-ba, -pa,* or *-le* mean, simply, "people of." Listed as they occur from east to far west Nepal, across the arc of the great Himalaya, they include: *Lhomi* (upper Arun river); *Sherpa,* i.e. *Shar-ba* (Solu-Khumbu, Rolwaling, and Helambu); *Langtang BhoTiya* (Langtang valley north of Kathmandu); *Nupri-ba* (northern Gorkha District, upper Buri Gandaki river); *Manangba* and *Nar BhoTiya* (Manang District, upper Marsyangdi river); *BaragaaUle* (Muktinath valley); *Lopa* (Mustang District, north of Muktinath and Thak Khola region); *Dolpa* and *Tarap BhoTiya* (Dolpa District, northwest of Thak Khola); *Mugu BhoTiya* (Mugu-Karnali valley); and *Limi-ba* (Limi valley, northwest of Jumla). There are other *BhoTiya* peoples in small, high-altitude valleys. Some northern area peoples *appear* to be *BhoTiya* in their dress and house styles; certain *Gurung* (in southern Manang District, for example); the *Tarali* (a northern *Magar* people in southern Dolpa District), and the *Byansi* (far northwest corner of Nepal) all reflect *BhoTiya* cultural affinities.

Some *BhoTiya* peoples, perhaps as many as fifty percent from areas like Muktinath and Mustang, for example, migrate south on trading trips during the cold winter months, when you may encounter them along the main north-south trails. Many are itinerant peddlers (of high mountain herbs and spices, woolen scarves, leather goods, and various trinkets and costume jewelry). Others are much more sophisticated traders or smugglers. The *Manangba,* for example, are reputed to have become quite rich at smuggling gold, electronic consumer goods, and fancy clothing into the country from Hong Kong and Southeast Asia. There are many *BhoTiya* peoples dwelling in the Thamel district of Kathmandu.

Human Geography

The Nepali people may also be grouped geographically in four regions: the Kathmandu Valley, east Nepal, central Nepal, and the west and far west of Nepal.

PEOPLES OF THE KATHMANDU VALLEY

The early inhabitants of the Kathmandu Valley were farmers and herders. The indigenous *Newar* are a mixture of those peoples and other migrants who found their way, over the centuries, to this fertile basin. Each conqueror of the valley, some from the eastern hills of Nepal (of *Kiranti* stock) and some from north India, added to the cultural heritage to make the ethnologically rich *Newar* culture and

Children playing on a ping *or Nepali-style ferris wheel. (Ane Haaland)*

society of today. *Newar* make up the bulk of the merchants and shopkeepers (alongside more recently arrived Indian merchants) in the three cities of Kathmandu, PaaTan, and BhatgaaU (Bhaktapur). *Newar* are also the predominant shopkeepers in outlying rural bazaars and, throughout the country, make up a considerable percentage of the Nepalese civil service.

Kathmandu Valley is also populated by large numbers of Brahmans and Chhetri. They too are farmers and many have become professional and civil servants in the capital city.

Other peoples often seen on the streets of the capital are Hindu peddlers from the Tarai, *Tamang* hill people who work as coolies and day laborers, *BhoTiya* (including many Sherpas) from the north, *Gurung* and *Magar* from central and west Nepal, and *Kiranti* (*Rai* and *Limbu*) from east Nepal. Since 1959, many Tibetan refugees have also settled in the valley. Monks and other Tibetan men and women are found in the Buddhist temples and monasteries of Baudhnath and Swayambunath, on the outskirts of Kathmandu, and at the refugee and handicraft center at Jawalakhel, near PaaTan. Tibetan handicrafts—especially articles of woolen clothing and colorful carpets—are well known to tourists in Nepal and in the export marts of Europe and America.

In medieval times, *Newar* craftsmen developed the distinct architectural and decorative motifs and religious arts of the valley and, not insignificantly, of Tibetan Buddhism as well. They became active traders when, for centuries, a main trade route between India and Tibet passed through Kathmandu and BhatgaaU. In time, *Newar* extended their craftsmanship and business enterprises to Lhasa and other Tibetan trade centers. After the defeat of their valley kingdoms by the Shah rulers from Gorkha in 1769, the *Newar* proceeded to take economic advantage of the Gorkha conquest. As Gorkha military and administrative outposts were established to tie the new Himalayan kingdom together, *Newar* merchants went along to set up shops. They created many of the hill bazaars that trekkers encounter throughout Nepal, and they continue to serve as suppliers for many of the still remote government outposts.

Not all *Newar* are businessmen or civil servants. Members of one subgroup known as *Jyapu* are seen tilling the vast fields of rice, wheat, and vegetables in the valley. Others are stone and wood carvers, carpenters, potters, goldsmiths, blacksmiths, butchers, and Hindu or Buddhist temple priests. *Newar* peasant communities are even occasionally found in the outlying districts. Most *Newar*, no matter how far dispersed, try to keep kinship and ritual ties with Kathmandu Valley because it is their homeland.

PEOPLE OF EAST NEPAL

The east is the indigenous home to *Kiranti* people (*Rai* and *Limbu*), *Tamang, Sunwar,* and *Jirel* people at the middle elevations, and to more recently arrived Brahmans and Chhetris who arrived in the wake of the Gorkha conquest of the eighteenth century. Sherpa, *Lhomi* and other *BhoTiya* people populate the high valleys of eastern Nepal, up to 14,000 ft (4000 m).

The *Kiranti* live in the easternmost districts, and are found even around Darjeeling in West Bengal. Like the *Gurung* and *Magar* farther west, the *Kiranti* are renowned for their exploits in the British and Indian Gurkha armies. They speak a number of interrelated dialects that are often unintelligible from one watershed village to the next.

Kiranti economy is fairly self-sufficient. (The description that follows fits the

Nepali hill peoples in general.) Rice is raised in lower, well-watered fields. Upland crops, such as corn, millet, barley, wheat, and potatoes, are raised on higher, drier and steeper or terraced hillsides. No mechanized farm equipment is found in the hills (except an occasional threshing machine or rice mill). Tilling is done either by hand with a short-handled hoe (seen most often in Kathmandu Valley), or with bullocks pulling iron-tipped wooden plows. All hillsmen eat what they raise, and market what little surplus they may have. Some supplement their incomes by selling oranges or fish. The wealthier may engage in moneylending. Others work seasonally in neighboring India as porters, Gurkha soldiers, policemen, or watchmen. In the far eastern hills bordering the Darjeeling district of West Bengal, there are tea plantations—Nepal's own brand of Ilam tea is exceptionally tasty. Many *Limbu* work the tea plantations on both sides of the border. Some hillsmen make and sell bamboo baskets and mats, and where sheep are raised on the higher slopes, the people weave and sell the woolen blankets, rugs, and felt-like capes and jackets that are often seen in Kathmandu's street bazaar. Trekkers are most likely to encounter *Kiranti-Rai* along the lower trail through Solu District on the trek to Mount Everest.

The *Tamang,* a very large and widespread hill group, are among the most recent groups to have settled along the northern border regions and higher hills, having come, it appears, from farther north and east. *Tamang* have retained much of their Tibetan and Buddhist heritage. They have many villages all around the Kathmandu Valley, especially north, towards Helambu, and east, on the Mount Everest trek. They also populate the upper Trisuli Valley, on the Langtang trek. *Tamang* are well known to Himalayan climbers, who hire them for the long haul into base camps. At the higher elevations, however, the Sherpas tend to dominate the portering.

Eastward, toward Mount Everest, there are also small ethnic enclaves of the *Sunwar* and the *Jirel* people. *Sunwar* inhabit the Likhu and Khimti valleys. Some of them have been recruited into Gurkha British and Indian regiments. The *Jirel* are found in the Jiri and Sikri valleys. These groups are difficult to distinguish initially from surrounding hill peasants.

Next to the Gurkha soldiers of Nepal, it is perhaps the Sherpas, famous as mountain guides and porters, who have attracted the most worldwide attention. Some Sherpas dwell in the remote Rolwaling valley, and as far west as Helambu region north of Kathmandu, but the most renowned come from the villages of Shar-Khumbu (Solu-Khumbu), along the upper valley of the Dudh Kosi and its tributaries, in the Mount Everest region. Sherpas are relatively recent newcomers to Nepal. Pangboche, their oldest village and one of the highest in the world, is thought to have been built a little over 300 years ago. The Sherpas speak a Tibetan dialect, dress like their Tibetan neighbors—or often like Western trekkers—and live as traders and agro-pastoralists, farming their high fields (mostly potatoes, wheat, barley, and buckwheat) and herding yak and sheep in alpine pastures up to 17,000 ft (5000 m). Their region is divided into three subregions: Solu, Pharak, and Khumbu. Solu, at the south, includes such villages as Junbesi and Phaphlu, and the monastery at Chiwong, in picturesque valleys at approximately 9000 ft (2700 m). Pharak is situated between Solu and Khumbu along the steep banks of the Dudh Kosi. Most Sherpa mountaineers hail from Khumbu, the highest and most northerly of the three regions, at elevations of 11,000 ft (3300 m) and up. Their villages include Namche Bazaar, Thami, Khumjung, Khunde, and Pangboche, as well as the famous and beautiful Buddhist monastery of Tengboche. Among the Sherpas, the practice of Tibetan Lamaism remains strong.

Their religion gives Sherpas a concern for all living things and for their Western clients on treks and expeditions. Their warmth of character, shared by many Himalayan peoples, is perhaps best displayed in their sense of hospitality. Visitors to a Sherpa house are considered guests of honor, for whom nothing is spared (sometimes to the point of embarrassment for Westerners). The best response to an outpouring of generosity by a Sherpa, or any Nepali host, is reciprocity—your own generosity and care in their regard.

Sherpa names of men often reflect the day of the week on which the boy was born. Nima on Sunday, Dawa on Monday, Mingma on Tuesday, Lhakpa on Wednesday, Phurbu on Thursday, Pasang on Friday, and Pemba on Saturday. Like any tradition this one is not strictly adhered to.

The Sherpas have received considerable attention from anthropologists, mountaineer-writers, and traveling journalists, so we need not go into detail here (see Recommended Reading). One facet of Sherpa culture not often described in the literature is the Namche Bazaar Saturday market, which is interesting from a traveler's perspective because of the chance to see several ethnic groups and a wide variety of local handicrafts and trade goods on display. If traveling toward Namche Bazaar immediately before a Saturday, trekkers may see many groups of lowlanders, mostly *Rai* and a few Brahman and *Chhetri*, carrying baskets of produce such as rice, corn, and fruits to sell or trade for highland produce such as wheat, wool, potatoes, *ghiu* (clarified butter, or ghee), and other animal by-products. This is part of the natural economic exchange that keeps each community supplied with the produce of the other. The lowlanders are easily singled out by their style of dress (light tie-across Nepali shirts and baggy trousers that fit snugly at the calves) from the Sherpas and Tibetans. Sherpa and Tibetan men, by comparison, prefer heavy woolen cloaks and trousers, with leather or woolen boots. And these days, some dress in down jackets as well. At the market itself, Tibetan boots and handicrafts of silver, wool, and leather are displayed. A market day is a lively occasion, a time when *Tibetans, Sherpas, Rai,* and others (including Western visitors) intermingle to trade, gossip, eat, drink, and even dance and sing in a spirited sharing atmosphere.

PEOPLE OF CENTRAL NEPAL

Central Nepal is the region extending from Kathmandu Valley westward to, and just beyond, Pokhara. It is the home of Brahman, *Chhetri, Magar,* and *Gurung* peoples, and of a number of northern border peoples, including the *Thakali* of the Thak Khola region of the Mustang District. The *Brahman* and *Chhetri* people are encountered especially in the lower valleys. Look for them in the vicinity of the old Gorkha kingdom and along the lower Marsyangdi Valley trail. *Newar* bazaars line the road between Kathmandu and Pokhara, and many other caste and ethnic people have been attracted to these new settlements. The *Gurung* inhabit the higher slopes of the Annapurna, Lamjung, Himal Chuli, and Ganesh Himalaya massif. There are many *Tamang* in the region as well, often indistinguishable from the *Gurung.* The *Magar* people live widely scattered, in both lower and higher hill areas.

The *Gurung* are most prominent on high ridges and upper valleys below the Annapurna and Himal Chuli massifs north and east of Pokhara, eastward beyond Gorkha. They are an enterprising upland farming and herding people; their sheep herds are often seen along the Manang trail on the Marsyangdi river route. They are subdivided into many clans, but except for the *Ghale* (pronounced like "golly"), who prefer to use the clan name, most call themselves, simply, *Gurung.* They, like their *Magar* counterparts, occupy some of the most inaccessible villages, high on the mountainsides above the trekking routes. Young *Gurung* men are often encountered as porters; older *Gurung* of distinction may have served in the Gurkha regiments, and many have interesting tales of exploits from World War II. If you happen to stop at a *Gurung* village for the night, you might see their colorful dances, or other ritual or festival activities, some of which display very ancient characteristics. Especially interesting are *Gurung* funerary rituals (called *arghun*), which are described later.

Tibetan *BhoTiya* groups of northern central Nepal come from Nupri (northern Gorka District, upper Buri Gandaki river), Manang (upper Marsyangdi river), Lo-Manthang (upper Kali Gandaki river), and from Dolpo and Tarap (north of the Dhaulagiri massif). During the winter months, large numbers of these high-mountain peoples trek south to the lower hills and are often encountered in and around bazaar towns, where they engage in trade and sometimes run inns and small shops. Many of the pony and donkey trains encountered along the Thak Khola trek route are operated by *BhoTiya* men from Lo-Manthang region, northern Thak Khola, and the valley of Muktinath, all in northern Mustang District.

The Thak Khola trek passes through villages of several ethnic and caste groups. Pokhara, the starting point for many central and west Nepal treks, is inhabited by all sorts of peoples—Brahman, *Chhetri, Newar, Gurung, Thakali, BhoTiya,* Tibetans, and many menial castes, as well as newcomers from the Nepalese Tarai lowlands and from India. The surrounding hills are dotted with *Gurung* villages. The wealth of ex-Gurkha soldiers among them is obvious from their large, cut-stone houses, with slate or corrugated metal roofs. There is a Tibetan refugee settlement at Pardi, near the Pokhara airport, and another at Hyangja, a half-hour walk north of the main Pokhara bazaar. Trekking north, one may encounter Hindu caste settlements at first, to be replaced on the higher hills by the ethnic *Gurung* and *Magar.*

The *Magar* are farmers and herdsmen who live along the tributaries of the Kali Gandaki river in Myagdi District both north, west, and southwest of Beni. *Magar* villages situated under the Dhaulagiri Himal seem to cling like postage stamps to the high cliffs. In some regions, indigenous *Magar* call themselves by clan names, such as *Pun, Chantel, Kaiki,* and *Tarali. Pun Magar* are renowned for rock-cutting skills, which are visible along the Kali Gandaki river trail. Some of the more northerly trails were cut out of the cliffs in the 1960s by Tibetan refugee *Khamba. Chantel Magar,* who also dwell below the south face of the Dhaulagiri massif, are herdsmen and farmers who are noted also for their skills in local copper mining. The culture of the northernmost *Magar,* the *Tarali* of Dolpo District, blends into that of the *BhoTiya.*

Above the dramatic gorge of the Kali Gandaki, north from the town of Ghasa, is the region known as Thak Khola. *Thakali* villages line the route north along the high Kali Gandaki Valley. Their language is very close to *Gurung* and *Tamang,* but their cultural history has been more influenced by Tibet. The *Thakali* are noted for their strong trading spirit, which they developed as middlemen in the formerly very active Nepal-Tibet rice and salt trade through their region. The largest town, until recently, was Tukche, the center of the *Thakali* ethnic culture and, for many decades earlier in this century, the regional center of the Tibetan salt trade. Since 1959, when the Tibetan border trade diminished, the Tibetan salt business has come to a virtual standstill in Thak Khola, and many *Thakali* have turned southward for other economic opportunities. Today, Jomosom, the district center north of Tukche, is much larger and at times Tukche appears almost abandoned. Some

Thakali have dropped their Tibetan and Buddhist predilections and have adopted Nepali culture and Hinduism. Some have moved permanently out of Thak Khola to take advantage of business ventures in the larger bazaars and trade centers of Nepal.

Despite uniform appearances, Thak Khola is actually the home of two similar ethnic groups, and one quite distinct group. The *Thakali* proper live between Ghasa and Tukche. North of them, and virtually indistinguishable, are a people known as *PanchgaaUle* (which literally means "people of the five villages"—Marpha, Syang, Chiwong, Cherok, and Jomosom-Thini). The *PaunchgaaUle* sometimes call themselves *Thakali* but intermarriage between them and their 'true' *Thakali* neighbors is not condoned. The third group are a *BhoTiya* people who inhabit the valley of Muktinath, from Kagbeni east to the Muktinath shrine at the base of Thorong Pass. They are also sometimes called the *BaragaaUle*, or "people of the twelve villages." Muktinath is a special place to these *BhoTiya* people, as it is a Hindu-Buddhist shrine of great significance. There are many religious observances throughout the year that attract Hindu and Buddhist pilgrims. The most important event to local Buddhists is the celebration of the Yartung festival in the fall, when the animals have been brought down from the high pastures for the winter. Yartung is highlighted by horse racing and great revelry. For Hindus, one of the largest events of the year falls on the occasion of Jani Purnima, the "full moon day (*purnima*) of the sacred cord (*janai*)." The sacred cord is worn by men of the highest twice-born Hindu castes, as a sign of their privileged social status and religious sanctity. More about Muktinath as a sacred center is given in the section on the Thak Khola trek.

Finally, north of Muktinath Valley, there are the *Lopa*, the *BhoTiya* people of upper Mustang District, in what was once the petty kingdom of Mustang. Their lives center around high, dry-land agriculture on oasis-like farmland wherever nearby streams can be diverted for irrigation water, and they follow pastoral pursuits with sheep, goats, and yak. In winter, many of them migrate south as traders and pony drivers. These people are Tibetan Buddhists, and some practice the pre-Buddhist religion called Bon. There are a number of small monasteries of both religions throughout Thak Khola and upper Mustang. In their northernmost walled town of Manthang, lives the king of the Lopa, the Raja of Mustang, whose allegiance is firmly with the government in Kathmandu.

PEOPLE OF WEST AND FAR WEST NEPAL

West and far west Nepal are less known to anthropologists than other parts of the country for several reasons—the difficulty of travel in the area, the remoteness from centers of trade and government, and the relatively low population, sparse settlement, and dearth of ethnic groups. These hills are drier, and the people suffer from more difficult environmental circumstances; their production is lower and it takes much more land to support the average family. The great distances and time involved to travel from either the Tarai towns to the south or the capital at Kathmandu also explain our relatively poor understanding of this region.

Part of the west is the home of the *Magar*, but only as far as the Sallyan District. Beyond that to the western border with India, Hindu caste groups predominate. In great measure these Hindu villagers are closely related to the *PahAARi* (hill people) of Almora, Kumaon, and Garhwal in the neighboring Indian sub-Himalaya. The Nepali language here blends into the central *PahAARi* dialect

Above: *Two Raute boys making a wooden box. The* Raute *of central and western Nepal are one of the last hunting and gathering tribes in Asia.* Below: *The* Raute *in dance costumes. (Johan Reinhard)*

of north India, and to some extent there is greater socio-cultural interaction with Indian neighbors than with the peoples of central Nepal or Kathmandu. In recent years the national government has taken a more active interest in the problems and potential of the far west. There has been a concerted effort to further integrate and unite all of the Nepali people as one nation and to improve the local standard of living.

Living north of the Hindu caste groups of the west and far west are more of the *BhoTiya* people, named after particular valleys in which they live, such as Limi, Mugu, Tarap, and Dolpo. Some of these have only recently been studied by anthropologists, and most accounts of them are found only in scholarly journals and dissertations.

This region offers some spectacular treks, particularly to the lakes (RaRa and Phoksumdo) and mountains. And there are equally interesting social systems, cultural patterns, and historic and archaeological reminders of the past.

This is the land of the ancient Malla Kingdom of the Karnali river basin. This region is literally "littered" with many of the cultural and historic artifacts of the Malla era, the twelfth to fourteenth centuries A.D. At one time, the Malla Kingdom included portions of western Tibet as well. After its decline, the *baaisi raja* (or twenty-two kingdoms) of west Nepal emerged and were not ceded to the expanding Gorkha kingdom until the nineteenth century. (Historians have postulated a relationship between the Malla kings of west Nepal, and those of the Kathmandu Valley just prior to the eighteenth century Gorkha conquest, but there is no consensus.)

Along the former "royal highway" of the Malla Kingdom of west Nepal, a walking route stretching north from the inner Tarai through Jumla and into Tibet, there are various inscribed stones that scholars have used to determine the nature and extent of the Malla domain. And there are ancient shrines to be seen throughout west Nepal dedicated to the prominent local deity called "Masta." On some trails in the west, one may see carved wooden spirit effigies, festooned with bells, flowers, and strips of colored cloth set out to appease the spirits that haunt each locale. Trekkers are admonished—*please*—to respect local customs here and throughout Nepal and to refrain from handling or taking souvenirs beyond what can be captured on film. Much of what is seen and admired here is sacred, and local feeling toward holy objects is not unlike the reverence and respect Westerners feel in the sanctuaries of the great cathedrals of Europe, or in their hometown churches and synagogues.

One fascinating cultural feature of some of the more northerly dwelling Hindus of this region is their apparent "Tibetanization." Unlike elsewhere in Nepal, some *Chhetri* and *Thakuri* of the west and far west are indistinguishable at first glance from their Buddhist *BhoTiya* neighbors. They wear the same style of clothing, construct similar flat-roofed houses, and pursue the same patterns of trade and subsistence economy. Their way of living is unlike that of their more "pure" Hindu caste neighbors to the south and east, who look down upon them in some respects. The *BhoTiya* cultural attributes noted here, and wherever they occur among non-*BhoTiya* people in Nepal, are reflections of the northern mountain environment.

There are also many true *BhoTiya* encountered on the trails of this region, along the Bheri and Karnali river routes, for example. They are typically high-mountain dwellers of Tibetan racial and cultural affinities, who prefer to spend their winters in the warmer, lower southlands of Nepal. At times, in the fall and spring, the trekker may encounter a kaleidoscope of people in caravans, including

Byansi ethnic traders, who live mostly in the Indian frontier district of Almora, and in adjacent border regions of far west Nepal.

The salt trade was once a flourishing business here. Salt from the great salt lakes of western Tibet was procured from Tibetan traders, then traded through several hands for cereal grain and other commodities in Nepal and India. Today, traders deal more often in wood products, animal byproducts (butter, hides), and cereal grains, as well as numerous manufactured goods, mostly of Indian origin.

Besides traders, the traveler may encounter devout Hindu pilgrims wending their way northward through far west Nepal. Their destinations are the sacred Mount Kailas and Lake Manasarowar, in western Tibet.

Despite the growth of tourism and travel throughout Nepal, and the government's increasing investment in rural development (new roads, schools, and other basic services), Nepal's west and far west districts remain remote from the national center. It is a region as exotic and romantic as its curious sounding place names: Dang, Dandeldhura, RaRa, Limi, Mugu, and Humla.

Religious Festivals and Sacred Observances

SECULAR FESTIVALS

Several national holidays are celebrated throughout the country. The most colorful from the standpoint of national culture and the prospect of photography is *Prajaatantra Divas,* or Nepali National Day, February 19. It is highlighted by parades on the Tundikhel (parade ground) in the center of Kathmandu. National ethnic groups, dancing troupes, the military, and various peasant, class, and cooperative organizations participate, all dressed in their traditional finery. There is much pomp and splendor.

At least three different New Year celebrations are held in Nepal annually. The Lunar New Year begins in the Nepali month of Baisakh (mid-April). The Tibetan New Year, called Losar, usually falls in February. It is heralded by feasting and celebration among the Tibetan community. The traditional *Newar* New Year falls in October and is celebrated by the preparation and sale of great amounts of sweet cakes and candies, and with colorful decorations throughout the streets of Kathmandu, PaaTan, and BhatgaaU.

Among the secular festivals in the hills, one of the most interesting is *Yartung* at Muktinath (Thak Khola trek). *Yartung* signals the return from the highlands of the animals, which are pastured in the lower valleys during the coming winter. It occurs in the fall and sometimes coincides with the full moon day of *Janai Purnima* (below), a Hindu sacred occasion. *Yartung* annually attracts the majority of *BhoTiya* people from throughout upper Thak Khola, northern Mustang, and from neighboring Manang District (over the Thorong Pass). The participants wear their traditional ethnic dress. Horse racing at Rani Pauwa, about a half mile (0.8 km) below the Muktinath shrine, is the main event, along with drinking, dancing, gambling, and a generally merry and festive good time. (See Buddhist Festivals, below.)

The *Yartung* is a kind of fair or *mela*. These rural fairs are countrywide and occur throughout the year at various locations. Many are held in the spring and in the fall after the harvest. Fairs are traditionally associated with local rural shrines, quite often for Hindus at the confluence (*beni*) of two sacred rivers or simply on the bank (*ghaaT*) of a sacred river. They usually coincide with a religious occasion, and include worship at a local shrine. Some *mela* are quite large and last several

A Rai girl making a flower and bamboo string to hang over the Dudh Kosi River during the festival of Tihaar. (Dave Hardenbergh)

days, attracting people from surrounding districts. Others are quite brief and limited to a small region.

HINDU FESTIVALS

Hindu festivals are celebrated in Kathmandu Valley and in many hill bazaars and villages. Only a few of the many smaller local festivals are mentioned here. Information about them and the exact dates of all festivals, which are reckoned by the lunar cycle, can be obtained in Kathmandu. The following Nepali words are often used in relation to certain festivals and religious occasions:

ekadasi, the eleventh day of every fortnight during the lunar year; observed by fasting, worship, and ceremonial bathing

jaatraa means festival or fair

yaatraa is more specifically a religious occasion that attracts pilgrims (*jaatraa* and *yaatraa* are sometimes used interchangeably)

pujaa means worship

A *Tikaa* is a mark of religious and decorative significance on the forehead of Hindus. They are given and received, particularly at festival and religious occasions, to express good wishes, friendship, respect, and honor. When a Hindu visits a temple or shrine, he or she often takes *Tikaa* from the officiating priest. One day each year, during the religious observance of *DasAAl,* the King gives *Tikaa* to the general populace. Outside of Kathmandu, the headman of a village substitutes for the King on this day of honor.

The major Hindu holidays include:

Shiva Raatri, literally "Shiva's Night," is observed in February at Pashupatinath, a famous large Hindu temple on the banks of the Bagmati river in Kathmandu Valley, northeast of the capital city. This festival attracts thousands of pilgrims from all over Nepal, the Tarai, and from India, who walk, fly, or ride buses into the valley for the occasion. The Nepal Army parades on the Tundikhel, and bonfires burn for several nights.

Holi is celebrated in early March. Its climax is on the full moon day when red powder is thrown and passersby are doused with colored water. It is not a day to wear one's best clothes, unless you are expecting to have them cleaned immediately anyway!

GhoRa Jaatra, held in late March, includes horse racing and athletic events on the Kathmandu Tundikhel.

Janai Purnima (or *Janai Purne*) is the full moon day of the late monsoon season (usually August) on which high-caste Hindus bathe ceremonially and men ritually change their sacred threads (*janai*), which are worn over the left shoulder. In addition, on this day priests give yellow threads, which for good luck are worn on the wrist until the Tihar festival, to all who wish them. Hardy and pious Hindus take pilgrimages on this day to bathe and worship at some of the high Himalayan lakes, such as Gosainkunda, north of Kathmandu, and to other equally auspicious holy sites such as Muktinath in northeastern Thak Khola. In Kathmandu, large numbers gather at the water tank of Kumbeshwar in Lalitpur, a site that has religious affinities with Gosainkunda.

Indra Jaatraa lasts eight days at the end of September and beginning of October. The center of activity in Kathmandu is Hanuman Dhoka (the square near the old royal Palace in Kathmandu), but preparations can be seen at various other places for many days prior to the main celebration. A tall pole is erected and a golden elephant is placed there, attracting worshippers with offerings of sweets, fruit, and flowers. The festival also features dancing troupes and drama productions. Families pay special tribute to those members who have died during the past years, parading through the streets carrying burning lamps and incense and chanting religious hymns. Various manifestations of the god Indra are shown throughout the city, the most famous being the huge head of Bhairab, at Indrachok, and the metal head gilded with gold, at Hanuman Dhoka. Each evening the temples of Hanuman Dhoka and the old palaces are lit with numerous oil lamps.

This festival and many others are especially important to the *Newar* people, and are celebrated in remote bazaars throughout the country. Travelers who happen to be in a *Newar* bazaar during *Indra Jaatraa* will see colorful masked street dancers who are thought to become possessed.

In Kathmandu, on *Raths Jaatraa,* the day before the full moon of *Indra Jaatraa,* thousands of Nepalis crowd the streets to glimpse the "Living Goddess," Kumari, and two "Living Gods," Ganesh and Bhairab, as they are paraded in ancient temple carts through the lower part of the city. The young virgin deity and her two boy attendants are especially selected from the Bada subcaste (silversmiths and goldsmiths) of the *Newar.* The Kumari is considered the protectoress of Kathmandu Valley.

DasAAI (Dusserah in India) lasts for ten days at the time of the new moon in mid-October. This is Nepal's most important festival. It commemorates the legendary victory of the goddess Durga (Kali) over the evil demon-buffalo, Mahisashur. One highlight is the ceremonial decapitating of buffaloes at the *kot* (fort) near Hanuman Dhoka on the ninth day of the festival. The tenth day, called *Vijaya Dasami* (literally, "Victorious Tenth Day") is the day of the *Tikaa* ceremony, and symbolizes victory by extermination of the buffalo demon by Durga. On this day, the King and Queen receive citizens at the Royal Palace, where they give *Tikaa,* and village leaders dispense *Tikaa* to their constituents in the hinterlands. Schools and government offices are closed during *DasAAI,* and the holiday is considered a time for family reunions all over the country. On rural trails, one will see women and children returning to their *maiti ghar* (or mother's home) during the time of *DasAAI* and/or during *Tihaar,* which follows. At this time of year, the Kathmandu Tundikhel is alive with goats and sheep brought into the valley from northern districts and with buffalo from the Tarai. These animals are for sale, and are ultimately used in the necessary sacrifices and feasting of the occasion. The whole *DasAAI* season is one of feasting and merrymaking.

Tihaar or *Diwali* is a five-day festival in mid-November. The last three days are the most interesting. The third day is *Lakshima Pujaa,* dedicated to Lakshmi, goddess of wealth and associated with light. Houses are trimmed with hundreds of tiny oil lamps, which transform Kathmandu at night into a beautifully lit city. Lakshmi's blessings are invoked, and a new business year is officially begun. In *Newar* communities, the streets are overhung with paper lanterns that are lit each evening. During *Tihaar* various creatures, including humans, are singled out for attention—on the first day, the crow; on the second day, the dog; on the third day, the cow; and on the fourth day, the bull. On the final day, *Bhaai Tikaa,* sisters ceremonially give their brothers *Tikaa* on the foreheads and wish them prosperity and long life. This is the only time of the year when public gambling is condoned, and one will see many crowds around groups of *juwaa* (cowry shell) players, or card players. During this season, girls and boys also carol in the streets and alleyways of towns and villages. Girls carol on the night of *Lakshmi Pujaa,* and boys carol on the next night. A popular treat during *Tihaar* is the rice flour doughnut, called *sel roti.* Finally, among the *Newar* merchant community, *Tihaar*

Swings are set up around the festival of DasAAI. (Dave Hardenbergh)

marks the beginning of their New Year, and *Newar* bazaars, in particular, are festooned with decorations and crowded with well wishers and merrymakers. At this time, the sweet shops are overflowing with pastries and candy treats.

Both *DasAAI* and *Tihaar* mark the end of the farming season, the bringing in of the harvest, and new beginnings. This time of year is especially joyous for individuals and families alike, and most people prefer to be at home with relatives and friends.

BUDDHIST FESTIVALS

Buddhist festivals are celebrated among the Tibetan and Buddhist *Newar* communities in the Kathmandu Valley and in outlying districts where these people are found. Secular and religious festivals among the Buddhists are commonly celebrated in the northern border districts, the principal domain of Nepali Tibetans (*BhoTiya*). Buddhist festivals include:

Losar, the Tibetan New Year, in mid-February. There are festive activities at Baudhnath and Swayambhunath temples in the Kathmandu Valley, and at the Tibetan refugee center near PaaTan. Festivals are also held in outlying Tibetan refugee communities such as in the Pokhara Valley, in Langtang Valley, and at Chialsa. Buddhist pilgrims visit the big temples and monasteries at this time, and family reunions—with feasting, drinking, and dancing—highlight home life.

Buddha's Birthday in May is a solemn occasion. Foreign dignitaries are usually invited to observances during the day at Swayambhunath, where Tibetan and *Newar* Buddhist monks perform elaborate rituals in their brightly colored robes. Observances are also held in other Buddhist temples and monasteries. Prayer flags fly overhead, and at night the Swayambhunath hilltop is brightly lit. The celebration of Buddha's Birthday is less elaborate in outlying Buddhist communities, where observances at the local *gomba* or monastery are common.

Dalai Lama's Birthday, on July 6, is a time for prayer, invocation of blessings, and feasting, especially by Tibetan refugees. For some refugees it is a time of patriotic expressions in remembrance of former times, when the Dalai Lama was the supreme ruler of Tibet. Prayer flags fly overhead, and within the monasteries, butter lamps are lit in the name of the Dalai Lama. Prayers are said for his long life and good health.

Mani-rimdu is a Sherpa dance drama performed in the Khumbu region. It is held annually at Tengboche and Chiwong monasteries during November or early December and at Thami each May. This colorful, uniquely Sherpa festival has its origins in ancient Tibetan theatrical genres. The performers are monks, but the occasion is highlighted by much gaiety and feasting by monks and lay spectators alike.

Yartung is a horse festival held annually at the end of the monsoon (August or early September) on the race grounds of Rani Pauwa, adjacent to the Muktinath pilgrimage site in Mustang District. *BhoTiya* people from all over BaragaaU (Muktinath or Dzong river valley), and Lo-Manthang (upper Mustang), and some from Manang (east of Mustang) and Dolpo (west) attend. The men of BaragaaU region compete in a day of horse racing, a raucous occasion spiced by drinking and gambling in tents set up on the hills around the small community below Muktinath. The day begins with processions of laymen and monks in colorful attire, some riding equally decorated horses, from each of the surrounding villages. The monks lead the processions to circle the Muktinath shrine, before the secular fun starts. Frequently, *Yartung* coincides with the Hindu pilgrimage of *Janai Purnima*, adding to the number of people present at the shrine during the day.

Other Festive Events

WEDDINGS

Hindu weddings can be observed almost any time, but most are held during the months of January and February. Wedding parties can be observed traveling to and from the bride's house, sometimes over a long distance and for several days. In rural villages, weddings are loud, colorful affairs accompanied by hornpipers, drummers, and dancers. Wealthy city weddings often include professional bands, and the house where the wedding feast is held is decorated with strings of lights at night. Hindu marriages are traditionally arranged by the parents of the couple; horoscopes are compared by a priest, and an auspicious date is set. Dowries are often demanded, and can be quite expensive. Child marriage, now prohibited, was traditionally the norm among orthodox Hindus.

Buddhist weddings in the hills and mountains are less elaborate, more relaxed affairs, with great attention paid to ostentatious display and reciprocity in gift giving. Among Sherpas, for example, a wedding is preceded, sometimes years earlier, by betrothal rites and often by the birth of a child. There is much beer drinking and dancing. Monks from a nearby monastery attend the actual ceremonial activities.

Today, throughout Nepal, the customs surrounding the securing of a marriage partner are greatly relaxed compared with the past. Love marriage and marriage between castes and ethnic groups are not uncommon. Nonetheless, arranged marriages of alliance between families in proper caste or ethnic categories are still contracted, especially among the more traditional and orthodox people.

FUNERALS

Funerals can be observed in the city and countryside at any time. Most Nepalis burn the dead, preferably at the riverside (*ghaaT*), within a few hours of death. Hill villagers, far from the river, prefer prominent hillsides on which to burn or bury the dead. Funeral parties are obvious from the presence of a white-shrouded corpse carried on a bier either prone or bound tightly into a sitting position. Male relatives at the funeral typically shave their heads; women frequently unloosen their hair, letting it hang unadorned down the back. Drumming is uncommon, except on the occasion of post-funerary ceremonies held sometimes months after death to celebrate the passage of the deceased's spirit into the afterlife. Such post-funerary rituals are common, for example, among the hill ethnic groups such as the *Gurung, Tamang,* and *Thakali.* These are occasions for great feasting, dancing, drinking, and serious and ancient religious rituals conducted by shamans and Bon or Buddhist monks. Such post-funerary events are sometimes known in Nepali as *arghun* in the hills of west and west-central Nepal.

PILGRIMAGE

The Himalaya are a great attraction to Nepalese, Tibetan, and Indian pilgrims. Pilgrimage sites are common—a high "milk lake" (*dudh pokhari,* or *kunda*), the confluence (*beni*) of sacred rivers, or an especially prominent shrine or temple. Some of the most famous pilgrimage sites for Hindus are at Gosainkunda, Dudh Pokhari, Panch Pokhari, and Baahra Pokhari. Muktinath and several other high mountain shrines are sacred pilgrimage attractions to Hindus and Buddhists alike. Likewise, there are many shrines and temples within the valley of Kathmandu—Swayambhunath for one—that are sacred to both religious groups. Baudhnath and

Pashupatinath, on the outskirts of Kathmandu city, are especially sacred to Buddhists and Hindus respectively.

Pilgrims come to Nepal from all over southern Asia, and as travel conditions allow, from Tibet. Hindu holy men stand out clearly by their attire (or relative lack of attire, as the case may be). The occasion of *Shiva Raatri* is especially significant both to holy men and Indian lay pilgrims, who flock to the Kathmandu Valley. Sometimes holy men may be encountered who are observing vows of silence; they sometimes go for as long as twelve years without speaking.

Lay pilgrims are commonly seen throughout the year on popular routes to the high-mountain shrines or lakes. For example, there are many seasonal events that attract pilgrims to and from Muktinath shrine above Thak Khola. Many of them have planned for years to come to a certain Himalayan Shaivite or Vaishnavite shrine (devoted to Shiva and Vishnu respectively). Others seem to come on the spur of the moment: some to cleanse themselves from sin or bad luck; others, just for the pleasure of doing something different and unusual, or to see the country. For Hindus, water is an essential element at pilgrim shrines, and bathing is a central feature of the ritual observances. Sometimes Hindu and Buddhist shrines offer other attractions, as well, such as natural gas fires, the presence of sacred fossils, hot springs, an ice cave, a sacred footprint or other holy mark or memory of the gods, or a rich mythology of sacred events that adds to the attractiveness of a place. Legendary accounts of sacred pilgrimage sites and events in the Himalaya are recorded in the ancient literature of Hinduism, some works dating back over 2000 years.

Jewelry

Jewelry and other body decoration is another fascinating aspect of Nepali culture that attracts the attention of visitors. As in most societies, jewelry is used for decoration; for women, it is their inalienable property and their dowry.

Such decoration shows affluence, but there is perhaps less individuality and idiosyncratic expression in jewelry worn by a particular ethnic group in an area than in some modern cultures. Nepali people are modest and disapprove of too much self-pride. At festivals and weddings, however, it is appropriate and necessary to wear all one has, for Nepal is very much a public culture.

Wearing jewelry is "auspicious" for women, who wear it at their ears, neck, and wrists. The religious implications are many, to honor is to adorn: men, their wives and daughters; hosts, their guests, with *kata* (scarves) and *maalaa* (flowers); and devotees, their gods, with red powder, *kata, maalaa,* and real jewelry, and stupas and mountain passes, with prayer flags and flowers.

Many styles are borrowed freely from adjacent groups. Occasional indicators of ethnicity are found: *Newar* never pierce noses; caste Hindus always do; only Sherpas and other *BhoTiya* wear striped aprons and the big silver hook clasps to hold them.

Jewelry is almost always handmade by a goldsmith. The metal is paid for by weight, and a small fee for craftsmanship. The gold, usually very pure, represents a safe investment.

Women pierce the nose on the left side (the female side) in the Hindu castes, and insert a discreet stud. Many hill ethnic groups—*Tamang, Gurung, Magar, Rai, Limbu,* and low-caste Hindus—pierce the left nostril and septum. You may find a ring on the left side, or a flat or dome-shaped plate of gold, with or without a colored stone. While the latter may be glass, or plastic because of its attractive color,

A Sanwar woman wearing cheptisun *earrings and two types of nose ornaments.
(Dave Hardenbergh)*

the gold is usually real and quite pure. Brass or alloy is occasionally seen.

Ears are pierced early in life, as earrings are considered auspicious and gold helps the ears to hear *dharma* and the mind to understand it. There is great variety in the ornaments worn on earlobes, with no clear representational design. Some earrings made in the Kathmandu Valley will have *makar* heads on either side, similar to the fish design of old water fountains. Large, up to 3-inch (8-cm) diameter, lightweight gold earrings, held stiff by their rim (*chepTisun*, meaning flat gold) are worn by *Tamang, Magar,* and *Gurung,* especially. The rings are put on by goldsmiths, and can only be removed by them.

In the hills, many groups (except Sherpas and other *BhoTiya*) wear large *dhungri* through the stiff center cartilage of the ear. These may be so heavy that the ears flop over, a traditional sign of beauty among some peoples. The ear rims of some individuals may also have as many as eighteen to twenty tiny holes for carrying little rings. Some men, notably the *Jyapu,* pierce the right (male) side of the ear, high up. *BhoTiya* men and women wear coral and turquoise on strings through the earlobes.

Necklace designs are shared among many groups. There may be large gold beads, wax-filled for strength and lightness, strung with coral, glass, or layers of velvet circles between them. While the necklaces were once silver, the trend is away from it to gold.

A *tilhari,* a long cylindrical beaten gold bead that hangs in the center of a few to a hundred strands of fine colored glass beads, is worn by married Hindu women. Red, followed by green, are the most popular color beads.

BhoTiya wear big pieces of coral (often imitation) and turquoise (almost always real) as well as large black and white *dzi* beads. These are believed to be the product of lightning striking. These people will also wear prayer boxes of gold and silver, often with bits of turquoise and fine filigree work. Colored, knotted strings, blessings from lamas, are also worn.

Many women wear bangles of gold, silver, and Indian glass on the wrists. Red is the most auspicious color, and the clinking is considered mildly erotic. Ankles are less commonly decorated than in the past. The *Tharu* in the Tarai may wear hollow or solid heavy gold anklets. *Tamang* wear gold with dragonlike (*makar* or *singha mukh*) designs. Anklets display high relief when new, but wear down over the years to become almost smooth. *Tamang* may wear similar pieces on the wrist.

A plain *Tikaa* of red or yellow powder is an essential part of *pujaa* (worship) for men and women. Black ones guard against spirits. Fancy ones are worn by women as decoration or make-up.

Colored powder, usually red and orange, is put on images of gods, thrown at *Holi,* and slapped on cheeks at festivals. This custom of Hindu origin is a sign of reverence that pleases the gods and delights people by expressing their connection with one another and with the gods.

Children, who need protection from the "evil eye" of witches and from ghosts and spirits, wear black *gaajal* at the eyes and black strings at the neck, wrists, ankles, and waist. Similarly, silver anklets are thought to help their legs grow straight. Amulets with mantra papers are worn at the neck. *Rudaaksha* (crinkly brown beads) are a sign of respect to Shiva, while *Narasimha* images of copper protect against lightning and fright.

APPENDIX A

Addresses

The following addresses, all located in Kathmandu, should be helpful for planning a trek in Nepal. Naturally, businesses come and go and addresses change, but these will at least provide a place for the reader to start. Inclusion in this list does not imply endorsement by the author or publisher.

Trekking (T) and River Rafting (RR) Agencies

(T)   Above the Clouds Trekking
Thamel
G.P.O. Box 3119
Cable: Clouds

(T)   Adventure Travel Nepal
Durbar Marg

(T)   Alpine Adventure
Majarajgunj, Phone 217806
Cable: Alpine Explorer

(T)   Amadablam Trekking
Jawalakhel, Phone 521732
G.P.O. Box 1954
Cable: Amadablam

(T)   Annapurna Mountaineering
and Trekking
Durbar Marg, Phone 21736
G.P.O. Box 795
Cable: Amtrek

(T)   Asian Trekking
Bagwati Bahal (Naxal),
Phone 212726
Cable: Astrek

(T)   Exploring Nepal
Ram Shah Path,
Phone 213017, 214424

(T)   Express Trekking
Naxal, Phone 213017
G.P.O. Box 339
Cable: Greatrek

(T)   Gaurishankar Trekking
Lazimpat, Phone 212112
Cable: Gotrek

(T)   Great Himalayan Adventures
Kanti Path, Phone 216144
Cable: Himadventure

(T)   Himalayan Explorers
Jyatha Tole, Phone 216142
G.P.O. Box 1737
Cable: Himexplor

(T)   Himalayan Journeys
Kanti Path, Phone 215855
G.P.O. Box 989
Cable: Journeys

(T)   Himalayan Rover Trek
Lazimpat & Hathisar,
Phone 212691
G.P.O. Box 1081
Cable: Rovtrek

(T)   Himalayan Shangrila Treks
Ram Shah Path, Puthali
Sadak, Phone 213303
G.P.O. Box 1985
Cable: Wildlife

(T)   Himal Trek
Maharajgunj, Phone
215561
G.P.O. Box 2541

(T)   Himal Trekking
Ram Shah Path, Phone
211808

(T)   Holiday Mountaineering
and Trekking
Jyatha Tole, Phone 212251
G.P.O. Box 3064

(T)   International Trekkers
         Durbar Marg, Phone 215594
         G.P.O. Box 1273
         Cable: Intrek

(T,RR)   Journeys Mountaineering
             and Trekking
         Kanti Path, Phone 213533
         G.P.O. Box 2034
         Cable: Jomtrek

(T)   Lama Excursions
         Durbar Marg, Phone 211786
         G.P.O. Box 2485
         Cable: Gaida

(T)   Manaslu Trekking
         Durbar Marg, Phone 212422
         G.P.O. Box 1519
         Cable: Manastrek

(T,RR)   Mountain Travel
         Narayan Chaur (Naxal) and
             Durbar Marg, Phones
             212808, 211262
         G.P.O. Box 170
         Cable: Trekkers

(T)   Nataraj Trekking
         Kanti Path, Phone 216644
         G.P.O. Box 1606
         Cable: Natours

(T)   Nepal Hiking and Mountain-
             eering House
         Jyatha Tole, Phone 216573
         G.P.O. Box 1632

(T)   Nepal Nature Trek
         New Road, Phone 215556
         G.P.O. Box 1852
         Cable: Nntrek

(T)   Nepal Trekking
         Thamel, Phone 214681
         G.P.O. Box 368
         Cable: Netrekking

(T)   Nepal Treks and Natural
             History Expeditions
         Ganga Path, Phones
             214446, 212985
         G.P.O. Box 459
         Cable: Neptrek

(T)   Sagarmatha Trekking
         Thamel, Phone 213239
         G.P.O. Box 2236

(T,RR)   Sherpa Cooperative Trekking
         Kamal Pokhri, Phone 215887
         G.P.O. Box 1338
         Cable: Sherpakeets

(T)   Sherpa Society
         Chabahil-Chuchepati,
             Phone 216361
         G.P.O. Box 1566

(T)   Sherpa Trekking Service
         Kamaladi, Phone 212489
         G.P.O. Box 500
         Cable: Sherptrek

(T,RR)   Summit Nepal Trekking
         Kupondole, Phone 521810
         G.P.O. Box 1406
         Cable: Summit

(T)   Tenzing Trekking and
             Mountaineering
         Thamel
         G.P.O. Box 1542
         Cable: Tentrek

(T)   Transhimalayan Trekking
         Durbar Marg, Phone 213854
         G.P.O. Box 283
         Cable: Transeview

(T)   Yeti Mountaineering and
             Trekking
         Bisalnagar, Phone 216841
         G.P.O. Box 1034
         Cable: Ymtrek

Pokhara Addresses

(T)   Himalayan Horizon
         Airport, Pokhara, Phone 253
         G.P.O. Box 35

(T)   Yeti Trekking
         Airport, Pokhara, Phone 283
         G.P.O. Box 40

Chitwan National Park
Tour Agencies (Kathmandu)

Gaida Wildlife Camp
Durbar Marg, Phone
    211786 or 215840
G.P.O. Box 2056
Cable: Gaida

Hotel Elephant Camp
Durbar Marg, Phone 213976
G.P.O. Box 1281
Cable: Elecamp

Jungle Safari Camp
Kanti Path, Phone 213533
G.P.O. Box 2154
Cable: Jscamp

Tiger Tops
Durbar Marg, Phone 212706
G.P.O. Box 242
Cable: Tigertops

Nepal Book Dealers (Kathmandu)

Educational Enterprise
Mahankal
G.P.O. Box 425

Himalayan Book Centre
Bhotahity, Phone 212725
G.P.O. Box 1339

Himalayan Booksellers
Ghantaghar
G.P.O. Box 528

Ratna Book Distributors
Bag Bazaar, Phone 213026
G.P.O. Box 1080

Ratna Pustak Bhandar
Bhotahity
G.P.O. Box 98

APPENDIX B

Glossary of Nepali and Tibetan Words

bhaat	cooked rice
bhaTmaas	soybeans
bhaTTi	traditional Nepali inn
BhoTiya	Buddhist highlander of Nepal
chaarpi	latrine
chang	locally brewed beer
chAUmri or zopkio	a cross between a yak and a cow
chautaara	rectangular resting platform on a trail
chilim	clay pipe for smoking
chorten	Buddhist religious cubical structure
daal	lentil-like sauce poured over rice
daru or rakshi	a Thakali distilled spirit
dhaami	measure of weight (approximately 6 lb, 2.7 kg)
dharmsala	rest house
Doko	conical basket for carrying loads
ghiu	clarified butter (ghee in India)
gomba	Tibetan Buddhist temple
goTh	shelter used by shepherds
haatisaar	elephant camp
himal	mountain
jAAR	locally brewed beer
kata	ceremonial scarf of white cheesecloth
khola	river
lekh	hill
loTa	vessel for carrying water to clean oneself after defecating
maanaa	volume measure (20 oz, 2½ cups, 0.7 l)
machaan	blind for observing animals
mani	prayer
memsahib	honorific title used by Nepalis for female foreigners
naamlo	tumpline
namaskaar	traditional greeting (very polite and formal)
namaste	traditional greeting (less formal)
paathi	volume measure equal to eight maanaa
paau	weight measure (8 oz, 0.2 kg)
paisaa	smallest denomination of money (0.085 U.S. cents)
rakshi	distilled spirit
rupiyAA	100 paisaa (about 8½ cents at 1980 U.S. exchange rate)
sahib	honorific title used by Nepalis for male foreigners
ser	weight measure equal to four pau (2 lb, 0.8 kg)
tal	lake
thangka	Buddhist scroll painting
tsampa	roasted barley flour, usually consumed by BhoTiya)
yersa	a cluster of goTh in Khumbu, but also applies to other northern regions
zopkio or chAUmri	a cross between a yak and a cow

APPENDIX C

Recommended Reading

Many people come, looking, looking. . .
some people come, see.

Dawa Tenzing, a Sherpa

Maximum enjoyment of Nepal will come through familiarity with its history, its culture, its geography, and people. This book is primarily concerned with the practical matters related to trekking. Those planning a trip to Nepal are encouraged to do some additional reading. Most of the books on the annotated list below focus on areas outside of the Kathmandu Valley, and should help the trekker learn more about the various regions of this country. I have included much more material than might be considered appropriate for the casual reader, but the interests of the peripatetic student can often be far ranging and lofty.

The books listed are either still in print, recently reprinted, or recently out of print. Those out of print can sometimes be purchased in Kathmandu. Those published in Nepal can normally only be purchased there. Some sources for ordering books by mail are listed in the Addresses section of the Appendix A. I urge you to buy the books you might want in Kathmandu before you leave Nepal. Books are often cheaper and easier to find there than at home, and you will avoid the hassle of mail ordering them later. Many of these books can be read at the Tribhuvan University Library in Kirtipur, Kathmandu.

BIBLIOGRAPHIES

Boulnois, L., and Millot, H. *Bibliographie du Nepal Volume 1.* Paris: Editions du Centre National de la Recherche Scientifique, 1969.

Boulnois, L. *Bibliographie du Nepal Volume 1 Supplement 1967-1973.* Paris: Editions du Centre National de la Recherche Scientifique, 1975.

Malla, Khadga Man. *Bibliography of Nepal.* Kathmandu: The Royal Nepal Academy, 1975.

GENERAL

Foreign Areas Studies Division. *Area Handbook for Nepal (with Sikkim and Bhutan). Washington: U.S. Army, 1972. A survey of the country in its many aspects.*

Hagen, Toni. *Nepal, The Kingdom of the Himalayas.* Berne: Kummerley and Frey, 1980. A large-scale, illustrated book by the first man to travel widely through the country.

Hamilton, Francis Buchanan. *An Account of the Kingdom of Nepal.* New Delhi: Manjusri Publishing House, 1819. A classic reprinted in 1971 in the Bibliotheca Himalayica series. It deals with much of Nepal's history and culture.

Hodgson, Brian. *Essays on the Languages, Literature, and Religion of Nepal and Tibet.* New Delhi: Manjusri, 1874. Another classic reprinted in 1972 in the same series. It was written by an incredibly eclectic scholar.

Hoefer, Hans Johannes. *Nepal.* Hong Kong: Apa Productions, 1983. One of the Insight Guides series, with contributions by experts, it is unquestionably the best guidebook to Nepal.

Kirkpatrick, W. *An Account of the Kingdom of Nepaul.* New Delhi: Manjusri, 1811. The account of the first visit to "Nepaul" by an Englishman. It was reprinted in 1969 in the Bibliotheca Himalayica series.

Landon, Perceval. *Nepal.* Kathmandu: Ratna Pustak Bhandar, 1928. Reprinted in the Bibliotheca Himalayica series in 1976. It is a veritable wealth of information on many topics.

Mierow, Dorothy, and Lall, Kesar. *This Beautiful Nepal.* Kathmandu: Sahayogi Press, 1981. A flood of images from Dorothy's wanderings in Nepal.

Nicolson, Nigel. *The Himalayas.* Amsterdam: Time-Life, 1974. A useful survey with excellent photographs.

Rieffel, Robert. *Nepal Namaste.* Kathmandu: Sahayogi Press, 1980. A detailed general guide to Nepal.

Rose, Leo E., and Scholz, John T. *Nepal: Profile of a Himalayan Kingdom.* Boulder, Colorado: Westview Press, 1980. An overview of Nepal since the overthrow of the Ranas.

Shirahata, Shiro. *Nepal Himalaya.* San Francisco, Heian International, 1983. A photographic record of the awesome mountains by view camera.

Shumshere, Pashupati; Rana, J.B.; and Malla, Kamal P. *Nepal in Perspective.* Kathmandu: Centre for Economic Development and Administration, 1973. A superb series of essays by distinguished Nepalis on diverse aspects of Nepal.

Stein, R.A. *Tibetan Civilization.* Stanford, California: Stanford University Press, 1972. The more you know about Tibet as it once was, the better you'll understand the people of northern Nepal.

Tucci, Giuseppe. *Tibet, Land of Snows.* London: Elek Books, 1967. Of interest here because so much of the culture, art, and ways of life of the northern people are Tibetan in nature.

ANTHROPOLOGY

Anderson, Mary M. *The Festivals of Nepal.* London: George Allen & Unwin, 1971. Mostly concerned with Kathmandu, but also helpful for the hills.

Aziz, Barbara Nimri. *Tibetan Frontier Families.* New Delhi: Vikas, 1978. A good source of information on Tibetan social life.

Berreman, Gerald D. *Hindus of the Himalaya.* Berkeley: University of California Press, 1972. Deals mainly with the Paharis of the Indian Himalaya, but also helpful in understanding the Hindus in the hills of Nepal.

Bista, Dor Bahadur. *People of Nepal.* Kathmandu: Ratna Pustak Bhandar, 1974. Presents an excellent synopsis of most of the ethnic groups found in Nepal. If a trekker were to restrict himself to one book, this should be it.

Caplan, A. Patricia. *Priests and Cobblers.* San Francisco: Chandler Publishing Company, 1972. Helpful for understanding the caste system in Nepal.

Caplan, Lionel. *Administration and Politics in a Nepalese Town.* London: Oxford University Press, 1975. Helpful for understanding a district center.

Ekvall, Robert B. *Fields on the Hoof.* New York: Holt, Rinehart and Winston, 1968. Deals with Tibetan nomads. It pertains to many of the Tibetan refugees found in Nepal.

Hitchcock, John T. *A Mountain Village in Nepal.* New York: Holt, Rinehart and Winston, 1980. The study of a particular hill ethnic group, the Magar, it contains a great deal of material relevant to many of the other hill people.

Hitchcock, John T., and Jones, Rex L. *Spirit Possession in the Nepal Himalayas.* Warminster, England: Aris & Phillips, 1976. A series of articles on shamans of Nepal. It is useful should you encounter any during your treks.

Höfer, Adras. *The Caste Hierarchy and the State in Nepal, A Study of the Muluki Ain of 1854.* Innsbruck: Universitätsverlag Wagner, 1979. This legal code governed caste behavior until recently and still underlies much interaction in the hills today.

Kuløy, Hullvard Kåre. *Tibetan Rugs.* Bangkok: White Orchid Press, 1982. A compendium of this traditional craft, it has helpful explanations of designs.

Macdonald, Alexander W. *Essays on the Ethnology of Nepal and South Asia.* Kathmandu: Ratna Pustak Bhandar, 1975. A far-ranging collection of material dealing with music, castes, and healing, among other essays.

Macfarlane, Alan. *Resources and Population.* Cambridge: Cambridge University Press, 1976. A study of economic and demographic change in a *Gurung* village.

Messerschmidt, Donald A. *The Gurungs of Nepal.* Warminster: Aris & Phillips, 1976. An excellent description of the social and political organization of these people.

Ortner, Sherry B. *Sherpas through Their Rituals.* Cambridge: Cambridge University Press, 1978. Useful for descriptions of Sherpa hospitality.

Von Fürer-Halmendorf, Christoph. *The Sherpas of Nepal, Buddhist Highlanders.* New Delhi: Sterling Publishers, 1979. An excellent account. A shortened version is available in the book *Mount Everest* (see Regional books).

_____. *Himalayan Traders.* London: John Murray, 1975. A look at changes in the economic patterns of Nepal's high-altitude dwellers.

_____. *Asian Highland Societies.* New Delhi: Sterling Publishers, 1981. A series of modern essays by distinguished anthropologists.

ART

Aran, Lydia. *The Art of Nepal.* Kathmandu: Shahayogi Prakashan, 1978. Deals primarily with the Kathmandu Valley, as do most books on Nepali art. It is also a useful guide to the art of this country seen through the religions.

Macdonald, Alexander W., and Stahl, Anne Vergati. *Newar Art: Nepalese during the Malla Period.* New Delhi: Vikas, 1979. Although dealing with Newari painting and architecture in the Kathmandu Valley, it relates to much of the country.

Sharma, Prayag Raj. *Preliminary Study of the Art and Architecture of the Karnali Basin, West Nepal.* Paris: Centre National de la Recherche Scientifique, 1972. One of the few art studies pertaining to Nepal outside the Kathmandu Valley.

Singh, Madanjeet. *Himalayan Art.* London: Macmillan, 1968. A survey of most of the Himalayan region with beautiful reproductions. There is a paperback edition published by UNESCO.

DEVELOPMENT, ECONOMICS, ENVIRONMENT, AND GEOGRAPHY

Blaikie, Piers; Cameron, John; and Seddon, David. *Nepal in Crisis.* New Delhi: Oxford University Press, 1980. A radical look at the development problems facing Nepal today, focusing on the building of roads.

Blair, Katherine D. *Four Villages: Architecture in Nepal.* Los Angeles: Craft and Folk Art Museum, 1983. An insightful look at structures and social ecology.

Eckholm, Erik P. *Losing Ground.* New York: W.W. Norton, 1976. A look at deforestation and world food prospects, with Nepal an example.

Shrestha, Badri Prasad. *An Introduction to Nepalese Economy.* Kathmandu: Ratna Pushtak Bhandar, 1981. A helpful survey.

Shrestha, Chandra Bahadur. *Cultural Geography of Nepal.* Bhaktapur, Nepal: K.K. Shrestha and K.L. Joshi, 1981. The seminal account.

Shrestha, Sharan Hari. *Simple Geography of Nepal.* Kathmandu: Educational Enterprise, 1983. A high school textbook.

Swiss Association for Technical Assistance in Nepal. *Mountain Environment and Development.* Kathmandu: SATA, 1976. A collection of essays on the Swiss development experience in Nepal.

Thapa, N.B., and Thapa, D.P. *Geography of Nepal.* New Delhi: Orient Longmans, 1969. A superficial account that nevertheless answers many of the newcomer's questions.

Toffin, Gérard. *L'Homme et la Maison en Himalaya.* Paris: CNRS, 1981. A collection of articles on village architecture in diverse areas of Nepal, mostly.

HISTORY

Regmi, Mahesh Chandra. *A Study in Nepali Economic History,* 1768-1846. New Delhi: Manjusri, 1971. Invaluable for understanding how life in the hills evolved.

_____. *Thatched Huts and Stucco Palaces.* New Delhi: Vikas, 1978. More on economic history in the nineteenth century.

Snellgrove, David, and Richardson, Hugh. *A Cultural History of Tibet.* Boulder, Colorado: Prajñā Press, 1980. Another example of a work dealing with Tibet that helps understand Nepal's highlanders.

Stiller, L.F. *The Rise of the House of Gorkha.* New Delhi: Manjusri, 1973. Provides an understanding of the problems involved in unifying Nepal in the 1700s.

_____. *The Silent Cry.* Kathmandu: Sahayogi Prakashan, 1976. A continuation of the author's study of the growth of unity in Nepal. It covers the pre-Rana period, 1816 to 1839.

LANGUAGE

Bell, Charles A. *English-Tibetan Colloquial Dictionary.* Calcutta: Sripati Ghosh, 1977. A reprint of the 1920 edition; it is worthless without instruction.

Clark, T.W. *Introduction to Nepali.* London: School of Oriental and African Studies, 1977. The only formal text. It is difficult to use, but valuable to those seeking a good knowledge of the language.

Goldstein, Melvyn C. *Tibetan for Beginners and Travellers.* Kathmandu: Ratna Pustak Bhandar, 1982. It is a place to start, but you need a teacher.

Hari, Anna Mari. *Conversational Nepali.* Kathmandu: Summer Institute of Linguistics, 1971. An excellent situational course, though not practical for use while trekking.

Karki, Tika B., and Shrestha, Chij K. *Basic Course in Spoken Nepali.* Kathmandu: published by the authors, 1979. Written for Peace Corps volunteers and stressing the situational approach. It may be useful for the serious trekker. Chij Shrestha's language institute in Naxal is also a source for language lessons.

Meerendonk, M. *Basic Gurkhali Dictionary.* Singapore: published by the author,

1960. An excellent pocket dictionary. Some grammar is needed to use it.

Pradhan, Yubaraj S., and Malla, Khadga Man. *Nepali Self Taught.* Kathmandu: Educational Enterprise, 1980. Based on the grammar translational approach, it would complement a transformative-situational book.

Shrestha, B.P., and Sharma K.R. *Speak with the Nepalese.* Kathmandu: published by the authors, 1982. Entirely situational, it is useful with a teacher.

LITERATURE

Dixit, Mani. *Come Tomorrow.* Kathmandu: Sajha Prakashan, 1980. A novel about the Gurkhas by a current prolific writer.

Rana, Diamond Shumshere. *Wake of the White Tiger.* Kathmandu: Mrs. Balika Rana, 1984. An English translation of this popular historical novel.

Rubin, David. *Nepali Visions, Nepali Dreams.* New York: Columbia University Press, 1980. Translations and commentary of the poems of the late Laxmiprasad Devkota, perhaps Nepal's finest poet.

NATURAL HISTORY

Bhatt, Dibya Deo. *Natural History and Economic Botany of Nepal.* Calcutta: Orient Longman, 1977. An excellent survey with a wealth of detail.

Fleming, Robert L., Jr. *The General Ecology, Flora, and Fauna of Midland Nepal.* Kathmandu: Tribhuvan University Press, 1977. A reprinting of this very useful work at last!

Fleming, Robert L., Sr.; Fleming, Robert L., Jr.; and Bangdel, Lain. *Birds of Nepal.* Kathmandu: Avalok, 1979. The comprehensive field guide. It can be ordered from Mrs. Vern Beieler, 1028 Crestwood Street, Wenatchee, Wash. 98801.

Gee, E.P. *The Wild Life of India.* London: Collins, 1964. Especially interesting for those visiting Chitwan National Park.

Gurung, K.K. *Heart of the Jungle: The Wildlife of Chitwan Nepal.* London: André Deutsch, 1983. Recommended for every visitor to Chitwan.

Hooker, J.D. *Himalayan Journals.* New Delhi: Today and Tomorrow's Printers and Publishers, 1969. A reprint of an account by the first scientist to travel in Nepal.

Lancaster, Roy. *Plant Hunting in Nepal.* London: Croomhelm, and New Delhi: Vikas, 1981. An account of a botanical trek up the Arun Valley and to the east.

Le Fort, Patrick. "Himalayas: The Collided Range; Present Knowledge of the Continental Arc," *American Journal of Science* (1975) 275-A: 1-44. An informative technical survey of the formation of the Himalaya.

Majupuria, Trilok Chandra. *Nepal—Nature's Paradise.* Bangkok: White Lotus, 1984. Another inappropriately titled collection of essays on non-faunal biology.

_____. *Wild is Beautiful.* Lashkar, M.P., India: S. Devi, 1982. A compendium of technical articles on Nepal's fauna written by experts.

Malla, S.B. *Flora of Langtang and Cross Section Vegetation Survey.* Kathmundu: Department of Medicinal Plants, 1976. One of several books published by the government. It is technical, but useful to those with botanical knowledge.

Mcdougal, Charles. *The Face of the Tiger.* London: Rivington Books, 1977. An ethnographic-like study of the Chitwan tiger.

Mierow, Dorothy, and Shrestha, Tirtha Bahadur. *Himalayan Flowers and Trees.* Kathmandu: Sahayogi Prakashan, 1978. Pictorial material to aid in identify-

335

ing plants. The notes in the back are helpful.

Mishra, Hemant Raj, and Mierow, Dorothy. *Wild Animals of Nepal.* Kathmandu: Ratna Pustak Bhandar, 1976. A useful species survey with line drawings.

Molnar, Peter, and Tapponnier, Paul. "The Collision between India and Eurasia," *Scientific American* (April 1977) 236: 30-41. Another look at the orogeny of the Himalaya.

Polunin, Oleg, and Stainton, Adam. *Flowers of the Himalaya.* London: Oxford University Press, 1984.

Prater, S.H. *The Book of Indian Animals.* Bombay: Bombay Natural History Society, 1971. Useful descriptions.

Regmi, Puskal Prasad. *An Introduction to Nepalese Food Plants.* Kathmandu: Royal Nepal Academy, 1982. Very helpful to those trying to identify exotic foods.

Schaller, George. *Stones of Silence: Journeys in the Himalaya.* New York: Viking Press, 1980. A book on the wild cats, sheep, and goats of the Himalaya. It is a fascinating synthesis of the author's observations and feelings about this ecosystem.

_____. *Mountain Monarchs: Wild Sheep and Goats of the Himalaya.* Chicago: University of Chicago Press, 1977. A volume more technical than the above. Those with a zoological background could appreciate it.

Sharma, Chandra K. *Geology of Nepal.* Kathmandu: Educational Enterprise, 1977. Very detailed. It is useful to those with a geological background.

Shrestha, Keshab Nepali. *Nepali Names for Plants.* Kathmandu: Natural History Museum, 1979. A compilation arranged by Nepali names in the order of the devanagari alphabet. It is one more tool in trying to understand Nepal's prodigious flora.

Shrestha, Tej Kumar. *Wildlife of Nepal.* Kathmandu: Tribhuvan University, 1981. A basic reference on fauna.

Shrestha, Tirtha Bahadur. *Gymnosperms of Nepal.* Paris: Centre Nationale de la Recherche Scientifique, 1974. A useful guide to the identification of conifers.

_____. *Ecology and Vegetation of North-West Nepal.* Kathmandu: Royal Nepal Academy, 1982. Useful to trekkers venturing forth from Jumla. I hope that similar publications dealing with the rest of Nepal follow.

Smith, Colin. *Field Guide to Nepal's Butterflies.* Kathmandu: Natural History Museum, 1981. Would that the photographs were in color!

Stainton, J.D.A. *Forests of Nepal.* London: John Murray, 1972. A detailed survey requiring knowledge of specific species.

POLITICAL SCIENCE

Mihaly, Eugene Bramer. *Foreign Aid and Politics in Nepal.* London: Oxford University Press, 1965. An early study. Its conclusions remain valid today.

Rose, Leo E. *Nepal Strategy for Survival.* Berkeley: University of California Press, 1971. A fascinating political history.

Shaha, Rishikesh. *Nepali Politics—Retrospect and Prospect.* Delhi: Oxford University Press, 1978. A controversial book. It is invaluable for understanding Nepal today.

REGIONAL

Chorlton, Windsor. *Cloud-Dwellers of the Himalayas: The Bhotia.* Amsterdam: Time-Life Books, 1982. A photodocumentary of life in Nar-Phu.

Coburn, Broughton. *Nepali aama: Portrait of a Nepalese Hill Woman.* Santa Barbara, California: Ross-Erikson, 1982. A sensitive look at life in a *Gurung* village, told by an old woman.

Downs, Hugh R. *Rhythms of a Himalayan Village.* New York: Harper and Row, 1980. A photodocumentary of a Sherpa village in Solu—a most helpful book for understanding Mani-rimdu and how Sherpas may view their land.

Gurung, Nareshwar Jang. "An Introduction to the Socio-Economic Structure of Manang District." *Kailash* (1976) 4:295-308. Very helpful in understanding the Manangba.

Hagen, Toni; Dyhrenfurth, Gunter-Oscar; Von Fürer-Haimendorf, Christoph; and Schneider, Erwin. *Mount Everest: Formation, Population and Exploration of the Everest Region.* London: Oxford University Press, 1963. The best single volume to take with you to Khumbu. It includes chapters on geology, mountaineering, and the Sherpas.

Hall, Andrew R. "Preliminary Report on the Langtang Region." *Contributions to Nepalese Studies* (June 1978) 5:51-68. An ecological analysis.

Hillary, Edmund. *Schoolhouse in the Clouds.* Harmondsworth, England: Penguin Books, 1968. An interesting account of Hillary's attempts to aid the Sherpas of Nepal.

Hornbein, Thomas F. *Everest: The West Ridge.* Seattle: The Mountaineers, 1980. Superb photographs and a sensitive text.

Jest, Corneille. *Tarap.* Paris: Seuil, 1974. A photodocumentary of life in a Dolpo Valley.

_____. *Monuments of Northern Nepal.* Paris: UNESCO, 1981. Helpful for the trekker to Thak Khola, Muktinath, Helambu, and Solu-Khumbu.

Rowell, Galen. *Many people come, looking, looking.* Seattle: The Mountaineers, 1980. A beautifully photographed look at trekking and climbing in the Himalaya.

Sestini, Valerio, and Somigli, Enzo. *Sherpa Architecture.* Paris: UNESCO, 1978. A record of this tradition, which is changing due to modern influences.

Shepherd, Gary. *Life Among the Magars.* Kathmandu: Sahayogi Press, 1982. An SIL family's experiences living amongst this ethnic group.

Snellgrove, David. *Himalayan Pilgrimage.* Boulder, Colorado: Prajñā Press, 1981. A chronicle of travel through north-central and northwestern Nepal in the 1950s. His wide range of interests and acute powers of observation make for fascinating reading.

Tucci, Giuseppe. *Journey to Mustang, 1952.* Kathmandu: Ratna Pustak Bhandar, 1977. Much of this early journey describes the popular trek to Jomosom. Read it to sense the changes.

RELIGION

Anderson, Walt. *Open Secrets: A Western Guide to Tibetan Buddhism.* New York: Viking, 1979; Penguin, 1980. Some may find this modern approach useful.

Bernbaum, Edwin. *The Way to Shambhala.* New York: Anchor Press, 1980. An exploration of the myth of the mystical kingdom hidden behind the Himalaya, believed in by many of Nepal's highlanders.

Blofeld, John. *The Tantric Mysticism of Tibet.* Boulder, Colorado: Prajñā Press, 1982.

Conze, Edward. *Buddhism, Its Essence and Development.* Oxford: Bruno Cassirer, 1951; New York: Harper & Row, 1959. A classic work on the basics.

Detmold, Geogrey, and Rubel, Mary. *The Gods and Goddesses of Nepal.* Kathmandu: Ratna Pustak Bhandar, 1979. Deals primarily with the Kathmandu Valley. But it is nevertheless very useful for Nepal in general.

Jerstad, L.G. *Mani-rimdu, Sherpa Dance Drama.* Seattle: University of Washington Press, 1969. Useful for an understanding of the festival. It also contains introductory chapters on religion and the Sherpas.

Sen, K.M. *Hinduism.* Harmondsworth: Penguin Books, 1961.

Snellgrove, David. *Buddhist Himalaya.* Oxford: Bruno Cassirer, 1957. An understanding of Buddhism is a prerequisite for this book. It deals with the Solu-Khumbu region and the Buddhism of Sherpas and of Kathmandu.

Tucci, Giuseppe. *The Religions of Tibet.* London: Routledge & Kegan Paul, and New Delhi: Allied, 1980. A comprehensive detailed account.

Von Fürer-Haimendorf, Christoph. "A Nunnery in Nepal," *Kailash* (1976) 4:121–154. Deals with Bigu Gomba in a scholarly fashion.

Zaehner, R.C. *Hinduism.* London: Oxford University Press, 1966.

TREKKING

Armington, Stan. *Trekking in the Himalayas.* Victoria, Australia: Lonely Planet, 1982. The title is misleading for it only deals with Nepal. Written to convince you to travel with an agency.

Baume, Louis C. *Sivalaya: Explorations of the 8000-Metre Peaks of the Himalaya.* Seattle: The Mountaineers, 1979. A fascinating detailed chronology for those interested in mountaineering.

Gurung, Harka. *Vignettes of Nepal.* Kathmandu: Sajha Prakashan, 1980. A fascinating account of a Nepali geographer's many treks in his country's remote regions. It is a source of inspiration for the veteran trekker looking for new horizons.

_____. *Maps of Nepal.* Bangkok: White Orchid Press, 1983. A detailed look at the history of cartography in Nepal. A fascinating resource but of no help for route finding.

Iozawa, Tomoya. *Trekking in the Himalayas.* Tokyo: Yama-Kei, and Bombay: Allied, 1980. Has good color photographs, sketches, detailed drawings, and maps. The English text is disappointing.

Kleinart, Christian. *Nepal Trekking.* Munich: Bergverlag Rudolf Rother, n.d., c. 1976. An attractive guide. It has sixteen fold-out pages containing brief route descriptions, maps, and excellent panoramic photos.

Lall, Kesar. *Nepalese Customs and Manners.* Kathmandu: Ratna Pustak Bhandar, 1979. Useful information.

Swift, Hugh. *The Trekker's Guide to the Himalaya and Karakorum.* San Francisco: Sierra Club, 1982. Ambitious in scope, it is enjoyable to read. An appetizer rather than a detailed guide.

TREKKING MEDICINE

Carey-Smith, K.A. "Diet, Habits and Living Conditions of 'World Travelers' in Nepal." *New Zealand Medical Journal* (February 27, 1974) 79, 696-701.

Hackett, Peter. *Mountain Sickness: Prevention, Recognition, and Treatment.* New York: American Alpine Club, 1980. A small but complete and useful booklet. The author is the medical director of the Himalayan Rescue Association.

Houston, Charles. *Going Higher.* Burlington, Vermont: published by the author, 1983. Invaluable for understanding what is going on inside you as you climb.

The author is the dean of researchers into human diseases of altitude. It can be ordered from 77 Ledge Road, Burlington, Vermont 05401.

Hultgren, Herbert N. "High Altitude Medical Problems." *Western Journal of Medicine* (July 1979) 131:8-23. An excellent review by a pioneering high altitude researcher. It is suitable for those with a medical background.

Postgraduate Medical Journal (July 1979), **55.** An issue devoted to the physiologic changes and episodes of altitude illness associated with a trek in Nepal.

Steele, Peter. *Medical Care for Mountain Climbers.* London: Heinemann, 1976. Comparable to *Medicine for Mountaineering* listed below, but somewhat simplified and reflecting the British point of view.

Summer Institute of Linguistics. *Field Worker's Medical Manual.* Huntington Beach, California: S.I.L. 1973. Comparable to *Medicine for Mountaineering.* It is directed to those dealing with medical problems in remote areas.

Ward, Michael. *Mountain Medicine.* London: Crosby Lockwood Staples, 1975. An excellent survey of problems associated with cold and high altitudes. It is not practical in clinical situations.

Werner, David. *Where There Is No Doctor.* Palo Alto, California: Hesperian Foundation, 1977. An immensely practical book that has also been translated into Nepali for use by health workers.

Wilkerson, James A. *Medicine for Mountaineering.* Seattle: The Mountaineers, 1985. A superb practical book designed for the layman, yet dealing with the entire spectrum of medical problems encountered in the mountains.

APPENDIX D

Questions to Ponder While Trekking

Nepal provides marvelous food for thought. A manifold society with almost un-fathomable ethnic diversity is layered over landscapes varying from tropical rain forest to snowy heights and desert. Paradoxically, the forces that shape Nepal are essentially very simple: its people endeavor to survive, while the land attempts to self-destruct through natural erosive forces.

There are too many facets to Nepal for an outsider to absorb in a single trip—or a lifetime. When I first came to Nepal, attracted by the incredible mountains, I was partially blinded to the people living among them. After spending more time in Nepal, however, I found the people—the culture, their ways of surviving in this harsh, upturned land—at least as interesting as the great peaks themselves. Once, some years ago, while I was working in western Nepal, a trekking group of expatriot school children from Kathmandu and their teacher visited my project. They peppered me with good questions about the work I was doing there. Indeed, I later learned that each of them had been given a list of questions to report on after their trek. But the questions they were asking me were not from the list. The listed questions had merely heightened their curiosity.

I wish to share similar questions with you, to use as you see fit. Please don't try to read all of them at once. But when the urge strikes, perhaps after a few days on the trail, you might read a few to see how they sit. They are not a test or catechism, but one way perhaps of organizing the myriad impressions and obser-vations that are accumulated during an extended trek in Nepal. There are no real answers for many of the questions, but I have occasionally indicated directions in which you may find it helpful to proceed.

Why are some villages composed of clustered houses, reminiscent of down-town Kathmandu, while others have dwellings either widely scattered over the hillside or within shouting distance? What factors influence this diversity? (Ethnic group? Terrain?) Why are some villages close to the main trail, while others avoid it? Why do some villages near the trail have shops, while others don't? Why do homes and villages face the directions they do? How have people adapted their town plan to the environment?

Have you noticed lines of communication in villages that follow an organized pattern? (Town crier?) What influence does the transistor radio have? What hap-pens if a printed note or letter arrives? What evidence do you see of modern improvements to people's houses? How well maintained are they? What non-locally produced materials are required for building? Who builds and maintains bridges, trails, water systems, other community projects? Why do so many of them seem in disrepair?

What evidence is there of governmental influence in remote areas? Can you imagine any recording of vital events (births, deaths)? Do you see many calendars in use? How many of the Nepali people you pass know the day, date, and year? How do people keep track of time? What are the greatest obstacles to better health among the Nepalis? What practices do the people undertake that promote good health? Are there differences in this regard among ethnic groups? What are the most constructive steps that can be taken to improve the health of the Nepalis?

Rumjatar High School class. (Dave Hardenbergh)

Who makes up the household? What happens to old people, the mentally retarded, the physically handicapped? How much evidence of alcoholism do you see? How much leisure time do people have and how do they spend it? Is there much obesity? How are bodies disposed of? Can you identify a person's caste or ethnic group without asking? What factors go into your hunch? (Facial and body hair? Facial shape? Eye folds? Jewelry? Dress? The way people interact with others? Where they locate their village? The kind of work they do?)

Do people wear makeup? Which sexes or ethnic groups? What materials do they apply? Do you see mirrors? Are people concerned about their appearance as much as you expected? What kind of body space do people have? How physically close can they be to one another without feeling uncomfortable? What about eye contact, body language, posturing, and physical contact? Is there much physical display of affection?

What distinctions do you see between gender roles and identity? Who does what work and how does this vary with ethnic groups? What do children do most of the day? What do you play with? Do they cry as often as you might expect? Do you see them sucking their thumbs? At what age are children weaned? How many children go to school? Mostly boys or girls? Are they in school during harvest times, or other periods of intense farm work? Where are the village schools built? How many of them function? Are the classes held inside the building? What supplies does the school have? What means of learning are used? How much teaching is done by chanting? What jobs are available to the educated?

What is the role of young unmarried women? Do you ever see them alone, or are they always in groups? Do you ever see them talking to single men? How do teenagers entertain themselves? What are the status and role of old people?

How much evidence is there of religious activity in the hills? Are there daily practices? How does this vary among ethnic groups in the same area? Do you see statues, symbols, or idols that don't seem to belong to one of the two major religions in Nepal?

What styles of walking and carrying loads do you see among the Nepali people? Slow steady pace? Many stops? What do they do when they stop? Estimate the weight of the heaviest porter load you see and compare it with his or her body weight. Try lifting it with the tumpline.

What role do pets have in Nepali people's lives? Do you see many cats? What do Nepalis feed their pets and how do they treat them? Are they affectionate towards them in ways you would expect?

What domestic animals are given status in the community? How big are they compared to similar breeds in your home country? Who cares for them? What evidence of disease do you see? Why aren't there more horses? What parts of the animals do they use? At what age can a child begin tending an animal? Are wild animals hunted? With what? Which animals are feared? What parts of wild animals are used?

What crop patterns produce maximum productivity for the land? What are the altitude limits for certain crops and animals? For what purposes are irrigation systems used, besides watering crops? How are they controlled?

What is a typical day like for an average person in the hills? How does this differ for men and women? How much do people rest? What are the sleeping arrangements in Nepali homes? What do people seem to talk about with one another?

What kinds of goods are available in local stores? If on the main trekking trails, what goods are purchased by the local inhabitants? Which are staples and which are luxuries? What is produced locally and what is imported? How dependent are the hill and mountain people on imported goods? What crafts are produced locally? Compare the use of the wheel in your society and in a remote area of Nepal.

Do you see any evidence of natural catastrophes? What factors contribute to erosion besides deforestation? What kinds of wood-cutting practices do you see in different areas? Do you see evidence of reforestation? What attempts do you see by the Nepalese to control erosion?

What physical hazards are hill people exposed to as they go about their daily lives? What tools are used, and how did they evolve to their present designs? Which items are made locally and which are imported? Do you suspect that local production has increased or decreased?

What modern consumer goods do you see in use? What did they replace, and how dependent are the people on them? How has this affected local craftsmen? How important is cash in trading and commerce? What are the major influences on the economy of the region you are passing through? What are the specific and general benefits as well as the negative influences that road building has brought? What will be the changes in this area in ten years, twenty years? How can *you* influence those changes positively?

What do the Nepali people you meet have that you don't? Materially? Otherwise? What do you think they would most like to have of yours? What about your encounter do you think they talk about among themselves after you have left?

Why do Nepali people seem to cling to old ways that may, on reflection, seem to be foolish or counterproductive? If your return home from Nepal was suddenly made impossible, which of your cultural trappings would you cling to most tenaciously? Which would you insist on passing on to your children and grandchildren? If you had to live in the Nepali village you are in, what changes would you want to make? Would you be successful? What would be the hardest part of adapting? What would be the joys of staying here?

If you have traveled in other mountain areas of the Himalaya, how do your experiences there compare with those in Nepal? Is there a distinct Nepali character or is it just a piece of a larger Himalayan mosaic?

APPENDIX E

After Trekking in Nepal, What Next?

Some people who travel to Nepal for the first time are smitten, hopelessly in love with one of the poorest countries in the world. They want a more serious involvement with Nepal than is provided by tourism. Numerous requests come my way for further information on opportunities for such deeper involvement. In the following pages I have listed various possibilities ranging from contributing to worthwhile projects in Nepal, to having a more intense learning experience, to working there.

WORTHWHILE PROJECTS TO SUPPORT

My criteria for worthwhile projects are somewhat stringent. Projects must spend little for administration, have a large component for local (Nepali) initiative, directly influence the most needy people, be sensitive to reasonable development or cultural needs and goals, and be small enough that modest contributions may make some difference. Inclusion here does not guarantee that these criteria have been met, nor does exclusion imply that they haven't. It is difficult to search out such projects, and I would be happy to be kept better informed.

NEPAL SCHOOL PROJECTS

The most remarkable example of a trekker working with the Nepali people to help themselves is Michael Rojik. On his first trek, this Toronto man realized that while Sherpas had many admirers and benefactors, the poor Tamang porters did not have any. Ten years ago, he embarked on a selfless plan to help build schools in poor hill villages. He raises funds by giving talks and appeals, and the donations are matched by the Canadian International Development Agency. The projects become local community efforts, with the villagers donating the site and voluntary labor. The money pays for construction materials, skilled labor, and school furniture. All the schools are staffed by Government of Nepal appointed teachers. Through the project, young Nepalis are also trained in construction trades. The current cost for building one school is less than you would pay for the cheapest new automobile you could buy in Canada or the United States. No funds go for administration. Mike's time is donated and his travel to and from Nepal is paid by the treks he leads there. To date, twenty-five schools have been built, every one of them still functioning. Contributions are tax-deductible in Canada. Checks should be payable to Nepal School Projects/TRAS, and can be sent to 63 Perivale Crescent, Scarborough, Ontario, Canada M1J 2C4.

THE AU LESHI SOCIETY

This society attempts to help the Nepali people maintain their traditional arts. Named after a great teacher and painter from Solu, the society has plans for patronage of traditional artists, as well as for education in those communities where these arts are no longer practiced. Its work has just recently begun. Contributions are tax-deductible in the United States and can be sent to The Au Leshi Society, Inc., 5681 Florence Terrace, Oakland, California 94611.

SAVE THE CHILDREN

My initial reaction to this organization was negative, because I felt it inappropriate to single out poor individuals and give them money. The word "poor" is one

A Jaishi Bahun *father and daughter. (Stephen Bezruchka)*

that the Nepalis now know through their contact with outsiders. Furtherance of that concept will help erode their self-respect, which may be their most valuable resource. However, I have come to learn that this organization and the one that follows use sponsorship as a means of attracting donors, but channel the funds directly into local development projects with considerable village input. No funds go directly to the sponsored child. For some people, helping fund development work by identification with a family and a child is important, and these two projects provide the means. Contributions are tax-deductible in the United States. For more information, write to Save the Children, 50 Wilton Road, Westport, Connecticut 06880.

FOSTER PARENTS PLAN

I believe that the information above also holds true for this project. Write to Foster Parents Plan, 155 Plan Way, Warwick, Rhode Island 02887, or Foster Parents Plan of Canada, 153 St. Clair Avenue West, Toronto, Ontario, Canada M4V 1P8.

CULTURAL SURVIVAL

Visitors to Khumbu will wonder what is happening to Sherpa culture. In fact, steps are being taken by the Sherpas themselves to preserve it. Much of the impetus comes from the Incarnate Lama at Tengboche, Nawang Tenzing, and a Sherpa Cultural Center has been constructed there. Further projects are planned and need support. For further information write to All Nepal Himalayan Buddhist Association, G.P.O. Box 576, Kathmandu, Nepal; or Lhakpa Tsering, Mountain Travel, G.P.O. Box 170, Kathmandu; or Cultural Survival Inc., 11 Divinity Avenue, Cambridge, Massachusetts 02138.

HIMALAYAN RESCUE ASSOCIATION

This group operates the Trekker's Aid Posts in the Khumbu and Manang areas, and its education programs have been partly responsible for the decrease in deaths of trekkers from altitude illness. The association subsists entirely on voluntary funding, supplies, and staffing. Donations (tax deductible in the U.S.) can be made out to Himalayan Rescue Association, P.O. Box 567, Bishop, California 93514.

INTENSIVE STUDY IN NEPAL

These programs can range from a several-month block of time to a year of college study. There may be other such programs in addition to the following:

The Experiment in International Living's School of International Training, Kipling Road, Brattleboro, Vermont 05301.

Joseph Elder, College Year in Nepal, South Asian Studies, University of Wisconsin, Madison, Wisconsin 54306.

WORKING IN NEPAL

There are many opportunities but it is not possible to go into great detail here. Many countries have volunteer organizations: Peace Corps, USA; VSO, United Kingdom; Japanese and German Volunteers, and so forth. There are numerous non-governmental organizations involved in Nepal, as well as bilateral (government to government) projects. I am most often asked about opportunities to work in the area of health. One resource I can provide is an article by John Dickinson, "Where Shall John Go? Nepal," in *British Medical Journal,* Volume 2, December 4, 1976, pages 1364-1366.

Physicians with appropriate backgrounds may wish to volunteer their services to the Himalayan Rescue Association's Trekker's Aid Posts. Applicants should send a *curriculum vitae* including credentials, wilderness and/or mountaineering experience, training in high altitude medicine (if any), site preference (Pheriche, or Ongre in Manang), and reasons for volunteering to:

David R. Shlim, M.D.
Medical Director, Himalayan Rescue Association
G.P.O. Box 495
Kathmandu, Nepal.

Qualified applicants will be interviewed before a final decision is made. Staffing arrangements are usually made 1 to 1½ years in advance for the pre- and post-monsoon seasons.

To work in Nepal is, I feel, a rare privilege. The Nepali people are quite capable of dealing with their problems on their own, as they have done for countless centuries. It is an extreme form of arrogance to believe that they must have our help. Development projects are often a two-edged sword. Often the greatest beneficiaries of these projects are the expatriots who have worked in them. In my own endeavors, I have always felt that I gained more from working in Nepal, providing health care, than the people gained from me.

INDEX

(Nick Langton)

As I write these last words, my thoughts return to you who were my comrades: the stubborn and indomitable peasants of Nepal. Once more I hear the laughter with which you greeted every hardship. Once more I see you in your bivouacs or about your fires, on forced march or in the trenches, now shivering with wet and cold, now scorched by a pitiless and burning sun. Uncomplaining, you endure hunger and thirst and wounds; and at the last, your unwavering lines disappear into the smoke and wrath of battle. Bravest of the brave, most generous of the generous, never had country more faithful friends than you.

> Ralph Lilley Turner, author of *Dictionary of the Nepali Language,** describing the Gurkhas with whom he served in the British Army. He learned Nepali from these soldiers, and wrote the definitive Nepali dictionary without ever having visited Nepal.

---

*Routledge & Kegan Paul Limited, London, 1931, 1965.

ABOUT THE AUTHOR

Stephen Bezruchka, a Canadian of Ukrainian descent, first went to Nepal in 1969, drawn by his interest in climbing and a desire to get close to the world's highest summits. He spent a year there between graduate studies in mathematics at Harvard University and the study of medicine at Stanford University. His fascination with Nepal soon transcended its lofty mountains to focus on the social-cultural matrix that is his lifelong passion.

He returned to Nepal for several years in the mid seventies to work as a doctor for a community health project in a high Himalayan valley in the remote western region. That most rewarding

(Suzanne Kurtz)

experience ultimately led to his current work of training Nepali doctors in a remote district hospital, a collaborative project between Nepal's Institute of Medicine and the University of Calgary.

Stephen Bezruchka has trekked far and wide in Nepal, including the jungles of the Tarai and the slopes of the highest mountains. In 1982 he was a member of the Canadian Everest Expedition. Between sojourns in Nepal, he has lived in Seattle and has also climbed in some of the world's remote mountain ranges. But the lure of Nepal, the land and its people, always calls him back.

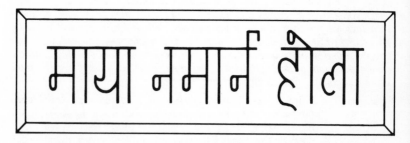

This message for trekkers, written in Nepali script on a sign north of Pokhara, reads "Come back again." The literal translation is "Don't let the love die."